TO MEND THE WORLD⎯⎯⎯⎯

Foundations of
Post-Holocaust
Thought

Emil L. Fackenheim

With a New Preface by the Author

Schocken Books   New York

Library of Congress Cataloging in Publication Data

Fackenheim, Emil L.
To mend the world.
Includes bibliographical references and index.
1. Judaism—Doctrines. 2. Holocaust (Jewish
theology) I. Title.
BM601.F29   296.3   81-16614   AACR2
ISBN 0-8052-0938-7 (pbk.)

Manufactured in the United States of America

First Schocken Edition published 1982

TO
MEND
THE
WORLD

OTHER BOOKS BY EMIL FACKENHEIM

Metaphysics and Historicity

Quest for Past and Future:
Essays in Jewish Theology

The Religious Dimension in Hegel's Thought

God's Presence in History:
Jewish Affirmations and Philosophical Reflections

The Jewish Return into History:
*Reflections in the Age of Auschwitz
and a New Jerusalem*

Encounters between Judaism and Modern Philosophy:
A Preface to Future Jewish Thought

Contents

To the Memory of
LEO STRAUSS

Acknowledgments

HOW does a Jew think of future Jewish thought? Of future thought? Of mending the Jewish world? Of mending the world? I confess that all this would be for me humanly impossible were it not for the reality that is Israel—the state, the land, the language, the people. For this reason I owe a quite uncommon debt to the Canada Council and the Social Sciences and Humanities Research Council of Canada for enabling me, a resident of the Diaspora, to spend, between 1972 and 1980, no less than seven summers in Jerusalem. As great is my debt to the Killam Program of the Canada Council for giving me an additional summer, as well as the two calendar years of 1977 and 1978 in uninterrupted leisure. To this the University of Toronto added yet another half year.

I cannot mention by name all the friends, colleagues, students and acquaintances who helped me in many ways. I must name, however, these Israeli friends: Yehuda Bauer who gave me a historian's help of confronting recent Jewish history "as it really was"; Moshe Davis who involved me in some of his numerous activities of building and rebuilding; and Pnina and Pinchas Peli who time and again opened for me aspects of the Israeli reality that I could hardly have come upon simply by myself. I must also thank Michael Morgan for reading and re-reading portions of the developing manuscript in stages when its meaning could be fathomed only by a reader of great fidelity. Finally

I must mention my family: my wife Rose, and our children, Michael, Suzy, David and—he arrived midway, a great disturbance to progress—Yossi. In the work on this book I was required to immerse myself in dark realities and to think dark thoughts. They gave me the strength and the perspective to look, in the darkness, for light.

In conclusion I must explain the dedication. It is a gesture long overdue. Ever since my student days, it was Leo Strauss—first, the author of books, later also the personal mentor, this even when I no longer saw him, but often kept thinking of him—whose example has convinced me, more than that of any other Jewish thinker alive in my own lifetime, of the possibility, and therefore the necessity, of a Jewish philosophy for our age.

Toronto
November 1981

Preface to the
Second Edition

T HE word "Holocaust" has not appeared in the title or
subtitle of any of my previous books, the first edition of the
present one included. Ever since I became seriously involved
in the subject in the late 1960s, it has seemed to me that its
name should be used sparingly, lest it be used in vain.

But the time for restraint is long past. The name is being used
in vain every day. Distortions, abuses, exploitations abound.
Yet the meaning of the word is clear and established. It refers
to the isolation-by-definition, ostracism, legalized spoilation
and eventual murder of every available Jew, for no reason other
than birth, by a German regime that came legally to power on
January 30, 1933, held undisputed sway until May 8, 1945, and
was recognized universally, a universality that came to an end
only on September 3, 1939, the day of the outbreak of the Second World War.

The regime was criminal from the start. In its twelve years—
like unto a thousand for its victims—it committed numerous
crimes other than the Holocaust, but also different in very definition. Had blacks ever become important, they would have
been defined and treated (as Poles and Russians were in fact)
as *Menschentiere* ("human animals"), to be used for work. To
work them to death was often desirable, for in the eyes of the
regime the sin of members of "inferior races" was that there
were too many of them. The sin of the "non-Aryan vermin,"

by contrast, was to exist at all. And who was "non-Aryan"? A
Japanese was an honorary "Aryan," and so was the "Semitic"
Mufti of Jerusalem, a welcome guest in wartime Berlin. With
the possible (but questionable) exception of a Gypsy, the only
"non-Aryan" was a Jew.

If the meaning of "Holocaust" is clear and established, why
is the subject surrounded by controversy, and the word prey to
obfuscation and abuse? Since *To Mend the World* is not a sociopolitical work but one that hovers between philosophy and
theology, both focused on ultimates, it is best for me not to be
diverted by lesser causes (including offensive, even obscene
ones), but to turn at once to the ultimate cause. To murder the
very last member of a well-defined group of human beings, man,
woman and child? To "comb" (an expression much employed)
Paris and Amsterdam, Warsaw, Vienna and, needless to say,
Berlin itself, lest even one be overlooked? To consider this task
so supremely important as to persist in it even as a Reich that
was to last a thousand years was, after a mere twelve, collapsing
in a nightmare of fire and death of its own people? Why, such
a thing is "not human nature"! Future historians may well
conclude what is already asserted by fake historians and other
scoundrels—that the Holocaust never happened: how could the
humanly impossible, way back centuries ago, ever have actually
occurred?

To rely on experience-tested beliefs about human nature is
itself human nature. It is therefore also natural for historians
and social scientists, for philosophers and theologians—to say
nothing of ordinary folk—to link the Holocaust with crimes and
disasters no less great, perhaps, but more readily intelligible.
The early historians of the Second World War were wont to
bury the Holocaust in footnotes. Now that any such interment
is impossible—made so by an army of Holocaust specialists—
some historians have fallen to flattening out the event through
a process of universalization. Why, Nazism was but one of the
several "fascisms," and the Holocaust (though deplorable, of
course) was not of its essence! To universalize further, "fascism" itself was but one manifestation of a still wider phenomenon, a "modern loss of transcendence," and for the historian

to rise to this view is to partake of philosophy! Most universalizing of all has been that self-styled master philosopher-
historian of them all, Arnold Toynbee. On a notable occasion,[1]
he declared that what the Nazis had done at Auschwitz was
"nothing unusual": it was but a case of Man's-inhumanity-to-
Man-in-wartime. Thus it has come widely to seem that the true
Holocaust criminal was not one particular regime but "Man";
that his victim was not one particular people but, once again,
"Man"; and that to hold otherwise is to be prey to an unphilosophical parochialism.

Philosophers, to be sure, universalize. But universalizing of
this kind is not philosophy but its opposite. Ever since Plato,
philosophy originates in wonder, a wonder aroused when what
to opinion is evident on reflection becomes a problem, a riddle,
an enigma. To universalize the Holocaust—to flatten it out into
one case among many, to link it with disasters and crimes no
less great, perhaps, but within the parameters of "human nature"—all this is therefore to avoid precisely what ought to
arrest philosophical thought. It is escapism-into-universalism,
in the case of the Holocaust the most fashionable escapism of
all. Philosophy—nay, an intellectual probity well within the
scope of ordinary, unphilosophical folk—thus makes it imperative, if and when the Holocaust is compared to other crimes
and disasters, to be arrested by the stumbling block of the
difference.

Not all are guilty of escapism who, on hearing of the Holocaust, start thinking and speaking of children in Hiroshima or
Cambodia then and there, or of other children here and now,
some starving in Africa, others languishing in refugee camps,
others still tortured and murdered in places of inhumanity. To
do such thinking and speaking is legitimate, however, only if
it is accompanied by the recognition that the subject is being
changed.

So tempting is such a change that it may occur even when it
is not in evidence. What the Western democracies did and did
not do; how Danes differed from Poles and Ukrainians when
their Jewish neighbors were carried off; whether or how the
victims themselves might have reacted in ways other than they

did: all this, to be sure, is part of the Holocaust. But the by-standers, accomplices, martyrs, resistance fighters and most of all the victims are viewed in a false perspective if the focus is on them and not the criminals. To shift the focus away from these and their crime, then, is also a change of subject.

The subject is sometimes changed even when the focus is and remains on the crime and the criminals—by historians when they place both into "historical perspective." To be sure, a historical perspective is necessary if the subject is how millennia of Jew-hatred made the Holocaust possible. An abyss still exists, however, between the background of Auschwitz and Auschwitz itself. To deny this abyss or even to ignore or belittle it—all this in the light of this or that historical perspective—is, then, yet another escape from the stumbling block of the difference and a change of subject: here the Holocaust is being tamed, as it were, in the process of being fitted into an academic curriculum. Yet this catastrophe, though in history—the history of the "humanly possible"—can never be made to be quite of it. As survivors have borne witness these many years, the Holocaust is a "kingdom" not of this world.

Establishing the facts, the historian must also explain them. Following the pioneering work of Raul Hilberg, others have therefore investigated the bureaucratic, legislative, technological, psychological, ideological and other methods by which, little by little, step by step, the regime made the "humanly impossible" possible after all. But few have shared his prudence—as Hilberg himself put it—in confining themselves to the "small" questions, for fear of giving "too small" an answer to the "big" question.

What are the small questions? The definitions, rules, regulations; the chain of command; the train schedules and the trains' operators; the supply and cost of the gas: in short, how it was done. What is the "big" question? Why it was done at all. Once, the only "good" Indian was the "dead" Indian, yet Indian reservations were allowed to remain: Jewish reservations in a victorious Nazi empire are inconceivable. In the First World War, Armenians were deported and murdered just as Jews were in the Second: yet no one "combed" Istanbul lest here and there an Armenian be overlooked. Some Cambodians have sent others to "killing fields": yet the fields neither killed all nor were meant to kill all. Once captains of ships that brought blacks to America gave pregnant female slaves a care denied others since, after all, they would soon be mothers of future slaves: a Jewish pregnancy at Auschwitz meant instant death for mother and unborn child. The stumbling block of the difference of the Holocaust, then, gives no rest to the historian of probity; and he stumbles when at last the "big" question comes into view. Why did they do it? "They wanted to do it"—but one does not do everything one wants to do. "They decided to do it"—but why did they make so "pointless"[2] a decision? "The point was ideology"—but why believe doctrines backed by little evidence, and incoherent enough to make a "Semitic" Mufti into an honorary "Aryan"? And why act on such doctrines to the bitter end, nay, even beyond: the main point of the Führer's "last will and testament" was that more must be done by surviving Germans to make the world *judenrein*.

Historians who lack Hilberg's prudence do answer the "big" question. But they all sooner or later come up with the smallest answer of all, smallest because it is a nonanswer: they were mad, they were possessed by a "biologistic insanity"![3] *This* is the answer? While Rome burned, a mad Nero fiddled—alone; in a burning Berlin, many little Hitlers fiddled with the one and irreplaceable one, and while this took place in the heart of the Reich, still other little Hitlers force-marched their victims from Auschwitz westward lest, liberated by the Russians, they survive. That Rome was set afire by a mad individual is an explanation. That the fires of the Holocaust are the work of a mass madness explains too little because it asserts too much; it is, in fact, but an admission (conscious or unconscious) that explanations have come to an end.

So long as he reflects on historical (or sociological, or psychological) explanations, the philosopher ministers to these disciplines. It is when these explanations have reached an end that the wonder in which philosophy originates comes into its own. So does the "abiding wonder" of the Israelites when at the Red Sea, their history almost ending violently when it had barely begun, they were "saved" by a "miracle."[4] The wonder, abiding then, continues to abide; it is experienced, year after year, when a Jew at Passover celebrates the fact that, saved by the beginning of his history, he continues to survive.

II

A Jew thinking of Hitler remembers Pharaoh, Amalek, Haman: closest is Haman. Pharoah enslaved the Israelites. Amalek attacked the weakest. It was Haman who planned to kill all the Jews. However, Haman failed, and Jews celebrate. They celebrate on Purim.

Christians, too, celebrate. Their greatest celebration is Easter. But just this Christian celebration has unhappy memories for Jews—and, after Auschwitz, for conscientious Christians also. Of these, one, a German pastor, once felt compelled to go so far as to begin his Easter sermon as follows: "This is the day on which we take vengeance on the Jews for killing Christ."

In 1967 Purim and Easter fell on the same day. It also so happened that for this Purim-Easter there was scheduled in New York a symposium, "Jewish Values in the Post-Holocaust Future," the proceedings of which, it was understood, were to be published.[5] One participant would be Elie Wiesel, the one writer then known to me who genuinely confronted Judaism with the Holocaust—and the Holocaust with Judaism. I, too, was asked to participate. All my instincts wished to refuse, but how could I? I accepted. It would be the first time for me to speak on the Holocaust—knowing that what I would write and say would subsequently appear in print.

I had been writing philosophical and Jewish essays for two decades. My *Religious Dimension in Hegel's Thought*[6] was about to be published. In these previous writings, I had said quite a lot about evil-in-general, even radical- and demonic-evil-in-general. References to Nazism, too, had not been absent, and when back in 1961 my *Metaphysics and History*[7] began with the threat of "ideological fanaticism," the allusion had been to Nazism. But just how easily a Nazism without Ausch-

witz becomes one-of-several-fascisms we have already seen
—how easily but falsely: when this particular "ideological fanaticism" was dying, the last message of its spiritus rector climaxed in the call, not for a resurrection of Nazism, but for a
continuation of the Holocaust. (Nothing even remotely similar
occurred when fascism died in Italy or Spain.) In my pre–1967
writings, then, I myself, though never flattening it out into "fascism," had treated only Nazism-in-general.

But now I would address the Holocaust, and the task was to
relate it to "Jewish values." Why had I wished to refuse? In all
the preceding years, why had I avoided the painful subject? As
I struggled with the now accepted task, this became all too clear.
A stumbling block for the historian, what if the Holocaust were
a stumbling block also for Judaism? The historian stumbles only
on the "big" question: what if a Jew confronting the catastrophe
had the Jewish faith destroyed—ever after? For two decades
one part of my thought—the other had been philosophy—had
been preoccupied with Judaism, the theological renewal of it
and return to it: what if I had been whistling in the dark? Jewish
thinkers still widely view the Holocaust as but another in the
history of Jewish destructions, and Hitler as but another Pharaoh, Amalek or—most appropriate—Haman. They are respected, and I respect them myself, for I had done much the
same thing for so long. But, in my struggle for Purim-Easter
1967, I could do it no more. Haman had failed; the new Haman
had not. For the one, the death-meriting offense had been an
act of one Jew; for the other, the birth of all. And as for viewing
the murder of Jews as more important than the very survival
of Persia, such an "insane" idea never entered the biblical vil-
lain's mind. Nor did it enter the minds of the great and numerous Jewish commentators who, though bearing the burden
of the many destroyers who had succeeded where Haman had
failed, elaborated on the wickedness of Pharaoh, Amalek and,
of course, Haman himself.

In preparation for the now unavoidable task, I desired two
things. If unable to stay—stay exclusively—with biblical pro-
totypes—Pharaoh, Amalek, Haman—I wished to stay at least
with precedents of past destructions, such as those of the two

temples, the expulsion from Spain, the seventeenth-century Chmelnitski massacres, for these, long absorbed as they were by the Jewish faith were, so to speak, safely past. Still more did I desire to keep the name of Hitler out. The rabbis add "may his name be wiped out" if and when they do mention Titus and Hadrian, the one a Roman who destroyed the Jewish state, the other another Roman who some six decades later sought to destroy Judaism itself. But could Hitler's name be mentioned at all? When Hadrian forbade the practice of Judaism on pain of death, Rabbi Akiba and the rest of the "ten martyrs" defied his edict, were caught and tortured, and died with the *Sh'ma Yisrael* on their lips: their martyrdom can be remembered even on Yom Kippur, the most solemn of Jewish festivals, for it has renewed the Jewish faith—and administered Hadrian a post-humous defeat. In the most painful possible contrast, Hitler's name could not be mentioned without the specter of posthumous victories for him. Hadrian's edict gave the ten martyrs the choice between life and the risk of death. But the new Jewish crime was not an act—the practice of *mitzvot*, the study of Torah, the ordination of new rabbis—but birth; and with Teutonic consistency the Holocaust was engineered so as to give few would-be Akibas the choice of how to die, and none at all that between life and the risk of death. For Judaism, then, the Holocaust is a destruction without adequate precedent: it is new.

Enough is recognized of this newness for Jews to have refused to mingle the commemoration of the Holocaust with that of other destructions: Yom ha-Shoah is set aside for the Holocaust alone. But how to observe it? A Jew may still fall back on past resources in memory of those left with the choice of how to die, the new martyrs with the *Sh'ma Yisrael* on their lips, the new heroes with guns in their hands. With birth being the new Jewish crime, however, the most characteristic new victims were those robbed of choice altogether: the children too young to choose, and the *Muselmänner* unable to choose any longer. Of the first, a Polish guard has testified that they were thrown into the Auschwitz flames without being killed first, that their screams could be heard at the camp. Of the second, Primo Levi has written: "One hesitates to call them living; one hesitates to call their death death." (See below, ch. II, section 4; ch. IV, section 13,D.) *Muselmänner* were those near-skeletons who, their feelings, thought and even speech already murdered by hunger and torture, still walked for a while till they dropped to the ground.

Has Hitler, then, succeeded where Hadrian failed? Jewish faith is renewed by the ten martyrs: is it destroyed by the screams of the children and the no less terrible silence of the *Muselmänner*? As I struggled with the now accepted task, Nietzsche's wise dictum kept coming to mind, about truths so terrible that they should be kept secret.

What emerged at length and was presented at the symposium was the (subsequently much quoted, but also misquoted, misunderstood and even distorted) "614th commandment," forbidding Jews to give Hitler posthumous victories. According to the classical sources, 613 commandments were revealed to Moses on Mount Sinai. Though never Orthodox, I have always revered the sources, and a (non-Orthodox and pluralistic) commitment to Sinai and Revelation has been first in my Jewish thought, and will, I think, remain with me to the end. Through the ages, rabbis not insensitive to new challenges have found it possible not to add to the 613. Though differing with them on much else, I would have much preferred to follow them in this particular: what commandment can be ranked with Sinai and Revelation, however "liberally" the two are understood? Yet to stay with the 613 now proved impossible. As honesty with the facts and fidelity to the victims was making something new—the naming of Hitler—unavoidable, along with it emerged a new necessity. It was forbidden to allow the posthumous destruction of the Jewish faith in Man, God and—this even for the most secularist of Jews—that hope without which a Jew cannot live, the hope which is the gift of Judaism to all humanity. To deny Hitler the posthumous victory of destroying this faith was a moral-religious commandment. I no longer hesitated to call it the 614th commandment: for post-Holocaust

Judaism it would be as binding as if it had been revealed to Moses at Mount Sinai. The long-avoided but now accepted task, then, did not destroy my Jewish thought but revolutionized it.

I remain with the 614th commandment to this day—as far as it goes. *To Mend the World* was conceived, written and published fifteen years later because, even with subsequent modifications and elaborations,[8] it does not go far enough. The necessity to deny Hitler posthumous victories is moral and religious, but is it an ontological possibility? If the Holocaust is "not human nature"; if the "humanly impossible" became real in the crimes of the criminals and the sufferings of the victims, how can the denial to Hitler of posthumous victories be a "possibility" that lies within "human nature"? When all is said and done, must not the Holocaust either cease to be a stumbling block for the Jewish faith, after all, in which case the 614th commandment is unnecessary, or else be and remain a stumbling block, in which to obey that commandment is "humanly impossible"? Must not Judaism either survive the Holocaust fundamentally as it was, or else, if not destroyed, at least be altered beyond recognition?

The question is not only theoretical, for philosophers and theologians. For sensitive Jews it has permeated the length and breadth of Jewish life all along and, as knowledge of the Holocaust is spreading, the second and third generations find it hard to avoid it. Yom ha-Shoah is established; the babies and the *Muselmänner* must be commemorated: then how can a Jew rejoice but a few weeks later in the Sinaitic gift of the Torah, as though the "covenant" then established remained "unbroken."[9] And then, when the year is done and Yom ha-Shoah approaches once more, how can he celebrate the Passover, as though the "wonder" of "salvation" reexperienced through the ages "abided" still? Must not the post-Holocaust Jew either fail to take Yom ha-Shoah with the seriousness it requires, or else have the knowledge of it permeate, alter beyond recognition, or possibly even destroy the whole of his Jewish life?

The 614th commandment failed to address this Jewish question. It was inadequate also in responding to a Jewish question and to this alone.

The martyrs, resistance fighters and most of all the victims are all viewed in a false perspective if the focus is on them and not the criminals.

I have made this assertion relative to history. It also applies to Jewish thought. Bar Kochba's fighters against Hadrian were inspired by hope; the ghetto-fighters against Hitler, by despair. When Hadrian had won, Akiba chose to risk death; when Hitler was winning, nameless Akibas could not choose whether but only how to die. Even these heroes and martyrs, then, are made different by the new crime. As thought—any thought—turns to the children and the *Muselmänner*, to avoid a shift to the crime and its newness becomes altogether impossible. How did the "humanly impossible" become a real "world" at Auschwitz, thus ceasing to be humanly impossible? If Auschwitz is "not human nature," what must be said of a world—*To Mend the World* calls it antiworld—in which the most "unnatural" crimes were the norms of daily behavior, and any show of ordinary decency, itself unnatural? These questions are not for Jews alone. They are not about storm troopers and kapos alone. They concern the whole human condition—and are for philosophers. Can philosophers carry on with their traditional business—the part of it in which human nature is involved—as though the Holocaust had not occurred? If carrying on, do they legitimately rise above or illegitimately evade the stumbling block of its difference? If the latter, does (as Theodor Adorno has said) that difference "paralyze" the "metaphysical capacity" (see below, ch. III, section 11), and if it does, must future philosophy confine itself to humanly irrelevant or trivial activities, such as symbolic logic, the philosophy of science, or the logic of such statements as "The cat is on the mat"? Philosophy, then, would seem to be faced with a question not much different from that faced by Jewish thought: must it be the case that either the Holocaust is no stumbling block for their discipline after all, or else, if a stumbling block it is and remains, that the humanly relevant parts of it are altered beyond recognition, if not wholly destroyed?

To Mend the World, then, could not be a book in Jewish

thought without also being a book in philosophical thought.[10] Moreover, if the 614th commandment was to be preseved, deepened and followed through the length and breadth of its implications, the book had to focus all else on a single problem. The Holocaust must be viewed as no less than a rupture, and this not only of Jewish faith and life but of all things hitherto considered "human"; is it possible to view it as such and yet affirm a "mending of the world"? The reader who does not recognize this as the fundamental problem of *To Mend the World* may understand much in the book but not its central problem. Whether it is solved in the book is for critics to debate. For my part, at any rate, I pondered its argument for nearly a decade before publishing *To Mend the World*. And as I reponder it five years after, find no fault in it.

                                   III

To Mend the World ends with chapters on rupture and mending, the one of philosophical, the other of Jewish, thought; the necessity of both has become obvious. But why a chapter on Christianity? Franz Rosenzweig's *Star of Redemption*, a "philosophical system," treats Christianity as well as Judaism. (See below, ch. II, section 3.) The present book can have no such ambition for—this is argued at its very outset (ch. I, section 2)—while the *Star* could still be a whole containing all things, now "systems are gone," leaving us only with the "systematic labor of thought" (ibid.). Hence, while as it moves to its end the book passes through thinkers bound up with Christianity—Hegel, Kierkegaard and Rosenzweig himself, to name only the most obvious—its end does not include "Concerning Post-Holocaust Christianity" so as to wind up, as it were, things Christian as well as Jewish. Then why is this chapter present? To write a Christian theology never entered even Rosenzweig's mind—at a time when a "philosophical system" was still possible.

Systems are gone. The *Star of Redemption* is not. A Jewish-Christian dialogue exists with it. It also exists without it, and as such is widely popular even among Jews and Christians unfamiliar even with Rosenzweig's name. After nearly two millennia of sterile Jewish-Christian disputes and worse, this dialogue comes upon old obstacles; it comes upon two new ones as well. Of these latter, one, the State of Israel, it is most urgent to remove. But the other, the Holocaust, is the most profound. Not long ago two high-ranking Catholics paid visits, the one to Yad Vashem, the museum in Jerusalem where the murder camps are overwhelmingly present, the other, the head of his church, to a murder camp itself. No Christian would be moved to visit either place except by care, and none would pay a visit without rehearing the screams of the children and the silence of the *Muselmänner*. Yet the response of both men was that this suffering, like that of the Christ, had been a redemptive gift to humanity, with Pope John Paul II spelling out the sufferers as "Christians, Jews and others." Few incidents could reveal more clearly the trauma of the Holocaust for the Christian faith. During the Holocaust my own teacher, the Catholic philosopher Jacques Maritain, had exclaimed that "the people of Christ had become the Christ of the people." The facts that "the people" includes children, and that children are not martyrs, continues to be unbearable for sensitive Christians; and, nearly half a century after Maritain, few of their theologians, Protestant or Catholic, have yet faced up to it. Why then is the Holocaust the most profound new obstacle to Jewish-Christian dialogue? Because it is a stumbling block for the Christian no less than the Jewish faith.

But must it be a stumbling block also in Jewish-Christian dialogue? No doubt for its superficial manifestations in which Jews, afraid of wounding Christian sensibilities, avoid a subject increasingly wounding to themselves. But what of serious dialogue? What of dialogue among friends?

Throughout life I have had good Christian friends, good Christians and good friends. To friends one owes truth. One owes truth even if it is bitter—and a helping hand. I would like to name some but cannot, for the oldest of them (unaware of these words being written) would wish at all costs to be anonymous. (He has been my wife's friend as well as my own, and this long before the two of us met.) He is a Protestant clergyman, a gifted theologian, and a preacher unlike any other either of us ever heard. When he preached the Bible, he was in the biblical scene he preached on, amid the personages, and so were his listeners. Soon after the war, he went to Europe to see for himself. He went, saw, read, and became what my wife calls an instant survivor. The years wore on. Then, one Sunday in the late 1960s, he preached a sermon on the Holocaust—and never preached again.

Must the Holocaust be a stumbling block between friends, the one a Jew, the other a Christian? Must it be a stumbling block in serious Jewish-Christian dialogue? May it not bring them together rather than set them apart, as they share the pain of rupture and struggle for a mending?

Why is "Concerning Post-Holocaust Christianity" in a book of Jewish thought? In order that such as our Christian friend, who way back became an instant survivor, may one day preach again.

IV

The book, if written today, would be shorter on Rosenzweig and Heidegger, but for different reasons. On Rosenzweig, I wrote at greater length than the book's argument requires in the joy of discovery. On Heidegger, as the years wear on, it becomes increasingly distasteful to write at all. More importantly, even in the age *post Hegel mortuum* as proclaimed by Rosenzweig, the stature of Hegel increases for me, while that of Heidegger is diminished. For all his stress on the historicity of Being, Heidegger ignored flesh-and-blood history—even the torture cellars of the Gestapo, to say nothing of the Holocaust. (See below, ch. IV, section 6.) In contrast, in his time Hegel passed through flesh-and-blood history before transcending it, and would have to attempt doing likewise today. Making the attempt with the flesh-and-blood history of Auschwitz, his thought would be (as Adorno's was) "paralyzed" by inevitable failure: to transcend the Holocaust is impossible.[11] And his own sphere of thought would stay paralyzed were it not for the astounding fact—for *To Mend the World* the crucial fact—that the very sphere of life that does the paralyzing also gives the basis for a mending. For if the wonder in which philosophy originates is turned into paralyzing horror by the "humanly impossible" crime of the criminals, its paralysis is mended by the wonder at the victims who resisted a crime to which resistance itself was "humanly impossible." Readers have understood the argument of *To Mend the World* if they recognize its crucial turning point (ch. IV, sections 8 and 9).[12] For a full understanding requires a recognition (possible even without a knowledge of Hegel) of the post-Hegelian character taken by the argument at its decisive turn.[13]

Hegel once said that the wounds of Spirit heal without leaving scars. He could no longer say this today. To speak of a healing has become inappropriate. Scars of the wounds of Spirit remain and will continue to remain. But a mending is possible, and therefore necessary.[14]

I

Introduction

1. Introductions

WHEN Franz Rosenzweig published his *Star of Redemption*, he left it without an introduction. He did not wish to behave like a chicken that clucks after having laid an egg. Yet four years later he had to write a belated introduction after all. Without it the book was unintelligible.[1] The present work, too, requires an introduction, and for much the same reason. Like Rosenzweig's work, it has a systematic, comprehensive purpose, and authors of philosophical or theological works with such a purpose face a difficulty: they cannot say everything they wish to say and that needs to be said. Nietzsche compares authors of philosophical systems to men descending into a bottomless cave, and asks why they did not descend further but stopped where they did. It does not seem to have occurred to him that a good many of these authors asked this question themselves—yet did what they did.

This difficulty would seem to leave an author with but three choices. He can, like Nietzsche himself, give up on systematic comprehensiveness altogether and resort to aphorisms and epigrams. Or he can lapse into the Germanic custom of composing prolegomenon after prolegomenon, without ever reaching the subject proper. Finally he can do what Rosenzweig did well and what Hegel did with unmatched mastery—point to what must remain unsaid in the context of what is being said, not only by hints and allusions spread throughout the work, but also, and above all, through the structure of the work as a whole. In that case, however, there is need for an introduction that is itself free of hints and allusions: if the work itself must somehow be esoteric the introduction must be exoteric.

The present introduction, in addition to doing what is always needful, must explain why a book with a systematic purpose came to assume so odd a form. And the exoteric explanation called for is a genetic one. What must be shown is how this book came to be written.

2. Systems

Among my first literary efforts was an outline of modern Jewish theology—the plan of a system.[2] This plan never got beyond the outline itself, for the whole project soon proved to be in principle misguided. A theological system that is premodern in spirit may base itself on dogmas accepted on authority. A theological work that is modern in spirit must spurn premodern authorities, and cannot be systematic unless it also involves philosophy; and the resulting system, inevitably too neat, is bound to place theology and philosophy alike into shackles that are unacceptable.[3] That this is so I might have known, in the case of philosophy, from its whole history. In the case of theology I might have derived it from the insight—I first came upon it in Buber's teaching—that revelation, as understood in Judaism, must be open-ended or in any case inexhaustible. However, the systematic impulse misled me for a time to underrate what I should have known and indeed did know. The lesson of this danger in the search for system has remained with me in my subsequent thought.

The immediate lesson, however, was not an outright rejection of system but rather a closer inspection of the circumstances in which, in a modern context, systems seem possible and necessary. In philosophy, this is when there is reason to believe that philosophical knowledge is complete; in theology, when the same is believed about revelation. (A theology that does not rest on revelation is part of philosophy.) Both these beliefs have found their greatest expression in the system of Hegel. The Hegelian system also suggests that the only theology that can ever be a system is the Christian, on the grounds that the Christian revelation alone lays claim—or lays a defensible claim—to completeness.

That this suggestion is not altogether true, even in modern times, was shown in the *Star of Redemption*, the "system" at once "Jewish" and "philosophical" of Rosenzweig. That Hegel's suggestion is not true at all of premodern times is shown by virtually all medieval Jewish thinkers, the most famous claim to completeness being Maimonides' thirteen principles. But, as has already been hinted, there is one great difference between the medievals and the moderns—and we cannot return to the Middle Ages. To be sure, Maimonides asserts the completeness of the Jewish revelation—that Moses is the chief of the prophets both before and after (principle 7), and that his Torah is unchangeable (principle 9). However, like his medieval Christian and Muslim counterparts, he bases this assertion on revealed authority. And since authorities, revealed or other, are mutually incompatible and rule one another out, this fact suffices to bar the systems based on them, by the standards of a critical, open-minded, antiauthoritarian modernity, from genuine comprehensiveness. (Rosenzweig terms an authority-based thought "fanatical"—a term which, incidentally, is meant to be purely descriptive and without derogatory connotations.) In contrast, in the explicitly "unfanatical" *Star of Redemption*, the Jewish people is the anticipating witness of the *whole*, *all*-comprehensive Truth, even though the witness himself and his testimony, being merely anticipating, are both fragmentary.

The *Star* is not only the most recent but also the last system, not only within the sphere of Jewish thought but also beyond it. Today there can be none, or none that is not an anachronism. This conclusion I long suspected but did not fully reach prior to the present work, in which the reasons for reaching it are fully spelled out. Then what remains of system when "systems" have come to an end? Kierkegaard found it necessary to set existential commitment above detached, systematic reflection: in this he set a task, whether for himself or others, of explicating the relation between this "above" and what is below it. On his part and by his own confession, Martin Buber philosophized not more than necessary; in this he left for others the task of philosophizing as much as possible. Systems are gone. What remains—in philosophy, theology, and the relation between them—is the systematic labor of thought.

3. Revelation

If the first, as it were formal, commitment of my thought that
was to remain permanent was to "system," the first lasting
commitment, so far as content is concerned, was to the Jewish
faith. By "Jewish faith" I understand now, as I did then, a
commitment to revelation; and by "revelation" I understand
now, as I did then, not propositions or laws backed by divine
sanction, but rather, at least primordially, the *event* of divine
Presence.

Of the German Judaism of the 1920s Leo Strauss has written
that "it was granted by all except the most backward that the
Jewish faith had not been refuted by science and history"; and
that this was so because revelation—the incursion in the human world of a divine Other—was not a supposed past fact
only but also, potentially, a present experience.[4] What was
true for Strauss in the 1920s was also true for my generation of
the 1930s—more intensely so, as it were, since the fateful year
1933 had intervened. The key question for us was whether
human existence in general, and Jewish existence in particular, is open or closed to the incursion of the Divine. And
whereas it was possible and necessary for philosophy to explore the implications of the two alternatives, the decision
between them—whether, in case of a *seeming* divine Presence,
it is *actual;* and whether, in case of a divine Absence, a Presence is *possible*—was a commitment, or an act of faith.

The "return to revelation," associated within Judaism mainly
with the names of Buber and Rosenzweig, by no means provided an all-at-once solution to theological and philosophical
problems. (Its main immediate merit was a new, exciting, ex-
hilarating access to the Jewish tradition, on terms including a
wide range of legitimate possibilities, from Buber's extreme
Halakhic liberalism to what might have become, in the case of
Rosenzweig had he lived, a wholly orthodox religious practice
based on new foundations.) It would be more correct to say that
the new way of understanding raised old (and also some new)
problems with a depth and seriousness unmatched since
premodern times. Among these problems were the following:

How to understand an event of incursion that was to be accepted as divine; how to relate it to a reception that interpreted the event yet is itself human; what roles were to be assigned to the human and the Divine in a new biblical hermeneutic; and, in and through all these questions, how to reach the content of revelation—and indeed, how to move from the sheer event of divine Presence to any content at all.

Momentous events have happened in Jewish life since the "return to revelation" of two generations ago. These events have also implicated theological thought since one cannot postpone, say, Halakhic solutions of Israeli problems until one's theoretical theological thought is complete. However, in the realm of purely theoretical Jewish thought, and despite claims in this or that quarter to having "gone beyond" Buber and Rosenzweig, the main characteristic of more recent Jewish thought is, by comparison, its low level. And the consequence is that the pioneering work then accomplished still waits for adequate successors.

If my own early efforts in this area[5] became, after a while, more hesitant, it was not because of second thoughts about the "return to revelation." (I remain committed to it to this day.) Rather, so far as I was concerned, the focus of the agenda had changed. In response to the challenge of modernity, modern (mainly nineteenth-century) Jewish thinkers had created a fateful split between the Jewish people and Judaism, in effect making the flesh-and-blood people over into a bloodless sect of "missionaries" to "mankind." (They had their nemesis in a secularist Zionism that made Judaism over into "Jewish culture" if it did not reject it altogether.) The "return to revelation" sought to heal this split. This is evident, in the case of Buber, in his embrace of Zionism; in the case of Rosenzweig, it appears most prominently in the arresting view that even the apex of Jewish spiritual existence is systematically impossible without a matrix in the flesh-and-blood people. Still, neither thinker wholly overcame the fateful split. Indeed, in some respects, they both deepened it. This is illustrated, in Buber's case, in a Zionism spiritualized in the extreme at the very time that the flesh-and-blood people—first, the Yishuv, later the State of Israel—were fighting for their lives. (The fight still is not over.) In Rosenzweig's case, it is evident in the fact that his doctrine takes the Jewish people out of history at the precise and historic moment when, after nearly two thousand years, this people—willy-nilly, but in any case inexorably and indubitably—has returned into history.

The focus of the agenda was changed, then, because the achievement of Buber and Rosenzweig had to be liberated from what may be called a fideistic one-sidedness. On the one hand, there had to be a closer affinity with *amcha**—the flesh-and-blood Jewish people with its concerns, day-to-day and not so day-to-day, religious but also secularist, outside Israel but also, and indeed above all, in the new Jewish reality that is Israel. On the other hand and at the same time, there had to be a certain disengagement from what had been, one might say ever since Spinoza, an undue proximity to Christian theology; indeed, a tendency to let Christian theology define the Jewish agenda.

These are the two aspects of what may be called the existential, religious Jewish liberation from fideistic one-sidedness. Its theoretical or philosophical aspects may be put succinctly as follows: after and despite Rosenzweig's encounter with Hegel, there was need for yet another. Hegel is the great, unmatched mediator of all things, and especially of all modern religious and secular things. He would be neither great nor unmatched, however, were it not for his insistence that the authenticity of no claim, however radical, may be compromised in the process of mediation. That Hegel's all-mediating effort failed is not surprising when the claims to be mediated include a Divine descent from heaven so radical as to grip, in Lutheran Protestantism, the human heart on earth, as well as a secularist self-confidence that does not satisfy its search for autonomy until it storms the heavens. Still, there is need for a new encounter with Hegel in what is rightly described as the

---

*Hebrew for "your people." The expression probably harks back to a time in Nazi-occupied Europe when Jews in hiding, unable to trust Gentiles they chanced to meet, would address in this way strangers who they thought might be Jews themselves.

age *post Hegel mortuum.** That this need is not confined to Judaism is suggested by one glance at the most recent career of Christian theology, from the fideistic anti-Hegelianism of such as Karl Barth to its current nemesis, in the odd phenomenon of a Christian Marxism.

A new, Jewish encounter with Hegel, meant for liberation from fideistic one-sidedness, would not achieve any kind of liberation unless it followed strictly, even stubbornly, its own Jewish exigencies. Yet precisely in this stubborn "particularism" it is bound to have "universal" implications. Hegel's mediation of all things is itself Christian or post-Christian. For that reason, and even while marking the end of Christian Constantinianism, it is also, and at the same time, the last non-anachronistic expression of Constantinianism. For these and related reasons, a Jewish testimony against *all* Constantinianism, Christian or post-Christian, given in the midst of the Christian or post-Christian world, is bound to play a pivotal role in the formation of post-Constantinian thought.†

Such was the stage of my thinking when I was forced to face an event that called into question all things—God, man, the ancient revelation and the modern secular self-confidence, philosophic thought and indeed any kind of thought. That event was the Nazi Holocaust.

4. The Holocaust

The events set in train in 1933, naturally, affected my thinking from the start. My first view of them, however, was of but another, if extreme, expression of human wickedness, Jew-hatred, and Jewish tragedy. To be sure, the case was extreme enough to make it no mere lapse from the progress of modern enlightenment. It seemed dealt with adequately, however, by categories that involved a critique of modernity itself. Nazism and all its works was a case of "the demonic" or "radical evil," and nothing more.[6] The possibility that the Holocaust might be a unique and unprecedented evil in Jewish and

---

*The expression, to be explained in context, is Rosenzweig's.
†On the immediately preceding assertions, see all of ch. III below.

indeed all history I did not consider seriously until more than two decades after the demise of the Third Reich.

No doubt psychological idiosyncrasies, individual or general, had their share in causing this long delay, among them the "denial syndrome" that quite rightly is given much weight by professionals in the field. So far as thought is concerned, I detect in retrospect three factors. First, it is hard to believe that a unique event of catastrophic import should have happened in one's own lifetime, all the more so when one is personally touched by it; it is more reasonable to suppose that the feeling of its uniqueness is the mere result of one's own traumas. Second, if nevertheless the event must be confronted by thought, then an appropriate category—in philosophy, radical-evil-in-general, in theology, the-demonic-in-general— seems sufficient to meet the case; the ingrained habit of thought resists the insight that, in case the event is in fact unique, these categories, simply *because* they *are* categories, are *not* sufficient to meet the case but are actually a means of escape from it. Third, there is the well-known philosophical problem of whether "the unique"—the unique of any kind— can be thought at all.

But what if the Holocaust *is* unique? I first faced this question when, yielding to moral pressure to participate in a symposium on the subject in the spring of 1967, I had no other choice. And my first response was to formulate a "614th commandment," to the effect that Jews are forbidden to give Hitler posthumous victories.[7] I would have much preferred to respond in terms of the traditional 613 commandments. Still more was I averse to mentioning the new, accursed name of Hitler rather than simply making use of the old symbol of Amalek. Still, if the Holocaust *was* unique there was no choice. As it happened, but a short time later the Jewish people collectively shared this perception when, faced with the threat of a second Holocaust in the weeks preceding the Six-Day War, they were, after a long period of repression, at length forced to confront the fact of the first. Thus the "614th commandment" became the only statement of mine that ever became famous.

But if the people shared this perception, this was not true, generally speaking, of the professors. To this day philosophers keep on acting as if, philosophically, there is no difference between the six million and one child dying of cancer, just as theologians keep on acting as if, theologically, the "case" of Auschwitz were "covered," respectively, by Good Friday or the ninth of Av. So far as most philosophers and theologians are concerned, there simply *is* no Holocaust. Or, alternatively, it is not single but manifold, one catastrophe to be classified with others, such as Hiroshima and Vietnam, Biafra and Cambodia. Such, to this day, is the behavior, and such are the arguments. As for the underlying stance, this comes to light with the charges made against "Holocaust theologians," such as the charge that they are "overemphasizing" the event, in so doing "disturbing Jewish-Gentile relations" and —this is the climax—replacing the "Sinai symbol" with that of Auschwitz. But is it *possible* to overemphasize the Holocaust? And if Jewish-Gentile relations are disturbed, is it not by the event itself, so that these relations can be set straight only by a shared Jewish-Gentile attempt to face it? And what needs to be faced is, of course, not the "symbol" Auschwitz but Auschwitz itself.

In making the attempt one does not practice "Holocaust theology," for there cannot be such a discipline. There is only a theology that is threatened by the Holocaust and that, spurning escapism, saves its integrity by self-exposure to it. *Mutatis mutandis*, I would apply also to philosophy* what Irving Greenberg has said about Judaism and Christianity: "The Holocaust poses the most radical counter-testimony to both Judaism and Christianity . . . . The cruelty and the killing raise the question whether even those who believe after such an event dare to talk about God who loves and cares without making a mockery of those who suffered."[8] Theologians refusing to face this question—and *mutatis mutandis* philosophers as well—merely seek refuge from a unique scandal in an unreal realm of abstract thought.

*The theme "The Holocaust and Philosophy," appearing sporadically throughout ch. IV below, receives concentrated attention in sections 6, 7, and 12.

For whereas "the uniqueness of the Holocaust" is a complex subject that will require much space in the present work, the basic facts are so plain as to be altogether beyond legitimate dispute:

1. Fully one-third of the whole Jewish people was murdered; and since this included the most Jewish of Jews—East European Jewry—Jewish survival as a whole is gravely in doubt.

2. This murder was quite literally "extermination"; not a single Jewish man, woman or child was to survive, or—except for a few that were well-hidden or overlooked—would have survived had Hitler won the war.

3. This was because Jewish birth was sufficient cause to merit torture and death; whereas the "crime" of Poles and Russians was that there were too many of them, with the possible exception of Gypsies only Jews had committed the "crime" of existing at all.

4. The "Final Solution" was not a pragmatic project serving such ends as political power or economic greed. Nor was it the negative side of a positive religious or political fanaticism. It was an end in itself. And, at least in the final stage of the dominion of the Third Reich (when Eichmann diverted trains to Auschwitz from the Russian front), it was the only such end that remained.

5. Only a minority of the perpetrators were sadists or perverts. For the most part, they were ordinary jobholders with an extraordinary job. And the tone-setters were ordinary idealists, except that the ideals were torture and murder.

One looks at this list (which could be expanded) and is hard put to find another catastrophe containing even one of these features. (The Armenian case comes to mind.) To find one containing them all is impossible. This is true within Jewish history. It is true outside of it as well. All this is by no means to deny the existence of other catastrophes equally unprecedented, and endowed with unique characteristics of their own. But to make this admission is only to say that these other catastrophes, too, must be confronted in their own right. To link Auschwitz with Hiroshima is not to deepen or widen one's concern with humanity and its future. It is to evade the import of Auschwitz and Hiroshima alike.*

But if the Holocaust is a unique and radical "countertestimony" to Judaism and Christianity (and, as we shall argue, to philosophy as well), how can there be a "commandment" to resist its destructive implications, to say nothing of the will and the strength to obey it? Must not Jewish and Christian faith (and also, *mutatis mutandis*, philosophical reason) be either, after all, *absolutely* immune to *all* threats or else destroyed by *this* threat? At one time, I did not hesitate to write the seemingly paradoxical statement that "religious faith can be, and is, empirically verifiable, but [that] nothing empirical can possibly refute it." (The statement required a careful explanation even then.)[9] Doubtless the greatest doctrinal change in my whole career came with the view that at least *Jewish* faith is, after all, *not absolutely* immune to *all* empirical events.† But what is the outcome once this admission is made? This has become for me the central question of all Jewish and indeed all "post-Holocaust"‡ thought, so much so that all else depends on how one grapples with it.

For my part, I should surely have shrunk from grappling with this question altogether had it not been for the discovery that while it is still barely asked in the sphere of thought it is already being answered—intermittently and often unconsciously, but for all that altogether decisively—in the sphere of Jewish life. One finds blurred traces of an answer even in the safe, Western "bourgeois" Diaspora, when it pursues such "secular" goals as safety for Israel or rescue for Syrian Jews

*This may be said to be the implicit subject of ch. IV, section 6.
†Cf. *Encounters*, ch. 1, where my new view is developed in the form of philosophical reflection. It has appeared in the form of religious immediacy ever since I was first forced to confront the post-Holocaust Jewish contradiction of being religiously obliged to have Jewish children, and morally obliged not to expose distant heirs to the danger, however remote, of being murdered solely on account of their Jewish ancestry. (See *Jewish Return*, pp. 30, 47 ff.) The majority of Jewish philosophers and theologians still maintain that the Holocaust has done nothing to alter Judaism. I know of hardly anyone who has addressed himself to the contradiction to which I have just referred.
‡Here and in the following this term refers to events, actions, beliefs, ideas that are not only located temporally after the Holocaust but also affected by it.

with a "religious" zeal. One finds clear proof of an answer among refusniks in Riga and Leningrad, Minsk and Moscow* when, though robbed of their Jewish past, they stake all on a Jewish future. And the proof assumes historic—nay, world-historical—proportions in a Jewish state, coming into being on the heels of the Holocaust. Israel needs no justification through a link with the Holocaust. What the link does is make the Jewish state at once a moral necessity and an ontological near-impossibility. Israel is a moral necessity: the bimillenial, unholy combination of Jew-hatred and Jewish powerlessness, always intolerable, is now *absolutely* so. (Hence the enemies of Israel must resort to absolute slander: the Israelis are "Nazis.") Israel is also an ontological near-impossibility: the faith and the courage needed for founding, maintaining, building *this* state, enormous in any circumstances, beggars the understanding in *these* circumstances—after a catastrophe calculated to destroy all faith and all courage, not only among the cousins of the victims, but wherever the news reaches and is understood. And since the faith and the courage are nevertheless actual, Israel is nothing less than an orienting reality for all Jewish and indeed all post-Holocaust thought.

Such were the considerations which at length led me to two conclusions. One is that, in our time, Jewish life is in advance of Jewish thought. The other is that Jewish life itself—intermittently and often unconsciously, but for all that altogether decisively—is in the grip of, and responding to, epoch-making events.

5. *"Foundations of Future Jewish Thought"*: Genesis of a Plan

How does thought stand related to life, and life to thought? This is a fundamental issue in recent philosophical and theological literature. Hegel affirms that thought can come only after life, and can only comprehend what already is, so that the owl of

---

*In 1977 my wife Rose and I spent two unforgettable weeks in these cities, conducting seminars on Judaism for refusniks. We went to teach, but received far more than we could have given.

Minerva rises to flight only with the coming of dusk. For their part, Marx, Nietzsche, and Heidegger (and also, according to rumor, Hegel on at least one occasion) all affirm that thought in some ways precedes and even helps shape forms of life, like a cock that announces a new day. For our part (as will appear again and again in these pages), we find it impossible to furnish the question with an unequivocal, sweeping, and definitive answer. However, if it is indeed the case that Jewish life in our time is in advance of thought, then it is clearly necessary for Jewish thought (and not for it alone) to go to school with life. To be sure, a pupil such as this—contemporary *thought*—would not absorb lessons handed to him without discrimination, but would rather come to school with questions of his own. The answers themselves, however, could not be constructed by thought, but only be given by life itself. In other words, thought has to become, after a fashion, empirical. Hence I set for myself the task of interrogating and listening to survivors and kibbutzniks, refusniks and resistance fighters, rabbis, professors, and taxi drivers. And I defined the whole project for myself as follows: "Radical Responses to Epoch-Making Events in Contemporary Jewish History."*

It gradually proved necessary to expand the scope of the inquiry beyond this "empirical" focus without, however, letting go of that focus. Even the most casual observation showed that what is or is not an epoch-making event depends, as the saying goes, on one's point of view. To go beyond this triviality, by the standards of what may be called pagan thought all things temporal vanish indiscriminately into the river Lethe, so that in one sense all events are epoch-making, and in another none are—a set of circumstances in which philosophical and theological thought must seek refuge from time altogether, in an eternity beyond it. On its part, what may be called normative Christian thought affirms one epoch-making event so momentous but already long actual, as to create doubt whether, ever since, there can be any others. And as for its Jewish counterpart—the "normative" thought of rabbinic Judaism and its

*This was the research project first submitted to the Canada Council in 1971, and pursued with the council's aid until it was expanded in 1976.

"Midrashic framework,"* this is generally thought to affirm
that nothing decisive has occurred, or can occur, between Sinai
and the Messianic Days. Not one of these "points of view" is
vulnerable to the challenge of epoch-making events that are
situated, not in past or future, but here and now.

No Jewish thinker can take lightly the stance of rabbinic
Judaism, or dissent from it without facing unforeseen, perhaps
unforeseeable, consequences. Yet simply to embrace it (as, up
to a point, I once had)[10] would be to prejudge rather than face
what we have called the central question for post-Holocaust
thought: to make Judaism *absolutely* immune to *all* future
events except Messianic ones is a priori to dismiss the challenge of contemporary events, rather than risk self-exposure.
Also, it would be a relapse into a fideistic one-sidedness
which, for my part, I was already in the process of rejecting.
For these and related reasons I had even prior to conceiving
the present work referred to Exodus and Sinai as "root experiences." Secular Jews may reject a miracle at the Red Sea and a
revelation at Sinai but, if committed to a Jewish future, cannot
reject the experience of their people. Moreover, a "root experience," as I then defined it, differs in quality from an "epoch-
making event," but at the same time is not absolutely immune
to its impact.[11]

Jewish thought in our time, then, must move forward, toward self-exposure to epoch-making events. Such a forward
movement, inevitably historically situated as it is, necessitates
a simultaneous backward movement, edging cautiously toward the view that rabbinic Judaism, its normativeness included, is *itself* historically situated: that it is permeated if
indeed not constituted by an epoch-making response to grave
historical events, among them the end of prophecy, the beginning of an exile, and the event that, more than any other, was
indisputable proof at the time that an age had come to an end,

*For all its immense internal varieties developed in a lengthy career, rabbinic
Judaism is both unified and authoritative enough to be considered "normative" even vis-à-vis modern liberal and conservative Judaism, both of which
may be viewed as largely being offshoots of it. That, for all *its* internal varieties, the rabbinic Midrash is unified enough to form a "framework" I have
argued in many places, see, e.g., *Presence*, ch. 1.

i.e., the destruction of Jerusalem in 70 C.E. The fact that rabbinic Judaism was not the only response to that catastrophe is evidenced by the simultaneous spread of plain despair, apocalyptic otherworldliness, and, of course, Christianity. That this response *was* epoch-making, outside Jewish history or at any rate inside it, is shown by the simple reflection that without it the Jewish people, except possibly for some scattered sects, would not have survived. A people cannot last in a disastrous exile unless it can view that exile as meaningful, and unless it has an abiding hope. In short, existence in *Galut* required *Galut* Judaism, defined by the beliefs that exile, while it lasts, must be patiently endured, and that its end is a secret in the keeping of God.

The rabbinic self-understanding takes its classical documents—Talmud and Midrash—to be wholly at one with the Jewish document, i.e., the Jewish Bible. Its own documents are "oral Torah," coeval with and mediating the "written" Torah; and since the Word of the living God is present in both, written and oral Torah alike, as it were, hover in their at-oneness *above* history even while present in it, minimally between the termini of Sinai and Messianic Days, and maximally even beyond them.* One contemplates these facts and concludes that for Jewish thought in our time to *situate* rabbinic Judaism *historically*—as an epoch-making response to an historic challenge—is no light matter. It is a fateful step.

To take this step is not necessarily to deny rabbinic Judaism the status of oral Torah, for a God that speaks *into* history can speak into *a particular* history. It is, however, to let the possibility come into view of a need, in a new epoch, for a *direct* encounter with the "naked"† biblical text, side by side, or even at odds with, the mediating tradition of an earlier epoch. Such a direct encounter is not to be confused with a lapse into fundamentalism, neo-Karaite or other. It may even be viewed as its extreme hermeneutical opposite. All forms of fundamentalism take the sacred text to be immediately accessible, so

---

*This alludes to the traditional doctrine of a preworldly Torah, a Jewish parallel to the Christian preworldly Christ.
†Rosenzweig's expression.

that a mediating tradition is both unnecessary and, in the last analysis, intolerable. On its part, and having been forced to suspend the mediating tradition, a Jewish thought that finds itself situated by epoch-making events also finds itself separated from the biblical text by an historical gulf of millennia, so that it can be accessible, if at all, only by acts of recovery.

A direct encounter with the naked biblical text, once admitted as a theoretical possibility, becomes for contemporary Jewish thought an existential necessity. The naked biblical text is *both* the account of a spiritual *Heilsgeschichte and* the flesh-and-blood history of a flesh-and-blood people. *And, for the first time almost since biblical times themselves, this duality is once again a collective experience—by the same, still existing people!* To be sure, the terms "historical gap" and "acts of recovery" are not confined to a Jewish hermeneutic. (We shall find them to be basic to all truly thoughtful contemporary hermeneutical teaching.)* However, as we shall also find, *this* relation between a present readership and an ancient book is hermeneutically unique. The Jewish return to Zion, in this of all incongruous ages, is in any case, and by all serious standards, astonishing. For Jewish thought in our time there is a special astonishment in the facts that neither "religious" nor "secular" Jews would or could have made this return were it not for that book; that despite the differences or even outright hostility between these two camps, they are committed to a shared future destiny; and that—so one must conclude after much pondering on this vital issue—the shape of this future destiny will depend in large measure on their ability to read the book together.†

Existentially, this backward movement of thought to biblical origins is ultimate. Theoretically, however, the forward thrust toward contemporary, epoch-making events requires a more radical backward move still—a basic, i.e., philosophical, inquiry into the concept "epoch-making event" itself. We have seen that for what was termed pagan thought the very possibil-

---

*See ch. IV, section 11.
†See further below, ch. V, section 5. However, an adequate treatment of this question belongs in Part II of the project as originally conceived, and is beyond the scope of the present work.

ity of epoch-making events does not arise, and that "normative" Judaism and Christianity are either immune to all future events or all except Messianic ones. A self-exposure to epoch-making events is a self-exposure to *history*, and this requires, on the part of the self-exposed thought, a backward-moving inquiry into the concept of *historicity* and the relevant concepts bound up with it, i.e., in the present case, "revelation," "secular self-assertion," and a "transcendence" without which, in the last analysis, neither revelation nor secular self-assertion is possible.

This final and most radical backward move to "first things"—basic "principles" or "presuppositions"—at length suggested a final forward move toward "last things," i.e., so far as is possible within the limits of an historical situatedness, to issues of eschatology. And the resulting overall plan was as follows:

Part I: Fundamental Investigations into (a) Historicity and Transcendence; (b) the Nature, Scope and Limits of Jewish Thought

Part II: The Recovery of Biblical Dimensions

Part III: The Midrashic Framework of Rabbinic Judaism

Part IV: Authentic and Unauthentic Responses to the Holocaust

Part V: Theopolitical Reflections on Israel, the Diaspora and the Religiosecular Conditions of the Modern World

Part VI: The Future as Sociopolitical Goal and Religious Anticipation*

Somewhat to my surprise I had arrived, in conception, if not at a "system," so at any rate at a project of systematic thought.

6. *"Foundations": From Plan to Execution*

But the neatness of the systematic project was soon to dissolve in the process of execution. Since the "going to school" was not

*This outline first appeared in a plan submitted to the Killam Program of the Canada Council in 1976.

to take place until the "empirical" Parts IV and V, the "a priori" reflections of Part I could at most only point to, but not deal with, lessons not yet learned, and such a proleptic stance became increasingly problematic. To come to the crucial problem at once, the difficulty mentioned at the outset—whether the unique can be thought at all—assumed the threat of a war between the epoch-making event most urgently in need of thought—the Holocaust—and the *concept* "epoch-making event," simply *because* this latter is a concept. This problem is neatly illustrated by the case of Hannah Arendt who, qua historian in *The Origins of Totalitarianism*,[12] saw the Holocaust as an unprecedented event and later, qua philosopher, argued that *every* free action is unprecedented, and that *all* events worthy of the name are initiated by free actions:[13] in this manner the unprecedented event of the Holocaust was lost in the concept "unprecedented event." If some such outcome was to be avoided, it could not be by first (in Part I) "defining" a set of concepts, and then (in Parts IV and V) "applying" them, but only if our thought placed itself, as it were, *between* the concept "epoch-making event" and *this* epoch-making event, prepared to be pulled in both directions. For this and other, less crucial, reasons, there had to be what may be called a selective anticipation of the "empirical" Parts IV and V in the "a priori" Part I. And as a result of this change the original Part I has become vastly expanded beyond the original intent, after a fashion comprehensive, and in any case a wholly self-contained work. It is the present book.

This is the change that occurred, on the way from plan to execution, at the "empirical" extreme. Another change of equal import occurred at the opposite, "a priori" extreme. Once before I had attempted to speculate in a philosophical vacuum until wiser counsels prevailed.[14] The same conversion was to take place now, for a second time. Rather than use an abstractly systematic approach, it turned out to be more modest, more prudent and, above all, more goal-directed to use an historical-dialectical approach, i.e., to seek out relevant thinkers of the first rank, and confront their thought with the events to which self-exposure is necessary. Of course, such a method is circular in that who is or is not a thinker either relevant or of the first rank depends on the author's own judgment. But provided this circle is recognized, and the recognition of it permeates the whole discourse, it merely illustrates what was said at the outset—that a philosophical writer with a systematic purpose cannot say everything that needs to be said.

As to who the great and relevant thinkers were, I had some surprises but in the end no doubts. Spinoza's greatness and Rosenzweig's Jewish relevance are unquestionable. But not until the present study did I appreciate adequately either the Jewish relevance of Spinoza, or the fact that, even by the highest standards of twentieth-century thought, Rosenzweig is in its first rank. A surprise too was the relevance of Hegel—his stature was never in doubt—in what is admittedly the age *post Hegel mortuum*. The conclusion resisted and suspended longest concerns the relevance and stature of Heidegger. One cannot ever quite rid oneself of the feeling that Heidegger's thought is flawed, and this quite apart from his bleak record, philosophical as well as personal, in the early part of the Nazi regime. Yet for all that there still remains in his thought a holding-together of a stern insistence on a human, historically-situated finitude with a profound self-immersion in the whole Western concern with transcendence. And since in its unyielding rigor this holding-together has no equal, the failure of Heidegger's historically informed, historically situated thought vis-à-vis one event—the Holocaust—extends in significance beyond his own thought, to the realm of thought as a whole.

In its present, final form, this book may give the impression of being a continuation of my *Encounters between Judaism and Modern Philosophy*. However, a comparison of the two tables of contents will suffice to remove this impression. In the earlier work (which was subtitled *A Preface to Future Jewish Thought*), thought is located between Judaism and modern philosophy, its objective being to expose each to the challenge of the other. In the second chapter of *To Mend the World* (which, as the subtitle indicates, seeks to go beyond a preface) thought is located between the extremes of Jewish modernity—secularism and the "return to revelation"—i.e., already *within* the modern Jewish problematic. The third chapter of the present work, unlike its counterpart in *Encounters*, does not end but begins with the breakdown of Hegelianism—in search, not of Hegel, but of what may be called a post-Hegelian, religiosecular truth. And that the fourth chapter of this book is not an inquiry into Heidegger *per se* is shown sufficiently by the fact that its last, largest and most important part takes leave of Heidegger and indeed all the thinkers who, until then, move somehow with us. In the grim but ineluctable task of a direct confrontation with the Holocaust, our thought receives much help from historians, novelists, poets. It receives more help still—indispensable help— from witnesses that survived the ordeal and told the tale. But so far as thought (philosophical or theological) is concerned, one still is, except for a few comrades-in-arms, alone.

7. Napoleonic and Related Strategies

In his belated introduction to the *Star*, Rosenzweig urged the reader to follow a "Napoleonic strategy." If bewildered by either the content or the purpose of the beginnings, he was to move on "bravely" to the end, to the "main center of the forces of the enemy," and the "fortresses" left behind unconquered would fall by themselves.[15] As it has turned out, a similar strategy is advisable in the present case: here too, to change the metaphor, things will fall into place only as the reader moves toward the end.

There, however, the resemblance ends. The *Star* is an anti-Hegelian antisystem, made necessary by the fact that the history of philosophy from Parmenides to Hegel has run its course.[16] The present work is made necessary by events, not in the history of philosophy but in history. And since one of these—the Holocaust—ruptures both history and the history of philosophy, there can be no question here of a system or even an antisystem. And even the systematic exposition alters at least in tone at the point of which it becomes necessary, first, to confront the rupture, and then to attempt to reach the other side. And the "main center" of the whole—what makes things fall into place—comes into view only on this other side. But can *that* side be reached at all?

We must, in any case, begin with *this* side and, so long as we stay on it, the main themes of the required Jewish thought (and also philosophical and Christian, insofar as they are relevant) are clearly recognizable, and so is a progression in our exploration of them. We begin with a clash between the extremes of Jewish modernity, i.e., secularism and a postsecularist commitment to revelation.* Thereupon—lest we be prey to an unconscious or uncritical "Jewish parochialism"—we widen our scope so as to consider this clash within modernity as a whole, thereby placing Jewish modernity in its context. Also and at the same time—this so as to remove fideistic and indeed all forms of one-sidedness—we consider ways in which the clash itself may be mediated.† Our systematic progression does not even falter as, next, we immerse our thought in historical finitude, this so as to let transcendence itself come under critical scrutiny.‡ However, when at last there remains no choice but an overt confrontation of thought with the Holocaust,§ there occurs a radical change, of which a change in tone is only the outward expression: thought must either flee from the event into unauthenticity or else suffer collapse, for, as Theodor Adorno has written, after Auschwitz the "metaphysical capacity" is "paralyzed." Thus we come to a dead halt, and our prior achievements or conclusions all remain suspended unless and until it is possible, nevertheless, to move on—unless we can both confront the abyss and reach the other side.‖

It is at this point that our going-to-school-with-life, occurring sporadically throughout, begins in earnest. Astoundingly, the world of the Holocaust, paralyzing our thought long after,

*See below, ch. II.
†See below, ch. III.
‡See below, ch. IV, sections 1–4.
§See below, ch. IV, section 6.
‖See below, ch. IV, section 7.

did not succeed in wholly paralyzing, even as the world held total sway, some of those most exposed to it. This enormous fact marks the beginning of our schooling,* and the going-to-school itself continues to take place to the end of the work and beyond. And only in this context can the "central question" of our whole inquiry be both asked and answered—how Jewish (and also Christian and philosophical) thought can both expose itself to the Holocaust and survive.†

I already once ventured an answer to the central question a good many years ago: the Commanding Voice of Auschwitz that *bids* endurance also *gives* the power *of* it.[17] This may be taken as a Kantian answer, to the effect that we *can* do what we *ought* to do. It may also be taken as a neo-orthodox (Jewish and Christian) answer, to the effect that a Grace that gives commandments also gives the freedom to obey them. But however taken, the answer is radically inadequate. In giving it I had lapsed into an unconscious glibness, for at the time I had yet to immerse myself adequately in that dark world to which we refer today as the Holocaust. This was indeed *a world*, and it was dominated by a "logic of destruction" that left untouched neither God nor man, neither hope nor will, neither faith nor thought.‡ And all brave talk today, *after* the Holocaust, such as "never again" or "we can do what we ought" or "faith is indestructible" either knows not what it says or else is haunted by the fear that, were it then and there rather than

*See below, ch. IV, section 8.
†See below, ch. IV, sections 12–14. A chapter "On Philosophy After the Holocaust" in a work of Jewish thought is sufficiently explained by its author's conviction (which permeates the entire present work) that one cannot be a modern Jewish thinker without also being a philosophical one. A chapter "Concerning Post-Holocaust Christianity" in such a work is more problematic, for one cannot be both a Jewish and a Christian thinker. The reasons for the presence of this chapter will appear in context later on. Here it suffices to say that the absence of such a chapter would lend comfort to both a Christian and a Jewish triumphalism: to the first, in fostering the opinion that whereas the Holocaust may rupture Judaism it leaves Christianity untouched; to the second, in fostering the view that whereas the rupture of Judaism can have a *Tikkun* ("mending"), Christianity is ruptured beyond repair.
‡Our self-exposure to Nazism occurs in this book in several stages; see below, ch. IV, sections 6 and 8.

here and now, its God and man, hope and will, faith and thought would all be indiscriminately prey to the Nazi logic of destruction. The most original, most characteristic product of the entire Nazi Reich were the *Muselmänner*, "the drowned . . . and anonymous mass . . . of non-men who march and labour in silence, the divine spark dead within them . . . . One hesitates to call them living: one hesitates to call their death death."[18] Who dares assert that, had he been then and there rather than here and now, he would not have been reduced to a *Muselmann*?

Only in this midnight of dark despair does post-Holocaust thought come upon a shining light. The Nazi logic of destruction was irresistible: *it was, nevertheless, being resisted.* This logic is a *novum* in human history, the source of an unprecedented, abiding horror: but resistance to it on the part of the most radically exposed, too, is a *novum* in history, and it is the source of an unprecedented, abiding wonder. *To hear and obey the commanding Voice of Auschwitz is an "ontological" possibility, here and now, because the hearing and obeying was already an "ontic" reality, then and there.** Pelagia Lewinska writes:

At the outset the living places, the ditches, the mud, the piles of excrement behind the blocks, had appalled me with their horrible filth. . . . And then I saw the light! I saw that it was not a question of disorder or lack of organization but that, on the contrary, a very thoroughly considered conscious idea was in the back of the camp's existence. They had condemned us to die in our own filth, to drown in mud, in our own excrement. They wished to abase us, to destroy our human dignity, to efface every vestige of humanity . . . to fill us with horror and contempt toward ourselves and our fellows.

. . . From the instant when I grasped the motivating principle . . . it was as if I had been awakened from a dream. . . . *I felt under orders to live.* . . . And if I did die in Auschwitz, it would be as a human being, I would hold on to my dignity. I was not going to become the contemptible, disgusting brute my enemy wished me to be. . . . And a terrible struggle began which went on day and night.[19]

*For these Heideggerian terms, see below, ch. IV, section 4.

It is symbolic of the universal significance of this statement that its author is not a Jewess but a Polish noblewoman, and also—so we shall have reason to assert—an honorary Jewess.

In substituting a theologically neutral "Commanding Voice" for my original theological "614th commandment" I had no wish to practice a theology of cooptation but, on the contrary, attempted to overcome fideistic one-sidedness, and in this had in mind Buber quoting Nietzsche to the effect that "one takes and does not ask who gives."[20] However, in 1967 I did not imagine (and Nietzsche and Buber in their time could not have imagined) circumstances in which such as Pelagia Lewinska heard orders not of their making, and found the will and the strength to obey them. But now that these orders, this will and this strength are all before our thought, it has no higher or more urgent task than to contemplate them. And, however long and deep its contemplation, it will never cease to be amazed.

8. Language

All writing about the Holocaust is in the grip of a paradox: the event must be communicated, yet is incommunicable. And the writer must accept this paradox and endure.

That this paradox has a special dimension for the philosophical writer was illustrated by Hannah Arendt's *Eichmann in Jerusalem*.[21] The philosopher must grasp a phenomenon as a whole. Attempting to grasp *this* phenomenon as a whole, Arendt adopted an "objective" stance of "clinical" detachment—and lapsed into irony. But for thought to detach itself from *this* phenomenon is *already* to distort it; and to lapse into irony is inadmissible.

Up to a point, the problem was solved in Terence Des Pres's *The Survivor*. Faced with "life in the death camps," Des Pres could not "write about terrible things in a neutral tone . . . [so as] to generate an irony so virulent as to end up in either cynicism or despair." At the same time, "to allow feeling much play when speaking of atrocity [was] to . . . reduce the agony of millions to a moment of self-indulgence." What remained was to write in an "archaic, quasi-religious vocabulary," for "only a language of ultimate concern [could] be adequate to facts such as these. [22]

But for the philosopher Des Pres solves the problem only up to a point. One can write in a quasi-religious vocabulary about the victims—those who endured the atrocity, lived with it, resisted it—for one can identify with them. But one cannot write in this way about the criminals—those who inflicted atrocity, gloried in it, preserved it on snapshots for the pleasure and profit of their children and children's children; and for a writer to identify with them would be his ultimate corruption.* Then how shall a philosopher write about the Holocaust in its totality, i.e., about the world that was the context of "the Survivor's" struggle?

One may wish to reply: by resorting to a thought and a language that enter into that world and also seek a transcending comprehension of it. Such was the strategy of Hegel, the master strategist vis-à-vis totalities. In his maturity (when in his view he had attained a transcending comprehension, not only of wholes but of an ultimate Whole of wholes) Hegel rose also above the language of involvement, and warned philosophy against the temptation to be edifying.[23] In his youth (when he was still on the way and indeed considered the goal unattainable) he exalted the language of involvement: since philosophy must "stop short of religion," one could speak of divine things only in a language of enthusiasm.[24]

But Hegel instructs only by way of contrast. His ultimate Whole of wholes is one of divine wonder. The Holocaust, on its part, is a whole of horror. A transcending comprehension of it is impossible, for it would rest on the prior dissolution of

---

*In a letter to me, dated April 16, 1976, Professor Des Pres writes in reply to my assertion that it is as necessary to write about the criminals as about the survivors: "I write through some sort of deep identification with my subject, and although I am quite willing to admit that in me as in all men there is the fullest range of good and evil, there is surely much damage and much danger to be borne if I use myself, as I did with survivors, to write about the criminals. I might even be able to do it well, but at what cost?" This profound statement should give food for thought to any writer about the Holocaust. For my part, I am greatly indebted to it.

a horror that is indissoluble. This horror leaves our thought and our language with but two choices. One is surrender—as we have said, the ultimate corruption. The other is the "no" of an ever-new, ever-again-surprised outrage.

This outrage, needless to say, would be lost by a "clinical" tone of "objective" detachment. It would be lost no less surely, however, by a "self-indulgence" in the writer's own mere feelings. The *facts themselves* are outrageous; it is *they* that must speak through *our* language. And this is possible only if one's feelings are subject to disciplined restraint. The language necessary, then, is one of sober, restrained, but at the same time unyielding outrage.

This language first forced itself on those most desperately concerned to communicate the incommunicable—the survivors. All writers coming after them will always remain in their debt. To be sure, novelists and historians, philosophers and theologians are often tempted to "go beyond" the survivors, to "transcend" in imagination or comprehension their "limited perspective." But one need only reread Jean Améry or Chaim Kaplan, Primo Levi or Elie Wiesel in order to realize that to attempt to go beyond witnesses such as these is to have remained behind; that, after what has occurred, the going-to-school of thought with *this* life is not a temporary necessity but permanent.

9. *Toward Future Jewish Thought*

We return to our theme: future Jewish thought. The impatient will ask: what are our post-Holocaust "options" *now*? Is truth to be found in the Whiteheadian God, infinite in goodness but finite in power, unable to destroy evil and hence *this* evil? Or is it in a mystical infinity, blotting out by its presence *all* history and hence *our* history? Or are there third or fourth or fifth options available for our choice? But "options" such as these, if true at all, are true not for our time but all time: by their standards, the Holocaust is not a new reality but merely a new debating point for old philosophies or theologies. As for the going-to-school by thought with life, this, if by their standards ever necessary at all, is over and done with now. Yet one glance at contemporary thought suffices to show that the necessary schooling has hardly begun. And the true question before us is whether a present attempt on our part, not to think future Jewish thought but merely to give foundations for it, does not, like Nietzsche's madman of a century ago, come too soon.

In Jewish history, this possibility is supported by compelling precedents. A third-century Midrash pictures God as waking up in the middle of the night and roaring in pain like a lion, for He has burned His temple and exiled His children: but it took almost a thousand years for this Midrash to be reflected in ritual.[25] Again, after the expulsion from Spain it took "almost an entire century" for its "tremendous implications [to] permeate ever more profound regions of being."[26] We must ask: is the Holocaust not a far more devastating catastrophe than these other two? Should there not be, then, a philosophical and theological moratorium on this subject, perhaps for centuries to come?

Grim necessities dictate otherwise. The victims of 70 C.E. and 1492 C.E were exiled or expelled but lived; the victims of the Holocaust, for the most part, were murdered. The earlier catastrophes were great but not beyond belief, and thus lived on in the memory of the generations until the time was ripe for a response. Our catastrophe, in contrast, is beyond belief and becomes ever more so with the passage of time. Hence already distortions abound on every side; and even the denial that it happened at all—it is all a Jewish invention, subserving a sinister plot—is beginning to find a respectful hearing. As these words are being written, the survivors are planning a worldwide conference in Jerusalem, in a last and desperate attempt to communicate their incommunicable truth. Their attempt is desperate: the world does not listen and would find it hard to hear even if it did listen. Their attempt is the last: in view of their ever-diminishing number, after this conference there will be none other.

In these circumstances, thought cannot wait for a ripeness of time that may never arrive. Rather than hope for a wisdom that comes only after a day of life is done, it is gripped by the necessity to announce and help produce a new day while there is yet night. And it cannot be deterred by the obvious fact that its announcing and producing, insufficiently wise as it is, must be both fragmentary and uncertain. In my earlier *Preface to Future Jewish Thought* I cited Rabbi Tarfon, to the effect that the day is short, the work great, the laborers sluggish, the wages high, and the Householder urgent. Now, almost a decade later, another saying of the same rabbi seems even more fitting for Jewish thought in our time:

לא עליך המלאכה לגמר

ולא אתה בן חורין להבטל ממנה

It is not incumbent on you to complete the work. But you are not free to evade it.

II

The Problematics of Contemporary Jewish Thought: From Spinoza Beyond Rosenzweig

1. Introducing Spinoza and Rosenzweig

ONLY two modern Jewish philosophers of the first rank considered their Jewish identity as a philosophical issue. The first—Baruch Spinoza—opted out of Judaism and showed his modernity by refusing to seek refuge in a religious alternative, i.e., for all practical purposes, in Christianity: he was a "free" man-in-general. The second—Franz Rosenzweig—was carried by his postmodern critique of modernity to the very portals of the church, yet returned to Judaism: he was a "free" Jew-in-particular. Events from Spinoza to Rosenzweig showed, for all with eyes to see, that in the modern world only Jews attempted, and were expected, to become men-in-general: the man-in-general was a chimera. Events since Rosenzweig have shown, for all with eyes to see, that the price for his return to Judaism can no longer be paid. Rosenzweig was able to carry out his postmodern return to the premodern Jewish faith only by making *all* Jewish existence ahistorical or, which is the same thing, by sacralizing it. (While much in world history was of great moment, in Jewish history nothing of moment had happened or could happen between Sinai and the Messianic days.) Yet, less than four years after Rosenzweig's death events began to unfold—events still far from over and done with—which, for better or worse, have cast the Jewish people back firmly, inescapably, irrevocably, back into history: not into sacred history, but rather into the flesh-and-blood history of men, women, and children—as Rosenzweig himself well put it, the history of *Mord und Totschlag*.* With this startling fact in contemporary history a new Spinoza might have been

*Of his teacher F. Meinecke he wrote: "he treats history as though it were a Platonic dialogue, not murder and manslaughter [*Mord und Totschlag*]" (*Life and Thought*, p. 17).

able to deal. However, the actual Spinoza in his time had opted out.

This gives a first indication of the problematics of present and future Jewish thought. It also suffices to show that, if we are not blinded by presumptuous folly, we cannot hope to understand or cope with that problematics unless we consider Spinoza and Rosenzweig. However, because of their profundity, radicalism, sobriety, and freedom from all self-deception we are able to confine our attention to these two thinkers. At least among modern Jewish thinkers we need attend, for the purpose at hand, to no one else.*

A comparison of two short treatises by these two thinkers will provide a preliminary clarification of the issues. Neither treatise was published by its author in his lifetime. Both contain the nucleus of the mature thought, in the one case as a blueprint for work yet to be done, in the other as a summary of work already done. In neither book is the author's Jewish identity so much as mentioned. Yet in both a certain stand toward this subject is clearly presupposed or implied. And since, astoundingly enough, the two works read as if written deliberately against each other, to read them together is to be vouchsafed a rare, not to say unique, insight into the way the issues are joined.

As indicated by its title, Franz Rosenzweig's *Understanding the Healthy and the Sick* seeks to heal some who are ill. Who are these ill? Those "paralyzed" by the "wonder" of philosophy. It may be natural for men to wonder. But it is not natural to be so "numbed" as to "retreat from the flow of reality into the protected circle of wonder,"[1] to a supposedly "true" reality behind "mere appearance," one to which all things are reducible. This may be a "Self" writ large, a "World" or "Nature" writ large, or a "God" writ doubly large since He is no longer *over against* self or world but rather is *the* "Reality" immanent in both.

In Rosenzweig's own mind, and for reasons of his own, other philosophical patients were higher on the priority list

*See above, ch. I, section 6.

than Spinoza. Yet objectively none is as much in need of the cure. No modern philosophical work, Spinoza's own *Ethics* alone excepted, resorts as speedily to a "true reality" behind all the "appearances" as that thinker's *Short Treatise on God, Man and His Well-Being.* And that reality—the Spinozistic God—is hardly affirmed when all things known and unknown reduce themselves to His—Its?—"attributes." Chance, free will, good and evil all are the product of mere opinion, and as opinion is transcended by "clear knowledge" we free ourselves ever more fully from the passions which flow from opinion so as, in the end, to reach oneness with God.

But on its own terms the *Short Treatise,* so far from inviting therapy, is itself a form of therapy. The "God" or "Substance" at the beginning, rather than being a shadowy "essence," is being *verified,* as it were, as the *Treatise* proceeds. And what verifies it is the passage of the mind from servitude to freedom. So long as a person is ruled by opinion he is ruled also by the passions which are its companions. It is as his reason transforms opinion into knowledge that he comes to dominate his passions which were hitherto, in a manner of speaking, other than his self, dominating *him.* And the increase in well-being, serenity, and reality thus achieved reach their climax when a person has climbed the "staircase" of reasoning and becomes united with the highest good "which union is our supreme happiness and bliss."[2] As for those who cannot see the possibility of this ascent or do not attempt to carry it out, they are the true patients. And as for philosophers who have considered the possibility and yet reject it in the name of a "return to common sense," their return is to "philistinism."

Such might be the case of Spinoza against Rosenzweig. Yet the words just cited are taken from Rosenzweig himself, and he writes them in order to stress that philosophy is the "enemy" only when it assumes "that it is possible for something to exist beyond reality."[3] However, this charge against the "guilty" philosophies would have real force in Spinoza's eyes only if a point were reached at which the mind's transcendence of passion is no longer a way to freedom and reality but rather an escape from both: a point, that is, at which "emotion" or "passion" must remain what they are, passively related to both world and God (in case God is) and compelled to accept them in their otherness. Moreover, this "must" will be rejected by the accused philosophy as a mere "maxim of weakness,"* unless the world and God accepted as other are in fact other: unless the disclosure of their otherness is even for the most critical mind one of truth.

The contrast between the two brief works, then, is clear. And it reaches its most revealing climax in their respective treatment of the phenomenon of surprise. In his examination of "what is good and bad in the affects or passions," Spinoza treats surprise as his first topic because, though neither good nor bad, it is an "imperfection" "arising either from ignorance or prejudice"; hence it makes a man vulnerable to evil even though, "through itself," surprise does not lead to evil.[4] For his part, as Rosenzweig turns from "diagnosis" to "therapy" he first considers a "sudden fright, an unexpected happiness, a blow of fate far beyond the ordinary"; and he asserts of these experiences that they "can dispel at once the delusions of the misdirected reason."[5] Spinoza views surprise as an imperfection—perhaps the most harmless of imperfections but an imperfection still—which is removed to the extent to which ignorance and prejudice are removed. In direct contrast, Rosenzweig considers surprise—or at any rate, some surprises, whether like joy for good, or like fright for ill—as a shock of recognition which can communicate reality when perhaps nothing else can. For Spinoza, surprise is a mere subjective feeling and hence a condition which is overcome to the extent to which ignorance and prejudice yield to knowledge. For Rosenzweig, surprise can have an objectively revelatory, ontological status. The issues could not be more clearly and dramatically joined.

Is this conflict arbitrary? And what philosophical bearing (if

*This phrase is used by Fichte in criticism of Kantians who maintained in Kant's name that thought had to stop somewhere in its attempt to free itself from the authority of "the given" (see Wissenschaftslehre of 1804, ed. Medicus [Leipzig: Meiner, 1922], p. 18). Since Rosenzweig's "therapy" aims at idealistic as well as Spinozistic seekers after "ultimate Reality," patients other than Spinoza head his priority list. Foremost among them, of course, is Hegel.

any) does it have, on the opting out of Judaism by the one thinker, and on the return to Judaism by the other? As we now turn to the main body of Spinoza's and Rosenzweig's works, both questions will be found to be inescapable. However, only to the extent to which the two answers are interrelated are they relevant to the future destiny of Jewish thought.

To the "pure" philosopher it may well seem that to assume an interrelation at all is already to beg a major question. Surely the *Ethics*—a "universalistic" work in which Judaism does not appear—is only accidentally related to the *Theologico-Political Treatise*—the only major work recognized by the history of philosophy in which Judaism appears so prominently that, were the references to it excised, the work would be destroyed!* And surely Rosenzweig's "anti-speculative," existential "new thinking"—which he himself associates with Schopenhauer, Nietzsche, Kierkegaard and, subsequently, Heidegger†—must stand or fall quite independently of his "particularistic" Jewish commitments to which it leads him! However, even the strangely parallel biographical facts relative to the two works suggest that the dichotomies are not so neat. Thus Spinoza was already at work on the *Ethics*—its blueprint, the *Short Treatise*, was complete—when he composed the *Treatise*. For his part, Rosenzweig had already returned to Judaism before completing his *Hegel und der Staat*,[6] his great work on (in his view as well as, incidentally, our own) the greatest and most modern of all the "old" thinkers. Thus we cannot dispose of the relation of either Spinoza's or Rosenzweig's Jewish and philosophical thought in terms of that most

---

*The recognition of the *Treatise* by the academic philosophical establishment may well be due to the prestige enjoyed by the *Ethics*. On the other hand, since the intrinsic philosophical merit of the work is no greater than, say, that of Maimonides' *Guide*, one cannot ever quite rid oneself of the suspicion that the *Treatise* is considered philosophical because it denigrates Judaism whereas the *Guide* is considered unphilosophical because it espouses Judaism. (Reputable scholars quite habitually praise Spinoza for having "outgrown" the "narrowness" of his tradition.) The Christian commitments of St. Augustine's *Confessions* or St. Thomas's *Summa Theologica* have rarely been a bar to the admission of these works to the category of philosophical classics.

†On the first three, see the opening pages of the *Star*. On Heidegger, see Kl.Schr., pp. 354–56.

beloved of philosophically-accidental explanations, the genetic-biographical. Indeed, we cannot dispose of it in philosophically-accidental terms at all.

2. Baruch Spinoza

Why does the author of the *Ethics*, who claims to rise above all bias and prejudice to nothing less than eternity, resort in his *Theologico-Political Treatise*[7] to the grossest distortions of the minority religion which he has left, especially and above all whenever he compares it to the majority religion which he yet refuses to embrace?* A few examples suffice. Judaism is "particularistic," whereas Christianity is "universalistic." The Mosaic ethics is only materialistic, utilitarian, and confined to the needs of a state, hence not truly moral. The ethics of Jesus (invariably referred to as Christ) is spiritual, universalistic, and thus truly moral. The Jewish religion is only a political religion, if indeed it may be called a religion at all. The Christian religion transcends political limitations and indeed—so it seems—actually makes possible a secular state. Moses was no philosopher, but Jesus, after a fashion, philosophized. And whereas the Jews followed Moses in this respect, it was the Gentiles who followed Jesus.

Thus none of the Apostles philosophized more than did Paul who was called to preach to the Gentiles. Other Apostles, preaching to the Jews, who despised philosophy, similarly adapted themselves to the temper of their hearers (see Gal. 2:11) and preached a religion free from all philosophical speculation.

---

*On Spinoza's refusal to embrace Christianity, see especially letter no. 76 (*The Correspondence of Spinoza*, ed. A. Wolf [London: Allen and Unwin, 1928], pp. 350–55). In a letter to Spinoza, Albert Burgh, himself a convert to Catholicism, had adduced the martyrs of the church as proof of the truth of Christianity. In the above-cited letter Spinoza replies that Jews "number far more martyrs than any other nation." He goes on: "I myself know, among others, of a certain Judah, whom they call the faithful, who in the midst of the flames, when he was believed to be already dead, began to sing the hymn that begins 'To Thee, O Lord, I commit my soul,' and died in the middle of the hymn."

Spinoza completes this passage (and ends the chapter) with this exclamation:

How blessed would our age be if it could witness a religion freed also from all the trammels of superstition![8]

One is tempted to reply: how blessed might Spinoza's philosophy have been had it transcended bias and prejudice against the religion which conscience had forced him to forsake!

For that there is any truth in these and similar comparisons between Judaism and Christianity can be seriously considered only by surviving members of a species of anti-Semite (primarily though not exclusively academic), which developed in modern times, largely under Spinoza's own influence.* In each of the cited examples, the exact opposite could be argued with equal plausibility. Judaism is "universalistic," for it teaches that the righteous of all nations enter the Kingdom of Heaven. Christianity is "particularistic," for it bars from the Kingdom all unsaved non-Christians, no matter how great their righteousness.† The Mosaic ethics is truly moral, for it demands only what man can do. The ethics of Jesus falls short of true morality, for it demands of men what they cannot do, and hence ought not to do. The Jewish theocracy in its time was harmless, for it did not last and, moreover, was limited while it lasted by a permanent conflict between king and prophet, power and spirit. The Christian theocracy, in contrast, is dangerous, for it has lasted (up to and including Spinoza's own tolerant Holland); and, more seriously, it has united power and spirit in an infallible papacy—and in the Inquisition. Finally,

*In a still authoritative essay Hermann Cohen asserted more than half a century ago that Spinoza remains to this day the accuser of Judaism *par excellence* before an anti-Jewish world. See *Jüdische Schriften*, ed. B. Strauss (Berlin, 1924), III, 290–372, esp. 363, 371. See also L. Strauss, *Preface*, p. 368. We shall refer repeatedly to Strauss's remarkable essay.

†When Adolf Eichmann was on trial, a Canadian missionary traveled to Jerusalem with the purpose of converting him. When asked whether a last-minute conversion would save Eichmann's soul he answered in the affirmative. When asked whether the souls of Eichmann's Jewish victims were saved, he answered in the negative.

whereas surely neither Moses nor Jesus were "philosophers," the rabbis expressed a poetic truth of sorts with the legend that Plato studied with Moses when, in contrast, St. Paul found himself forced to tell his Greek listeners that his message was foolishness in their eyes (I Cor. 18 ff.)

If such apologetics in behalf of Judaism are foolish, they are surely no more so than the Spinozistic attacks by which they are provoked. *But is Spinoza foolish?*

To add to the puzzlement, *does this of all philosophers act in bad faith?* According to his own claims a close student of the Jewish Scriptures, Spinoza surely knows that the commandment or permission to hate one's enemy, a New Testament charge against Jewish teaching, is not found in these Scriptures. And the onetime rabbinic student surely also knows that his attacks on "the Pharisees," like those of the Gospels, are quite unfounded.*

It seems, then, that when writing of Judaism, and in particular of Judaism in conjunction with Christianity, Spinoza not only writes falsely but does so *against his better knowledge.* But is Spinoza—a secular saint unable either to recant or convert, one compelled to leave the synagogue and yet to stay outside the church, and content to suffer the consequences—is he no better than all the Jewish opportunists who showed their old Jewish knowledge and new Christian zeal by slandering the Jewish writings?

Perhaps Spinoza's knowledge of Jewish tradition, though better than that of most Gentile philosophers who accepted his views, is not good enough. Perhaps one must consider the fact that his community consisted of former Marranos—long forced to practice Christianity outwardly, returned to the open

---

*See Cohen, p. 358. Spinoza quotes Matthew 5:43 ("Love thy neighbour and hate thy enemy," Tr., ch. XIX, p.250), referring to evidence adduced in ch. XVII. In the evidence adduced, however (Ps. 139:21, 22) the Psalmist expresses hatred for those who hate God. He does not say (as Spinoza makes him say) that "other nations" are "God's enemies" (Tr., ch. XVII, p. 229). Perhaps the most damning evidence of bad faith on Spinoza's part is his identification of the rabbis with "the Pharisees" as stereotyped in the New Testament. (See esp. Tr., ch. III, pp. 52 ff.; ch. IV, p. 72.) Does Spinoza wish to ingratiate himself with Christians who accept the stereotype?

practice of Judaism but recently, and hence inwardly and out-wardly insecure. A noted Spinoza scholar writes:

Everyone else in Europe was born into pre-determined categories of thinking, Jews into the categories of law and justice, Christians into the categories of original sin and redemption. Here, however [i.e., in the Amsterdam Jewish community] there is for the first time a group of people without pre-determined categories of their own, a people with a ruptured consciousness. From this rupture of consciousness emerged modern consciousness. A people looked for the coasts of the old homeland—and Spinoza discovered a new world.[9]

There is little doubt that in their insecure grasp of the "old homeland" Spinoza's teachers so narrowed its borders as to affront their sensitive young student. And there is less doubt still that the *Treatise* is the work of one who, at home in no land yet found, seeks to discover a "new world." Much can be said for this way of viewing Spinoza. He would be neither the first nor the last Jew who was at home neither within nor without the Jewish community of his time—and shook the world.*

What, then, is the "new world" sought in the *Treatise*? It is a state—so Spinoza tells us in the Preface—in which free thought and hence "worship . . . as conscience dictates" is both possible and necessary: in short, a liberal state. The liberal state stands or falls with the distinction between the public duty of civic obedience and the private right to belief and its free expression. The liberal state stands by this right. It must fall unless the right is vigorously used. For the state is threatened by no greater danger than the political exploitation of the superstitious fears of the multitude. Masking these fears with the "specious garb of religion," "despotic statecraft" can induce men to "fight as bravely for slavery as for safety, and count it not shame but the highest honor to risk their blood and their lives for the vainglory of a tyrant." Hence when

---

*The most obvious examples are St. Paul before Spinoza and Karl Marx after him. On St. Paul viewed in this perspective, see *Kl.Schr.*, p. 531. On Marx, see H. Liebeschütz, *Von Georg Simmel zu Franz Rosenzweig* (Tübingen: Mohr, 1970), pp.209 ff.

"opinions are put on trial and condemned on the same footing as crimes," despotism either prevents the liberal state from arising or is in the process of destroying it.

The Treatise, then, sets out to demonstrate that "not only can freedom [of opinion] be granted without prejudice to the public peace, but also that, without such freedom, piety cannot flourish nor the public peace be secure."[10] No wonder all kinds of Jews were to be in the forefront of those following Spinoza into his new world. Members of the minority faith par excellence in Christian countries, they could expect freedom of opinion, or at any rate of its expression, from none but the liberal state. As for Spinoza himself, he was doubtless concerned with freedom for Jews as well as Christians; "while he may have hated Judaism he did not hate the Jewish people."[11] His battle was on behalf of all men.

Spinoza's main aim in the Treatise, then, is to defend the liberal state. His main problem is this: What if true piety rests on a body of truth which is publicly revealed, i.e., the Jewish and Christian Scriptures? The problem arises because a truth, if divinely revealed, is surely binding, and because the revelation, if public, must threaten the distinction by which the liberal state stands or falls. Spinoza proposes to solve this problem by demonstrating that it results from the illegitimate mixing of the Scriptures with philosophy; that if Scripture is read in the light of Scripture alone it teaches "nothing repugnant to our understanding"; and that this is so partly because Scripture conforms to our understanding, but, more importantly, because, whereas the object of philosophy is truth, that of revelation is obedience. Hence "everyone should be free to choose for himself the foundations of his creed, and . . . faith should be judged only by its fruits."[12]

Such is Spinoza's program as stated in the preface. One need not go beyond one expression in the preface itself—"the Universal Religion, the Divine Law revealed through the Prophets and Apostles to the whole human race"[13]—in order to anticipate problems in the execution. No Jew would accept this definition. (Jews need Moses as well as the prophets but not the apostles in order to achieve righteousness, and "righteous Gentiles" need neither prophets nor apostles but only the laws of Noah.)* Nor would, for obvious reasons, non-Jewish non-Christians accept it. Must we say, then, that Spinoza's thesis that religion teaches morality and not truth presupposes one truth from the outset: that Christianity—however interpreted and whether or not leaving room for a Judaism of sorts as well—is revealed?

This question, in fact, haunts the entire *Treatise*. And it takes its most poignant (or, at any rate, in our context most significant) form in the uneven treatment meted out to Judaism and Christianity. By any standard, Spinoza has the task to criticize Jewish and Christian bigotry. But by the standard he applies he criticizes Christian bigotry as a practice in contrast with Christian teaching whereas, when criticizing Jewish bigotry, he does not hesitate to criticize the teaching itself, and not merely the practice: certainly that of "the Pharisees," but also (though more circumspectly) the Jewish Bible itself.

This lack of evenhandedness has far-reaching consequences. To this day Spinoza is celebrated as a pioneer in biblical criticism, if not as its founder. His own critical practice rests on the famous principle that "just as the interpretation of nature consists in the examination of the history of nature . . . so Scriptural interpretation proceeds by the examination of Scripture"; that what Scripture does or does not mean can be discovered not by adducing "the speculations of the Platonists and Aristotelians"[14]—or, for that matter, the rabbinic "oral Torah" or Spinoza's philosophy—but only through Scripture itself. This principle itself, however, rests on the prior rejection of Scripture as revealed *truth*: if Scripture is one source of truth, and philosophy another, might it not be possible, indeed mandatory, to interpret the two in the light of each other?

To answer this question one need not go beyond Spinoza's own treatment of Christianity or, more precisely, beyond his treatment of Jesus and Paul. Spinoza spends much time and effort on castigating Maimonides for reconciling the Jewish Bible with Aristotelian philosophy. On his own part, however,

*According to rabbinic teaching, Noah was given seven laws, and "righteous Gentiles" observing these laws have a share in the world-to-come.

he habitually—one might almost say, systematically—rec-
onciles the teaching of Jesus and Paul with the true philosophy,
i.e., his own. And since this is decidedly *not* "interpreting
Scripture in the light of Scripture," *Spinoza emerges not as the
founder of biblical criticism but rather as the founder of "Old
Testament" criticism only.* Only concerning the Jewish Bible is
the formerly single inquiry—into the meaning of Scripture, and
ipso facto into its truth—to be split in two. Concerning the New
Testament, or at any rate concerning Jesus and Paul insofar as
they are treated in the *Treatise,* the formerly single inquiry is to
remain single. One might go so far as to say that it is not biblical
criticism, but rather this discriminating stance, that is original
with Spinoza. And traces of this particular discrimination remain among Bible scholars to this day.

We are thus driven back, with increased urgency, to our
original question: why does the author of the *Treatise* resort to
distortions and discrimination against the minority religion
which he has forsaken, especially and above all when compared to the majority religion he has yet refused to embrace?
Bearing in mind all the aforesaid, many answers to this question can no longer be given.* And any answer which *can* be
given must come to this: the discriminating treatment is somehow necessary for the achievement of the fundamental goal of
the *Treatise*—the fostering of the liberal state. The work is
addressed to would-be philosophers who, at the same time,
are still believers, i.e., potential or actual bigots. And the goal
is to actualize their potential for philosophy and to destroy
their bigotry or susceptibility to it.

But why should this noble goal require means which, if
used against the author's better knowledge, are ignoble, and, if
based on insufficient knowledge, bar the work resting on it
from serious attention?

This question has a "Machiavellian" answer.† Christian

---

*Among these is, of course, the view that there *is* no distortion but rather
truth. This view survives, for example, in the Marxist doctrine that whereas
all religions are false, Judaism is more false than Christianity.
†The profoundest exponent of this view is Leo Strauss. In addition to his
Preface, see esp. "How to Study Spinoza's Theologico-Political Treatise," in
Persecution and the Art of Writing (Glencoe: Free Press, 1952), pp. 142 ff.

would-be philosophers exceed Jewish in number and—more importantly—in power. Spinoza can hope to free Christians from their prejudices only by appealing to them. And since these include prejudices against Judaism, he resorts to the tactic of making the Jewish elements in Christianity, and more specifically the "Old Testament, the scapegoat for everything he finds objectionable in actual Christianity." If this is the correct answer, then Spinoza must indeed be presumed to write against his better knowledge. Moreover, one must judge that he "plays a most dangerous game" and that his tactic, whatever its motive, is "amazingly unscrupulous." That the motive is to foster the liberal state is obvious, as is the corollary that such a state is tolerant toward Jews as well as Christians. However, grim hindsight knowledge teaches us that one does not foster tolerance of Jews through slanders of Judaism. When we consider the countless academic anti-Judaic heirs of Spinoza in both the liberal and the Marxist world, we must conclude that his tactic backfired.[15]

But the Machiavellian answer cannot be the sole or ultimate answer.* More precisely, the end—which is to liberate Jews as well as Christians from religious tyranny—is more important than the means, the unscrupulous ones included. Hence while, like his liberal-academic heirs, Spinoza spiritualizes the Hebrew prophets, thus exempting them from his general strictures against the "carnal" Old Testament, unlike these heirs he attributes to them a morality no less exalted than that of Jesus and the Apostles, and a universality more restricted not in quality but only in the accidental scope of their audience. And the purpose of this exercise is disclosed when at last he confesses to having

no further fear in enumerating the dogmas of universal faith or the fundamental dogmas of the whole of Scripture, inasmuch as they all tend . . . to this one doctrine, namely, that there exists a God, that is, a Supreme Being Who loves justice and charity, and Who must be obeyed by whosoever would be saved; [and] that the worship of this Being consists in the practice of justice and love towards one's neighbor.

*Until this point our interpretation is much indebted to Strauss.

The seven "dogmas" that follow are meant for obedience more than for knowledge. For since reason by itself induces in few the "habit of virtue," we should "doubt of the salvation of nearly all men" if we did not have "the testimony of Scripture."[16] To this we may add—a point supremely important both for Spinoza and for our own inquiry—that, since these seven dogmas are taught equally by *both* Testaments, Jews and Christians may equally be virtuous citizens of the liberal state.

This is not to say, however, that Jews and Christians must pay an equal price in order to achieve the civic virtue referred to. Christians need merely shed their bigotry: they must privatize their religious beliefs insofar as they go beyond the seven dogmas. In contrast (since the religion of Moses is a political constitution also, and Jews cannot be members of two nations) Jews must abandon rather than merely privatize the "ceremonial laws" of Moses that once made them a nation. To be sure, in Spinoza's own eyes this requirement may be a blessing in disguise. (He views the laws of Judaism as having lost their binding force since the destruction of the Jewish state, and more a curse than a blessing when they were binding.)[17] However, even a critic of the Halakhah may wonder what, except for the denial of the Christ, would distinguish a Judaism resulting from Spinoza's criticism—a Judaism "liberal in the extreme"[18]—from a liberal Christianity. Such a question, to be sure, did not disturb those eighteenth- and nineteenth-century German-Jewish disciples of Spinoza who in all seriousness proposed to embrace Christianity provided it was purged of the dogma of Christ, imagined that their proposal would be accepted in Christian circles, and yet expected or hoped for a survival of Jews.* Not given to delusions such as these, Spinoza may be said to have advocated straightforward assimilation. Yet, as we shall see, he also advocated Zionism.

If these reflections concerning Spinoza's "dogmas of universal faith" produce wonder as to the sacrifices they demand of Judaism, the inspection of the seven dogmas themselves pro-

---

*One thinks especially of David Friedlaender (1750–1834), a respected German-Jewish communal leader who made this offer on a famous occasion.

duce wonder as to the sacrifices they demand of Christianity as well. There is no problem about the first four, concerned, respectively, with the existence, unity, omnipresence, and omnipotence of God. There is a problem, however, concerning the last three, for these, concerned as they are not with God but with the divine-human relation, cannot avoid the subject of the Christ. It is true that Jews and Christians may seem equally able to accept Spinoza's last three dogmas. (The true worship of God consists of true morality. Morality saves. The sins of those who truly repent are forgiven.) Yet Spinoza finds it necessary to end his account of the seventh dogma as follows:

He who firmly believes that God, out of the mercy and grace with which he directs all things, forgives the sins of men, and *who feels his love of God kindled thereby*, he, I say, does really know Christ; according to the Spirit, Christ is in him.[19]

This passage gives rise to a grave dilemma. *If any or all of Spinoza's seven dogmas imply his concluding affirmation, then Jews, no matter how "liberal," cannot accept them. And if they do not imply that affirmation, then Christians can accept them only at the price of making their own central affirmation superfluous.* We began by considering Spinoza's attempt to define a "Judeo-Christian" dogma which would be suitable for the liberal state. The result of this attempt, it now seems, cannot be *both* Jewish and Christian, and most probably must be neither.

Reflections such as these make two central, but deliberately postponed questions no longer postponable: *Does Spinoza believe in revelation? If not, does he claim to have refuted it?*

Some answers to these momentous questions are already implicit in the foregoing. Thus, first, Spinoza does not claim to have refuted revelation, for the simple but weighty reason that in many though not all relevant passages he affirms it. Second, he *does* claim to have refuted the *proofs* for revelation. Such proofs could come either from Scripture itself, in which case (even if they were not inherently circular) his own practice of biblical criticism, however limited, would be enough to dispose of them. Alternatively, they could come from ecclesiastical authorities. But one of the main purposes of the *Treatise* is to undermine *all* authority in matters of religious conscience. Indeed, one reason for Spinoza's attack on "Pharisaic" authority is surely to rob papal authority of its precedent. And one reason for singling out for attack the conveniently remote Papacy is surely to be able to pronounce in Protestant but not omnitolerant Holland no less radical a doctrine than the following:

As the supreme right of free thinking, even on religion, is in every man's power, and as it is *inconceivable [sic]* that such power could be alienated, it is also in every man's power to wield the supreme right and authority in this behalf and to explain and interpret religion for himself. [My italics.][20]

This "inalienable" right to interpret the *content* of the revealed Scriptures cannot come to an abrupt halt at the question of their *status* as revealed, a fact which, at long last, leads us to the climactic question. Spinoza does not claim to have refuted revelation. *But does he believe in revelation?*

This question may be considered through an interpretation of the passage just cited, taken in its full context. The individual has the "supreme right" of free thinking vis-à-vis both the content and the status of the revealed Scriptures. But this right, though "inalienable," poses a problem. On the one hand (unless the main issue is to be prejudged), the individual must be free to opt for as well as against the revealed status of the Scriptures. On the other hand (since individuals in their free thinking are no less prone to superstitious interpretations of the Scriptures than are ecclesiastical authorities), this free-thinking individual must be given "rules" that prevent his religion from becoming "superstition" rather than "religion." In this dilemma Spinoza has no difficulty in deciding that "the rule for such interpretation should be nothing but the natural light of reason which is common to all—not any supernatural light nor any external authority."[21]

The implications of this decision are much more far-reaching than may at first sight appear. Ever since Philo, Jewish and Christian thinkers alike permitted reason to interpret Scripture. However, unless they dissipated revelation in the process of interpreting it they were forced to choose between the Jewish and the Christian Scriptures. Spinoza, as we have seen, rejects this choice. As we see now, he is able to reject it by means of a hermeneutic of the natural light of reason. This, and the use of it, are designed to prove that the content of the two Scriptures, to the extent to which they still can lay claim to validity, is identical. Spinoza, insofar as he identifies himself with the results of his hermeneutic, is at once Jew and Christian, and therefore neither. For it is all too obvious that *the identity of the Jewish and Christian Scriptures can be asserted only on the basis of a prior rejection of the revealed status of both.* In other words, Spinoza's "universal religion, the Divine Law revealed through the Prophets and Apostles to the whole human race"[22] paves the way for a *still* more universal religion, a religion of mankind revealed in *all* scriptures and therefore *no* scripture. The "new world" Spinoza has discovered has its outer court in the liberal state. Its inner sanctum is inhabited by individuals who are men-in-general, i.e., no longer Jews or Christians. They are philosophers who can no longer accept revealed Scriptures and no longer need any, for they are "free" men.

This radical conclusion discloses two strange, not to say paradoxical, aspects of Spinoza's teaching, one concerning the outer court, the other the inner sanctum. Spinoza so interprets—or operates on—the Jewish and Christian Scriptures as to make Jews and Christians equal citizens in the liberal state; yet the operation has the unequal result of making orthodox into liberal Christians while robbing Jews of every incentive (if indeed not the right) to remain Jews at all. (Hence Spinoza himself—so it seems—aware of this injustice and indeed inhumanity, balances his "assimilationist" with a "Zionist" proposal which latter, however, cannot yet be understood.) More startling still, he immerses himself in the claims of revelation with an energy matched only by Hegel among modern rationalists; yet, unheard of in any great modern rationalist, *he rejects*

*revelation without claiming to have refuted it.** Hence it is true
that the "*Tractatus* is Spinoza's introduction to philosophy"[23]—his *Ethics*—if this latter work is understood as pre-
supposing the *rejection* of revelation. However, the *Treatise*
could not function as such an introduction if the *Ethics* required the prior *refutation* of revelation. Indeed, there is a
sense in which the *Ethics*—or the *Short Treatise* which precedes it—is the hidden introduction of the *Treatise*. Lesser
thinkers might reject, indeed imagine themselves to have refuted, revelation on trivial grounds such as textual inconsisten-
cies in the Scriptures, rival claims made in behalf of other
scriptures, and the real or imagined resemblance between revelation and magic or superstition—all difficulties long recognized and dealt with by medieval commentators.† A thinker of
Spinoza's profundity, once having faced the claims of revelation, is able, in the final analysis, to reject it only in behalf of a
claim rivaling it in magnitude.‡ That claim is made in the *Ethics*—the work to which we now must turn.

The *Ethics* is often viewed as a system of true propositions
deduced and proved from self-evident principles. However,
that the geometrical method is in truth a mere method of exposition is sufficiently illustrated by the fact that Spinoza employs this same method to expound the Cartesian philosophy.
For our part and for our special purposes, we shall therefore not
dwell on the beginning of the work but rather move toward the
end and, moreover, do so with haste. However, we must not
move so speedily as to overlook significant stages on the way.

*It is worthy of note that few modern rationalists of the first rank attempt
such a refutation. Descartes and Leibniz accept revelation. Kant examines
religion critically "within the bounds of reason only." Schelling rejects or
even refutes revelation only in his Fichtean and Spinozistic periods. Hegel
transfigures revelation. Only Fichte was bold enough to write a "Critique of
Revelation"—in being a "critique," ipso facto a refutation.

†After giving a fairly large number of examples, St. v. Du. Borkowski writes:
"Possibly there is not a single textual-critical remark in the ... *Treatise*
which is not inspired by an ancient Talmudic teacher or exegete" (*Der junge
Spinoza* [Münster, 1913], pp.123 ff.)

‡This enormous assertion concerning man's relation to transcendence cannot
be defended at this point in the developing argument of the present work but
only in the context of chapter IV, when Transcendence itself comes under
explicit scrutiny. See also above, ch. I, sections 6 and 7.

The definitions which open the *Ethics* are as much declarations as statements—declarations of war although, to be sure, of a war which is to end in a profound peace. The equations *Causa Sui*-Substance-God-Nature, in the beginning empty abstractions, all find their whole richness and polemical power only as the work moves, inexorably, toward its end. And the same is true of the subsequent disposal of thought and extension among the infinitude of attributes. In a different context Spinoza himself "begs" his readers to "accompany" him "slowly, step by step, and not to pronounce on [his] . . . statements till they have read to the end."[24]

Some of the polemical power of the initial abstractions emerges already in the first part of the work. If "God or Substance" alone *is*, then all that ought to be already is, and the beginning of wisdom is neither fear nor hope—both geared to the future*—but rather the transcendence of both, by means of the insight that everything actual or possible *other* than Substance already *is* in Substance. Thus with a single blow Spinoza disposes of Creation—the ultimate precondition of the revelation taught by his Jewish forefathers; redemption—its ultimate consequence; and hence he also disposes of revelation itself.

What makes the single blow radical is that "Substance" *is* "God," an assertion which, according to Feuerbach, makes Spinoza the "Moses" of the "modern free spirits." However, in praising Spinoza as a "materialist" (who gets rid of God and also of man) Feuerbach is less sound than Hegel, who blames him for being an "acosmist" (who saves God but loses the world, and hence man as well). But the central question is put to Spinoza neither, at one extreme, by Feuerbach (or his disciple Marx) nor, at the other, by Hegel. It is put by Rosenzweig's *Star of Redemption*. And this question is: Does Spinoza's equation of God with Substance rightly transform or wrongly abandon the three realities bound together through

---

Ethics, Part III, Definitions of the Emotions, XII and XIII. Our expression "beginning of wisdom" is an allusion not only to Scripture (Ps. 111:10; Prov. 9:10) but also to Hegel's allusions to both Scripture and Spinoza (*Phil. R.* II.i.93 ff., *Hist. Phil.* III, p. 257). See below, ch. III, section 2.

revelation—God, world, man? And if the latter, has he sold his ancient Jewish birthright for a mess of modern pottage?

Spinoza's claim to wisdom would remain an empty gesture unless it is made good, and the wisdom made good would be worse than the empty gesture if it were a flight from reality, that is, a rise by the mind into Substance in which the body, unraised and unraisable, is simply left behind. However, the first two parts of the *Ethics* (which make extension as well as thought into attributes of Substance) already declare war on all mental flights from the body. And the remainder of the *Ethics* is meant to be the road to victory.

Substance alone *is*. Part of the subsequent task is to "deduce" the implications of this thesis. But, as the course of the *Ethics* clearly shows, one task is decisive if the otherwise merely hypothetical thesis is to become categorical.* This is the answering of two questions. One is: If "the actual being of the human mind is the idea of some particular thing actually existing," can it, being finite, rise to "absolute thought"? If so, having a finitude parallel to that of the human body,[25] can this rise avoid an arbitrary break away from this parallelism? As we have said, while forced to hasten toward the end, we may not be so indiscriminate in our haste as to overlook, bypass, or treat lightly, questions such as these.

Can the human mind rise to absolute thought? This first question has a clear answer. Already at an early stage Spinoza flatly declares: "The human mind has an adequate knowledge of the eternal and infinite essence of God."[26] The preceding propositions (together with some earlier hints) may prepare this assertion carefully.[27] Nevertheless, there is at this stage a suspicion of what may be called an abstract circularity. The mind can rise to an "adequate" knowledge of God because God *is*, is *Substance*, and hence *is immanent* in the mind; and God is, and is Substance, and is immanent in the mind, because the mind *recognizes* these truths as it rises above the determination by the "fortuitous play of circumstances" to a stage where it transforms "inadequate" into "adequate" knowledge.[28] This is

---

*Our use of the terms "rise" and "hypothetical" is controversial; but our justification will appear in context.

an obvious circle. And it is abstract because between the truth presupposed at the start and the knowledge attained at the end there lies a gulf, composed of the whole length and breadth of human life—a gulf which cannot be bridged. It may be objected that the un-Spinozistic term "rise" has un-Spinozistic connotations; that Spinoza, teaching as he does that Substance *is* in all things, the mind included, asserts that the mind *already has* knowledge of God; and that it is merely required to make the "inadequate" knowledge "adequate." The fact still remains, however, that this requirement involves a *transformation*; that to have made this transformation is to *know* oneself to be in a circle in which one already *is*, one's "inadequate" knowledge included; and that hence the circle is concrete rather than abstract only if one can bridge the gulf between the place in human life and ("inadequate") knowledge which is the *terminus a quo*, and the ("adequate") knowledge—and, possibly, form of life—which is the *terminus ad quem*.

The *Ethics* begins to move toward this goal when, having abstractly affirmed the highest knowledge, it turns to a consideration of the emotions. All knowledge of the emotions diminishes bondage to them and increases mastery over them, which latter is freedom. The highest knowledge produces the highest freedom. Since this knowledge sees itself in God, the freedom produced by it is itself in God: it is not restless striving, but rather "acquiescence," the "blessedness" of free surrender to necessity. And because mastery over the emotions is their transformation rather than their destruction, the highest knowledge does not dissolve emotion but rather produces the highest emotion. This is the intellectual love of God.[29]

With this love, of course, Spinoza's teaching reaches the end of its road and its goal. It is instructive to compare it with the Jewish teaching that he has rejected. This too has its goal in the love of God. But whereas the Spinozistic love drives out all fear, that of God included, its rabbinic counterpart, though driving out other fears, only deepens the fear of God.[30] In Spinoza's view he who still fears God while claiming to know and love Him, has neither the necessary love nor the knowledge. In the rabbis' view, the gulf that separates man and God is recognized the more deeply the closer one comes to Him, which is why the love of God, if and when it occurs, is not only rare but also astonishing. For Spinoza, too, the love of God is rare. But it is not astonishing, for there exists no gulf between God and those loving Him. Indeed—a proposition unheard of for the rabbis—the mind's love of God and God's self-love are identical.[31]

With this enormous claim the *Ethics* reaches its climax. One must ask, of course, how this claim can be justified. But it would be wayward to look to mathematical demonstrations. Doubtless the *Ethics* makes its case more systematically than the rabbis made theirs, or cared to make it. Its proof, however, lies beyond the "system"—in the life lived by the wise man.

That this proof, like "all things excellent," should be "as difficult as it is rare" one will readily accept.* The question is, however, how such a proof is possible at all, and what is involved on the rare occasions when it is achieved. This cannot be answered without at least the bare listing of some of the intermediate theses, summing up stages of the road.

First, emotion is both a "modification of the body" and "ideas of [such] modifications": it is a process at once physical and mental. Second, emotion may "increase" or "diminish" both the "active power" of the body and the ideas thereof: emotion can be both active and passive. Third, the mind, while confined to "confused and fragmentary knowledge" so long as it is "determined from without . . . by the fortuitous play of circumstance," is capable of "adequate knowledge" when it is "determined from within"; and since God is in all things, adequate knowledge is knowledge of God in all things. Finally, as there is an increase of the mind's power to understand all things, its own emotion included, "an emotion which is passive ceases to be passive."† It either is transformed into an active emotion or else vanishes.

*An allusion to the celebrated last sentence of the *Ethics*.
†Part III, def. 3, prop. 1; Part II, prop. 29 Corollary and note; Part V, prop. 3. It is important to stress that Spinoza claims total originality for the doctrine just outlined. He writes: "No one, so far as I know, has defined the nature and strength of the emotions, and the power of the mind against them for their restraint" (Part III, opening paragraph).

Much more could and perhaps should be said. But the above suffices to show why the love of God, though rare and difficult, is not impossible: first, there is a *road* to this love; second, emotion *as such* has a passive *and* an active potential; third, *every* mind has *some* power both to "restrain" and transform emotion. Thus Spinoza can make the sober admission that even the wise man does not live by the love of God alone but remains "prey" to passive emotions. And he can also give the life-enhancing message that the many who cannot hope to reach the goal are still able to embark on the road.

One would wish to dwell at length on Spinoza's goal. For the purpose at hand, however, it is necessary (as well as more instructive) to revert to the road. For whereas the goal may be taken (or mistaken) for a return to a premodern piety that finds fulfilment in contemplative surrender, the road has the unmistakable hallmark of the "new world" that Spinoza has "discovered." Long ago, we came upon one crucial component of that world, Spinoza's modern-liberal state. We have now, at last, come upon its most genuine citizen, the enlightened, modern, "free" man.

This man, once again, may be but briefly described, this time, however, without fear of misunderstanding. For, partly owing to Spinoza's own influence, the shape of this man is familiar. Knowing himself to be subject to the emotions, this man neither blindly submits to them, nor vainly attempts to reject them nor again does he indiscriminately slander them. Instead, he seeks to understand and thus to master the emotions. This he does by weakening those that negate or diminish life, and by enhancing those that affirm and expand life. He aims at strength of character composed of courage and high-mindedness. And he *can* aim at this *high* virtue only because he regards self-preservation as his *first* virtue. (Unless he exists he can have no virtue; and unless he *himself* is the preserver of his existence he is not his own master.) Given neither to pride nor to humility, this man aims at self-approval as "the highest object for which . . . [he]can hope."[32]

Such is the stance of Spinoza's free modern man. His religion reflects this general outlook. While accepting the fact of "wonder," he does not "come to a stand" with it, for it is a mere "distraction." And what it distracts from is rejection of false religion and acceptance of the true. It is "superstition" and not "religion" that glorifies pain and slanders pleasure. And it is a "spurious piety" that gives rise to "abasement," when it is in fact no better than pride which is its opposite. True religion flows from, or conforms to, the two prime virtues of courage and high-mindedness. Of these virtues, already referred to, Spinoza writes as follows:

All actions flowing from emotion, which are attributable to the mind by virtue of its understanding, I set down to *strength of character (fortitude)* which I divide into courage *(animositas)* and high-mindedness *(generositas)*. By *courage* I mean *the desire whereby every man strives to preserve his own being in accordance solely with the dictates of reason.* By *high-mindedness* I mean *the desire whereby every man endeavours, solely under the dictates of reason, to aid other men and to unite them to himself in friendship.* Those actions, therefore, which have regard solely to the good of the agent I set down to courage, those which aim at the good of others I set down to high-mindedness. Thus temperance, sobriety, and presence of mind in danger etc. are varieties of courage; courtesy, mercy etc. are varieties of high-mindedness.[33]

Such, in outline, is Spinoza's image of the new man in his new world—of the best inhabitant of the liberal state. He is quite unlike the best inhabitant of the Jewish community which Spinoza has found himself forced to leave. Spinoza cannot view *its* best inhabitants—direct teachers such as Morteira or Menasseh Ben Israel or indirect teachers, the greatest of whom is Maimonides—as anything but prey to a passive memory of a long-lost glory and to a no less passive hope for its miraculous return. That the mass of men should wait for miracles or good luck, rather than resort to resolute action, would cause Spinoza neither surprise nor upset. The passivity of the best, however, produces dismay and calls for a cure.

In Spinoza's view, the best in the Jewish community have come to consider passive waiting as a religious duty, and resolute action as a heinous sin. They take pride in self-abasing humility and useless repentance, and their activity is confined to impotent prayer. The Jewish religion, so Spinoza asserts, has emasculated the Jewish people.

It was not always thus, for when this religion was the constitution of a state, it was, like all constitutions, not an apotheosis of pious passivity but rather the framework of action. Hence, speaking the language of imagination, Spinoza concedes that God once showed favor to the Jewish people. Hence, too, he can see a future for this people in his own new world if only their religion were cured of its effeminacy. He writes:

The sign of circumcision is, I think, so important that I could persuade myself that it alone would preserve the nation forever. Nay, I would go so far as to believe that if the foundations of their religion have not emasculated their minds they may even, if occasion offers, so changeable are human affairs, raise up their state afresh, and that God may elect them a second time.*

With this conclusion, the chief topic that has eluded us throughout this discourse has at last come into view—Spinoza's vision of a Jewish future in his "new world." In effect, he places before the modern Jew two fundamental options. One is to reject the Jewish past as a dead relic and become a man-in-general among men-in-general. The other is for him to take his Jewish destiny into his own hands and restore the ancient Jewish state. As for *Galut* Judaism, however—defined by Spinoza as a hankering after the past and a passive, hence empty, hope for its future restoration—this, to be sure, may continue to exist in the modern as it did in the premodern world, for all things historical are contingent. But as for it having a share in this world, this is impossible.

---

*Tr., ch. III, end. Because of the importance of this passage we cite it in the original: "Nisi fundamenta suae religionis eorum animas effeminarent, absolute crederem, eos aliquando, data occasione, ut sunt res humanae mutabiles, suum imperium erecturos, Deumque eos de novo electurum."

L. Feuer reads his own prejudices into Spinoza when he comments: "the backwardness of the Jewish religion was, in his opinion, an obstacle to the restoration of the Jewish state" (*Spinoza and the Rise of Liberalism* [Boston: Beacon, 1958], p. 23). Spinoza's reference to circumcision is enough to prove that something quite other than "backwardness" is at stake.

Beside these possibilities, one can perceive only dimly yet a fourth, which was in fact to become dominant for the next several centuries in the world which Spinoza helped shape: a modern Jew for whom dispersion is no longer an ancient curse but rather a modern blessing; who does not wish to belong to a people apart but only to a religion apart; and who, in defining that religion, relies largely on the tools forged by Spinoza and his non-Jewish philosophical heirs and successors. For his part, Spinoza, to be sure, would have defended the right of a Jew to practice such a religion on a basis of total political equality. But he would have been puzzled as to why any Jew should wish to make use of that right.

3. Franz Rosenzweig

This was not puzzling in the milieu into which, just about two hundred years after Spinoza's death, Franz Rosenzweig was born. Rosenzweig was brought up as a Jew in Wilhelminian Germany. While assimilation and intermarriage proceeded at a steady pace, the "baptismal epidemic" of the early nineteenth century had long passed. The Jewish religion was recognized by the state which, indeed, collected taxes for it as it did for all recognized religions. To belong was respectable so long as one did not belong too much. It was rather overt apostasy to Christianity that was not respectable, and even to have oneself legally declared konfessionslos ("unaffiliated") was unprincipled, for its motive was either to save taxes or to run from the anti-Semites. The young Franz Rosenzweig was equally at home in music and art, jurisprudence and literature, history and philosophy. He grew up as close to being a modern man-in-general as was possible in Germany before the Great War.

Yet what was not puzzling to fellow-Jews in his milieu puzzled Rosenzweig himself, and did so in one way just as it would have puzzled Spinoza in another. When in 1909 Hans Ehrenberg, Rosenzweig's cousin and friend, underwent baptism, he reacted as follows:

About Hans we simply do not see eye to eye. . . . We are Christian in everything. We live in a Christian state, attend Christian schools, read Christian books, in short, our whole "culture" rests entirely on a Christian foundation; consequently a man who has nothing holding him back needs only a slight push . . . to make him accept Christianity. In Germany today the Jewish religion cannot be "accepted," it has to be grafted on by circumcision, dietary observance, bar mitzva. . . .

This letter to his parents had been preceded by another a few days earlier:

Because I am hungry, must I on principle go on being hungry? On principle? Does principle satisfy hunger? Can being non-religious on principle satisfy a religious need? Or can the empty notation at the registry office, "Religion: Jewish" satisfy a religious need? If I am given the choice between an empty purse and a handful of money, must I choose the purse? Again on principle?[34]

Thus even at the age of twenty-three, Rosenzweig took a positive attitude toward baptism not, like the Jewish intellectuals of the age of the "baptismal epidemic," because he did not take religion seriously, but precisely because he *did* take it seriously. Coincidentally or not so coincidentally, this was also the time when, disillusioned with the philosophical epigones of his age, he turned to the study of the great German masters—Kant, Fichte, and, above all, Schelling and Hegel. This fact is worthy of note, for the two last-named philosophers were Spinozists in at least one respect: they believed to have found something more ultimate than "religious need" and its satisfaction. As for the greatest of Germans (viewed as such by Rosenzweig to the end of his days—and an avowed Spinozist), he had written: "Whoever possesses science and art, ipso facto has religion as well. Whoever lacks these two— let him have religion!"[35]

Three steps separate the twenty-three-year-old Rosenzweig from the author of the *Star of Redemption*: the discovery in himself of a religious "hunger" no less great than that of his friend and cousin; the discovery that Judaism is no more an "empty purse" than Christianity; and the conclusion that the transreligious reality embraced by the Spinozists is spurious: that the religious sphere, far from being confined to "needs"—moral, psychological or "existential"—is *itself* the sphere of ultimate *truth*. This last-named conclusion (which encompasses the earlier two discoveries) does not find full expression prior to the *Star of Redemption*, a work matching the *Ethics* in depth and power. As for the earlier two discoveries that preceded it, they may have developed gradually; yet each had its moment of truth. In an all-night discussion (July 7, 1913) with two friends, both Christians of Jewish origin, Rosenzweig found in them a faith so genuine, and in himself a hunger so profound, that he gradually reached the decision that he, too, must convert to Christianity.* And during a single day (October 11, 1913, attending Yom Kippur services in a small Orthodox synagogue in Berlin, since he would come to Christianity only as a Jew), he made the astounding discovery that "Religion: Jewish" was not, after all, an empty notation at a registry office, but nothing less than the unique relation between the Jewish people and the God of the world.

The published materials do not say what happened to Franz Rosenzweig on that fateful Yom Kippur. Even the unpublished materials may never disclose it.† It would be characteristic of this man to have written much about himself but nothing about his "road to Damascus." But perhaps to know what happened we need only study the *Mahzor*—the Yom Kippur prayer book. Perhaps he spent this day standing directly before the divine Other in all His awesome otherness—the God

---

*See *Briefe*, pp. 72 ff.; *Life and Thought*, pp. 23 ff. The two Christians in question were his cousin Rudolf Ehrenberg and Eugen Rosenstock, this latter a major influence on Rosenzweig. The important correspondence between the two men is contained in the appendix to *Briefe*, and is translated into English in *Judaism Despite Christianity*, ed. Rosenstock-Huessy (Alabama University Press, 1969).

†The closest we currently have may well be a passage in a recently published letter which, written almost seven years after the fateful Yom Kippur, contains the following: "It is a great act of mercy that God has once uprooted me out of life during my life. From July to September 1913 I was quite willing to die—to let everything within myself die. *But this may not be made into a rule . . .*" (*Judaism Despite Christianity*, p. 76; my italics). On this subject, see further R. Horwitz, "Franz Rosenzweig's Unpublished Writings," *Journal of Jewish Studies* (1969), pp. 57 ff., and also N. N. Glatzer's Foreword to *Star*.

above both world and man that is yet present *to* Israel *among* men *in* the world, sternly demanding repentance and gently bestowing forgiveness. Countless Jews before him had spent this day in just this manner, among them not a few who, *Ba'ale Teshuva* like Rosenzweig himself, were to spend the rest of their days studying the words of the Torah and following them. There was just one difference. *This Ba'al Teshuva* was to become the greatest Jewish philosopher since Spinoza.

This could never have come to pass had Rosenzweig attempted, along with a return to premodern Judaism, a return to the premodern world and its philosophy. Instead, he applied to himself what he wrote of his teacher Hermann Cohen—that his critique of Spinoza's philosophy, to be sure, struck "with deadly accuracy" at its "Achilles' heel," but was at the same time "deeply unjust," not because it was not objective enough but rather because it was not subjective enough. Cohen had been insufficiently aware of the fact that "the age which had produced and educated him would have been impossible without Spinoza."* On his part, Rosenzweig himself did not lack in this awareness. Hence while he sought to recover, against Spinoza, the Jewish God of revelation, he was no more able than Spinoza (or Cohen) to submit to premodern authorities (and hence, for example, in principle to reject biblical criticism).† Nor was he willing or able to turn his back on that liberal state of which Spinoza had been the first philosophical protagonist. Hence Rosenzweig's own "Archimedian point in philosophy"—"whether and how one could distinguish revelation from purely human cognition purely philosophically, or in general by means of identifiable criteria"—could not be pre-Spinozist, nor could it be simply anti-Spinozist. It had to be post-Spinozist as well. His is a post-Spinozism which cannot for a moment forget that the idea of revelation—"the incursion of a higher content into an

---

*Kl.Schr., pp. 352, 353. Spinoza's Achilles' heel is "the inability to say 'and' when necessary, but always only 'sive.' "
†On this latter subject see a famous letter, *Briefe*, pp. 581 ff.; *Life and Thought*, p. 158. Rosenzweig's attitude toward the Bible is to concern us in a future work (see above, ch. I, section 5) but is beyond our present scope.

unworthy vessel"—may be a "terrible stumbling block" for all "paganism," ancient as well as modern. For modern (i.e., Spinozist) paganism, however, it is, in addition, positively "insulting."*

At first sight, to be sure, Rosenzweig's thought appears to be simply anti-Spinozist. Above, the definitions and propositions which open the *Ethics* were said to be not so much statements as declarations of a war to be won—if at all—only at the end. The same is true of the radically antithetical "elements" "God-world-man" which are treated in the first part of the *Star of Redemption*. Spinoza urges his reader not to judge his assertions until he has read to the end. Rosenzweig gives the same advice, though much more explicitly and in much stronger terms.[36] There is need, then, not to dwell on the "elements" of the "eternal proto-cosmos," but, on the contrary, every need to rush forward from that declaration of war on to victory. Indeed, in this case the rush may and must be still greater. It *may* be greater because the military terminology and strategy we were forced to foist on Spinoza is urged upon us by Rosenzweig himself.† It *must* be greater because the *Star*'s symphonic prolixity threatens to distract us from our own necessary course even more drastically than the mathematical economy of the *Ethics*. That our own course is itself not off course, however, can be assured by a quality shared (albeit oppositely manifested) by the two works: their systematic rigor.

The *Star* introduces itself as an expression of an activity termed "new thinking." The difference between this and the "old" is not that the "old thinking" is an "objective rational theory" and the "new" a "subjective irrational commitment." (This would make both into caricatures of philosophy, the "old" thinking, as is maintained by positivism, into a precur-

---

Kl.Schr., pp. 357, 285. The qualitative distinction made by us between ancient and modern paganism is warranted by Rosenzweig's reference to the modern (i.e., Kantian) notion of the "autonomy of moral law." The text in which this reference occurs is lent special significance by the fact that it is his first major literary expression (1914) after Rosenzweig's return to Judaism in 1913.

†He uses expressions such as "Napoleonic strategy" and "chief battle for understanding" (pp. 376 ff.). See above, ch. I, section 7.

sor or ape of the natural sciences, the "new" into activities so arbitrary as not to deserve the name of thinking.) The difference is rather that the "old" thinking, having carried the mind above time and existence, causes it to dwell in eternity, whereas the "new," having carried the mind to things eternal, perceives these latter to be empty abstractions, and is plunged by this perception back into existential limitations, now known to be untranscendable.

This contrast—especially if it is not spelled out—may lead the two ways of thinking to misunderstand both themselves and, when confronted, each other. Thus Spinoza writes:

I do not presume to have found the best philosophy. I know that I understand the true philosophy. If you ask in what way I know it, I answer: in the same way as I know that the three angles in a triangle are equal to two right angles.[37]

This does not outdo Rosenzweig, who writes:

We know in the most precise way, we know with the intuitional knowledge of experience, what God taken by Himself, what man taken by himself, what the world taken by itself, "is."[38]

These antithetical claims are shocking in their bold extremity. If taken at face value, the philosophies so taking them— "old" and "new" thinking—cannot understand, let alone recognize each other. Moreover, they do not understand themselves: that Spinoza's geometrical method is not one of proof was already seen; yet to be seen is that Rosenzweig's "experience" is not self-authenticating. We must therefore advance the dubious claim of understanding the two philosophies better than they understand themselves. However, since the claim is indeed dubious, we shall confine it to a single point: *Only because Spinoza considered history to be indiscriminately meaningless—irrelevant to philosophic truth—could he believe that, in matters religious and philosophical, the geometric method is the method of truth. And only because Rosenzweig considered history—or at any rate, Jewish history—to be indiscriminately meaningful could his "absolute empiri-*

cism" be overwhelmed by subsequent history. Jewish history
was meaningful for Rosenzweig, and indiscriminately so, in
this sense, that not until the Messianic age could anything happen that would affect the Jewish faith.*

In Rosenzweig's case our better understanding will not have
to be better by much. It will mean "placing into an historical
perspective," and such a placing, while alien to Spinoza, is by
no means wholly so to Rosenzweig. His own new thinking
sees *itself* in an historical perspective vis-à-vis the old. However, the perspective in which it sees itself cannot be the same
as ours.

The "new thinking" sees itself as related to the "old" as
follows. The old thinking must be opposed insofar as it misdi-
rects mind and man, thought and life, toward a shadowy "essence" of all things—a reductionism which dissipates man
and God into world (ancient period), man and world into God
(medieval period), God and world into man (modern period).†
However, the "new" thinking would destroy itself along with
the "old" if, rather than "letting count fully the spiritual labor
of the past in all its accomplishments," it simply "destroyed it
in a riot of blind destructiveness." Instead, the new thinking
views the old as being, as it were, an experiment at once
necessary and predestined to disclose, once it had exhausted
(in Hegel) all its possibilities, its own inevitable failure. This
experiment was necessary because philosophical thinking is
an activity of uniting. It had to fail because this process of
uniting, if truly radical, abstracts "naked unities"[39] from the

---

*The claim to understand an author better than he understands himself is
always dubious, may serve as an excuse for careless reading, and was vulgar-
ized in the extreme by nineteenth-century historicism. Yet at times the claim
may have to be made. In any case, Rosenzweig supports it. He writes: "The
other [i.e., the reader], if for no other reason than that he is other, will always
be permitted to attempt, in Kant's bold words which are not all that bold, to
understand Plato better than he understood himself. I for one do not wish to
deprive any reader of mine of this hope." (Kl.Schr., p. 397).

†Kl.Schr., p. 378. The weakness of this account of the history of philosophy,
i.e., its schematic nature, should not obscure its strength: it represents an
attempt to make a *radically* new, "existential" start in philosophy which is
yet neither rationally arbitrary nor historically groundless. In both respects
Rosenzweig may be influenced by Schelling.

richness of contingent actuality. And the new thinking can itself *be* a thinking—the new *thinking* after the old has run its course "from Ionia to Jena"[40]—only because it is not the simple foe of the old but rather its dialectical nemesis and successor. Such, in brief, is the relation between the old thinking and the new, as seen by Rosenzweig. Interpreters who deny or ignore that relation must regard the three "elements" of Part 1 of the *Star of Redemption*—God, world, man—as mere "postulates," at least the first of which is wholly arbitrary. And this view of Part 1 in turn compels them to view the rest of the work (which moves ever closer from abstract thought to concrete experience) as at most a phenomenology of religious experience, illegimitately projected into a realm of transcendence. However, the three "elements" are not "postulates." They are—so Rosenzweig contends—the positive result of the demonstrated failure of more than two millennia of Western metaphysics to reduce all things, respectively, to God, world, and man.

Rosenzweig does not claim originality for this conception of the "new thinking." (His main debt is to Schelling.)* He *does* claim, however, to have written the first nonfragmentary—i.e., systematic—book which is both "Jewish" and "unfanatical." He writes: "I am regarded as the 'Jewish fanatic,' and yet I have written the first unfanatical Jewish book I know of (that is to say, Jewish and yet unfanatical, unfanatical and yet Jewish)."[41]

This claim is altogether fundamental and must be kept in mind until the end. Compelled to opt out of Judaism, Spinoza had been able to admit a modern "vocation of the ancient Hebrews," if at all, only by insisting that "in regard to intellect and true virtue, every nation is on a par with the rest."[42] Compelled to return to Judaism, Rosenzweig was able to accept and embrace the uniqueness of Jewish destiny only within a framework free from all—but especially philosophical—"fanaticism," that is, by means of a philosophy whose universal scope did not come to an arbitrary halt at the wall of a re-

---

*Rosenzweig writes: "[Schelling's] *Ages of the World* is a great book from beginning to end. Had it not remained a fragment, the *Stern* would deserve no attention, except on the subject of Jews" (*Briefe*, p. 399).

vealed authority.* Hence the *Star of Redemption*, while in one sense a "Jewish book," is in another sense "merely" a "system of philosophy" which deals with Judaism "no more fully than with Christianity, and hardly more fully than with Islam."[43]

So much for the general characteristics of Rosenzweig's "new thinking" and its relation to the demonstrated failure of the "old." The question is, of course, whether this failure *is* demonstrated, and if so, how Rosenzweig's three "elements" (to which we now turn) emerge from the failure. Against Rosenzweig's (and Schellings's) first contention—the failure of the "old" thinking—one might cite such twentieth-century thinkers as F. H. Bradley, Bergson, and Whitehead; against the second contention—God as one of the "elements"—such "new" thinkers as Marx, Nietzsche, and, perhaps, Heidegger; and against both together, such philosophical skeptics as have always rejected the "old" metaphysical rationalism and would therefore reject out of hand Rosenzweig's (and Schelling's) "new" "absolute empiricism."[44]

Such external objections will require some attention subsequently. The present internal exposition is faced with enough difficulties of its own, especially and above all at the start. Like the opening definitions and axioms of the *Ethics*, the three "elements" with which the *Star* opens will find their "verification" and indeed their full meaning only at the end. However, there is a great difference. Spinoza's "cosmological-naturalistic" Substance is meant to be a reality—indeed, *the* Reality—from the start, and so is the "theological" Substance of the "preceding epoch" and the "anthropological" Self of the "succeeding" one between which, according to Rosenzweig, Spinoza is "*the* important mediator."† In contrast, it is

---

*The standard medieval argument is that the 600,000 Israelites present at Mount Sinai were too many to be mistaken, and that between them and us is an unbroken chain of trustworthy witnesses. Rosenzweig's disposal of this argument will be found further below.

†See *Kl.Schr.*, p. 379: "In handing over, at the beginning of his work, the scholastic concept of Substance to the great idealists of 1800, Spinoza becomes the important mediator between two epochs of European thought, precisely because he did not, like the preceding epoch, understand this concept theologically nor, like the period to come, anthropologically, but rather cosmologically-naturalistically. Thus he formalized the concept and made it alterable."

not enough to say that the "point" of Part 1 of the *Star* is "to teach that none of these three basic concepts of philosophical thought can be reduced to another . . . , that each can be reduced only to itself." Since this thinking is "new" thinking and not a species of the "old," the "elements" it constructs as "new" thinking at the beginning—in Part 1—must somehow point beyond themselves, to something more real and concrete that is found when, in Parts 2 and 3, thinking is no longer "mere" but turns into "experiencing philosophy."[45] The elements of Part 1 are abstractions—and yet must also somehow be the basis of what is to come.

The precise nature of the "abstractions" involved accounts for much of the admitted "difficulty" of the first part of the *Star*. Rosenzweig advises us to conquer it by means of a "Napoleonic" strategy. Following his advice we rush on to the "short conclusion" of Part 1:

If a "real Nought" corresponds to the Nought of our knowledge, as we presumably must admit, then they are mysterious for us beyond any reality that will ever be visible to us, occult powers that are at work inside God, world and man before ever God, world and man *are revealed*. [My italics.][46]

This seemingly obscure or even nonsensical passage (like others similar to it) results in fact from an utterly precise reflection. As conceived by Part 1 of the *Star*, "God," "world," and "man" cannot be three real "entities." (This would make the part, not a propaedeutic to the "new thinking," but a mere specimen of the "old"—indeed, not only old but ultimately unintelligible. First, Rosenzweig would merely be following the time-honored, tired practice of pitting "pluralism" against "monism." Second, unlike other pluralists, he would arbitrarily confine his "many" to three. Third, like other pluralistic metaphysicians he would need no experiencing philosophy subsequent to the metaphysics itself. Indeed, that very notion would be meaningless.) But neither can the three elements of Part 1 be the "nought" of merely subjective concepts—concepts that claim no counterpart in reality and are therefore wholly arbitrary. What, then, are these "noughts" that are arrived at by the "smashing of the All" into the components

God-world-man? They are each, Rosenzweig replies, a "Not-Yet," i.e., ontologically "occult powers" which *are* not but, as it were, *strive* to be. And to this ontological status corresponds, epistemologically, a "knowledge" that remains ignorance until the striving-to-be has *revealed itself as being*.*

The reflections leading to the "difficult constructions"[47] of Part I of the *Star*, then, whatever their nature and tenability in detail, are precise in general purpose. Yet they also involve a complex dilemma that is reflected throughout the whole work. This dilemma may be put as follows. If revelation is a self-authenticating experience (a view which we believe to be untenable) then we arrive, not at Rosenzweig's "absolute" empiricism, but rather at empiricism plain and simple,† and the whole complicated structure of the *Star* is unnecessary, impossible, or even meaningless. And if revelation is not self-authenticating, we arrive at a logical circle. Revelation can *be* revelation only if the "noughts" in question are "real" noughts rather than random subjective conceits; yet these noughts can be *known* to be real only in and through revelation—and this is not self-authenticating. This circle, to be sure, does not exist so long as revelation rests on revealed authority. However, it is precisely the rejection of such authority (shared by Rosenzweig with Spinoza) that makes the "new thinking" imperative if revelation is to be reaffirmed; and it is just this rejection that underlies the *Star*'s claim to being not only a "Jewish" book but also an "unfanatical" one.

Perhaps nothing else testifies quite so much to Rosenzweig's stature as a thinker as his clear awareness of the above dilemma—and the fact that, like Schelling before him, he chooses the second alternative without hesitation. This is proved by the goal-directed clarity with which he seeks to free the logical circle involved in this choice of its seeming or actual viciousness by means of a thoroughgoing step-by-step,

---

*Doubtless this concept of "nought" is influenced by Schelling. For a brief account of the meontological tradition, see my MH, pp. 30 ff.

†In ch. I of *Encounters* I argue against the doctrine of self-authenticating religious experiences, and against the view that Martin Buber subscribes to it or implies it. That it is false to the *Star* is an essential part of the argument of the present exploration.

increasingly concrete "confirmation" or "verification." This is the process by which this "system of philosophy" is to become both "unfanatical" (i.e., do justice to all experience) and yet "Jewish" (i.e., make Jewish experience indispensable and indeed somehow central.)

That so monumental an effort cannot be wholly successful is not surprising. Thus it is doubtful whether a system of philosophy whose "heart" is revelation* can be *wholly* "unfanatical" toward paganism, Hinduism, and Confucianism, which do not accept a revelation, or toward Islam, which claims revealed status but is denied it by the *Star*. (At least in the last-named case the *Star* would seem to lapse, by its own standards, into fanaticism.) However, if these problems are serious, the decisive one is whether Jewish experience can *itself* emerge inviolate. Like Spinoza, Rosenzweig cannot return to premodern thinking (which permits revealed authority to call a "fanatical"—i.e., philosophically arbitrary—halt to the freedom of thought). Yet unlike Spinoza, he will not sell his ancient Jewish birthright for a mess of modern pottage. The question is therefore whether the *Star* does not combine the uncombinable; and this abstract question will become increasingly concrete as we are forced to ask whether the book can remain both "unfanatical" and "Jewish" without one sacrifice—the fragmentation of the "system."

A "system" both "Jewish" and "unfanatical" is in any case possible only by virtue of the celebrated "double-covenant" doctrine which has always been recognized as the attractive-yet-dubious (and in any case unprecedented) feature of Rosenzweig's "Jewish book." Its author knows this feature to be dubious and without precedent. And he is neither weakhearted nor soft-minded enough to be misled into dubious doctrines merely by their seeming or actual attractiveness. *Only if a mutually complementary relation obtains between the Jewish and the Christian experience is a "system" possible that is "unfanatical" toward all experience.* This will be the key point on which the fate of the *Star*, taken as a system

---

*Rosenzweig describes Book II of Part 2 of the *Star* as the *Herzbuch* of the whole (*Kl.Schr.*, p. 386). Its subject is revelation.

and as a whole, depends. Toward this point we must therefore hasten and, as in the case of Spinoza, with our special purpose in mind and with the greatest speed. However, equally as in Spinoza's case, we must not hasten blindly toward our goal, so as to overlook indispensable stations on the way.

The first such station must obviously be paganism. One asks: How can there be any truth or value in paganism, when the central truth to be "confirmed" or "verified" is that "terrible offense to paganism, new as well as old—the *difference* between God and man, the insulting idea of revelation, the incursion of a higher content into an unworthy vessel"?[48]

Rosenzweig replies: While the "actual Greek" may have prayed to Zeus or Apollo, he was heard—if heard he was—by God. Once Schiller had written that the sun of Homer still shines upon us. At once exposing and opposing this apotheosis of pagan Greece so prevalent in German culture, Rosenzweig writes that our sun—the sun of the "created world"—shone upon Homer as well.* It is trivially obvious that the Greek pagan does not know of creation, for he lacks the revelation which alone could disclose it. Equally obvious is that—if creation is a reality—he is, his ignorance of it notwithstanding, himself a part of it. Neither trivial nor obvious, however, is the concession that a prayer addressed to the gods may be heard by God. What is more, while a good many Jews may wish to make this concession on behalf of Zeus and Apollo—the precursors, after all, of the God of Plato and Aristotle—they must surely be alarmed by the ease with which Rosenzweig extends it to Moloch as well. He writes:

The temples of the gods have rightly decayed. Their statues are rightly to be found in museums. Their service . . . may have been a monstrous confusion. Yet the prayer ascending to them from a tortured heart, and the tear shed by the Carthagenian father *as he led his son to the sacrifice of Moloch* cannot have remained unheard and

---

*Schiller had written: "The sun of Homer, behold, it smiles also on us." Rosenzweig rejoins: "when the real Greek prayed he was of course not heard by Zeus or Apollo but by God. And he did not live in the cosmos but rather in the created world whose sun—our sun—shone upon Homer as well" (*Kl.Schr.*, p. 381).

unseen. Or should God have waited for Sinai or even Golgotha? [My italics.][49]

So lightly does Rosenzweig pass over the weighty distinction—considered weighty by the rabbis—between paganism-in-general and idolatry-in-particular! He could surely not have done so had he not considered both as safely past.* The passage, already cited, concerning "secret forces" and "dark powers" goes on as follows: "But in becoming revealed, all those mysterious, generative powers become a thing of the past."[50]

Rosenzweig does not share the modern folly which considers idolatry to be a mere species of superstition, always harmless and done away with by modern enlightenment. (In his own time Spinoza did not consider it harmless, for unlike later Enlightenment thinkers, he regarded enlightenment as a rare achievement.) Even so, Rosenzweig does cause us to wonder—so early in the *Star!*—whether his "unfanatical" system, in order to be unfanatical, is not forced into unacceptable concessions in behalf of Sinai (which opposes idolatry) and Golgotha (which claims to have vanquished it). Can a Jew make this concession at any time? Can a Christian make it in our time? It is premature for us to consider the Holocaust. Even so, once idolatry is mentioned, there appears the spectre of Auschwitz, and with it the end of the age-old Christian claim that idolatry is vanquished.

Such reflections, premature though they are, raise with renewed emphasis the question of the Jewish-Christian complementarity in Rosenzweig's "unfanatical" system. Yet just one more time this climactic question must be postponed. For there arises before us the spectre of what may be called a Judeo-Christian fanaticism: a common front in behalf of "revealed truth" against revelationless falsehood. Such a front would be fanatical (in Rosenzweig's sense of the term) because it would be arbitrary, no less so for the fact that the front is common. Moreover, unlike a possible premodern precursor,

---

*On this subject, see ch. 4 of my *Encounters*—and, of course, the whole of this book.

this fanaticism would be bankrupt, for its premodern foundation—revealed authority—has vanished.*

In Rosenzweig's view, the spectre of a Judeo-Christian fanaticism can be laid because the time is ripe for a new inter-
play between philosophy and the theology of revelation. Having passed through a dissipation of faith by an historically
motivated skepticism concerning every rise *to* God, theology
now both can and must reclaim the God who *comes to man.*
This act of reclaiming, however, will be arbitrary unless it is
philosophically justified. This is the deeper reason why "the
clamor for philosophy becomes audible in theology along its
whole length."[51]

This is the theological situation. What of the philosophical?
Philosophy has exhausted with Hegel the possibilities of
"one-dimensional" systems. Hence philosophy "*post Hegel
mortuum*"† can avoid "an abyss" only by means of "deliberate self-fragmentation" into "multi-dimensional" aphorisms.
In these latter a conscious, self-critical, deliberate subjectivism
reaches its extreme. In just this extremity, however, philosophy can maintain itself *as* philosophy only if it receives "support from elsewhere," from outside its own sphere, from the
sphere "most objective of all." And "the bridge from the most
subjective to the most objective is provided by the theological
concept of revelation."[52]

One cannot claim that the above is more than the sketch of a
doctrine, and it is doubtful that it would become much less
sketchy were one to develop it in full. Its main points, however, negative and positive, are clear enough. The negative:
Part 1 of the *Star* has the motto "*In philosophos*" because it
smashes all systems, while Part 2 has the motto "*In theologos*"
because it shows that revealed *authority* (if, to be sure, not

---

*In the Introduction to Part 2—the part that deals with revelation—the *Star*
cites the traditional arguments for the authority of the Torah (see above, p. 66n)
but immediately passes from an objective witness that testifies to a fact to a
subjective one—ultimately a martyr—that testifies with his life (*Stern*, pp. 123
ff.; *Star*, pp. 96 ff.)

†A favorite expression of Rosenzweig and his friends, indicative at once of
their keen historical sense and the pivotal role they ascribed to Hegel's
philosophy.

revelation) is a thing of the past. The main positive point is that a "system" both "Jewish" and "unfanatical" has these requirements: a philosophy and a theology which are both free and interrelated; a "bridge" between them provided by the "concept of revelation"; and a concept of revelation wide enough both to include Judaism and Christianity, and to do justice to all experience.

Note well: the *concept* of revelation. The "new thinking" cannot wait until it turns to Sinai or Golgotha—the subjects of Part 3 of the *Star*. Rosenzweig states that whereas the old thinking had "set up for itself the problem of whether God is transcendent or immanent," the new thinking "narrates how and when the far God becomes near, and the near God far."[53] Thus in Part 2 of the *Star* philosophy becomes "narrating." The narrating, however, is as yet, as it were, an abstract narrating. It is confined to the "far" and "near" God as such and in general. Only in such abstract generality can the philosophico-theological narration of revelation point backward to Creation as its own presupposition (thus doing justice to paganism); point forward to Redemption as its own goal; and lay the foundation for a Jewish-Christian relation which is not a case of "fanaticism," separate or joint, but rather a road with different and even antagonistic roles, the difference and antagonism of which, however, is transcended in a goal in which all things, those pagan included, are transfigured and redeemed. No wonder the middle part of the *Star*—Creation, Revelation, Redemption—is the "heart" of the whole, and the middle of the middle—Revelation—its heart of hearts.

We have mentioned that Part 2 has the motto: *In theologos*. Rosenzweig cites the standard medieval theological proof for revelation at Sinai—the authority of the 600,000 witnesses and the authority of a tradition unbroken between them and ourselves.[54] He would, however, lapse into an obsolete premodern "fanaticism" destructive of his whole purpose if he himself accepted that proof. Instead, he moves at once from "objective" to "subjective" witnesses, i.e., from reliable reporters of an event to martyrs willing to die for a truth. He makes this move even though he must know that Spinoza had shown long before that martyrdom "proves," not the truth of the martyr's belief but only his fanaticism.* Spinoza could reject revelation but not refute it. On his part, Rosenzweig can reject Spinoza's rejection and accept revelation. He cannot, however, return to the premodern proofs, for these Spinoza has long refuted. As for the "proof" supplied by the martyrs, this must be—for the modern Spinoza and Rosenzweig, if not for the premodern Saadia, Yehuda Halevi, and Maimonides—accompanied by the insistence that it is not meant to supply what is objectively inaccessible. Indeed, as Spinoza implies, these "subjective" proofs can avoid a war of mutual destructiveness only if they merge into a single history. Hence Rosenzweig quotes "Augustine's famous appeal from all individual reasons to the *present* overall manifestation, the *ecclesiae authoritas*, without which he would not credit the testimony of Scripture."[55] The Jew Rosenzweig cites the Christian Augustine, and he does so with approval. For he himself can "credit the testimony of [the Jewish] Scripture" only because it is *being testified to* by "the present overall manifestation of the Jewish people."†

This theological shift from a premodern objective proof to a modern committing testimony links up with a philosophical shift from the "old" to the "new" thinking. A theological thinking resting on proofs of objective witnesses could once link up with a metaphysics that inquired whether God is immanent or transcendent, if only because, when necessary, it could impose external limits on philosophy. A thinking arising from a committed existence (whether the *ecclesia* or the Jewish people) would find an "immanent" and a "transcendent" God equally irrelevant, the one because He is indiscriminately accessible, the other because He is indiscrimi-

---

*Letter no. 76, see above, p. 38n. This (nontechnical) sense of fanaticism must be distinguished from Rosenzweig's technical sense.

†Rosenzweig thus makes a fundamental shift from the traditional givenness of the Torah to the givenness, however fragmentary, of the Jewish testimony to the Torah. The following will show that we disagree with Strauss's view that Rosenzweig makes this shift "because he looks for a Jewish analogue to the Christian doctrine of the Christ" (*Preface*, pp. 360 ff.). However, Strauss himself is dissatisfied with his own account, for he adds: "the same change would have been effected if the starting point had been mere secularist nationalism."

nately inaccessible. It is quite otherwise with a God (and a thinker concerned with Him) who can *move* from "farness" to "nearness" and back.

How *does* the "far" and "concealed" God become "near" and "disclosed"? From the start of Part 2—Creation—it is clear that the "narrating" thinking *is* new thinking. The "old" thinkers would ask: Is Creation an arbitrary act extraneous to the divine Essence? Or is it part and parcel of that Essence? As for narration (if narration there was), it would begin with history—whether with Adam and Eve or Abraham or the Exodus—i.e., at the point when the metaphysics is ended. In the new thinking, in contrast, narration boldly invades the formerly metaphysical realm. *Qua* "far" or "concealed," God could have refrained—could forever refrain—from the act of creating. *Qua* "near" or "disclosed," God could not—forever cannot—do *other than* create. As for "narrating" thought, it shows how the "far God has become"—ever again becomes—"near."

A consideration of the nature of this bold invasion of narration into metaphysics would lead too far afield. Its consequences, however, direct us to our purpose. A "transcendent" God (who creates by a whim extraneous to his Essence) would rival the Epicurean gods—pagan gods!—in "apathy": He would be indifferent to the world. A God "overflowing" into the world would be "immanent" in it, thus robbing it of its independence. In contrast to both, the "far" God forever moving toward "nearness" *creates an independent world and affirms it in its otherness. And only in a world thus affirmed can revelation take place.*

If "Creation" narrates what always *has been*, and (as will be guessed) "Redemption" will relate what always *is yet to be*, then "Revelation," as found in the *Herzbuch* of the *Star*, narrates what always *is:* in contrast to recovery and anticipation, it is present experience. More precisely, the *Herzbuch* narrates what is always present when *He* is present. This "narration" Rosenzweig justly considers the "heart" of the whole, for it does nothing less than reaffirm in one grand sweep the age-old Jewish commitment to God's presence in history. Moreover,

this reaffirmation, as made at this point, is made in grandiose
and sovereign disregard of all that may have to be said subsequently about *actual* history: the *Star* here affirms the love
between God and man as reflected in the *Song of Songs*. And
since this reading of this biblical book (and its inclusion in the
Canon) is itself not biblical but rather a deep and bold act on
the part of rabbinic Judaism, held fast to by countless Jewish
generations until Spinoza's "new world" came to challenge it,
one may view Rosenzweig's move at this point as one deep
and bold act making contact with another, in order to make an
end to a modern alienation which may once have been necessary, but whose day is gone.

We call this act deep and bold, on the part of both Jewish
tradition (as well as Christian tradition which has its parallel)
and Franz Rosenzweig. For it takes hold of a book that expresses the most intimate love between human equals and
does not hesitate to make it into an allegory of a love whose
partners are wholly incommensurate, for the one is human,
and the other, Divine. Yet in at least one respect Rosenzweig's
boldness exceeds that of Jewish and Christian tradition alike.
These latter stress that the divine-human love, like the human
love it allegorizes, is radically particular. Rosenzweig goes further. Since sexual love, while particular, is at the same time
also the most universal, this is true also of the love it allegorizes: this too is radically universal even as it is radically
particular, so that revelation is not Jewish or Christian only
but also universally human. This step is not accidental. *Rosenzweig can reclaim the* Song of Songs *in the modern, post-Spinozist world only by claiming it in behalf of the whole human
race.* Here is the fundamental doctrine that makes the *Star* not
only a "Jewish" book but also an "unfanatical" one. That it *is*
Jewish as well as unfanatical, of course, still remains to be
shown.

We must now identify the "concept of revelation" that the
Star discovers in the *Song of Songs*. For the "new thinking,"
Creation is *already* Revelation, a manifestation of the "far"
God who cannot be "near" unless He is also *known* to be near.
What, then, is revelation in the narrower sense, and why is it

necessary? It is necessary as a "second" revelation to "secure" the "first" from a "relapse into the night of mystery." And this goal is achieved by its being "nothing but revelation, revelation in the narrower, indeed, its narrowest sense." This narrowest sense discloses the *concept* of revelation—what revelation as such is. It is the love of God.

This love has one thing in common with its Spinozistic counterpart. It is sheer, unalloyed, joyous Presence, "ever-young" and "ever-first." There, however, the resemblance ends. In Spinoza's love of God, man makes the first move and cannot expect a divine countermove. In Rosenzweig's counterpart the first move is a divine "self-opening of a locked-up-ness," an act which—a startling and, to all Spinozists, a shocking notion!—can only be thought of as one of divine humility; and the primordial human countermove is the reception of the divine gift. Spinoza's love of God makes an end to mutuality, for the human love of God, become one with God, is at the same time the divine self-love. Rosenzweig's love of God is the start of all mutuality, for it is not only itself intimately mutual but is also the source of all mutual love between humans. The love of God for man is also and at the same time the "discovery of the thou"; and the "commandment of commandments" is: "Thou shalt love the Lord thy God, with all thy heart, with all thy soul and with all thy might" [Deut. 6:5].[56]

This divine love would remain an empty abstraction if it were for man-in-general. The human "thou" addressed in love is always particular, indeed, singled out. There is a falsely universal "all-love" which loves everyone and no one. God shows the truly universal love of the "Not Yet":

Revelation knows of no all-loving Father; God's love is ever wholly at the moment, to the point at which it is directed, and only in the infinity of time does it reach one point after another, step by step, and informs the All.[57]

In this manner we are at length led to the weightiest—or at any rate, for contemporary Jewish thought the most fateful—difference between Spinoza's and Rosenzweig's thoroughly antithetical affirmations. The *Ethics* culminates in Spinoza's kind of love of God, for through it all things are seen *sub specie eternitatis:* thus *history is reduced to a sphere of fortuitousness.* The *Star of Redemption* does not culminate with Rosenzweig's kind of love of God, for this is a love which does not raise man above time but rather carries God *into* it: *thus any purported human rise above time becomes a mere form of escapism.*

The consequences of this fateful difference will emerge only gradually. One consequence, however, emerges at once. One asks: How can God's love be universal when a rise above time is impossible, when one time differs from another, and when many if not most times are dark and unloved? This question reminds us of the fact that we have as yet only the *concept* of revelation. This concept is no more a mere human conceit—a man-made abstraction—than the "elements" God-world-man dealt with earlier. *Qua* concept it is unreal and yet deep within reality, for it is the source of the "ever-renewed birth of the soul."* This, the pristine expression of the concept, doubtless "already" has sporadic reality in ecstatic moments of individual souls. The divine love, however, is not for ecstatic moments or individual souls, but rather for flesh-and-blood men, women, and children. And this can only mean that the concept of revelation, like the elements God-world-man, has the incomplete reality of a Not-Yet, pointing not to eternity-above-time but a future within it.

This conclusion is of considerable systematic significance. If "confirmation" of the "system" is what is wanted, both by Rosenzweig himself and ourselves, this may seem to be found in ecstatic moments of individual souls, for through these divine love is revealed. This, however, by itself, remains profoundly ambiguous. Thus at one extreme the soul in ecstasy may seem to be raised to what the *Star* considers a spurious eternity. At the other extreme, this ecstasy may be dismissed as being, not a "rebirth of the soul" through the love of the divine Other, but rather a solitary disport of the soul, un-

---

*This is the subtitle of the *Herzbuch.*

reborn, with its own empty conceits. That there *is* or *can be* a rebirth of the soul, through the presence of the divine Other, *itself* requires confirmation, and this can come only when the "Not-Yet" gives way to a revelation that, going beyond its mere concept, *already is.* Thus we are led at length to the decisive "verification" or "confirmation" of the *Star* as a whole—the Jewish-Christian double covenant.*

We need a "confirmation" or "verification." This must be empirical and historical in some sense of these terms. However, if it were empirical and historical in their ordinary sense, it would "verify" not Creation, Revelation, or Redemption, but at most only human *beliefs* about these subjects. Rosenzweig wants not an ordinary history, but rather a divine-human one. And his empiricism is not of the ordinary form but what he terms "absolute empiricism."[58]

That the "absolute" in this empiricism and the "divine" in this history cannot be proved but only be witnessed to is, after the above, in no further need of exposition. The witnessing itself, however, must have empirical-historical facticity. What if the Jewish people were other than what the sought-after "confirmation" required—or if they even ceased to exist? (Christian thought distinguishes between the visible and the invisible church: what if the visible church had reached the vanishing point?) Clearly, it is the empirical aspect of Rosenzweig's "absolute empiricism"—the human aspect of his divine-human history—that, at this point, requires attention.

What makes Judaism the "fire," Christianity the "rays"? Not the individual Jew or Christian. (Not every Jew is "with the Father," and a Christian, though "coming to the Father only through the Son," may have reached Him.)[59] Not the Jewish origins of Christianity. (Rays vanish when the fire goes out. But its Jewish origins have never prevented Christianity from

---

*While Rosenzweig holds that truth is one, he also asserts that our truth must be manifold. Truth turns from being true (*wahr*) into wanting and needing to be *bewährt* (confirmed, tested, proving its mettle). The word play *wahr-bewährt* can be preserved in English only with "verification," but this has a scientific rather than an existential connotation. Hence we generally use "verification or confirmation" for Rosenzweig's *Bewährung.*

considering Judaism as dead.) Not, finally, Jewish-Christian
relations in history even at their most positive. These have
often been likened on both sides to a mother-daughter relationship. However, the Christian "daughter" has rarely recognized her continued need of the Jewish "mother." As for
this latter, she has never been able to recognize the older
"daughter"—Christianity—without also, unlike Rosenzweig,
recognizing the younger one, i.e., Islam. Is the double-
covenant "theory," then, a mere theory *about* history? This,
however, is totally alien to Rosenzweig's "absolute empiricism" and, indeed, would be utterly illogical. How can the
Jewish-Christian double covenant "confirm" everything—confirm *anything*—when what is or is not a divine-human covenant is decided by a mere theory? There is an altogether basic
need, then, for an *empirical given.*

*A Jew is born into the Jewish covenant, whereas a Chris-
tian is baptized into the Christian covenant. This is the decisive "empirical"—by itself insufficient but altogether basic
and indispensable—"confirmation" of the whole Star of
Redemption.* *

We have reached a pivotal point. And, having reached it, we
shall pause for a proleptic assertion: Whether or not our Jewish
thought today will be able to stay with Rosenzweig, the point in
his thought just reached is essential to all future Jewish
thought, to say nothing of its being essential to any future authentic Jewish-Christian relationship. We have seen Spinoza
point to a restoration of the ancient Jewish state as the sole
genuine way of remaining a Jew in the modern world, with
only a weak concession to a universal "prophetic Judaism"
bound to dissolve into a still more universal "religion of mankind." From now on Rosenzweig will emerge as the first Jewish
thinker since Spinoza to point to another authentic alternative.
As for Jewish thinkers between Spinoza and Rosenzweig, they
found themselves faced with a gulf, created not by them but by
the modern world for them, between a "Judaism" that is universally true if it is true at all, and a "Jewish people" that is

---

*As early as 1914 Rosenzweig describes the Jewish people as "the *Herzstück*
of the faith" (*Kl.Schr.*, p. 290).

a particular people like other peoples if it is at all. As Jewish thinkers, they were bound to close this gulf. However, they were able to close it only by means of a doctrine—ad hoc and unauthentic, intrinsically unbelievable and rarely if ever believed—which made the flesh-and-blood Jewish people over into abstract "missionaries to mankind." And the nemesis of this doctrine—secularist Zionism—was no cure, for in trying to close the gulf from the other side, it made Judaism over into "Jewish culture" if it did not reject it altogether. As for Rosenzweig, his stature as a thinker both Jewish and philosophical is shown by the fact that he makes no attempt to close the gulf created by the modern world for Jewish thought. He rather removes it: it is both an alien import into Jewish existence and intrinsically questionable. This bold thinker does not hesitate to ascribe religious significance to the very existence of the Jewish people, quite apart from its beliefs, hopes, actions— simply by virtue of the fact that this people *is*. This is also, incidentally, why, despite his own vigorous non-Zionism, he is able to sense the unauthenticity of his contemporary anti-Zionist "German citizens of the Jewish faith."*

We proceed. Rosenzweig's turn to the Jewish covenant is, of course, a return to a premodern doctrine. It is to be accomplished, however, by a modern, post-Spinozist way of thinking. The premodern "old" Jewish thinking accepts the covenant on the authority of the Torah, and is necessarily incompatible with the old Christian thinking whose authority is the Christian Scriptures. Spinoza's "old" thinking refutes all premodern authorities and rejects (although it does not refute) each and every revelation. On his part, Rosenzweig can reaffirm the Jewish revelation only by means of a shift from the centrality of the Torah *itself* to the centrality of an Israel *witnessing* to the Torah, a shift that removes the necessity of conflict between a "new" Jewish and an equally new Christian *thinking*, while at the same time reaffirming as strongly as ever the difference (and possibly even the incompatibility) between Jewish and Christian *existence*. And the indispensable (albeit, as has been

*See above, ch. I, section 3, on the broader implications of the proleptic assertion just made.

said, by itself insufficient) basis both of the compatibility in the thinking and the difference in the existence, is that whereas one *becomes* a Christian, a Jew is *born*. Rosenzweig writes:

The son is born so that he bear witness to his father's father. The grandson renews the name of his forebear. The patriarchs of old call upon their last descendants by his name which is theirs. Above the darkness of the future burns the star-strewn heaven of the promise: "So shall thy seed be."

There is only one community in which such a linked sequence of everlasting life goes from grandfather to grandson, only one which cannot utter the "we" of its unity without hearing deep within a voice that adds: "we are eternal." It must be a blood-community, because only blood gives *present* warrant to the hope for the future. . . . All eternity not based on blood must be based on the will and on hope. Only a community based on common blood feels the warrant of eternity warm in its veins even now.

And again:

It is the Jew, accepted into the Christian world, who must convert the heathen within the Christian. For hope which love would like to forget and faith believes it can dispense with lives as a matter of blood-inheritance only in Jewish blood.[60]

On the basis of passages such as these Rosenzweig has been suspected of racism. (As will be seen, nothing is further from the truth.) His actual doctrine begins to emerge with a comparison between two institutions, i.e., Christian confirmation and Jewish bar mitzvah. At the time of baptism Christian parents can only *hope* that their child will be confirmed. On their part, at the time of circumcision, Jewish parents *know* that if not their own son then other Jewish sons will be b'nai mitzvah, for this occurs automatically at the age of thirteen. As a convert from paganism, the Christian is forever tempted to flee from his uncertain Christian future, either backward into paganism or forward into eternity. (It does not much matter which, for the longing is either for a "love" that "would like to forget" the future, or a "faith" that believes that it can "dispense with it.") For this reason the Christian stands in intrinsic need of an external nourishment. This he can receive only from the Jew, for the Jew, and he alone, has *the future hoped for* inextricably bound up with a love and a faith both of *which are wholly present;* indeed (since he is born a Jew), all things hoped for are bound up for him with what is most present of all—*existence itself.* In the case of the Jew alone, love, faith, and hope, on the one hand, existence, on the other, are all but inseparable.

All but inseparable: regardless of traditional Jewish legislation concerning Jewish identity, Rosenzweig must concede that "individual Jews" and their children may fall away from this eternity-in-the-present.[61] Hence unless he is to lapse into a natural determinism of the blood (a racism destructive of all action and commitment, divine as well as human) or into a supernaturalist determinism of divine decrees (destructive of human if not divine action), he must and does grant that what happens to "the individual Jew" could conceivably happen to the whole people. And it would be obtuse for him to rejoin that this possibility is improbable.* (His "absolute empiricism" does not and cannot rest on probabilities.)

At this point Rosenzweig, so to speak, approaches his Rubicon. The "fanaticism" of the "old" thinking had been able simply to accept the Torah, and with it its teaching that the divine-Jewish covenant is eternal, regardless of whether the people does or does not decide to keep it: Jewish choice is limited to two alternatives, willing or unwilling participation—but participation in either case. However, as we have seen, the "unfanatical," "new" Jewish thinking must shift the focus from the authority of the Torah to the Jewish people and its commitment to the Torah, its authoritativeness included. As a result, this thinking is now faced with a crucial dilemma. *Either Judaism is the individual Jew's free commitment*—an act of human will, a reception of divine Grace, a togetherness of the two; *but then this free commitment in the long run determines Jewish existence and indeed survival as well. Or else Jewish existence not only precedes the commitment to*

---

*The hope for a future, however probable, is qualitatively distinct from the present experience of eternity.

Judaism but also in some way determines it; but then the question is whether, in determining the commitment, it does not destroy the freedom in it. Rosenzweig must reject the first alternative, as perpetuating the unauthentic modern gulf between "Judaism" and "Jews" which can generate no authentic Jewish thought or life. He is therefore ineluctably driven toward the second alternative.

The alternative rejected as untrue to Jewish existence is much rather true to Christian existence. It is the Christian who "would be lost if Christ were not born in him, even if he were born a thousand times in Bethlehem." On its part, Jewish life "is the exact reverse. Here birth, the whole natural 'here,' natural individuality, immediate participation in the 'world' is always-already-there." The contrast between Christian and Jewish existence is expressed strikingly as follows:

Bearing witness (zeugnisablegend) [Christian faith] . . . is the first generator (Erzeuger) of the eternal way in the world. Jewish belief, on the other hand, follows after the eternal life of the people as a product (Erzeugnis).[62]

This passage startles not by what it says about Christianity but by what it seems to say about Judaism. Is Rosenzweig's "new thinking" driven, perhaps against its will and by the dilemmas it faces, into elevating Jewish "life" quite apart from "faith" to "eternity," and into making "faith" a mere product of "life"? This would be racism after all—a fanaticism quite different from that rejected, but far more deadly. Yet the word play on Zeugnis ("testimony") and Erzeugnis ("product") would suffice to suggest that this interpretation is wrong.

We cannot detect what is wrong (or discover what is right) unless we make a foray, as it were, to the end of the Star, where Judaism and Christianity are both transcended. More precisely, what occurs then is that the Jewish "fire" and the Christian "rays" are looked at from the standpoint of the "Star, or the eternal Truth." Rosenzweig writes:

Before God . . . Jew and Christian both labor at the same task. He can dispense with neither. He has set enmity between the two for all time, and withal has most intimately bound each to each. To us [Jews] he gave eternal life by kindling the fire of the Star of his truth in our hearts. Them [Christians] he set on the eternal way by causing them to pursue the rays of the Star of his truth for all time unto the eternal end. We [Jews] thus espy in our hearts the true image of the truth, yet on the other hand we turn our backs on temporal life. They [Christians], for their part, run after the current of time, but the truth remains at their back; though led by it, since they follow its rays, they do not see it with their eyes. The truth, the whole truth, thus belongs neither to them nor to us. For we too, though we bear it within us, must for that very reason first immerse our glance into our own interior if we would see it, and there, while we see the Star, we do not see—the rays. And the whole truth would demand not only see- ing its light but also what was illuminated by it. They [Christians], however, are in any event already destined for all time to see what is illuminated, and not the light.

And thus we both have but a part of the whole truth. But we know that it is in the nature of truth to be imparted, and that a truth in which no one had a part would be no truth. The "whole" truth, too, is truth only because it is God's part.[63]

The Star here clearly rises above Jewish and Christian exis- tence alike so as to see how each partakes of "the Truth." This gives us pause. Does not a thought thus rising understand both Jew and Christian differently from the self-understanding achieved by either? Does it not, in consequence, incongru- ously both assert "enmity between the two for all time" and, achieving its own higher viewpoint, make an end to that en- mity from that time on? Above all, in seeing the Jewish and Christian "part" in the "whole" truth from the standpoint of the whole truth, does the "system" not, at long last, relapse from the "new thinking" into the "old"? In the age post Hegel mortuum, is Hegel, after all, resurrected?

That the Star has many Hegelian (as well as Schellingian) features in undeniable. Yet there is no final relapse from the "new" thinking into the "old." For just as we have made a mere foray into the realm of eternal truth, so does the Star itself. To think the trans-Jewish, trans-Christian truth is, as it were, to think the unthinkable, and it is to do so only in order to be cast from eternity back into time. If, therefore, the Star is nevertheless to be both a "system" and "unfanatical," eternity

must somehow be "verifiable" or "confirmable" in the midst
of time. And since the verification can only be Jewish or
Christian, and Rosenzweig is a Jew, the "unfanatical" verification looked for must be the Jewish testimony to eternity in
the midst of time. Not accidentally, Jewish existence, though
dealt with fully earlier, reappears in the last pages of the Star.
And not accidentally, the Star—a philosophical and ipso facto
"unfanatical book"—is also described as being not a Christian
or "Judeo-Christian," but rather a Jewish book.

The Jewish "confirmation" or "verification" looked for exists
in the liturgical life of the synagogue. We must therefore turn to
this theme, as yet untouched, and do so with some degree of
explicitness. Jewish life—the life of the synagogue—is the celebration of eternity in the midst of historical time. Time: who if
not the Jew knows that it both needs redemption and has yet to
find it? Thus the Sabbath, the feast of Creation, anticipates
redemption; and whereas the cycle of Sabbath makes the year
into a cyclical eternity, each Sabbath yields, ever again, to the
workaday week. Thus time is untranscended.

This is true also of history. History: who if not the Jew has
received redemption in history rather than from it? Thus he
knows that, if history does point to an ultimate redemption, a
distinction remains between redemption which is yet to be
and revelation which already is. The Jewish people is the
"carrier of revelation," a "destiny" celebrated on the "historical festivals" of Pesach, Shavuot, and Succot. These form a
liturgical whole composed of three stages: "the people is
created into a people; the people is endowed with the words
of the revelation; the people wanders through the wilderness
of the world." So long as all history is unredeemed, the "eternal people" consists of "eternal wanderers."[64]

The climax of the liturgical year are the "Days of Awe."
Successfully or not, Rosenzweig has managed to find liturgical
parallels between the Jewish "fire" and the Christian "rays."*
In the case of the Days of Awe he can find no parallels: these

*Thus, for example, Christmas parallels Pesach, Easter Shavuot, and Pente-
cost Succot (Stern, pp. 457 ff.; Star, pp. 363 ff.).

days are unique.* For they represent nothing less than "eternal redemption," i.e., *absolute* transcendence in the very midst of time.† Here what is abstractly affirmed and sporadically experienced in *all* revelation is concretely and coherently *confirmed in the prayer-life of a whole people: that love is strong as death.*‡

The climax of the Days of Awe is Yom Kippur. On this day the Jew dons a shroud, stands out into death itself—and finds that love is its match. Death is the boundary of Creation. Revelation transcends that boundary with the *knowledge*—its own primordial knowledge—that love is strong as death. This is "the only thing that can be said, stated, narrated 'about' love . . . , everything else can be spoken only *by* it." And what is stated and narrated is that "one day all the dead past and future will be devoured by . . . [a] victorious today, [by a divine] love [which is] the eternal victory over death." For the Christian, this is his hope. This Christian hope would be groundless and anchorless unless for the Jew on Yom Kippur it were *already* a present experience:

Death meant to mow down all life lest it live on to eternal life. He had presumed that no end could be reached except by dying. But the eternal people is held up to him as a triumphant proof that the end can also be experienced by living. With that the scythe of the grim reaper breaks.[65]

This is the *ultimate* "confirmation" found in Rosenzweig's *Star of Redemption*. It is both of a way of being and of a way of thinking at once Jewish and unfanatical. *Of a way of being:*

*Stern, pp. 460; Star, p. 366: "What is the type of festival which would correspond to the Days of Awe? None." Subsequently Rosenzweig mitigates this somewhat by granting that Christmas, the Sunday of Sundays, has some resemblance to Yom Kippur, the Sabbath of Sabbaths (Stern, p. 461; Star, p. 367).

†"There is no festival of redemption as such in Christianity. In the Christian consciousness . . . the clear distinction which exists for us between revelation and redemption is obscured" (Stern, p. 462; Star, p. 368).

‡Stern, p. 199; Star, p. 156. This sentence—a quotation from the *Song of Songs* (8:6)—opens the *Herzbuch* which, as will be recalled, treats of revelation. Rosenzweig describes the *Song of Songs* as the *Kernbuch* (focal book) of revelation (Stern, p. 257; Star, p. 202).

this is Jewish life as lived by the Jew through the ages, climaxing in the Yom Kippur. *Of a way of thinking:* this is the *Star of Redemption*, a "system" itself rooted, in the ultimate analysis, in a way of being climaxing in the Yom Kippur. The ultimate confirmation of *both:* this lies in the fact that on this day the Jew stands in as "naked a solitude"[66] before God as *any* human being stands before death—but naked before Him with the promise of universal love.

Our search for the "confirmation" needed by Rosenzweig's thought, then, has ended. This being so, his "absolute empiricism" must now yield its secret if ever it is to yield it. Above we saw Rosenzweig reject the notion of self-authenticating experiences which would imply empiricism plain and simple, and make superfluous and unintelligible his "new thinking" in general and the *Star* as a system in particular. And, as a result of this rejection, he saw himself driven into a logical circle.[67] Now that we have reached the Jewish liturgical year as the ultimate required confirmation, this rejection and this circle may be specified as follows. First, is the divine-human relation that is said to be manifest in the Jewish liturgical year real rather than illusory because it is experienced as real? Or is the experience valid because the relation is real rather than illusory? If self-authenticating experiences cannot be maintained, clearly the first alternative is false, so that, if it were embraced, the confirmation of Rosenzweig's whole "system" would reduce itself to being at best a mere phenomenology of Jewish experience. Rosenzweig, however, embraces—as he has done all along—the other alternative: the experience is valid because the relation is real. As a result the logical circle reappears. For unlike the "old thinking" Rosenzweig's "new thinking" cannot *step outside* the experience in its attempt to *know* that the relation is real, whether the stepping be toward metaphysical proofs or revealed authority. The knowledge, or such knowledge as is possible, can be attained only *in and through* the experience. This means nothing less than that the logical circle which has been with us all along is inescapable. *It would be incurably vicious unless it were openly admitted. Jewish religious existence, as described in the Star, is shot* through with risk. *As for the "system" which is the Star of Redemption, far from overcoming or removing the risk, it fully shares in it.**

This conclusion might have been expected. The "fanatical" "old" Jewish thinking had been able to affirm the eternity of the divine-Jewish covenant on the authority of the Torah which contains the divine promise. The "unfanatical," "new" Jewish thinking can affirm this eternity only through the Jewish experience *of*, or commitment *to*, the Torah and its divine promises. Given this necessary shift from a start with the Torah to a start with the "Jewish nation," the *Star*, except for the open admission of the built-in risk, would degenerate into the idolatry of the "religious genius" of "the nation." However, Rosenzweig knows his Schleiermacher.

The risk built into Rosenzweig's "absolute empiricism" might have been discovered ever since we first came upon the logical circle which is part of it. Nevertheless, nothing really fruitful could be discovered unless the discovery was postponed. So long as it was only revelation-in-general that needed "confirmation" by experience-in-general, we could come upon nothing philosophically more instructive than the circle-in-general, and nothing empirically more palpable than ecstatic experiences-in-general. Now that the *Star*'s ultimate confirmation has emerged—the divine-Jewish covenant, its eternal reenactment in the Jewish liturgical year, and the Yom Kippur as its climax—the confirming experience *shows itself as having a structure, the unique characteristic of which is to be based in something that precedes all experience—the fact of Jewish birth.* Here is an irreducibly empirical datum for the *Star*'s "absolute empiricism."

---

*Leo Strauss has offered the most searching account of Rosenzweig's shift from the "old" to the "new" Jewish thinking. He has also argued powerfully for a return, after and despite Rosenzweig's new thinking, to the old, i.e., to the authoritativeness of the Torah. Yet in an unpublished lecture given just prior to his death, Strauss not only argued for the irrefutability and moral nobility of traditional Orthodoxy (in its Mizrachi-Zionist form) but also admitted his inability to regard it as more than a noble illusion. Thus the most powerful Jewish philosopher since Rosenzweig came to testify that the new thinking is intellectually inescapable. See further below, ch. IV, p. 264n.

With this conclusion, the spurious problem of "Rosen-zweig's racism" discloses its spuriousness. Above we wondered whether the Jewish testimony, as taught by the *Star*, might reduce itself to the mere product of "blood"—a doctrine both intrinsically objectionable and contrary to Jewish teaching. (A convert becomes a child of Abraham.) Now Rosen-zweig's true teaching has emerged: *the "confirming" Jewish experience which is the climax of the Star has the unique characteristic of extending beyond experience itself, so as to include the fact of birth. It is, then, not Jewish "blood" or "existence" that "confirms" the "eternity" of both itself and the Jewish faith. It is rather the structure of the Jewish faith-experience that confirms the "eternity" not only of the experience but also of what is prior to experience—Jewish existence in "blood."*

But how can the *experience of* eternity confirm *existence for* eternity? Here the risk built into the *Star's* whole series of confirmations—of Judaism, Christianity, and retroactively of creation, revelation, redemption and indeed the "elements" God-world-man—shows itself in its most acute and decisive form: *the Star must admit that the experience of eternal existence cannot warrant eternal existence.* Its power to give warrant is limited as follows:

All secular history deals with expansion. Power is the basic concept of history because in Christianity revelation began to spread over the world, and thus every expansionist urge, even that which consciously was purely secular, became the unconscious servant of this expansionist movement. But Judaism, and it alone in all the world, maintains itself by subtraction, by contraction, by the formation of ever new remnants. This happens quite extensively in the face of the constant external secession. But it is equally true also within Judaism itself. It constantly divests itself of un-Jewish elements in order to produce out of itself ever new remnants of archetypical Jewish elements. . . . In Judaism, man is always somehow a remnant, . . . always somehow a survivor.[68]

This passage, of course, restates the ancient doctrine of the holy remnant. It does so, however, in the form required by the "new thinking." In this new form it lacks the *total* warrant present in the old. It does not rest on the divine promise. It rather rests on an *experience*, forever renewed and rejuvenated, the structure of which includes a *human commitment* to a divine promise. And so far is this latter from an "objective" warrant resting on "supernatural facts" that it *can* be rejuvenated only by an ever rejuvenated radical surprise.* With this final conclusion of the present exploration we have come full circle—to the way it began.

The "empirical" verification of the whole vast edifice of the *Star of Redemption*, then, is far from absolute. Yet to Rosenzweig it must have seemed sufficient. Perhaps it could be sufficient. For from Haman to Hitler it was, to be sure, imaginable (and imagined) that someone might plot to exterminate the whole people, including and above all the holy remnant. It was not imaginable, however, that he might succeed (or very nearly succeed) in doing it.

4. Spinoza and Rosenzweig Today

To mention the accursed name of Hitler is to awaken from Rosenzweig's thought—profoundly philosophical, profoundly Jewish, profoundly modern—as if, nevertheless, from a dream. Yet we cannot (as some theologians would have us do) fail to mention the accursed name. For we dare not ignore Eichmann's boast that in murdering East European Jewry he effectively destroyed Judaism as well. *This* time it was precisely the holy remnant that did not survive—and history may yet prove Eichmann right. Something radical has happened in our time, not only to Jews but also to Judaism.

Exactly what has happened we shall be unable to explore until we are ready to immerse ourselves in the vast, unprecedented catastrophe known as the Holocaust. Some questions, however, can be answered at once. Can Jewish faith reconcile itself to the loss of the many because of the faith of the few? Is a system of Jewish thought tenable that rests on the pillar of a

---

*The pious Jew is surprised every day that the Creation is renewed; every Sabbath that the Redemption is anticipated; every Yom Kippur that he is given new life—as it were, in the midst of death.

holy, eternal remnant? Not ever since events have put in
doubt any kind of remnant. In destroying the holy remnant the
Holocaust also suspended, for the post-Holocaust world, the
idea of a holy remnant. As for the "contracting" dynamic of
the *Star of Redemption*, this is overrun by events; indeed, it is
imperative that it be reversed.*

The idea of reversing the "contracting" dynamic of Jewish
existence is barely glimpsed as yet in the sphere of thought. It
is already actual, however, in the sphere of Jewish life. In
response to the great catastrophe, the Jewish people took the
one collective step that was able to avert wholesale despair: it
restored a Jewish state. This monumental act altered the lives
of a part of the Jewish people; it also altered the Jewish condition as a whole. The Jewish state requires a dynamic of ingathering, and this in turn requires a dynamic of expansion.
That there must be more Jewish children, and more *Olim*
among those in the Diaspora, is an obvious sociopolitical necessity. (This is shown by one glance at the newspapers or the
map.) After what has occurred, it is also a moral imperative
and an act of faith. In his own time, Franz Rosenzweig gave
the most profound modern account of the Jewish people as a
remnant, of this remnant as the "eternal people," and of this
people as eternal because it was in history but not of it. In our
time, he would have to recognize that—for better or worse but
in any case inevitably and irrevocably—this people has returned into history.

It is instructive to note that the *Star*'s new Jewish thinking,
in decisive respects destined to remain ours, is in some respects more dated today than the old Jewish thinking of rabbinic Judaism. Like Rosenzweig, the rabbis may belittle the
valor of the Maccabees, but they do not wholly repress it: for
Rosenzweig the Jewish people "waits," "wanders eternally,"
and "cannot take seriously war."[69] Again, the rabbis may con-
centrate most if not all tragic Jewish memories on the one date
of the ninth of Av, thus lending plausibility to Rosenzweig's
view that the "distinctively commemorative festivals" of the

*The above assertions, here merely proleptic, will be fully spelled out in
chapter IV, section 14.

Jewish people have become "as rigid . . . as the history of—
[the] people" itself.[70] Yet historical memory remained sufficiently alive to cause Jews to go to die in Jerusalem when they
could not live there. Or yet again, while in waiting for the
Messianic days the rabbis are out of history, they are also, in
working for them, in history; for Rosenzweig, Jewish existence
is a "vigil for the Day of Redemption," and nothing else.
These and similar differences all point to a single question:
The rabbis accept the fact of exile but also work and wait for
its end; then why does Rosenzweig elevate Jewish wandering
to the status of the essential Jewish destiny?*

This question about Judaism is best treated in conjunction
with a corresponding question about Christianity. In his youth
Rosenzweig had rejected Constantinianism, never the most at-
tractive feature of Christianity, dubious already then, and
wholly discredited in our own age of rising non-Christian civilizations. Yet in the *Star* a Constantinianism of sorts reappears.
Corresponding to the Jewish "contraction," an "unrestricted
expansion"—missionarizing in history and of history—is described as essential to the very being of Christianity: "Christianity, as the eternal way, *has* to spread further. Merely to preserve its status would mean for it renouncing its eternity and
thus would be death."[71] The rabbis recognized a divine cove-

---

*Some four years after Rosenzweig's death, his friend Martin Buber was
forced to write to the Nazi Christian theologian Gerhard Kittel as follows:
"Authentic Jewry, you say, remains faithful to the symbol of the restless and
homeless alien who wanders the earth. Judaism does not know of such a
symbol. The 'wandering Jew' is a figure in Christian legend, not a Jewish
figure" ("An Open Letter to Gerhard Kittel," reprinted in *Disputation and
Dialogue,* ed. F. Talmage [New York: Ktav, 1975], p. 53). Kittel had invoked
the image of the wandering Jew, not only to justify the Nazi reversal of the
emancipation of German Jews but also to argue that "authentic" Jews (and,
needless to say, Christians) were religiously required to accept it. Close to
forty years later Father Daniel Berrigan asserted that in Israel "the wandering
Jew became the settler Jew . . . the slave became master and created slaves,"
and "the classic refugee people is now creating huge numbers of refugees"
("Fr. Berrigan's New Left Antisemitism," *Christian Attitudes on Jews and
Judaism* [Feb. 1974], pp. 12–13). Just as Kittel had no need to investigate
whether German Jews had behaved like a "foreign people" (Talmage, p. 51),
so Berrigan had no need to find out whether kibbutzniks were "settlers," and
Israelis in general "masters" who "created" refugees. In both cases the "eternal wanderer" stereotype was enough.

nant with Noah, hence with all men. On occasion they would recognize in Christianity and Islam providential means to bringing mankind to the One God. But not until Rosenzweig did a Jewish thinker assert that all except Jews must seek the Son if they are to find the Father. Rosenzweig, in short, gave a Jewish endorsement to Christian Constantinianism—just before this, too, was overrun by events. One asks: What leads Rosenzweig, a lover of rabbinic Judaism, into some modern doctrines more dated today than their premodern counterparts? This question in the end has but a single serious answer: *He sought a "system" at once "Jewish" and "unfanatical."**

This aim was not unreasonable. All modern thought must be, in Rosenzweig's (and Spinoza's) sense of the term, "unfanatical," i.e., reject intellectual authorities, whether human or divine. All Jewish thought is genuine only if it is intrinsically Jewish, i.e., if it lives by its own resources rather than the borrowings of an extraneous philosophy. Most arresting is Rosenzweig's reason for wanting a "system." The systems of the "old" thinking were gone. So were "fanatical" theologies resting on revealed authority. *In the age post Hegel mortuum the "new thinking" needed a system if it was to escape from what Rosenzweig termed the "curse of historicity."*† It was this third goal, in conjunction with the other two, that could be reached only at a price which even in Rosenzweig's age was too high and which, today, can no longer be paid. And the result is that *historicity, whether a curse, a blessing, or something of both, has become inescapable for Jewish thought.*

What exactly was Rosenzweig's price, and why was his *Star* forced to pay it? When Spinoza, the first great modern philosopher of Jewish origin, helped initiate the "new world," he saw no place for a nonanachronistic Jewish existence other

---

*Quite inadequate answers are that the cause is "undue Christian influence" in a thinker "whose return to Judaism was never complete," or that "he conceded too much to Christianity." This was rightly rejected by Rosenstock (*Judaism Despite Christianity*, p. 71).

†Kl.Schr., p. 289. According to Glatzer (*Life and Thought*, p. xxi) Rosenzweig first uses this term in 1914. The "curse" is an all-encompassing historical relativism which, in their first encounter, had been the main issue between him and Rosenstock.

than an implausible modern restoration of the ancient Jewish state. No profound alternative to Zionism was spelled out in thought until the advent of Franz Rosenzweig, the second great modern philosopher concerned with his Jewish identity, and he identified the alternative as synagogue-Judaism. However, he was able to assert this Judaism *within* and *against* modern history only by raising it *above all* history, with the claim that nothing significant could happen in Jewish history between Sinai and the Messianic days. *Thus Rosenzweig sacralized Jewish history or (which is the same thing from a different perspective) made Jewish existence ahistorical. (Yom Kippur is eternity in the midst of time and, in the last analysis, all Jewish existence is geared to it.)* Such, in short, is the price paid by Rosenzweig for a "system" at once "Jewish" and "unfanatical." One looks at this price and is driven to a startling conclusion. The ancient rabbis had responded to the grim reality of *Galut* (exile) with *Galut*-Judaism. Exile was punishment for Jewish sins, vicarious suffering for the sins of others, or in any case a meaningful if mysterious fate. Being meaningful, a Jew had to bear it in pious patience: One could pray or work for its end but not try to force it. And the patience was possible because the Gentiles, even when they oppressed the Jewish people, could be counted on to "fear God" sufficiently to resist the temptation of (and oppose) wholesale murder. The rabbis embraced *Galut*-Judaism. *But only Rosenzweig elevated it to a metaphysical level—and he did so just before Galut-Judaism (if most assuredly not the Galut) came to a violent end.**

This startling conclusion turns us from Rosenzweig back to Spinoza—the modern philosopher of Jewish origin who could see no place for *Galut*-Judaism in his "new world." Let us recall that thinker on "self-preservation." Spinoza teaches that self-preservation is the first and most indispensable virtue;

---

*This is of course a thoroughly controversial assertion. It can be substantiated only when it will become thematic. However, the present proleptic account suffices to make intelligible the claim that the Holocaust would have made an end to *Galut*-Judaism even if the fact of Israel had not altered the whole Jewish condition. See further below, ch. IV, section 14.

that "only by uniting their forces can [men] escape from the dangers that beset them on every side"; and that, if and when the dangers are extreme, no unity can provide safety except a military one, i.e., a state.[72] Such is Spinoza's teaching in his own time. In our time he would be faced with the facts that at Auschwitz Jews were murdered solely because of their Jewish origin; that no one came to their aid; and that their abandonment and murder were possible because they lacked every means of practicing of all virtues even the first and most indispensable. From these facts Spinoza today—unless he either betrayed his principles or suspended them in the case of Jews—would deduce the necessity of a Jewish state. In his own time, this was for him a minor and improbable option. Today it would be inescapable. Theodor Herzl was not wrong in considering himself a Spinozist.

This is not to say that Spinoza's own major option—the Jewish man-in-general—has disappeared. (Indeed, he is conspicuously present.) But this too requires a fresh look—at Spinoza's principles and new realities. In his own time, Spinoza expected all enlightened men to become men-in-general. Today this is expected of no one but Jews. In the Soviet Union, Russians, Ukrainians, and even Germans are allowed their own language and culture; to Jews these are denied. In the West enlightened men can be Englishmen, Frenchmen, or Americans; to Israelis this is not readily granted. And whereas it is considered natural that black Americans identify with Black Africa, Jews are zealots if they identify (or identify too much) with Israel. During the Holocaust, Jews were murdered by their enemies as Jews. When their friends came to liberate the survivors they recognized their Jewish identity only reluctantly or not at all. In the Soviet Union today all but a single memorial flatten out the six million murdered Jews into "victims of fascism." And when the Western Allies liberated Bergen Belsen they set up a huge memorial, with legends inscribed on it in many languages. But they forgot Hebrew and Yiddish, and mended their mistake only after survivors protested.

From these and many similar facts Spinoza today would deduce that the Jewish man-in-general remains a possibility but not an honorable one. For if the first Spinozistic virtue is self-preservation, the highest is self-respect, and this for a Jewish man-in-general is unattainable in our time. When at Auschwitz Jews had no choice but death, Jews elsewhere had no honorable choice but to use every means of coming to their aid. When Israelis today have no choice but to fight for life, Jews elsewhere have no honorable choice but support of their struggle. As for apologies to any quarter, they are out of place now just as they were then. Anti- or non-Zionism remains a possibility for Jews today. But it is a possibility without self-respect.

Doubtless Spinoza today would be surprised by these turns of events, less so, however, than by yet another: *the Jewish religion, in its most authentic forms, no longer emasculates.* If in his own time Spinoza hated Judaism, the essential reason was that, as he saw it, this religion had come to seek refuge from life in impotent prayer and a self-abasing humility; that it considered passive waiting as a duty and resolute action as a sin. This was so in his time. Hence, when considering the religious Zionism of our time, Spinoza today—for him "true piety and religion" are bound up with "courage and high-mindedness"—could hate Judaism no more. He might not love it, but by his own principles, he would be bound to respect it.

All this is, of course, not to say that Spinoza today would return to Judaism, despite all the surprises in store for him. For Rosenzweig, surprise is an ontological category, such that a shock of recognition can "dispel . . . delusions of a misdirected reason" and—so his "new thinking" testifies—lead to a return to the God of Judaism. For Spinoza, however, surprise is only a subjective feeling; and, being due to ignorance, it inspires a search for ever greater knowledge even if complete knowledge—and hence the end of all surprises—is in principle unattainable. And since in any case "human affairs are changeable," the changes between his and our world would cause him no *absolute* surprise. Thus, there is nothing to suggest that Spinoza today would not remain the chief philosophical source of inspiration of a Jewish secularism.

Yet the radical events of our time would not leave the foundations of his secularism unshaken, a point disclosed by yet another fresh look at Spinozistic teachings. In his own time, Spinoza rejects the biblical God (whom he does not refute), in the last analysis and at the deepest level, on the grounds of an antithetical love for an antithetical God. Moreover, this maximal achievement by the "God-intoxicated" author of the *Ethics* requires the minimal conditions discovered by the "Machiavellian" author of the *Theologico-Political Treatise*, among them not only the possibilities of good government but also limits of bad government; and among these limits a crucial one is that the "wise man" can "live under every form of government."[73] With these limits in mind, Spinoza writes:

No one can ever so utterly transfer to another his power and, consequently, his rights as to cease to be a man; nor can there ever be a power so sovereign that it can carry out every possible wish. It will always be vain to order a subject to hate what he believes brings him advantage, or to love what brings him loss, or not to be offended at insults, or not to wish to be free from fear, or a hundred other things of this sort, *which necessarily follow from the laws of human nature*. . . . If it were really the case that men could be deprived of their natural rights so utterly as never to have any further influence on affairs, except with the permission of the holders of sovereign might, it would then be possible to maintain with impunity the most violent tyranny which, I suppose, *no one would for an instant admit.* [My italics.][74]

One reads this passage and marvels, for a second time in this exploration—the first was with Rosenzweig—as if awakened from a dream. For what in Spinoza's view no one would for an instant admit today no one can for an instant deny. The absolute and "most violent" tyranny which he considers impossible is, in our time, actual. *Nineteen Eighty-Four* is a household word. Spinoza's science of "human nature," though Machiavellian, is not Machiavellian enough.

But something far graver is at stake here than insufficient Machiavellianism. Spinoza's tyrant is motivated by greed and lust for power. Our age has seen one tyrant—the Führer of the Third Reich—who was motivated far more deeply by ideals. The subjects in Spinoza's tyranny are manipulable by dint of their blind fears and base instincts. The subjects of the Führer's tyranny typically needed no manipulation, for they *chose* blindness, and obeyed in a spirit of willing sacrifice. These ideals and these sacrifices, however, were unheard of in human history: whereas elsewhere the twentieth-century concentration camp is a means, here it was an end as well. As for the Nazi murder camp—we shall find it to be the inmost essence of the Third Reich as a whole—this was doubly unprecedented, for it was not only the practice of torture and murder on a scale hitherto unknown; it was also, unbelievably, the worship of both. In due course, we shall be forced to confront the startling fact that the mind accepts the possibility of Auschwitz, in the last analysis, solely because of its *actuality*.* Here (when this confrontation is premature) it is already clear that the Holocaust challenges far more than merely Spinoza's version of a science of human nature. Called into question is the very idea of such a science: "Human nature" after the Holocaust is not what it was before. Thus, for a second time in this exploration, historicity—whether a curse, a blessing, or something of both, emerges as inescapable.

Perhaps one can still affirm that a Spinozistic sage in our time can reach or approximate the "blessedness" of Eternity. What can no longer be affirmed is that a "wise man" can exist in every state. The counter-testimony is too compelling. One philosophically minded survivor—Jean Amery—testifies that at Auschwitz "the intellect . . . lost its basic quality: its transcendence."[75] Another—Primo Levi—writes as follows:

On their entry into the camp, through basic incapacity, or by misfortune, or through some banal incident, they are overcome before they can adapt themselves; they are beaten by time, they do not begin to learn German, to disentangle the infernal knot of laws and prohibitions until their body is already in decay, and nothing can save them from selection or from death by exhaustion. Their life is short, but their number is endless; they, the *Muselmänner*, the drowned, form the backbone of the camp, an anonymous mass, continuously renewed and always identical, of non-men who march and labour in silence, the divine spark dead within them, already too empty really

*This subject will not become thematic for us until ch. IV, section 6.

to suffer. One hesitates to call them living; one hesitates to call their death death.[76]

We must heed this profound, if shocking, testimony. (Indeed, we shall have to recall it again and again.) The Nazi state had no higher aim than to murder souls while bodies were still alive. The *Muselmann* was its most characteristic, most original product. He is a *novum* in human history. And how many Spinoza-like sages were made into *Muselmänner* will never be known.

These grim facts can be explored only subsequently. Even now, however, it is clear that a Spinoza today cannot ascribe his attainment of eternal blessedness to wisdom alone. Grimly, sadly, it is also due to luck. And this fact would suffice to make it impossible for him to abide in the serene state of his blessedness. He would have the duty of solidarity with his luckless fellows. He would be honor-bound to fight their fight. With this insight, Eternity itself is invaded by historicity: The plunge into history is complete.

5. Conclusion

With this plunge, our present exploration is itself complete. We have thus far been guided by Spinoza and Rosenzweig. The commitment, in antithetical ways, of both these thinkers to Eternity—their spurning of history—marks the limit of their guidance. Radical events have happened to both Jews and Judaism in our time. When the Romans destroyed Jerusalem, the rabbis recognized and responded to catastrophe. Future Jewish thought must follow their example. Jewish life is *already* responding to the great catastrophe of our time. Jewish thought must do its share.*

But the plunge by thought into history is by no means necessary because of the great catastrophe alone. Spinoza's modern Jewish secularism and Rosenzweig's modern Jewish neo-orthodoxy are divided by the shibboleth of revelation. Revela-

---

*See below, ch. IV.

tion is the great shibboleth still. But in a new Jewish reality
the shibboleth both survives and is transformed. In the State
of Israel the modern religio-secular conflict does survive: Perhaps it has even reached a new extremity. (In a liberal democracy orthodox and secular Jews can stay out of each other's
way. In a Jewish state this is impossible.) At the same time,
there is also a new, shared commitment. It is impossible for
Jewish thought to predict the outcome of this togetherness of
conflict and sharing. But it is necessary for it to consider ways
of mediating the conflict—a task that plunges us into history.*

The self-immersion of thought is not in Jewish history
alone. The Holocaust is a Jewish catastrophe—but also one of
all humanity. Revelation is the great shibboleth of Jewish modernity—but also the great shibboleth, directly of Western
and indirectly of all modernity to be sure. Jewish thought may
not dissolve its native exigencies in a spurious universality.
But a Jewish thought devoid of universal significance, or cut
loose from it, would not deserve the name of thought at all.
The problematics of modern Jewish thought are intertwined
with the problematics of modernity as a whole.†

*See below, ch. III.
†See above, ch. I, section 6, where the plan of the remainder of this work is
spelled out.

III

The Shibboleth of Revelation: From Spinoza beyond Hegel

1. Rosenzweig on Hegel

WE have thus far treated Spinoza as Rosenzweig's chief philosophical antagonist. In Rosenzweig's own mind, however, this role was played by Hegel rather than Spinoza, and at least in one respect he was right: Of the two antagonists, Hegel is the more dangerous. Spinoza's Achilles' heel may be "to say always 'sive' and never 'and.' "[1] Through this very sive, however, he at least says a simple no to the God of the revealed Scriptures. In contrast, Hegel claims to overcome this either/or concerning the God of revelation—no either/or could be more ultimate!—by means of an all-mediating, all-reconciling "both/and." As Rosenzweig puts it:

[For Hegel] philosophy is, as it were, only the consummator of what is promised in revelation. Nor does it exercise this office only sporadically or at the height of its career; but in every moment, as it were with every breath it breathes, philosophy confirms the truth of what revelation has declared. Thus the old quarrel seems settled, heaven and earth reconciled.*

If, then, the great sickness of the "old" thinking was a "retreat from the flow of reality into the protected circle of wonder,"[2] Spinoza at least expels the God of revelation from that circle, leaving Him free, as it were, to retaliate. Hegel, in contrast, draws this God into the fatal circle. No escape is left.

In the present context we concede from the start that Hegel's philosophy fails respecting its highest objective and therefore as a whole, and that Rosenzweig is right in speaking of an age

---

*Stern, p. 12, Star, p. 7. I have used this passage as one of three mottos in my RD. The other two, with much the same message, are by Karl Barth and Hegel himself.

post Hegel mortuum.* But what does that historical location
signify? Here it would seem that, focusing his polemical attention as he did on Hegel's unacceptable goal, Rosenzweig paid
insufficient attention to Hegel's way toward his goal,† and
that this neglect led him to reject Hegel *in toto* when reject
him he did. To put it in more precise (and more Hegelian)
language, he did not consider sufficiently the possibility that
the failure of Hegel's enterprise might be a "process" with
dialectical "results."

One glance at the contemporary scene suffices to suggest
that these results are more alive than it seemed to Rosenzweig
when he wrote: "It is a pity about him [Hegel]! Only Nietzsche
(and Kant) pass muster."[3] (Does Kant pass muster today? Does
Nietzsche? Can the import of either thinker today compare
with Hegel's?‡) Before considering such results, however, we
must inquire into the concept "dialectical result" itself. The
heart of Hegel's whole enterprise is the mediation of all
things, and above all of those things that are highest. What

*For an account of Hegel's pursuit of his objective, see my *RD*. For an
encounter between Hegelianism and Judaism in which both are allowed to
speak, see my *Encounters*, ch. 3. My present occupation with Hegel, though
it relies on the two previous ones, is independent of them. In *Encounters*
thought is located *between* Judaism and Hegelianism, seeking a "preface" to
future Jewish thought. In "Foundations," thought is located *within* Jewish
existence from the start and occupied with "post-Hegelian" thought because
modern Jewish existence is bound up with modernity as a whole; and because in my view the bravest philosophical expression of modern-secular
self-confidence is what I term "post-Hegelian." See further above, ch. I,
section 6.

†This judgment, fundamental to the whole following exploration, underlies
my *RD* in its entirety. The implicit argument of that work is that whereas
Hegel's philosophy takes itself to *be* at its goal—the Absolute and Absolute
Thought—we on our part can neither understand nor critically appraise his
philosophy unless we watch it seek and reach its goal. On this point, see also
my exchange with James Doull, "Would Hegel Today be a Hegelian?," *Dialogue*, 9 (1970), pp. 222–26.

‡Kant's categorical imperative fails to pass muster on account of its unhistori-
cal abstractness (see further below, ch. IV, section 12). This failing initiates the
move from Kant in the direction of Hegel. In a way, this move is reenacted in
Sartre's turn from his own earlier to his later thought. On Nietzsche, Karl
Löwith writes in part as follows: "He is still close to us, yet already quite remote. . . . He coined maxims with an unheard of harshness of which in his personal life he never was capable, maxims which entered into public consciousness and then were practised for twelve years." (Quoted in *Quest*, p. 297.)

renders his enterprise profound and serious (rather than merely clever and frivolous) is the determination to do justice to all things in the process of their mediation. This is why Hegel's system, in case it fails, does not vanish without a trace. "Systems" come and go. Since, even by its own standards, Hegel's system fails to do *complete* justice to the things it mediates, it also goes. But since it metes out a great deal of justice it does not vanish without results. Indeed it leaves us with a host of fragmentary and fragmented mediations. Philosophy in the age *post Hegel mortuum* must cope with these. As for Rosenzweig's thought, to the extent to which it ignores or denies the significance of the results of Hegel's philosophy, it would require reconsideration even if events between his time and our own had not overrun so much of it. After Rosenzweig's historic encounter with Hegel, yet another is required by Jewish thought in our time.*

2. Hegel on Judaism and Spinoza

By his own admission and insistence, Hegel's philosophy must do justice to the things it mediates. It must therefore do justice to Judaism. This is despite the fact that the standpoint at which Hegel metes out his justice is explicitly Christian. Perhaps it is because of that fact. For whereas most modern philosophers are semi-, crypto-, or quasi-Christian, Hegel is virtually alone in *explicitly* drawing Christianity *into* his philosophy. Indeed, he makes it *a* or even *the* decisive factor without which his philosophy would not be possible. Thus it is doubly noteworthy that Hegel does greater justice to Judaism than any other modern philosopher of the first rank.

Hegel mediates between all things as he does justice to them. His mediating activity therefore extends to Judaism. However, it also extends to the conflict between Judaism and Spinozism—this latter a phenomenon which requires justice in Hegel's scheme of things far more obviously although (as will be seen) not more urgently. We shall begin by focusing

*See above, ch. I, section 3.

attention on this particular mediation. Indeed, it will be wise for us to stay with this focus, as far as possible, to the end. On the negative side, the wealth of Hegel's thought might otherwise lead us astray from our own proper task. On the positive side, Hegel's mediation between Judaism and Spinozism, together with the results of its failure, contains all the essential elements of the two questions that occupy us in the present exploration. One is: How does revelation function as the shibboleth in Jewish modernity? The other is: What can be made of the claim that this conflict between the religious Jewish affirmation of revelation and its secularist Jewish denial is mediated at a standpoint higher than both? (This claim, if borne out, would render anachronistic this whole conflict and, indeed, the two antagonists themselves.)

What, then, of Spinoza? Hegel writes:

What constitutes the grandeur of Spinoza's manner of thought is that he is able to renounce all that is determinate and particular, and restrict himself to the One, giving heed to this alone.[4]

This modern philosophical Jew has "renounced all that is determinate and particular." He has therefore renounced the thoroughly particular—i.e., singling out—religion of his ancestors, and become through this double renunciation—particularity as such, and his own Jewish particularity—a man-in-general. As such he stands in the most startling contrast to just these ancestors who hold fast to their Jewish "determinacy" and "particularity" with what is, on the one hand, a "fanatical stubbornness," but also, on the other, an "admirable firmness."[5] To be sure, like their apostate modern philosophical descendant, they "renounce" all to "the One." But whereas in the one case this One is "Substance" *containing* all, in the other it is "Lord" *over* all. And whereas in the one case we see a "thought" *at one* with Substance, remaining in its self-renouncing stance and turning into a self-effacing love, in the other we behold a "service" *of* "the Lord," renouncing itself *over against* Him, and, unable and unwilling to persist in this stance, turning into a "renunciation of renunciation."[6] It is this last move which, for the present, requires closer inspection. This is a *double* move of renouncing *renunciation* even while being *self*-renouncing. And it is *both* aspects of this move that make up the believing Jew's "absolute confidence" or "infinite faith" that "he who does right fares well." This is what constitutes the "admirable" Jewish "firmness." This is what prevents Abraham and his seed from dissolving into either "Substance" or "mankind" but rather remain a particular "family even when expanded into a nation." Otherwise put, this "family" remains so totally opposed to becoming men-in-general as to remain Jews-in-particular even in the presence of the universal God. Indeed, it is in His presence above all that it remains particular: its particularity is ultimate. To be sure, the external critic may wish to dispose of this stern ultimacy with the idea that this God is only one god among gods, that YHVH is god of Israelites just as Athene is goddess of Athenians. But, as Hegel has it, any such idea is wholly dispelled *by the Jew himself in extremis*—the figure of Job:

Submission, renunciation, the recognition of God's power restores Job's earlier good fortune. Pure confidence, the intuition of Power, of the sheer or unpurposive power of God is first. However, it carries in train temporal happiness.*

Job submits to a Power that has laid the foundations, not of Athens but of the whole earth (Job 38:4), yet is restored in his own particularity.

*Phil.Rel., II, i, pp. 79, 98. One cannot exaggerate the importance of holding fast to Hegel's view that Judaism contains not only "renunciation"—the surrender of the human servant to the divine Lord—but also a "renunciation of renunciation" whereby the finite human is restored in his finitude. (Hegel's Job thus is not unlike Kierkegaard's Abraham.) This is all the more important since Hegel himself does not always hold fast to this view. Thus he asserts that since in Judaism and Islam God is Lord only, "the finite does not receive its due," and that to give it its due is the function of "pagan and polytheistic" religions. In a similar context Spinoza appears as a Jew "with an oriental view." (Enc. #112 Zus., #151 Zus.) But one must notice that the context here is the *Logic* that abstracts from existence. A different and more adequate account appears in *Phil.Rel.* and *Hist.Phil.* which do not abstract from existence. Here Judaism appears not as part of the Orient but rather as its climax, and as an equal partner in the historic meeting with the Greek-Roman West. (See *RD*, pp. 133–38.) As for Spinozism, this appears not as an oriental intruder into Western philosophy but rather as its initiation into modernity.

Hegel holds that this Jewish "fear" of the "Lord" is the beginning of all *ancient religious* wisdom. He also holds that "the placing itself at the standpoint of Spinozism is the essential beginning" of all *modern philosophical* wisdom.[7] Thus the relation between Judaism and Spinozism is of vital importance to Hegel himself, not only to ourselves. The great difference is, of course, that whereas for us the relation is one of conflict, with revelation as the great shibboleth between them, Hegel proposes to mediate just this conflict, undismayed if indeed not inspired—in the precise Hegelian sense of the term—by its very extremity.

3. Revelation as Shibboleth

As thus far stated, the conflict would appear to give rise to a dilemma which may be stated as follows. Either the "Lord," worshipped in Judaism as wholly other, is in fact wholly other than His human servant, in which case it is far better to be a "slave" with and for Him than a "free" man without or against Him; but then Spinoza's rise in thought to Substance stands exposed as the work of a superficially Promethean yet ultimately puny pride, and the Substance itself as a sham. Or Substance is "the Truth" even though it is not the "whole Truth,"[8] and Spinoza's thought has in fact the "grandeur" which Hegel ascribes to it; but then the Lord-worshipped-as-other is, after all, not *wholly* other if indeed He is not a mere man-made projection, and the more-than-human awe in which He is held shrivels into a less-than-human, animal fear.

From the standpoint of either of the two positions, the conflict is obviously absolute. On reflection no less clearly (though on account of prevailing academic prejudices somewhat less obviously) an "objective" standpoint external and neutral to both is in principle unavailable. The conflict can be mediated, if at all, only at a standpoint sufficiently immersed in *both* the Jewish "admirable firmness" *and* the Spinozistic "grandeur" as to do justice to both, *and yet also* superior to both. Here for the first time in this book the possibility comes into view that a way of thought might come on the scene that both *enters into*

Jewish existence from its own internal point of view, *and also* rises so unmistakably *above* it as to render it obsolete. However, once Hegel's attempt to encompass and transcend Jewish existence has failed, this possibility will not reappear. For Hegel's attempt is unequaled and unsurpassed, and indeed unsurpassable.

4. The Basis of Hegel's Mediating Thought-Activity

For, of course, the standpoint superior to both Jewish "firmness" and Spinozistic "grandeur" is Hegel's own. *How can it be superior?* The textbook answer would cite Hegel's famous statement, already alluded to, to the effect that "the True must be grasped and expressed not only as Substance but just as much as Subject."[9] The "grandiose" Spinozistic "renunciation" is only the beginning of modern philosophical wisdom, for it is an "acosmism" which surrenders both world and self. Hence it is contradicted by the Kantian-Fichtean assertion of the primacy of selfhood. This latter, however, asserting as it does a "subject" over against the realm of "object," remains, unlike Spinozism, at a standpoint of finitude. Hence there is need for a fulfillment of the wisdom whose beginning is Spinozism. This fulfillment may equally be described as the elevation of selfhood to infinity and the transfiguration of Substance into Subject.

But what of the "Lord" of Judaism and His otherness? The textbook wisdom just cited, sound as far as it goes, is not sound or wise enough for our purpose. That it is not wise enough for Hegel's own purpose is evident from his critique of the thought of his own immediate predecessor and onetime friend. Some years before Hegel, F. W. J. Schelling had already affirmed an "Absolute" which was at once self raised to infinity and Substance transformed into Subject.* Yet in the same text which calls for just this achievement Hegel also, hinting at Schelling, writes derogatorily about a "night in which all

*In his writings between 1800 and 1804.

cows are black."[10] To be sure, unlike Spinoza's Substance, Schelling's Absolute is to *contain* rather than to "renounce" the "determinate and particular." It also is to be Subject just as much as Substance. However—so runs Hegel's criticism— since all this is only *asserted*, Schelling's assertion remains an empty thought, and all difference, and with it all reality, falls outside it.* On our part, we ponder all this and ask: What difference can be more radical than that between a God who is wholly other-than-man and a worshiper who remains all-too-human?

We therefore progress to a deeper wisdom within Hegel himself when we accept his account of both the Absolute itself, and the thought grasping it, as a "union of union *and* nonunion."† The implications of this progression are vast. Only some can be considered in this context. For the present there is no need to go beyond our immediate theme: Only if Hegel's own thought is a union of union and nonunion can it do justice to, and mediate between, Judaism and Spinozism. For the "admirably firm" Jewish "service" of the "Lord" remains a "nonunion," and, on its part, the "grandiose" Spinozistic Substance renounces everything "determinate and particular" to a sheer "union."

But Hegel's union of union and nonunion would hardly constitute progress of any sort if it were confined to *thought alone*. For all one knows, thought might well extend its bounds beyond all previously recognized limits so as to unite what had hitherto been considered ununitable. The union thus achieved would still be exposed as being one of *mere* thought by a *sheer* nonunion persisting *outside* it. To be sure, a whole host of nonunions might be viewed as trivial and contingent. (Even so they would not be beneath philosophical notice.)‡ However, one could hardly so view a nonunion between a God accessible only as Lord because of the absoluteness of His transcendence,

---

*For the relation between Schelling and Hegel, see *RD*, pp. 26–30.
†*E.Th.Wr.*, p. 312. On this crucial passage see *Encounters*, p. 243, and *RD*, pp. 26, 32, 82, 175 ff., 184 ff., 190, 227 ff.
‡On Hegel's notion of contingency, see *RD*, pp. 114 ff.

and a man finding access to Him only as servant because of his persistence—honest as well as stubborn—in his human finitude. Indeed, no protest against a union in the sphere of thought, coming from the sphere of life, could be more ultimate and, unless coped with, more devastating.

We therefore make a genuine advance in thought only with the recognition that in its own self-understanding Hegel's philosophy does not come on the scene in an historical vacuum. That it exists in no vacuum in the history *of philosophy* might have been guessed from our earlier recognition that it accepts and supersedes Spinozism, the beginning of *modern philosophical* wisdom, by a process of reconciling it with the Kantian-Fichtean protest against it. The crucial advance we seek comes with the question: How can Hegel's union of union and nonunion (which is in the sphere of thought) encompass also a nonunion which is in the sphere of life?

The answer can only be this: There *already is* just such a union in the sphere of life *itself*, and without this as its presupposition Hegel's philosophy could not reach its goals. Hegel fulfills the philosophical wisdom of which Spinoza is the beginning: there already is a fulfillment of the religious wisdom whose beginning is Judaism. This latter beginning, as we have seen, is a radical "nonunion"—the Jewish "fear" of the "Lord." The love in Christianity that fulfills this beginning is by no means a "union" only. Manifesting a Divinity that has entered into the extreme of immanent particularity—a single flesh-and-blood man—from the extreme of its own transcendent universality, it is a union of union and nonunion. And in the sphere of life it is ultimate.*

Evidently Hegel's philosophy cannot mediate the conflict between Judaism and Spinozism by dint of its Christian presupposition alone. On grounds such as these Judaism would testify as firmly (and successfully) against Hegel's philosophy as, throughout the ages, it has held its ground against Christianity. As for Spinozism, this would simply reject the Chris-

---

*This interpretation is fully developed and defended throughout *RD* and indeed may be said to be the chief theme of that work.

tian revelation as it rejects all revelation. And these two testimonies would jointly declare that the conflict between revelation—a descent of God into time—and modern autonomous
reason—the ascent by thought to eternity—is absolute. We
would, in short, remain at an impasse.

We go an important step beyond this impasse in noting that
Hegel does not identify either Judaism or Christianity as "revealed" religions.* Hegel denies *absolute* distinctions between religions—not only that between "true" and "false" but
also that between "natural" and "revealed." Moreover, his denial of such distinctions is not, and cannot be, simply *brought
to* religious realities but must *already* be present *in* them, even
though it is partly or wholly unrecognized. Otherwise put,
mediation, as brought by thought *to* the sphere of religious
life, must already be a process *within* that sphere, even though
philosophy is necessary both to complete the process and
bring it to consciousness. And, so far as Hegel is concerned,
the complete mediation, insofar as it can be real in religion,
exists in Christianity. He writes:

Over against this God [of Judaism] all other gods are false. But this
distinction between true and false is quite abstract. *The other gods
are not recognized as gods, and rightly so. The same is true in Christianity.* But the exclusion is here such that the worship of other gods
is regarded as darkness, rather than as a dawn containing a show of
light. . . . Since religion . . . is of the spirit, it may be ever so errone-
ous, yet it contains the Affirmative—a stunted, abstract truth, yet
Truth. *In this sense there is a divine presence in every religion, a
relation of divine love.* [My italics.][11]

This is a crucial passage, and it indicates, not only Hegel's
denial of absolute distinctions between "true" and "false" or
"natural" and "revealed," but also why, in the following, the
topic of revelation must nevertheless remain central. Hegel is
often taken as a "rationalist" who minimizes, waters down, or

*Enc. ## 564 ff. is entitled "The Revealed Religion." *Phen.* refers to Christianity as the "manifest" (*offenbare*) religion. The section on Christianity in
Phil.Rel. is entitled "The Complete or Manifest, the Absolute Religion." The
last-named designation expresses Hegel's meaning most exactly. Judaism is
for Hegel the "religion of Holiness."

even denies the claims made by revealed religions on behalf of revelation. *In fact, however, he does not deny revelation or take a reductionist stance toward it, but rather expands its scope.* This was well understood by Rosenzweig when he wrote that in its self-understanding Hegel's "philosophy . . . consummates what is promised by revelation."*

5. Spinoza and Hegel on Revelation

A comparison between Spinoza and Hegel on the subject of revelation serves to spell this out. The precondition of Spinoza's rise to philosophic truth is the rejection of revealed truth, Jewish or Christian. The precondition of Hegel's rise to philosophic truth is the acceptance of revealed truth, directly the Christian and indirectly the Jewish as well. Having rejected revealed truth, Spinoza has no further philosophic but only "theologico-political" truck with revelation. Having accepted the revealed Christian truth, Hegel is faced with what may well be described as the central problem of his whole philosophy. If the divine incursion into the Christ, *passively accepted* by Christian faith, *remains as* accepted by Hegel's philosophy, then this latter surely falls philosophically far short of Spinoza's self-active rise to eternity; it may indeed, by the highest modern philosophical standards, destroy itself as philosophy altogether. Yet if it emulates or surpasses Spinoza's self-active rise to eternity, then it surely retroactively negates its own acceptance of the Christian revelation, and indeed negates that revelation itself. This dilemma must seem inescapable unless, in its self-active ascent to the Divine, philosophy *transfigures* and thus *preserves* the Christian "content" instead of destroying it: and unless, moreover, it not only *ascends* to divinity *above* time but also *reinstates* the divine descent *into* it. The question is, of course, whether this is possible. It is the central question not only of Hegel's philosophy of religion but, as I have suggested, of his philosophy as a whole.

*See above, p. 105n.

6. The Core of the Hegelian Mediation

The question may be reformulated as follows. Aristotle's pagan thought denies the otherness of the Greek gods and in so doing both destroys Greek-immanentist religion and rises above it. Hegel's own Christian (or post-Christian) thought cannot deny the otherness of the Christian God, for divine otherness is real in the Christian union of union and nonunion. Then what makes possible Hegel's *self-active* rise to the ultimate union of union and nonunion, when Christian faith itself remains *receptive* of that same union of union and nonunion? And if this rise is nevertheless possible how can it fail to destroy the Christian God just as Aristotle (and, of course, other Greek philosophers before and after him) destroyed the gods of Greece?

Just how seriously Hegel takes the otherness of the Christian God appears from his view that the Incarnation, though an indispensable condition of his philosophy, is far from sufficient and that its immediate effect was to widen rather than close the gap between the human and the Divine. In medieval times, an abyss came to yawn between a "sacred" heaven and an "unsanctified" earth; and, corresponding to this, philosophical thought, free in pagan Greece, became subservient to ecclesiastical authorities. Not until heaven and earth showed themselves to be not two realities but rather tensions and contradictions in *one* reality did the times become ripe for modern philosophic wisdom *in history*. And not until, without relapse into ancient paganism, thought overcame ecclesiastical authorities did the necessary ripeness become real in the *history of philosophy*. This modern wisdom begins when such as Spinoza "rise to the sun like a young eagle, a bird of prey that strikes religion down." And the wisdom is fulfilled when in Hegel philosophy "does justice to faith and makes peace with religion."[12]

What is this peace? *Hegel's philosophy rises in thought from the human to the divine side of the Christian union of union and nonunion. But what from the human side of this relation is passively received as the ultimate incursion of the divine*

Other *is, from the divine side (and in the philosophical thought re-enacting it) a divine* self-othering *in man and world.* This philosophical reenactment brings about three results. First, it gives the religio-secular diversity, already "implicitly" united in the sphere of life, explicit unity in the sphere of thought. Second, in uniting the Christian union of union and nonunion (already actual but passively received) with modern secular realities (*already* self-active but *ever yet to be* made actual), philosophical thought (itself the highest form of self-activity) gives the Christian "true content," its "true"—i.e., philosophical—"form," thereby transfiguring it. Third—since life cannot be reduced to thought—philosophic thought *reinstates* modern secular-religious life with all its diversities.

7. Hegel's Mediation between Spinoza and Judaism

It is at this standpoint—the standpoint that "consummates" what was "promised by Revelation"—that Hegel mediates between Judaism and Spinozism. At his own standpoint, the religious Jew may see himself covenanted to the God of the world, free over against Him as Father as well as subject to Him as King, and in both aspects of the covenantal relation geared to a Messianic future* By the standard of a divine self-othering *in* the human, *any* freedom is servile that remains human in its relation to a transcendent Divinity, just as, correspondingly, this Divinity is *nothing but* Lord if it remains other-than-human in the relation. Again, by its own standards Spinozism may see itself as the timeless truth, which, moreover, does justice to all phenomena. By Hegel's standard it represents the Jewish principle within a philosophy whose modernity could arise only in the modern Christian world. Only because it is within the Christian world can Spinoza's thought rise as it does from the human to the divine side of the divine-human relation. And only because it completes the

*See further below, section 12. How Judaism from *its own* point of view might respond to Hegel's mediating activity, done from *his* point of view, is the subject of ch. 3 of *Encounters.*

Spinozistic beginning by reenacting in thought a divine self-othering (already actual in life and witnessed to by Christian faith) can Hegel identify Spinozism as only a beginning.

This stance enables Hegel's thought to mediate between Judaism and Spinozism while "doing justice" to both. In this mediation both appear as witnesses to the divine Unity. Their testimony, however, finds opposite, and hence mutually antagonistic expressions. For such as Abraham, Moses, or Job, the One remains Other; however, these biblical figures compensate for this lack by "renouncing renunciation" even while practicing renunciation: thus they regain the world even as they serve its Lord. On its part, Spinozism overcomes the Jewish "non-union," for it becomes one in thought with the One. However, it pays a monumental price for this monumental achievement. This is its "acosmism"—the loss of the world. Doubtless in Hegel's view Spinozism emerges from this mediation with the higher rank. Yet Judaism by no means emerges with a lesser weight. Spinozism does have the higher rank, for whereas Judaism is no true part of the modern world, Spinozism does no less than initiate the philosophical dimension of it. However, in so doing Spinozism loses the world. In contrast, and like Hegelianism itself, Judaism holds fast to the world.

Such, in brief, is Hegel's mediation between Judaism and Spinozism. And it leads us to three conclusions. First, as Hegel sees it, this mediation is possible only in the modern world, and within it only by Hegel's philosophy. Second, this mediation is central to his philosophy as a whole. To be sure, Judaism and Spinozism are each a beginning only, the one of the ancient religious wisdom, the other of the modern philosophical one. *But in each case the beginning must continue to be reenacted as the wisdom finds its consummation.* Only if the Christian revelation retains the Jewish otherness of the Divine can it remain revelation rather than shrivel into a neopagan immanentism. And only if the modern philosophical Subject retains the principle of Substance can it avoid fragmentation into a multitude of finite subjects. It is surely a weighty fact that in Hegel's "consummation of what was promised by revelation" his mediation between Judaism and Spinozism is indispensable.

But one fact is more striking still, and this is our third conclusion. *In the context of Hegel's all-mediating philosophy, Judaism, Spinozism, and revelation insofar as it is the shibboleth in the conflict between them, are all preserved and yet, as such, superseded.*

8. The Failure of Hegel's Mediation and Its Dialectical Results

But what if Hegel's philosophy cannot keep its promise? We have shown elsewhere, and in this discourse conceded from the start, that Hegel's philosophy fails in its maximal aim and thus as a whole. Hence what is required here is only to redirect Hegel's own doubts, present in apprehensions about his own age, onto ours. Hegel's thought can arise only from a "modern world" composed of an unconquerable Christian faith and a boundless secular self-confidence; and only such a world can it wish to reinstate. Yet in his own age Hegel saw "religious unity vanished" and secular life "inactive and without confidence." Hence, robbed of a vital bond with a vital world in both its ascending and its descending moves, his philosophy came to seek refuge in a "separate sanctuary" inhabited by philosophers—an "isolated order of priests."[13] According to Hegel, precisely such a recourse to a worldless God-of-thought had characterized ancient Neoplatonism, but need not and cannot characterize his own philosophy. Indeed, his thought stakes all on its ability to *stay with* the modern world. Thus Hegel's final doubts have implications catastrophic for his philosophy as a whole.

In his own age Hegel's apprehensions remained peripheral. In our age they would have to become central. It is premature, at this point, to mention the Holocaust, a modern catastrophe undreamt of in Hegel's thought. Not premature is the introduction of a kind of spiritual decay of modernity which is already noticed in his own writings. Hegel attributes the decay of his age to the power of "the understanding," a fragmenting, alienating principle that is yet indispensable; and even in his time he perceived technology as the characteristically modern form of it. Yet how far his world is from ours is sufficiently illustrated by a single example. To Hegel technology still is a humanizing factor in warfare: Unlike with a spear, with a rifle one can kill a person without hating him. Clearly this example is enough to raise doubt as to whether Hegel himself today could be a Hegelian.

Then what is the abiding power of his philosophy? And in what sense, other than a trivial chronological one, is this the age *post Hegel mortuum*? In the wake of its so-called "collapse," its foes on both right and left came to view Hegel's philosophy as an aberration to be left behind without a trace— a "panlogistic" denial of "existence," an "idealistic" blindness to "reality" and the like. But in our time it is obvious that Hegel's thought *has* left traces, and that it remains significant enough to make its foes on right and left into post- rather than simply anti-Hegelians. This significance has many aspects. The aspect that concerns us here may be described as follows. *Hegel's philosophy is no aberration. It is rather an experiment that failed; and the experiment was historically necessary. Once Spinoza had come upon the scene and, in behalf of a rival God of autonomous modern Reason, had rejected the God of the revealed Scriptures*—without, however, refuting Him—*there was, as it were, a philosophical necessity for the attempt to overcome this harsh either/or, placed unsurpassably by Spinoza before the modern (Jewish and Christian) mind, and to seek to reconcile the most radical (i.e., orthodox) claim on behalf of the God of scriptural revelation with the most radical (i.e., autonomous) claim on behalf of modern reason.* The experiment failed. Yet this *is* the age *post Hegel mortuum*. For the failed experiment has dialectical results.

9. The Move toward the Extremes*

The failure of Hegel's experiment suggests that revelation, after all, *remains* the great shibboleth, and that it is necessary

*In the following the terms "right" and "left" refer exclusively to the post-Hegelian (Christian or Jewish) reaffirmation of revelation and its "humanistic" negation. The Kierkegaard- and Marx-interpretation offered in this section is so sweeping—not to call it a tour de force—that documentation, unless it is

to move from the Hegelian middle to post-Hegelian extremes. These extremes are embraced in various forms by numerous thinkers, but by none as impressively as, respectively, Sören Kierkegaard and Karl Marx.

Kierkegaard's commitment to the Christian revelation announces its post-Hegelianism in the admirably precise formula "immediacy after reflection." Immediacy—or the only immediacy worth Kierkegaard's agonized struggle—is the believing reception of Grace in the Christ. Post-Hegelian is only this, that it is "after reflection." Thought, having failed in its Hegelian endeavor to rise to the divine side of the divine-human relation, falls back to its human side and indeed, being mere thought, falls *outside* and *below* that relation altogether: it is no longer divine-human speculation but "reflection" which is only human. However, having attempted and failed in the speculative enterprise, it transcends its limits even while remaining confined to them, *pointing to* faith—the human participation in a relation with the Divine—as *lying beyond* it. And since it is itself outside that relation, this latter can be reached only by a *leap*. Hegel's speculative thought which *contains* the reality of faith has reduced itself to an abstract "reflection" that has lost it. The reality of faith can be regained only through a *decision*.

Kierkegaard's leap into faith becomes involved in what may be called the existential circle. Revelation is the *gift* of the *divine Other* for human faith to *receive*. Yet faith is not a simply-passive experience but rather a *commitment* and an

---

in a formidable detail that wholly transcends our present scope, makes no sense at all. For the present purpose it may suffice to say that the most authoritative source of our Kierkegaard interpretation is his *Concluding Unscientific Postscript* (Princeton University Press, 1941), and that the best Marx anthology for our purpose presently available is F. L. Bender, *Karl Marx: The Essential Writings* (New York: Harper Torchbooks, 1972). Bender's companion volume, *The Betrayal of Karl Marx* (New York: Harper Torchbooks, 1975), contains documents relevant to our criticism of Marxian thought, including proof to the effect that the so-called betrayal of Marx begins with Marx himself. As Leo Strauss aptly puts it, "It is foolish to say that that policy [i.e., of the USSR] contradicts the principles of communism, for it contradicts the principles of communism to separate the principles of communism from the communist movement." (*Preface*, p. 352.)

act. Under no circumstances may this act *posit* or *produce* the gift; to do so would be to do away with revelation, its God, and human faith in both. Yet that there *is* a gift (and no mere pseudo-gift) is known only *in* and *through* the act of faith: without it there is no revelation of a present God but only a mass of physical and psychological facts. Thus faith is an "objective uncertainty" shot through with risk.

This circle assumes a paradoxical character because of what revelation is and must be. It is no mere gift of this or that but rather all-encompassing. It therefore encompasses faith itself. Hence the decision of faith is at the same time no decision at all but rather the gift of a Grace that is merely received. And yet faith—the passionate commitment to the "highest Truth"—also remains, of all human decision, the most momentous.

Kierkegaard holds fast to this paradoxical circle of faith and revelation with an admirable single-mindedness, a trait that lends historic significance to his thought. Spinoza has served as our prime, incorruptible witness that modern thought can reject revelation but not refute it. Kierkegaard will serve as our prime, incorruptible witness that modern thought cannot dialectically so overcome the God of revelation as to reduce all surviving belief in Him to a mere anachronism. Yet for this achievement Kierkegaard pays a price that is destructive and, in the end, self-destructive as well.

Hegel's Christian faith is self-exposed to the modern-secular world. On its part, Kierkegaard's circle of faith and revelation, first, seeks immunity from external assaults, and finds it by moving into a fideistic extreme that is indifferent to history and lets go of it. Second, resting as it does not on revealed authority but on a leap of faith, Kierkegaard's thought fulfills generally the modern requirement to be "unfanatical"; yet it is forced to behave fanatically toward other faiths. Its stance toward Judaism is especially instructive. Though heir to a strongly anti-Jewish German tradition, Hegel can do a justice of sorts to the Jewish Job, for if faith is in history and of it, religious truth can have many forms and degrees. On his part, and although heir to a Danish tradition only weakly anti-Jewish if anti-Jewish at all, Kierkegaard, to be sure, makes Abraham a central figure, but co-opts him as a proto-Christian: if faith is not *of* history, and is *in* history only in the form of isolated "knights of faith," then the truth of faith is one and absolute or not at all.

The third consequence of Kierkegaard's self-protective stance is most serious, for it is self-destructive: he lets go not only of secular and non-Christian history but of "sacred" history as well. This, to be sure, makes him the unequaled critic of established churches, including and above all his own. However, threaten as it does the invisible along with the visible church, it also isolates him from fellow-Christians and, indeed, by a gulf of nearly two millennia, from the Christ himself. Kierkegaard gave his life to the single question of how one becomes a Christian. There is reason to doubt that he ever answered it.

We pass from one post-Hegelian extreme to the other. Karl Marx emerges as a left-wing Hegelian if one considers, not just this or that Marxian fragment, but rather what may be called the Marxian whole. This we sum up as follows: (1) All past history consists of conflict, the root of which is economic. (2) The conflict is not between individuals but rather classes, and these are constituted as such by antagonistic relations to the privately owned instruments of production. (3) To overcome private property is to overcome both class conflict and classes themselves; and this overcoming (which is at the hands of the propertyless proletariat) is not only desirable but also, sooner or later, inevitable. (4) The state is an instrument of oppression in class-conflict; hence with the end of class-conflict—the advent of the classless society—the state will wither away. (5) Class-conflict manifests more than merely men-in-conflict. Ultimately, it is nothing less than man-in-self-contradiction. Hence the classless society will produce not only new human relations but also a new man. He will be the New Man.

The last-named thesis is not only additional to the others. It is also the soul of the Marxian whole, giving as it does the first two above theses their full meaning and the last two their entire meaning. Marx puts this, his deepest principle, as follows: Man's entire historical "existence" has been alienated from his true "species-being" or "essence"; this latter is a being-for-each-other rather than a being-against-each-other: and man's task in history and the goal of history is the overcoming of this alienation. Marx owes this principle to Feuerbach, his predecessor and one-time mentor. However, whereas for Feuerbach the alienation of human existence from its essence, as well as the overcoming of it, involves hardly more than the mind, for Marx it involves the whole man. What is at stake is not the transformation of mere ideas but of the real human world.

So radical a transformation—what is at stake is the self-creation of the New Man—involves an absolute or religious (or rather, in this case, anti-religious) dimension. And so real a transformation involves not mere ideas of God but God Himself. Hegel has negated the otherness of the God of revelation—but rather than negate God Himself he has internalized Him in an act that raises thought itself to absoluteness. Kierkegaard rejects Hegel's absolute thought, causing thought to fall back to the level of a merely human and abstract reflection that points to existence outside and above it—but the existence pointed to is a reinstated faith in a reinstated God. Marx, like Hegel and unlike Kierkegaard, negates the otherness of the God of revelation, but unlike Hegel he negates this God *himself* and indeed all gods.* And since his thinking, like Kierkegaard's, is abstract, finite, and merely human, its negating would be unsubstantial unless it pointed to a negating existence beyond it. The true left-wing Hegelian counterpart to Kierkegaard's leap into faith is the Marxian revolution.

Marx's historic significance, like that of Kierkegaard, lies in his radicalism: All post-Marxian thought that sets limits to

---

*Marx is orthodox enough in his left-wing Hegelianism to consider all other gods overcome by the Christian God before this latter is in turn Himself overcome by the new, post-religious Man. See further, *Encounters*, pp. 134 ff.

man's modern-secular potential must henceforth demonstrate its innocence of conservative timidity or even outright "reactionary" villainy. At the same time—this too like Kierkegaard—just this radicalism has consequences both destructive and self-destructive. Kierkegaard protects (and must protect) his circle of faith and revelation by handing over all history to a realm of irrelevance. On his part, Marx makes (and must make) a *total* claim on *all* history. And this has its nemesis.

Marx's claim on history is total. His revolution, unlike that of Feuerbach, involves the whole man. His "dialectical" socialism, unlike the "utopian," does not look to mere "ideas" to affect a "reality" that is itself alien to them—a view that makes the conflict between ideas and reality permanent. Rather does it see a "new world" emerge from the "womb" of the "old"—both its own seeing and the acting to which it points are part of the process, as well as the completion of it. There is no deeper expression of the Marxian claim on all history than in its self-assumed task to both "interpret" the world and to "change" it—and the claim that "theory" and "praxis" are inseparable. And since all efforts at change are vain unless embodied in a political instrument, communist "theory"—Marxian thought—and praxis—the politics of the communist party—are inextricably intertwined. This is not only the deepest expression of Marx's total claim upon history but also a doctrine by which the Marxian whole either stands or falls.

That it has a destructive and self-destructive potential showed itself even in Marx's own lifetime, in the factional disputes of the movement he founded. Its true nemesis, however, is communism-in-power. There the destructive potential of Marx's total claim upon history is evident in the existence of divergent and mutually antagonistic communist states that accuse each other of heresy. And the self-destructive potential is fully revealed when the advent of the New Man—post-revolutionary, post-alienated, post-political, liberated—is officially proclaimed by the state that, of all states currently existing, shows the fewest signs of withering away.* One might object reasonably—though not without being involved in theoretical difficulties—that Stalin's or even Lenin's and Brezhnev's Soviet Union has "betrayed" Marxian thought. However, a Marxian thought that keeps being betrayed by communism-in-power finds itself driven into either withdrawing from history altogether, into "principles" unsullied by it, or else into becoming frozen in a stance that guarantees it the purity of powerlessness.† Either stance, however, is in conflict with Marxian thought itself. Claiming, as it does and must, all history, it is self-exposed to judgment by it.

The failure of Marx's affirmation of the New Man inspires a critical look at his negation of all the old gods. Marx has a sharp eye for religion insofar as it diminishes man—servile fears, escapist otherworldly hopes, the uses made of such "opiate" by oppressors. To religion insofar as it enhances man, he is wholly obtuse. Indeed, one may doubt whether any thinker of stature has ever given so sorry an account of himself in this particular sphere. Where is Marx's account of the God of the prophets, or the God that liberates in the Exodus? Or of the love of God shown by as diverse witnesses as Talmudic rabbis, Christian saints, Spinozistic sages? Marx asserts that the more a person gives to God the less he has left for himself. Even a thoroughgoing skeptic may recognize in *homo religiosus* one who, the

---

*See Leonid Brezhnev, *Report of the CPSU Central Committee . . . XXVth Congress of the CPSU* (Moscow: Novosti, 1976). Brezhnev said *inter alia:* "Finally, there is a Soviet man, the most important product of the past 60 years. A man who, having won his freedom, has been able to defend it in the most trying battles. A man who has been building the future unsparing of his energy and making every sacrifice. A man who, having gone through all trials, has himself changed beyond recognition, combining ideological conviction and tremendous vital energy, culture, knowledge and the ability to use them. This is a man who, while an ardent patriot, has been and always will remain a consistent internationalist." (p. 104). Although Brezhnev claimed that "socialism is impossible without a steady development of democracy," as well as that this latter was in process through an "ever fuller participation by the working people in running all the affairs of society" (p. 102), he also admitted that communism had not yet been attained (p. 104). Perhaps this was in explanation of why the Soviet state has yet to wither away.
†The first of these two positions is generally characteristic of Western anticommunist Marxian thought; the classic example of the second position is Trotskyism.

more he gives, the more he has to give. We have seen that Marx's total claim on history, in behalf of secular self-affirming Man, collapses in self-contradiction. This is confirmed by an open-minded contemplation of religious self-giving man—a contemplation that, unlike the Marxian, *remains* open-ended.

10. The End of Constantinianism and the Turn to Dialogical Openness

These results at the extremes suggest the necessity of moving toward what may be called the post-Hegelian broken middle. The middle is "broken," first, in that there can be no thought of a return to Hegelianism, a possibility which, if it ever was real, is gone beyond recovery; second, in that there can be no thought of compromising the integrity of the extremes—the God of revelation and a modern self-confident secularity—in a flat, un-Hegelian syncretism; third, in that the extremes, with a new un-Hegelian sense of their fragmentariness, show a new, post-Hegelian openness toward each other. As for philosophic thought, this cannot either (as in Hegel) rise above the extremes, or (as in Kierkegaard and Marx) point to one extreme so as to overwhelm the other. It must rather locate itself *between* the extremes; and if it can dwell in this precarious location and is not torn asunder, it is because the extremes show a new willingness to be vulnerable. This new willingness is a crucial feature of the age *post Hegel mortuum*. It marks the end of Constantinianism.*

Constantinianism is the theopolitical praxis of two beliefs: that the Christian revealed truth is the complete revealed truth; and that truth itself is not divided into "religious" and "secular" but rather is one and indivisible. Hegel's philosophy may be viewed as the climax of modern Constantinianism and yet already foreshadowing its end. It is the first because it both

---

*This assertion applies only to Christian Constantinianism, and even there in the sense not of empirical fact but only of any claim to legitimacy. As for Constantinianism in Islam, it is beyond our present scope. (The use of the term is odd—but Islam too does claim a revealed truth.) And only marginal to our purpose is a post-Constantinian Constantinianism that can arise when the God of revelation is overcome by the New Man.

separates religious and secular truth and reunites them; and because it not merely asserts its own comprehensiveness but *demonstrates* it. But precisely in this demonstration it also foreshadows the end of Constantinianism. This latter, resting as it does on authority, asserts itself *against* other faiths and ways of life, and does not hesitate either to use armed force or to become imperialistic. For Hegelianism any self-assertion *against* another is ipso facto proof of its own one-sidedness. And a true comprehensiveness demonstrates itself only through a mediating process which metes out justice to all things mediated. It is true that Hegel's mediating activity metes out unilateral justice only, i.e., by Hegel's standards and not those of others: this is what *makes* his philosophy Constantinian. Yet because every external protest testifies against Hegel's whole enterprise and continues to testify until its claim is mediated, there is a true justice of sorts in Hegel's mediation—enough to make his philosophy anti-imperialist. Moreover, in case Hegel's whole experiment fails, its failure marks the end of Constantinianism.

A residual Constantinianism remains in the post-Hegelian extremes. No great Christian thinker may seem less Constantinian than Kierkegaard, who, rather than seek a Christian conquest of the world, renounces the world. Yet his move which makes faith invulnerable to the world makes it obtuse also to other faiths. By the logic of his Christian faith—it rests not on revealed authority but rather on a commitment—it should be open to the testimony of other faiths, no less committed and genuine than his own. Yet of this openness his "knight of faith"—out of history, alone with his God—shows not a trace.

A residual Constantinianism is equally present on the post-Hegelian left. Marx too is an unlikely Constantinian, for he seeks a secular state in which religion is privatized. Yet his own communist state (and the communist overcoming of the state) has Constantinian traces of its own. Whereas all religions are false, some are more false than others. Lutheranism is the last religion; and Marx, "the last of the Lutherans," is also the last of the Constantinians. Not accidentally, Western

Europe is the center of Marx's universe; no less accidentally, Jews in that universe, standing as they do in Marx's view in greater need of "human" emancipation than Christians, can receive it only if, ceasing to be Jews, they become men-in-general.

This residual Constantinianism is overcome only through a move to the broken middle that is open to dialogue.* A truly post-Kierkegaardian witness to the Christian truth makes himself vulnerable to the claims both of the modern-secular world and of non-Christian faiths. And a truly post-Marxian witness to the New Man makes himself vulnerable to surprise, not, perhaps, by Divinity, but at any rate by an unexpected Grace in humanity. And in both cases the openness is genuine only if the outcome of the dialogue is not known before it is begun.

Such, in brief, is the character of the age *post Hegel mortuum*, and such are the dialectical results of Hegel's experiment that failed. When we speak of this "character" and these "results" we do not, of course, speak of a universal empirical condition. (Indeed, the post-Hegelian world is threatened by tyrannies without and within that dwarf, or threaten to dwarf, all the old.) What we do speak of are the convictions, religious and secular, that are honestly possible—and that are accompanied by the faith that, however fragmentarily and precariously, they can prevail.

It can hope to prevail because the age *post Hegel mortuum* does not come empty-handed to the dialogue to which it is self-exposed. It is true that dialogical openness, a current fashion in the Western world, all-too-often reflects nothing better than a lack of conviction and failure of nerve. A post-Hegelian openness to dialogue is not so empty; it *brings with* itself what is of all Hegelian ideas the most completely non-

---

*Commitment to dialogue is a widespread phenomenon in our time. But only rarely—e.g., Feuerbach in the nineteenth century and Rosenzweig in the twentieth—do its proponents explicitly connect it with Hegel. To place it into a post-Hegelian setting does more than merely serve historical accuracy. All genuine dialogical thought begins not in a vacuum but "where one is." Its post-Hegelian setting makes this "where one is" more than an arbitrary personal given but also, and at the same time, a given in the Western religious-secular situation.

negotiable. This is the idea of Overcoming. It is the Hegelian Idea. In Hegel himself it conjoins a religious aspect—the world-already-overcome (John 16:33) with a secular aspect—the world-ever-yet-to-be-overcome through human self-activity: This is why Hegel can give contingency free rein, yet see it conquered. This conquest of contingency survives at the right- and left-post-Hegelian extremes, for the one is an Overcoming of man by God, albeit withdrawn from the world, and the other, an Overcoming of God by a man, who through this act conquers the world. It is true that, as post-Hegelian thought moves from the extremes toward the broken middle, contingency is conquered no longer, for the overcoming has become limited and fragmentary. Moreover, the trust in an overcoming is challenged in our time, not only by natural catastrophe without and the undiminished strength of destructive passion within, but also, far more deeply, by products of self-activity itself that, meant to help spirit overcome nature, now threaten to destroy it. Even so, an authentic Hegelian response to the problems of the present age is to bid men summon their religious and secular strength, address the problems of a world increasingly technological, and overcome.

11. Catastrophe

In 1964 the great Auschwitz trial began in Frankfurt. Two years later, this trial stirred a philosophically-minded survivor to speak after twenty years of silence. Jean Améry subtitled his book "Attempts at Overcoming by One Who Is Overcome." What was to be overcome, he wrote, was a novum in history. Auschwitz was a world dominated by a "logic of destruction." In the "meeting" which that world created for the victims "between spirit and horror," spirit, after a brief period of total disbelief, "abruptly lost its basic quality: transcendence." Even dying was not what it was in other worlds, for whereas, for example, the life of the soldier "was not worth much," the state "did not order him to die but to survive"; in contrast, "the final duty of the [Auschwitz] prisoner . . . was death, that of an animal intended for slaughter." Moreover, to the murderers this death was an end in itself, for it was in behalf of a Germany that found "self-realization" in it. As for the ideal SS man, he "had to torture and annihilate, in order 'to become great in enduring the suffering of others.' " In an age marked by torture in many countries Nazi torture was, nevertheless, unique.

The Nazis tortured, as did others, because by means of torture they wanted to obtain information important for national policy. But in addition they tortured with the good conscience of depravity. They martyred their prisoners for definite purposes, which in each instance were exactly specified. Above all, however, they tortured because they were torturers. They placed torture in their service. But even more fervently were they its servants.

Améry's final conclusion must have been that it was impossible to overcome Nazism and its most characteristic, most original works. On October 17, 1978 he committed suicide.*

Other witnesses confirm that the Holocaust was a *novum* in history. Confining himself in his reflections, as he did, to the victim's conscious experience unto "the mind's limits," Améry himself was reluctantly forced to exclude the *Muselmann* from consideration.[14] But we have already cited another philosophically-minded survivor, to the effect that the *Muselmann*—"one hesitates to call them living; one hesitates to call their death death"—was a new way of living and dying, of being human.†

And, as a form of murderous self-realization on the part of the Third Reich, the manufacture of the *Muselmann* found a worthy rival only when, with the Auschwitz "extermination of the Jews in the gas chambers at its height, orders were issued that children were to be thrown straight into the crematorium furnaces, or into a pit near the crematorium, without being gassed first." Such was the testimony of a Polish guard at the Nuremberg trials. To the Russian prosecutor's question as to why this was done he replied: "It is very difficult to say. We do

---

*Améry, pp. 10, 6, 7, 16, 31. The subtitle quoted by us does not appear in the English translation. The title of the work in the original German is: *Jenseits von Schuld und Sühne: Bewältingungsversuche eines Überwältigten* (Munich: Szcesny, 1966).

†See above pp. 99 ff. Primo Levi and Jean Améry were comrades in suffering.

not know whether they wanted to economize on gas, or if it was because there was not enough room in the gas chambers."[15] Much evidence could be adduced to the effect that the Pole's opinion should not be taken as authoritative. Doubtless, in the new way of murdering children, utilitarian considerations played a role. But utility, in this case, was synthesized with idealism—the "becoming great in enduring the suffering of others." As for the identity of these others, they included political enemies—but on occasion even German communists saw the light. They also included "inferior races"—yet inferior Slavic women could occasionally become superior and be chosen to serve the Reich's Aryan breeding policies. Only in the case of "non-Aryans" was there no room for ambiguity or compromise in the Nazi philosophy; and, except for some quibbling by Nazi scholastics, a "non-Aryan" was a Jew.

The survivors testify on the basis of experience. Their testimony is supported by a few clear-sighted thinkers that have only their minds, among them some Hegelian enough to be otherwise wholly committed to the idea of overcoming. Thus one maverick Marxist—Isaac Deutscher, a self-declared "non-Jewish Jew"—concedes that the Holocaust becomes increasingly unintelligible with the passage of time.* Another maverick Marxist, Theodor Adorno, asserts that the "real hell" of Auschwitz "paralyzes the metaphysical capacity."

With the administrative murder of millions, death has become something that was never to be feared in this way before. The last possi-

*He writes: "To the historian trying to comprehend the Jewish holocaust, the greatest obstacle will be the absolute uniqueness of the catastrophe. . . . I doubt whether even in a thousand years people will understand Hitler, Auschwitz, Majdanek and Treblinka better than we do now. . . . Posterity may understand it even less than we do. . . . There was still some human logic in the Inquisition. . . . The fury of Nazism, which was bent on the unconditional extermination of every Jewish man, woman and child within its reach, passes the comprehension of the historian. . . . It is not my personal involvement in the Jewish catastrophe that would prevent me, even now, as a historian, from writing objectively about it. It is rather the fact that we are confronted here by a huge and ominous mystery of the degeneration of the human character that will forever baffle and terrify mankind" (The Non-Jewish Jew and Other Essays [New York: Oxford, 1968], pp. 163 ff.).

bility has been taken of making death part of the experience of the individual as in some way harmonizing with its course. The individual is robbed of the last and poorest that until then still remained his own. In the camps it was no longer the individual that died: the individual was made into a specimen. And this fact necessarily affects the dying also of those who escaped the procedure.[16]

This dying was a *novum*, affecting all dying ever after. And this *novum* "paralyzes."

The view that the Holocaust cannot be overcome is, of course, not shared by all believers in an overcoming. In 1945 the death camps were liberated and revealed to the world. Four years later Karl Barth, writing at the post-Hegelian Christian right, recognized the Holocaust as the greatest Jewish catastrophe—but failed to ask whether it might also be a Christian catastrophe.[17] Responding to Adorno on the left, a German Marxist proceeded in 1970 from the "negation" of Auschwitz on an "ascent from the negation of the negation to affirmation," such that "Auschwitz" became an "ideological turning point, the birthplace of something better, higher, more valuable that must come after Auschwitz." And since his "humanistic vision" rested on "Marxist-Leninist foundations" one gathers that in the German Democratic Republic this "birth" was already actual.[18] Thus in both the post-Hegelian Christian right and Marxist left alike, Auschwitz is long overcome.

It was overcome before Auschwitz had ever occurred. In the 1949 essay Barth asserted that "the evil that had come to the Jewish people was the result of its unfaithfulness"; that the Jew "pays for the fact that he is the elect of God"; and that the Jewish nation is "no more than the shadow of a nation, the reluctant witness of the Son of God and the Son of Man." Barth wrote about Jews as though the Holocaust had not happened: for his Christianity it *had* not happened. Only the original Good Friday was before Easter. Every subsequent Good Friday, Auschwitz included, is after Easter, overcome in advance. On this if on no other point, orthodox Marxism is in agreement with orthodox (or, in this case, neoorthodox) Christianity. The Holocaust is a by-product of Nazism, which in turn is a species of fascism, which in turn is the final, desperate expression of capitalism, the overcoming of which by communism is preordained where it is not already actual. Jewish cemeteries all over Eastern Europe bear the inscription "To the Victims of Fascism." Thus a double lie—Nazism is "fascism" and Jews are victims-in-general—is the price paid for the left-wing Hegelian overcoming of the Holocaust before it ever happened. It would not be difficult to find the corresponding price paid on the right-wing ortho- dox (or neo-orthodox) Christian right. Doubtless this takes many forms, but all are variations of deafness to Jacques Maritain's cry, "The people of Christ have become the Christ of the peoples."

But is not, as a German proverb has it, the event so long ago that it is no longer true? And, to cite another proverb, is it not the exception—a terrible exception to all things human and divine—that proves the rule: a malfunctioning of the social machinery that confirms that all is well with its normal func- tioning? Améry (who employs this last-named metaphor) also foresees a time not too distant when the survival of such as himself, too, will be considered a malfunctioning of the ma- chinery—a disturbing reminder that malfunction the machin- ery once did.

Thoughts such as these may be part of a pagan conscious- ness for which all things vanish without discrimination in the river of forgetfulness. They can be no part of a dialectical consciousness. Here the past is taken up in the present; and, if the past is a "negation," the taking up is through a "negation of a negation," i.e., an overcoming. Hence Hegel cites the above German proverb about the past no longer being true— but only in order to reject it. And as for irregular catastrophes that prove the validity of the realm of regularity—on this, in conjunction with the German proverb, Kierkegaard writes as follows:

Should we say, "There have elapsed now nearly two thousand years since those days; such a horror the world never saw before and never again will see; we thank God that we live in peace and security, that the scream of anguish from those days reaches us only very faintly;

we will hope and believe that our days and those of our children may pass in quietness, unaffected by the storms of existence? We do not feel strong enough to reflect upon such things, but are ready to thank God that we are not subjected to such trials."

Can anything be imagined more cowardly and more disconsolate than such talk? *Is then the inexplicable explained by saying that it has occurred only once in the world? Or is not this the inexplicable, that it did occur? And has not this fact, that it did occur, the power to make everything inexplicable, even the most explicable events?* [My italics.][19]

Writing as he does about the fall of Jerusalem in 70 C.E Kierkegaard overcomes the catastrophe through the "edifying" thought that man is always wrong over against God—a turn of thought even then possible, perhaps, only because he has withdrawn from history into the privacy of his soul. Our own catastrophe, however, cannot be overcome even at such a price. The edification of our soul is disrupted by the cries of the children, the no less terrible silence of the *Muselmänner* and, above all, by those who became great through enduring the suffering of these victims—and were yet human like ourselves. We therefore conclude: *where the Holocaust is there is no overcoming; and where there is an overcoming the Holocaust is not.* Indeed—here Kierkegaard is our witness—so long as no way is found to confront the Holocaust and yet endure, it has the power to render questionable all overcoming everywhere.

The Holocaust cannot be overcome by the post-Holocaust world; neither is this possible for the post-Holocaust Jewish people, heir to the most unequivocally singled-out victims. This is the testimony of Jean Améry, a thinker minimally Jewish in that "solidarity in the face of a common threat" is all that "binds" him to his "Jewish contemporaries." It is the testimony also of Martin Buber, the deepest and most representative Jewish thinker to live through the twelve-year Third Reich (its years were equal to a thousand). In April 1933, Buber wrote that the Jew was the inwardly most exposed man of the contemporary world, that he was being torn in two by the tensions of the age, and that, after the test was over, there would not be two but one—the Jew who had overcome. After

1945, Buber no longer wrote of overcoming. It had become impossible.*

12. The Shibboleth of Revelation in Jewish Modernity

We must therefore suspend, for the present, the subject of the Holocaust and resume—albeit with a tentativeness born of our brief encounter with that subject—our present exploration, i.e., the modern shibboleth of revelation, its Hegelian mediation, and the dialectical results of its failure. Now, however, we must shift our focus from modernity-in-general to Jewish modernity. We have hitherto exposed Jewish modernity to the most courageous and most characteristic claim of all modernity—the Hegelian (and right- and left-wing post-Hegelian) Idea of Overcoming. In what remains of the present exploration we shall by no means let go of that idea. However, we shall now be required by expose it to the deepest, most lasting, most characteristic experience of Judaism.

Such an exposure would hitherto have been premature. We have seen Hegel's mediation between Judaism and Spinozism mete out a justice of sorts to both—but also that this justice was unilateral, and that it was meted out at a standpoint higher than both at which both were seen to be superseded. So long as the Hegelian mediation could maintain itself as unbroken, this unilateral justice was inevitable: At Hegel's standpoint, the pious Jew's finite, merely-human freedom was "servile" when it stood over against an Other that was infinite and divine; and Spinoza's philosophical thought was "acosmic" when it achieved oneness with the divine Substance by ignoring, by-passing or denying the Divine self-othering in the world. However, with the Hegelian middle broken—and Constantinianism of every kind giving way to dialogical openness—mutual jus-

---

Die Stunde und die Erkenntnis (Berlin: Schocken, 1935), p. 35. On Buber and the Holocaust, see further below, ch. IV, section 7. Since where there is overcoming the Holocaust is not, the grim necessity of confronting the event is here postponed, until we reach a more radical self-immersion in history in which even a fragmentary overcoming of history that gives it meaning is not presupposed.

tice has become imperative. Hence while the Idea of Overcoming will remain with us, we must not let it overwhelm either Judaism or Spinozism or the relation between them. Rather must we let all these stand *over against* that idea, in order that a *Jewish* modernity—if such there be—may reveal its secret.

This cannot be done unless Hegel's own mediation is confronted not at marginal points or in dialectical results, but rather at its own inmost core. We therefore give the following summary:

1. Every genuine religion is an actual relation between the human and the Divine; it is by no means a merely subjectively-human, but objectively-illusory experience. On its part, every genuine philosophy has an actual dimension of infinity; the claim to infinity—if and when it is made—is by no means subjectively-arbitrary, objectively-false. Hence religion and philosophy are both "worship."

2. They are therefore, implicitly from the start and explicitly at the end, identical in "content." They are, however, radically antithetical in "form." In religion, the Divine is "represented" as Other, and *remains* in representational otherness to the end. On its part, philosophy is an infinite—i.e., divine-human—self-activity from the start and remains in the "form" of self-activity even as it particularizes itself to the extreme in finitude. A clash between religion and philosophy is therefore inevitable. And the clash is, in the end, between religious divine-human otherness and philosophical divine-human sameness.

3. The conflict would be absolute and incapable of mediation were it not for the fact that one religion—the Christian— is not singly-representational but *doubly* so. My (i.e., the Christian's) making myself "fit for the indwelling of Spirit within me . . . is *my* labor, the labor of man." But it is also the "labor of God, from *His* side," for He "moves toward man" even as men "move toward Him." In the Christian religion, this is "*one double* activity." In the philosophical "notion," however, this same activity is reenacted as "single." *In the "absolute" or Christian religion a divine self-othering in the human is receptively experienced at the side of the human. In*

the "absolute" or Hegelian philosophy, this same "content" is reenacted in thought from the side of the Divine. And this same, absolutely-true content is the "identity of the human nature and the Divine." Here lies the ultimate core of Hegel's mediating philosophy.

4. It is a core that enables and requires Hegel's philosophy to be all-mediating, i.e., not only between relatively-true religions and the "absolute" religion but also between the religious sphere of life as a whole and that of secular freedom. The former is constituted by human representational receptivity to the Divine. The latter, like philosophy, is constituted by self-activity—although, unlike philosophy and like religion, it is a sphere of life rather than thought. For this reason, a conflict seems possible or inevitable between the religious and secular spheres of life; and the conflict may seem to be radical and inevitable when the two, as it were, meet in the same space: when Christian Grace, no longer content with a premodern heaven, descends into the Lutheran heart on earth; and when secular freedom, no longer content with a premodern earth, becomes a revolutionary storming of heaven. Yet because of the identity of the human nature and the Divine, mediation occurs precisely in the sameness of space. In his own age, Hegel seems to observe the beginning of a religio-secular mediation in the sphere of life. And the mediation becomes complete in his own absolute thought.*

Such, in brief, is the Hegelian mediation, and such is its core. As after the breakdown of both, Jewish experience is permitted and required to appear in its own right, our post-Hegelian thought makes an astounding discovery. *The Jewish religion, unlike the Christian, cannot accept the identity of the human nature and the Divine. When encountering any such teaching, whether in Christianity or elsewhere, it rejects it passionately and emphatically. Yet it too is doubly-representational, and this despite the fact that the "double activity" is not "one" but two.* The Hegelian God of Abraham, in order to become accessible to Abraham and his tribe, shrivels into a deity that is itself

---

*On the above, see further RD, passim, and Encounters, pp. 159 ff.

tribal. The Jewish God of Abraham is indeed Abraham's God— but *blesses all nations in his seed.* The Hegelian Moses is a mere "unfree" instrument of the Divine. The Moses of Judaism confronts the people on behalf of God —*and God on behalf of the people.* And whereas Hegel can understand Job's self-assertion against his God only as a "renunciation of renunciation" that follows after the most thorough-going renunciation, the Job of Judaism—however this many-sided, enigmatic figure may be understood—cannot be understood at all unless, God's absolute power notwithstanding, *his protest is central.* Hegel has achieved a superb—among non-Jewish philosophers virtually unique—grasp of the incommensurability within Judaism of a divine Presence that is and remains infinite and universal to a humanity that remains unyieldingly finite and particular. That this togetherness can be anything but a "strange, infinitely harsh, the harshest contrast"—a contrast unmediated and in its own terms incapable of mediation—is a possibility that remains, and must remain, outside the Hegelian universe of discourse. It is equally outside the universe of the right- and left-wing post-Hegelian extremes.

Yet a divine-human moving-toward-each-other in Judaism is not merely asserted by us, on the basis of texts culled, possibly arbitrarily, from the sources. It is also the persistent, authoritative, Jewish self-understanding. In a characteristic Midrash we read:

When God created the world, He decreed that "the heavens are the heavens of the Lord and the earth is for men." (Ps. 115:16) But when He intended to give the Torah He repealed the former decree and said, "The Lower shall ascend to the Upper, and the Upper shall descend to the Lower, and I will make a new beginning," as it is said, "And the Lord came down upon Mt. Sinai, and He said unto Moses, 'Come up unto the Lord.' " (Exod. 19:20)[20]

One would wish to dwell on the teaching of this Midrash. (It teaches a primordial infinite distance between the divine Creator and the human creature; a "new beginning" manifest in the meeting of the two; and a "descent" of the one and "ascent" of the other, even as both remain other to the other.)

One would wish to pursue and test that teaching throughout the length and breadth of Midrashic literature, as well as other literature matching it in authoritativeness.* In our present context, however, our task is to confront it with the Hegelian Idea of Overcoming, in order that a Jewish modernity may come to light.

This task was already undertaken by Franz Rosenzweig's modern-Jewish, post-Hegelian thought. Rosenzweig did not consider his own age post-Hegelian in respect to Christianity only. The Hegelian experiment that had failed was relevant—at least insofar as they were in the modern world—also to Jews and Judaism. (One glance at the world half a century later—to mention but two factors, the worldwide role of technology, and the Marxism invoked by large parts of the so-called Third World—proves this judgment correct.) Jewish existence is in the modern world, even if, as will be seen, it must challenge decisively some reigning ideas of it. A post– rather than simply anti-Hegelian thinker, Rosenzweig did not simply reject the Hegelian Idea of Overcoming. Indeed (as we have seen), as claimed by Christianity he not only endorsed it but gave it so large a scope as to lapse, on Christianity's behalf, into a Constantinianism already anachronistic in his time and wholly so in ours. That nevertheless he is far from surrendering to that Idea—whether in its Christian, Hegelian, or right– or left-wing post-Hegelian forms—appears in his account of Judaism. Rosenzweig's Jewish militancy is so strong as to make him claim—possibly extravagantly—that the "rays" of the Christian Overcoming require—indeed, cannot survive without—the "fire" that is Judaism. And what makes this a militancy over against all forms of Hegelianism (as well as over against Christianity of course) is that Judaism, as Rosenzweig portrays it, is not and cannot be an Overcoming.

Rosenzweig makes the last-named point so radically—again possibly extravagantly—as to deny to Judaism, at least prior to the eschatological Overcoming, any kind of progressive development. Jewish existence is the perpetual, "eternal," experi-

*On this as a future project, see above, ch. I, section 5.

ence of the same. Here the "old" is not overcome by the "new" but rather forever renewed. Moreover, Rosenzweig's post-Hegelian espousal of Judaism (understood as an eternal renewal of the old in the sphere of life) is itself an instance of such a renewal in the sphere of thought. What is pitted against the Hegelian Idea of Overcoming is the Jewish Idea of *Teshuva*.

Teshuva in Judaism is a many-sided experience. Its core, however, is a divine-human turning-toward-each-other, despite and indeed because of their persistent and unmitigated incommensurability. This, as the above-cited Midrash illustrates, is the central experience of Sinai. It is also the experience of countless generations that, alienated from the God of Sinai, found themselves ever turning, and ever being turned, back to Him. And when the Yom Kippur discloses a love strong as death itself, it lends to *Teshuva* so large a scope as to make it encompass *all*—hence also *modern*—human history. Rosenzweig was a *Ba'al Teshuva* as a person. *Teshuva* was also the core of his post-Hegelian, modern (or post-modern) Jewish thought.

However, as we have asserted from the outset, Rosenzweig paid insufficient attention to the dialectical results of Hegel's failure. Perhaps in consequence of this, his own post-Hegelian thought moved into a one-sided, fidestic extreme. (The name of Karl Marx does not appear in the *Star of Redemption*.) Our own, second Jewish encounter with Hegel, now nearing completion, requires us to move from that fidestic extreme toward the middle. (Kierkegaard then emerges as our prime witness to the effect that modern dialectical thought cannot so overcome the God of revelation as to make Him an anachronism; Marx, as our prime witness to the effect that modern thought may set limits to man's free modern-secular potential only if it can prove itself innocent of conservative timidity or reactionary villainy.) Moving toward that middle, our Jewish thought now comes face to face with the fact of Jewish secularism.

This fact, of course, is not in doubt. A secular Jewish culture flourished among the East European masses until, together with these masses themselves, it fell prey to Nazi murder. Still, despite its unquestioned actuality, one could question the historic significance of the phenomenon, disposing of it as the mere product of nostalgia within and necessity without.* (Russian Jews could not all emigrate to America—and at home were denied emancipation, and hence the possibility of assimilation, by Czarist tyranny.) But at least vis-à-vis one product of Jewish secularism so cavalier an attitude is impossible. This is modern Zionism and its result, the State of Israel.

That the Zionist impulse is genuinely Jewish in nature is undeniable. That it is also genuinely modern is equally undeniable if only the standards of modernity are applied without discrimination. Throughout the present work the chief hallmark of modernity has been a confident, self-active self-reliance whose courage does not falter even before formidable obstacles. By that standard, the Zionist movement and the State of Israel need fear comparison with no modern phenomenon.

The authentic modernity of Zionism and the State of Israel is not, of course, universally recognized. In a different context we have mentioned that much liberal thought still considers Jews, and Jews alone, as men-in-general. In the present context we must mention that most Marxist thought considers Zionism, and Zionism alone, not as a liberation movement but as an anachronism. On occasion it may admit that, at least ever since the Holocaust, the Jewish people stand in need of a state of their own. (Indeed, this was Andrei Gromyko's chief point in support of his U.N. vote in 1947.) Far more characteristic, however, is the Marxist view that Zionism and a Jewish state are intrinsically reactionary, even in comparison with Syria, Libya and Saudi Arabia. Yet Israel is a secular-democratic state, and the kibbutz, among the few twentieth century achievements of which Marx, were he alive today, could wholly approve.

The *Realpolitik* aspects of this phenomenon are outside our present scope. (Arab states are large in number and rich in oil. All Marxist politics is anti-American even when it is not totally pro-Soviet. And Soviet politics itself, unlike the American, can afford to be—and is—totally unscrupulous.) Well

---

*The late, fideistic Jewish thinker Will Herberg once remarked that by the logic of their convictions secularist Jews in our time ought to assimilate and disappear.

within our scope, however, are the ideological aspects. As we have seen, Marxian thought makes—must make—a total claim on history; and so total a claim on behalf of so radically a New Man requires—cannot but require—the overcoming by the human of the Divine. This latter, however, requires the prior achievement of the identity of the human and the divine, and that achievement—Christianity completed in Lutheranism—requires the prior overcoming of all other gods by the Christian God. It requires, above all, the overcoming of the Jewish God, for between Him and the human is the "harshest"—indeed, "infinitely harsh"—"contrast." Hence even a surviving Jewish religious life is in the Marxist mind far more "reactionary"—if presumably much more harmless—than a surviving Christian religious life. As for the Zionist impulse that transforms the old religious life into a new secular reality—the *Teshuva* to the old land that creates a new state—this is so dangerously outside that universe as to make, by the standards of it, even the most progressive (but affirmatively Jewish) kibbutz more reactionary than Libyan colonels and Saudi princelings. Only a post-Marxian thought that has repented of Marxian Constantinianism can achieve a dialogical openness that does justice to the reality of Israel.

Zionist thought itself cannot easily do that reality justice. Thus if Zionism were nothing but an escape from persecution, or a flight from economic abnormality, or a variant of modern nationalism, or a Jewish contribution to the Revolution, the Zionist impulse should have led to Uganda or Argentina, Biro Bidjan or Moscow.* Yet whereas these other projects were all tried but failed only the impulse that led to Zion became a reality. Only through a secular counterpart to Rosenzweig's recovery of *Teshuva* can Zionist thought do justice to its own subject. Herzl, a Spinozist of sorts, wrote a book entitled *Old-Newland*. (For Spinoza human affairs are so radically "change-

---

*An allusion, respectively, to the plan to establish a Jewish state in Uganda rather than Palestine; to attempts to "normalize" Jewish life through agricultural settlements in Argentina; to the Soviet project of a Jewish province; and to Ernst Bloch's claim that Moses Hess, were he alive in our time, would (or should) seek his Zion in Moscow rather than Jerusalem. (See *Presence*, pp. 58 ff.)

able" that history can repeat itself, and that—Spinoza uses the
language of imagination—"God may elect them [i.e., the Jewish
people] a second time.")[21] Perhaps more significant here is that
kibbutz thought (except at its most slavishly orthodox-Marxist)
never shared the presumptuous Marxian vision of the state
withering away. Perhaps most significant of all is that Moses
Hess, the first and according to some the greatest Zionist
thinker, was a left-wing Hegelian that yet found it necessary to
hark back to Spinoza. Like other left-wing Hegelians, Hess ascribed meaning and direction to history. He also shared the
left-wing, socialist vision of human being as a being-
for-each-other. If nevertheless he felt compelled to hark back to
Spinoza it is—so it would seem—because modern Jewish existence, though in a post-Hegelian world, *was not itself post-Hegelian: in bypassing the Christian Overcoming, it bypassed
also its Hegelian (and right- and left-wing post-Hegelian) results and derivatives.**

The Zionist impulse, then, though in the modern world, is a
renewal-of-the-old *within* it. It is a *Teshuva* that in our time has
produced a return of the dispersed from all corners of the
world; a relearning of the political and military arts of self-preservation after long centuries of disuse; the rebuilding of a land
desolate through the ages; and a giving of secular flesh-and-
blood to a language long confined to the sphere of piety. Zionist
thought must do justice to these realities, and to the impulse
that is within them. It is no wonder that the justice it has been
able to do them—they are still in the making, and this in a
world that largely fails to recognize them when it does not
actually slander them—has only been partial and fragmentary.
And it can hope to do better justice only if, before all else, it
allows itself to be filled—ever again be refilled—with an abiding astonishment. Only thus can the *Teshuva* that is in these
realities find expression in the sphere of thought.

It is between the extremes of a modern-religious *Teshuva* to
the old God and a modern-secular *Teshuva* to the old land
that future Jewish thought must assume its location. Earlier in

---

*In conversation with Professor Shlomo Avineri, I was pleased to find him
agreeing with this interpretation.

this exploration we saw contemporary thought move into a post-Hegelian broken middle. Now we perceive contemporary Jewish thought assume a similar location. One must add, however, that the shibboleth of revelation is not the same. To come to the key difference at once, in the Jewish case the extremes, united as they are by a shared destiny, are intimately intertwined: the Zionist impulse could not either have come to be or succeeded without both. (Without an originally-religious inspiration, the modern-secular impulse to self-liberation would not have led to Zion; and without the impact of secular self-activity, religious Jews would have continued to pray for the rebuilding of Jerusalem, rather than taking a share in rebuilding her.) A conflict between the extremes is, of course, for all that possible and actual. But there are no winners in this conflict. It is, for both extremes, self-destructive.

One cannot rule out the possibility of the two extremes pulling ever further apart. In that case a Jewish thought that is located between them and seeks to mediate between them, would itself be pulled apart. This is a risk that Jewish thought must assume. It must do so in behalf of a Jewish future. Could it be also, perhaps, in behalf of a human future? Throughout the present exploration, we have perceived much of present humanity as bound up with the shibboleth of revelation. As at length we came to focus our attention on Jewish modernity, and on the role of the shibboleth of revelation within it, it emerged that the secular-religious conflict that elsewhere in the modern world exists *between* the extremes exists, so far as modern Jewish existence is concerned, *within* it. This has been vaguely felt in all the modern Jewish identity worries that came into being when the first Jew ever accepted emancipation—and along with this, modern secularity—while at the same time struggling to remain faithful to a Jewish destiny. However, not until religious and secular Jews chose a shared destiny in a modern Jewish state did the Jewish shibboleth of revelation assume a modern form that was both unambiguous and inescapable.*

---

*In a letter addressed in 1939 to Mahatma Gandhi, Martin Buber writes as follows: "Dispersion is bearable; it can even be purposeful, if there is some-

Unlike the Hegelian owl of Minerva, Jewish thought in our time is geared to a future. But unlike the Marxian cock, it cannot predict a future. Hence Jewish thought in the age *post Hegel mortuum* can do no other than culminate in an open-ended wonder. And in our time it wonders whether perhaps an epoch-making event occurred—within Jewish history but also beyond its limits—when, following the liberation of Jerusalem in the Six-Day-War, religious and secular Israeli soldiers embraced in front of the Wall.*

---

where an ingathering, a growing home center, a piece of earth where one is in the midst of an ingathering and not in dispersion, and whence the spirit of the ingathering may work its way into all the places of the dispersion. When there is this, there is also a striving common life, the life of a community which dares to live today because it may hope to live tomorrow. But when this growing center is lacking, dispersion becomes dismemberment" (reprinted in *The Writings of Martin Buber*, Will Herberg, ed. [New York: Meridian 1958], p. 281).

*In accordance with the considerations given above (ch. I, sections 5 and 6), the exploration now completed was compelled to have in mind throughout, and toward the end to deal proleptically with, "empirical" realities that can be treated adequately only when they come into view in their own right. (In the present case, the prolepsis is of "Part V" of the original project, entitled "Theopolitical Reflections on Israel, the Diaspora and the Religio-Secular Condition of the Modern World.") If only in clarification of our future course, we may here add to the foregoing the following bald judgments—"bald" because a justification, other than what is implicit in the foregoing, is here impossible. (1) Jewish anti-Zionism of every kind—secular or religious, outside or inside Israel—is of all phenomena in contemporary Jewish life the one most clearly anachronistic. (2) Israeli phenomena such as neo-fundamentalism on the right and Canaanism on the left are "fanatical" by the standards developed in the present work, and deserve much attention practically but none theoretically, for they are intellectually untenable. (3) Reconstructionism, or Israeli counterparts of this American-Jewish phenomenon, bespeak a deep sensitivity to Jewish history but are inadequate as theoretical schemes of thought: rather than confront the shibboleth of revelation, Reconstructionism simply denies it, and in so doing fails to do justice to the extremes of Orthodoxy and secularism. (4) Impulses such as the Israeli *Gesher*—a bridge between the extremes—are the hope of the Israeli and indeed the whole Jewish future but depend for their success on their ability to avoid being cooptational in practice and theory. To supply the theoretical basis of the *Gesher*-practice could be described as the chief goal of the present exploration.

IV

Historicity, Rupture, and *Tikkun Olam* ("Mending the World"): From Rosenzweig beyond Heidegger

C
1. Spinoza, Rosenzweig, and Heidegger on *Death*
ONCERNING death, Spinoza writes as follows:

> The more of things spirit knows according to the knowledge of the second and third kind [i.e., reason and intuition], the less is it subject to those emotions which are bad, and the less does it fear death.[1]

Few statements in the history of the "old" thinking speak so confidently of the power of thought to transcend the ultimate limit of human existence. Few authors of statements such as this have ever matched *this* author in the nobility with which they demonstrated the power of thought in their own personal lives.* Yet it is just this confidence of the "old" thinking that the "new" assails as being without foundation. The opening page of the *Star of Redemption* attacks the age-old claim of metaphysicians to "bear us over the grave which yawns at our feet with every step."[2] And Martin Heidegger's *Being and Time*—perhaps the only philosophical work contemporaneous to the *Star* and of comparable spirit that can be mentioned in the same breath—asserts that our thought-access to *Sein* is inseparable from *Zeit*, for the *Dasein*† in which it is rooted is being-toward-death.

With regard to stern sobriety, it must seem that *Being and Time* surpasses the *Star of Redemption*. Rosenzweig's work, insist though it does on man's time-bound creatureliness, finds eternity "confirmed" in the midst of time, climactically so in the Yom Kippur. On its part, *Being and Time*—and on this point its author shows no signs of wavering in all his subsequent works—finds eternity "confirmed" no more with-

---

*Whereas Socrates comes to mind first, his life-negating stance—he owes a debt to Asclepius for being about to cure him of the disease of life—has no place in Spinoza's philosophy. Of course, Socrates may be practicing his irony.
†This Heideggerian term has become part of English philosophical usage.

in time than the mental eye of the "old" thinking had intuited it in a realm beyond it.[3] Rosenzweig confronts what he terms the "curse" of historicity and—so he claims—masters it. In *Being and Time* historicity emerges as permeating man's very being, and hence as inescapable; yet far from being a curse, its core—man's being toward death—is the decisive condition of all true human freedom. Man is free to live his own life only because he is free to die his own death.

It is necessary to test Rosenzweig's "new thinking" in the light of this stern sobriety. What is more, this testing must extend, either directly or by implication, to all the thinkers hitherto considered. Spinoza has rejected but not refuted the revealed God of the Scriptures, in behalf of a rival, "secular" God who remains Himself undemonstrated. Rosenzweig has reaffirmed but not demonstrated the scriptural God if only because his "new thinking" cannot fall back on the premodern authorities of the "old." On his part, Hegel has reconciled the two Gods, but his "demonstration" of this "whole truth" depends on the assumption that each is already in its own right a partial truth. And as for his right- and left-wing successors—Kierkegaard at one extreme, Marx at the other—these, while refuted to the extent to which they refute themselves, have each remained with a claim, the one antithetical to the other, to a transcendence of his own. The task, then, is clear. To be sure, the above thinkers have already been tested in the foregoing, for our enterprise is not a study in the history of philosophy but a search for truth. Not one of them has been tested, however, in the light of a thinking that calls radically into question a claim advanced by them all, however different their ways. This is an access to transcendence.

It cannot be said with assurance that Heidegger—a *Denker in dürftiger Zeit**—matches in stature the greatest of the above thinkers. (Only time will tell.) If nevertheless he must be the

---

*Heidegger writes: "It is the time of the gods that have fled *and* the god that is coming. It is the time of *need*, because it lies under a double lack and a double Not: the No-more of the gods that have fled and the Not-yet of the god that is coming" ("Hölderlin and the Essence of Poetry," *EB*, p. 319.) Our above formulation alludes to the title of Karl Löwith, *Heidegger: Denker in Dürftiger Zeit* (Göttingen: Vandenhoeck and Ruprecht, 2nd ed., 1960), a title which in turn alludes to Hölderlin.

central figure in the following exploration (or at any rate of its first part), it is because, beginning with *Being and Time* and to the end, he holds together with an exemplary tenacity two basic commitments which for most if not all other thinkers fall radically apart. One is that the *Weg* of present and future *Denken* is indissolubly bound up with a recovery of the Western philosophical tradition "from Ionia to Jena" and beyond.* (This is the way of Athens, one of the two occidental claims to transcendence, the second being the way of Jerusalem.) The other is so radical and thoroughgoing an insistence on the historicity of human *Dasein* that none of its dimensions is exempt from it. The historicity of man's *Dasein*, therefore, encompasses man's philosophical thought, and hence Heidegger's own.

2. Historicity

Being and Time excites the thoughtful reader, no less so today than at the time of its first appearance two years before Rosenzweig's death. The work is imbued with two fundamental convictions. One is a skepticism concerning the age-old search for Being known as Western metaphysics—a skepticism no less radical than that of any positivist. The other is a profound and abiding inability to believe that a tradition so long, so deep, so venerated, is a mere tissue of obfuscating nonsense, to be disposed of by a few easy lessons in scientific, logical or linguistic enlightenment. This togetherness encourages the belief, little short of intoxicating, that the metaphysical enterprise, for all the arduous labors spent on it for so long by so many, has a hidden ground which has yet to disclose itself; that to pave the way for this disclosure is the task of present and future occidental thought; and that—at least if man is and continues to be the *animal metaphysicum†*—the performance of this task is of momentous, nay, world-historical significance. Whatever the fortunes of his later thought, Heidegger

---

*Among many other things, Heidegger shares with Rosenzweig an exalted opinion of German Idealism: not German Idealism "collapsed" but rather the spiritual strength of the age that followed it was not adequate to the greatness, breadth, and originality of that philosophy (*EM*, pp. 34 ff.; *IM*, pp. 45 ff.).
†"As long as man remains the rational animal he is the *animal metaphysicum*" ("Was ist Metaphysik," in *Wm*, p. 197).

remained true to these initial convictions to the end. As for *Being and Time* itself, it has altered the philosophical land-scape—permanently, so far as one can tell. It speaks highly indeed for Franz Rosenzweig's astuteness that, though virtu-ally on the threshold of death when the work appeared, he did not fail to recognize its significance.[4]

Being and Time has had many thoughtful readers, and hence much thoughtful understanding. Perhaps it has also had much thoughtful misunderstanding.* But however the work has been understood or misunderstood, there could not be any doubt that never before had human historicity been taken so seriously, held fast to so relentlessly, grasped so profoundly.

Ever since the nineteenth "century of history," it has been fashionable in the enlightened general public to assert its own superiority over all *Weltanschauungen*, past and present, by affirming their universal historical relativity. Not to be out-done, the professors of philosophy, no longer "naive" enough to love wisdom themselves, began to write "critical," schol-arly tomes about previous philosophies marked by just such a naïveté. (The Heidelberg chair once occupied by Hegel was given to Kuno Fischer.) Both the general public and the pro-fessors fancied themselves, even while asserting or implying the "historicity of all things," as having attained an "objec-tive" standpoint outside or beyond these things.[5] This stance, itself naive, was at least partly overcome once the spectre of historicism—for Rosenzweig, a "curse"—was permitted to come to consciousness, a fact evidenced by ceaseless attempts to "overcome historicism."† But not until *Being and Time*

---

*Otto Poeggeler writes: "SuZ widely occasioned basic decisions. Some saw in it the attempt of man, at last carried out radically, to base himself entirely on his solitary self. To others it became an aid to making human speech about God, or even God's address to man, hearable in a new way. For many seeking young people SuZ pointed a way, even if they learned nothing more from this book, in the darkness of revolution and war, than how to die their own death. On his part, however, Heidegger could consider this kind of attention to his work . . . only as a misunderstanding" (*Heidegger* [Pfullin-gen: Neske, 1963], p. 7).

†As a young student, on being told that the great philosophical task was to "overcome historicism," I studied a work of that title by Ernst Troeltsch, only to find that the promise of the title remained unfulfilled in the book.

burst upon the scene was there a thoroughgoing attempt to explicate radically the historicity of human *Dasein* as such and as a whole—an explication radical enough to dispose of the easy notion that, despite the "historicity of all things," man qua thinker could somehow stand over against or above it all. Man's existence and his truth are inseparable. His thinking as well as his *Dasein* is toward death.[6]

We may ask whether so stern a reduction of human being to so stark a finitude does not dispose without further ado of one of the three "elements" of the *Star of Redemption*, with the result that Rosenzweig's "Man's-Being-With-God-in-the-World" reduces itself at once to "man's-being-in-the-world." But could one's critical reductions stop at this point? Man's being "in" the world is said by Heidegger to consist of his inability to transcend his situatedness-in-the-world: in the final analysis this is his being-toward-death. However, this latter is "unauthentic" when it is toward death-in-general, and "authentic" only when it is *each* man's being-toward-*his*-own-death. Are not, then, "man-in-the-world-in-general" and "history-as-a-whole" mere products of unauthentic flights? And must not a sternly limited *historicity* fragment human *history* into a multitude of individual *histories*, the scope of each of which does not transcend the limits of anticipated death, recollected memories, and whatever commitments (or lack thereof) are situated between these two termini? (This fragmentation surely is in no way altered by the fact that each *Dasein* is a *Mitsein** with others; for the focus of each *Dasein* is itself alone, with no focus more ultimate available.) In short, must not the historicist reduction performed by this "new thinking" dispose of the *Star's* "Man" and "World" just as surely as of its "God"? And must the truths attained by it (assuming that the term "truth" may be retained) not be merely autobiographical?

But it is not easy to see why a philosophical search for truth, "new" or "old," should move in any such direction. It is the plainest common sense that some objective knowledge is at-

*"Being-with," see SuZ, p. 263.

tainable—perception, for one thing, the sciences, for another.[7] The proverbial man in the street might ask what such knowledge has to do with the fear of death. As for the student familiar with the history of philosophy, he may wonder whether the connection is, perhaps, nothing better than a hankering after the "old" metaphysical verities, despite all brave protestations. In that case, the true sobriety demanded by a truly "new" critical thinking would not consist in an attempt to connect mortal man's yearning after transcendence with an actual transcendence, but rather a stance that, however it deals with the yearning, gets rid of the transcendence.

3. *Historicity and Transcendence*

Such a new critical sobriety, anticipated in part in the premodern world by such as William of Ockham, may be said to have first been laid down as a modern principle by Francis Bacon.* Along with this, Bacon laid down a second principle—that the new critical sobriety can dominate nature as well as know her—that "knowledge is power."† One look at modern technology suffices to show how well the second Baconian principle has been applied. And one glance at the history of modern empiricist philosophy suffices to convince us of the power of Bacon's irreverence—in striking contrast with Heidegger's resurrected reverence‡—toward the great metaphysical tradition. (We should note, however—for the present only in passing—that Bacon and at least some of his empiricist followers found it necessary to place the Christian revela-

---

*Ockham's "razor" affirms that "entities may not be multiplied beyond necessity." Bacon writes: "another error proceeds from too much reverence, and a kind of adoration paid to the human understanding, whence men have withdrawn themselves from the contemplation of nature and experience, and sported with their own reason and the fictions of fancy" (*Advancement of Learning and Novum Organon* [London and New York: Colonial Press, 1900], p. 22).

†See, e.g.: "That which must dignify and exalt knowledge is the more intimate and strict conjunction of contemplation and action" (Bacon, *Advancement of Learning*, p. 23).

‡The reverence obvious in Heidegger's later writings is already foreshadowed in SuZ; see, e.g., pp. 22 ff.

tion beyond the destructive grasp of both empiricist criticism and technological domination.*

The greatness of the empiricist principle lies in its simplicity. It is plain common sense that knowledge comes to us through the five senses. Not quite so plain, but still common sense, is the fact that we possess some knowledge of our psychic states—not quite so plain, for it is not easy to point to the relevant, so-called "inner sense." Less plain still is the justification, in empiricist terms, of mathematics and the natural sciences, although it *is* common sense that they, too, must somehow be justified. However, whatever the theories that will make this plain, it is and remains common sense that backs up the principle that a knowledge rooted in the senses cannot extend beyond them. Empiricism—so it seems—is not, as in this whole work thus far it must have seemed to be, a case of illegitimate "reductionism." It results from the necessary wielding of Ockham's razor.

The weakness of empiricism is not that it is too critical but that it is not critical enough. It sees knowledge as both originating and terminating in "data." But it fails to bring to critical consciousness the knower of these data, a lack of acumen which is by no means corrected when reflection, turning inward, is prepared to notice and recognize data of an "inner" as well as "outer" kind. It was a strange lapse for so subtle a thinker as David Hume to write of the mind as "a kind of theatre where several perceptions successively make their appearance," when this very image suggests a spectator—who in Hume never receives his due.[8]

But perhaps this was no lapse after all. Perhaps to have extended critical consciousness to the "self" would have

---

*Bacon and Hobbes may be said to have established a tradition that combines empiricist skepticism with Christian orthodoxy; and the contrast between "empiricist" Britain and the "speculative" Continent may be partly understood through the fact that the one found it possible to separate knowledge from the Christian revelation while the other did not. Even the carefully-limited four chapters of Kant's *Religion within the Bounds of Reason Alone* all end with "general observations" which Kant himself calls "parerga," i.e., beyond the bounds of reason and yet looked at, however cautiously, by reason itself.

meant shattering the empiricist principle. This was done by the second founder of philosophical modernity—a thinker more radically critical than all empiricism.

In his critical radicalism René Descartes did not hesitate to go beyond all common sense. Attempting to distinguish between knowledge and mere opinion—"mere" however commonsensical—he proposed to doubt whatever it was possible to doubt. In carrying out this proposal he did not shrink from doubting sense knowledge as such and in principle, thus committing himself (if but temporarily) to an absurd—i.e., wholly noncommonsensical—solipsism. He then proceeded to doubt all rational knowledge, thus committing himself (if again but temporarily) to what may well appear to be, for a thinker of any kind, an absolute and absurd impasse. (How can one think the thought that calls into question the validity of all thought?) Yet this very radicalism rewarded Descartes with an insight that escapes the empiricist. The one thing that the philosopher could not doubt in his all-doubting solitariness was his own all-doubting activity itself, i.e., the existence of his doubting self. Never before or after in the history of philosophy did the self move so splendidly, terrifyingly, inescapably into the center of a solitary, critical thought-activity. Admittedly the speed with which (as though nothing had happened) Descartes restores all things, divine as well as human, comes as a startling anticlimax.[9]

But, as Schelling was to observe,[10] whereas Descartes focused attention on the "that" of the self—the inability to doubt one's existence while in the act of doubting—he hardly noticed the far deeper question of the "what" of the self—the question of the self's nature. (Descartes's identification of the self as a *"res" cogitans*, alongside the *res extensa*, is a philosophical scandal.) It remained for Immanuel Kant to make two discoveries. One was that the existing subject could *be* existing only if there was, alongside and over against it, a world of objects: this—a refutation of solipsism—was the source of his "empirical realism." The other was that an empirical "datum" could not become an *object*—part of a *system* of objects—unless it was constituted as such by and for a subject: this is the source of his "transcendental idealism."[11]

But, as Fichte was to observe,[12] while Kant philosophized radically, he failed to philosophize sufficiently about philosophy itself. On his part, Fichte did philosophize sufficiently about philosophy. So did Schelling and Hegel—this latter the thinker in whose thought the whole revolutionary movement set in train by Kant reaches its completion. And the abiding and radically self-critical question from Kant to Hegel is this: *To philosophize is to think neither about objects nor about subjects but rather about the subject-object relation; to do so is to transcend that relation: but how is such a transcendence possible for a subject that is a subject only by virtue of* standing *in that relationship?*

This is a Kantian-Fichtean formulation of the question. A broader, more Schellingian or Hegelian formulation would be as follows. Philosophy is an inescapable thought-activity *about* experience; as such it transcends *all* experience: but how is this inescapable activity possible for a self existing *in the midst* of experience? This formulation is broader because the term "experience" has come to have connotations wider than the cognitive subject-object relation.* Indeed, once the post-Kantian problematic requires more encompassing connotations one wonders how they can fail to become all-encompassing. Above we observed—then merely in passing—that such empiricist thinkers as Bacon and Hobbes left the Christian revelation untouched by their criticism. The same is true of rationalist thinkers such as Descartes and Leibniz. Even Kant will still criticize religion only "within the bounds of reason" but will not—a widespread impression to the contrary notwithstanding—criticize the Christian revelation beyond these bounds. Such a self-distantiation is no longer possible once, beginning with Fichte and on account of Kant, philosophy philosophizes radically about itself, i.e., about its necessary claim to transcendence. The immediate choice before philosophy is either, with Fichte, to produce a "critique of revelation" that is ipso facto destructive of revelation or else, with Hegel, to incorporate revelation in the totality of experi-

---

*The subject-object scheme is adequate when (as with Kant and Fichte) cognition and morality are the focus of discourse. It begins to become inadequate when Schelling transforms Fichte's ethical into an aesthetical idealism.

ence and—in case Christianity emerges as the "absolute" religion—to reinstate the revelation.* Such are the immediate alternatives. Merely to state them is to imply an expansion of the term "experience" to all-comprehensivenss. It is also to bring to light that just this expansion implies the answer to the key question, stated above, that is explicit in modern philosophy since Kant, and implicit ever since it took its whole modern-critical turn. *Philosophical thought can transcend all experience only because there is already a transcending dimension within experience. Philosophy both requires, and is supplied with, what may be called an experiential matrix, although, to be sure, its own proper task is to rise above that matrix.*

This fundamental answer to the fundamental question of modern critical philosophy-become-self-critical goes far toward explaining the dynamic of the movement, at once supremely humble and supremely presumptuous, that begins with Kant and culminates in Hegel. More central to our present purpose, it also casts into clear relief the enormous achievement of *Being and Time*, once Hegelianism has broken down. After that breakdown, the many attempts to return to empiricism or Kantianism are lapses into semi-critical positions long surpassed. Right- and left-wing post-Hegelian positions, as was seen above, are self-destructive extremes which point toward a broken middle. And while the spectre of a universal historical relativism appears in that middle, to yield to it by embracing "historicism" is a mere, gross lapse by the standards of critical philosophical self-consciousness ever since Fichte. Historicism is a philosophy that fails to philosophize about itself: it asserts the historical relativity of all things, those philosophical included; yet it claims or implies that it is itself exempt.

---

*A "critique" is of experience, whereas revelation is the incursion of the *Other* into experience; a critique of revelation, therefore, ipso facto does away with revelation. It is thus a fact of great significance that Kant never wrote a critique of revelation, but only his *Religion within the Bounds Alone*. That Hegel does not "reduce" revelation to experience but rather lets experience be expanded by revelation, is asserted above in ch. III, and is the main burden of my *RD*.

Being and Time sweeps aside all these lapses into anachronism and halfheartedness when, in effect—to reduce, for the purpose at hand, the great complexity of its scope to its simplest form—it commits itself to these assertions: (1) To think about *Dasein*-as-such is to transcend in thought *Dasein*-as-such. (2) This possibility cannot be denied, for to deny it is itself to transcend in thought *Dasein*-as-such. (3) The German idealists rightly asserted the necessity for an experiential matrix of such a transcending thought, but wrongly found it in forms of experience that themselves transcended finitude: *Dasein is and remains, bound to finitude, and is nowhere able to transcend it.*

These fundamental assertions culled from the complex work produce for us a climactic question: *How can philosophical thought (inevitably a transcending activity) be a possibility for* Dasein *when this latter (and hence the matrix of transcending thought) is confined to finitude—i.e., when* Dasein *is being-toward-death?* Doubtless the question as thus formulated, or at any rate the characterization of it as central, may be viewed as yet another misunderstanding of the intention of *Being and Time*. (Almost certainly it would be so viewed by Heidegger himself.) Yet surely Heidegger himself would assent to this account in a context in which the task is to test various claims to transcendence—directly those by Rosenzweig's "new thinking," and indirectly also those of crucial other thinkers, both "old" and "new."

For our purpose, then, the question is central. For a grasp of Heidegger himself, it also serves as a link connecting his thrust toward the future with his reverence toward the past, i.e., his modern insistence on a universal historicity with his renewal of the ancient quest for Being. And the connecting of these seemingly unconnectibles produces a decisive insight that is without precedent. *A hidden transcendence dwells, not in the human rise above finitude but precisely in the endurance of it.* Animal finitude may manifest itself as fear of this or that. Human finitude, *qua* human, manifests itself as anxiety-about-being-in-the-world-as-a-whole. Like the animal, man is in the world; but unlike the animal he *knows* that he is in-the-world, and this knowledge constitutes part of his being. The animal must die. Only man's *very being* is toward-death: *this very "toward" is its transcendence.** Hence Heidegger reaches these definitions: "Transcendence is the being-held of *Dasein* into Nothingness, grounded in a hidden anxiety which rises above what-is-as-a-whole." And: "Metaphysics is the quest beyond what-is, in order to regain it as such and as a whole for comprehension.[13] These assertions, and many others like them or dependent on them, have been much debated, attacked and ridiculed, exalted and revered. One thing, however, is surely certain: the excitement created by *Being and Time* remains justified to this day. The work's unique to-getherness of historicist sobriety and reverence for the tradition continues to encourage the belief that tradition has as yet hidden resources, that precisely for the sake of the most new it is worthwhile, if indeed not imperative, to seek out the most old. For to be in history is not simply to be swept along by the river of time. To be within history is at the same time to be capable of a transcending grasp of it.† *Historicity is itself inseparable from transcendence.*

The image of a "river" of time, nevertheless, serves to indicate that, as thus far sketched, the "historicity" of *Dasein*—its being-toward-death—is indistinguishable from its "temporality." Heidegger in fact affirms not only that the historicity of *Dasein* is rooted in its temporality but also, more significantly, that "the interpretation of . . . [its] historicity is *nothing but* a more concrete exposition of its temporality."[14] What basic features emerge from such an "exposition"? First, while in its "less concrete" temporality being-toward-death is *situated,* in its "more concrete" historicity it is fated to be situated *with others.* Second, this fate does not fragment itself into a mere side-by-sideness of isolated, individual "fates" but may also be—to venture no more—the shared destiny of a "community," indeed—so Heidegger incautiously says in at least one

---

*See SuZ, pp. 240, 247: whereas the animal "perishes" (*verendet*) only man "dies."
†In SuZ, p. 426, the "stream of time" is characterized as an unauthentic conception of temporality.

instance—a *Volk*.[15] These are significant features. But perhaps yet a third is most significant of all. Even in its less "concrete" temporality *Dasein*, situated in the present but also transcending the present, is capable of a free recovery of its own past as it is geared toward future possibilities. In its "more concrete" historicity, this capacity for recovery discloses itself as extending, albeit problematically, to a past which is not *Dasein's* own but rather "inherited." Thus emerges a notion of *tradition*. Heidegger writes: "Recovery is explicit tradition, and this means the going back into possibilities of *Dasein* which once were *da*."[16] In this manner we receive our first inkling as to how a being which is toward-death might have a recovering access to the age-old, traditional quest for Being.

We have said above that it is the togetherness of skepticism and reverence toward the philosophical tradition that assures *Being and Time* its abiding stature. We are now able to identify the grounds of both this skepticism and this reverence. The skepticism is rooted in the stern assertion of human finitude, i.e., its being-toward-death. The reverence has its roots in two characteristics of that finitude, of which the first is associated with its "temporality," whereas the second comes into view only once this latter is expounded "more concretely" as "historicity." Even in its "less concrete" temporality, *Dasein*, anxious about being-in-the-world-as-a-whole, transcends by dint of this anxiety a mere being in the world and thus is not only capable of metaphysics but is willy-nilly *the animal metaphysicum* par excellence. However, it is the second characteristic, emerging with the "more concrete" historicity of *Dasein* that is, in the end—and for better or worse—bound to be more weighty and significant: the quest for Being is not abstractly temporal but can only be concretely historical, for all "tradition" is history. Its relation to tradition, and hence to history, may limit Heidegger's new quest for Being; or it may, on the contrary, enrich it. But whether it is one or the other (or something of both), it is in any case impossible for Heidegger's quest to sever itself from history. It cannot soar above history to supposedly freer, more universal realms. Nor can it wish to do so. For the mere wish would already be a resort from the task assigned by the historical situation to a flight from it.

4. The Ontic-Ontological Circle

This may suffice as an account, deliberately nontechnical, partial, and hence presumably not free of either superficiality or bias, of the stern radicalism with which Heidegger's being-toward-death challenges all claims of the "old thinking" to transcendence, not because it repudiates transcendence but, on the contrary, because of the manner in which it affirms it. A simple rejection of any and all transcendence on the grounds of human finitude could be simply rejected in turn. (One might invoke against it, for example, the venerable, age-old metaphysical tradition. One might also invoke—once again this is mentioned, for the present, in passing only—the faith, no less venerable and age-old, in the revealed Scriptures.) Conceivably one might even *refute* such a simple rejection, with the argument that to assert an unqualified human finitude is ipso facto, through the assertion itself, to transcend finitude, and thus to contradict oneself.* However, Heidegger does not reject the metaphysical tradition; he accepts it—and finds its ground, hitherto hidden, in being-toward-death. And if this is to be taken seriously as a *finding*, a *discovery*, it is because being-toward-death is seen at the same time as both the *ultimate* manifestation of human finitude *and also* as a way—the *only possible* way—of transcendence. The anxiety which, as such, is *in* the world is also, and at the same time, *about* being-in-the-world-as-a-whole.

We must now consider somewhat more closely (and hence somewhat more technically) the price paid by Heidegger for his achievement, at this state of his thought. The fundamental goal of *Being and Time* is what Heidegger calls an "ontological" analysis of human *Dasein*-as-such; this uncovers its fundamental temporality, and is termed *existenzial*. (This analy-

---

*My attempt in *MH*, pp. 77 ff., to give such a refutation was inadequate.

sis is in turn preliminary to the reopening of the ancient quest for Being—and the work is subtitled "first half.") This "onto-logical" inquiry, however, would by Heidegger's own most fundamental commitments be "rootless and groundless" (*bo-denlos*) unless it had what is termed an "ontic" matrix, i.e., a matrix in a human *Dasein* which, prior to all philosophizing, the Heideggerian included, *already has* a "foreknowledge" of its own fundamental temporality. (*This* knowledge is termed *existenziell*.)[17] Our above account has already stressed the ne-cessity—though the terms were not used—of an "ontic" ma-trix for "ontological" thought. Indeed, we have suggested that, in becoming self-critical, *all* modern philosophy points to-ward this most indispensable of all Heideggerian assertions.

This ontic-ontological relation implies a distinction which has already been mentioned but thus far left unconsidered. All men are mortal. Presumably all rational men know that they are mortal. But not everyone agrees with Heidegger's account of this knowledge, to say nothing of the role he ascribes to it in the scheme of things human, those philosophical included. To emphasize this last point we need go no further than to the claim advanced by the "old thinking" (assailed, as we have seen, on the very first page of the *Star of Redemption*), to "bear us over the grave which yawns at our feet with every step." If *Dasein*-as-such is toward-death, then the *Dasein* of the "old" as well as the "new" thinker is toward-death. And if, nevertheless, the first can make claims which are rejected by the second *in behalf of* Dasein *itself,* then one altogether fundamental conclusion is inescapable: *there is "unauthen-tic" as well as "authentic"* Dasein. There is, to be sure, an "authentic" anxiety which, *qua* anxiety, is *in* the world and which, *qua* anxiety-about-being-in-the-world-as-a-whole, achieves the transcending grasp of the truth that no transcen-dence other than just this grasp is possible. But there is also a plethora of "unauthentic" ways of distorting this anxiety or denying its ultimacy; and among these is the "old" thinking assailed by Rosenzweig and Heidegger.

The distinction between authenticity and unauthenticity, then, is necessary. It gives rise, however, to what may be de-

scribed as an ontic-ontological circle. Presumably it is the ontological analysis that distinguishes between authentic anxiety
and the plethora of ways of distorting it or evading its ultimacy. Yet this analysis is itself "rootless and groundless" (*bo-
denlos*) unless it has a matrix in ontic foreknowledge, and this
must be authentic anxiety. The circle is obvious.

This circle may well seem to produce the following dilemma. Either ontology provides the standards of authenticity
and unauthenticity. But then the *existenzial* analysis arrogates
unto itself arbitrarily the decision-making power—makes an
"authoritarian pronouncement" (*"Machtspruch"*)—"about *existenziell* possibilities and liabilities,"[18] cuts itself off from its
own ontic roots, and thus degenerates into a mere species of
the "old" thinking. Or else the ontological analysis becomes a
mere expression of the ontic foreknowledge. But then the standards of authenticity yielded are surely at worst conflicting,
and even at best so radically pluralistic as to dissolve the
whole project of an *existenzial* analysis of *Dasein*-as-such-
and-as-a whole.

Heidegger, of course, is aware of both the circle and the dilemma. Also, he quite rightly rejects an escape from the circle
by means of a return, after all, to the "old" thinking. Instead, he
proposes to leap into the circle, affirming that it loses all sem-
blance of viciousness if only the leap is conscious, "basic and
complete." And it *is* nonvicious because *Dasein* is *itself* circular, i.e., always in-advance-of-itself and cast-back-on-itself.
Anxious *about* being-in-the-world, it forever returns to
being-in-the-world. And since the *ultimate* boundary of this
advance is death, the *original* source of all authenticity is an
ontic foundering upon this boundary, and a falling back from
this foundering into a consciously finite freedom-toward-fate.
Thus the *original* ontic foreknowledge of *Dasein* both *yields*
the standards of authenticity and unauthenticity, and is itself
subject to them.[19]

A student and critic of Heidegger has asserted that his
former teacher deprives the ontic-ontological *circulus* "too
rashly of its predicate *vitiosus*." Arrestingly enough, this assertion occurs in a context in which Heidegger's stern, pagan

(or quasi-pagan) being-toward-death is contrasted with Rosenzweig's "Jewish vigil for the day of Redemption."[20] In a
different context we have ourselves contrasted Heidegger's authentic being-toward-death with two stances which may well
seem to have no lesser claims to authenticity, i.e., an honest
Stoic's choice of death when life is no longer worth a wise
man's living, and a genuine Jewish Abraham concerned, not
with his own death but rather with his Isaac's life.[21] In the
present context, however, another course is clearly called for.
As we have indicated from the start, our present task is not to
confront Heidegger's being-toward-death with Rosenzweig's
Eternity-in-time but rather to *test* this latter by the standards
of a philosophical sternness that has repudiated the "Platonic
Sun" and the "Christian Rebirth" alike and that, if it noticed it
at all, would do the same with the "Jewish vigil for the day of
Redemption."[22] Hence Heidegger's sternness, if it is somehow
wanting, must *show itself* to be so *internally,* not merely be
judged as such by an external testimony. Otherwise put, any
"rashness" on his part in disposing of the threatening viciousness of his ontic-ontological circle must reveal itself as such in
an internal nemesis.

The nemesis—or at least the premonition of a nemesis to
come—is not far to seek. The ontic-ontological circle exists
because the ontological analysis (which must claim universal
validity) rests on an ontic foreknowledge (which is radically
particular); and it is said to be nonvicious because the ontic
foreknowledge *itself* rises to universality: thus in *my own* ex-
istenziell being-toward-death is disclosed the *existenzial*
meaning of all temporality. This assertion seems acceptable
enough but is in terms of the "less concrete" temporality.
However, Heidegger becomes less acceptable, not to say ominous, when his circle is considered in terms of the "more
concrete" historicity. In so doing we add such characteristics
as *Mitsein*-in-fate (a community or, possibly, a *Volk*) and the
"recovery of inherited possibilities," or "tradition." The ontological analysis of these too must claim universality; it too
rests on an ontic foreknowledge: but can the "more concrete"
ontic foreknowledge too rise to universality? Can *my own* tra-

dition—or community, or *Volk*—disclose a universal truth about *all* tradition, community, *Volk*? Heidegger does not immerse himself in *history*. At the same time, his ontological analysis of *historicity* must have an ontic *Boden* in it. Thus he hovers between the extremes of historicity and history.

This uneasy hovering has many consequences. The most fateful was to be a hovering between the extremes of an ontological *decisiveness* and an ontic *decision-making*. We have already seen that the ontological or *existenzial* analysis cannot arrogate unto itself a decision-making power "about *existenziell* possibilities and liabilities." (This lies within the province of the ontic.) We have also seen that the distinction between authenticity and unauthenticity is central to the *existenzial* analysis; and this distinction would dissolve into triviality unless authenticity were a matter not of fate, heredity, or chance but rather within *Dasein*'s decision-making power. The ontological analysis must therefore stress and indeed exalt *decisiveness* and the making of decisions; at the same time it must disqualify itself from laying down standards (other than authenticity itself) for the *making* of decisions. (If "be authentic" is a categorical imperative of sorts, it has a greater abstractness than any dreamt of by any Kantian.) Exalting as it does a "historicity" "more concrete" than an abstract temporality, Heidegger's *Being and Time* points to actions of great moment that are not in mere time but rather in history. But what, other than having the characteristic of authentic decisiveness, these actions ought to be or will be, the work cannot say.

This was the condition of Heidegger's thought when his own *Volk* made a fateful decision, and when the ontological thinker Heidegger made an ontic decision of great consequence—the only such decision he was to make during his whole life.

5. *1933: Year of Decision*

On January 30, 1933, Adolf Hitler came to power. The *Reichstag* fire of February 27, 1933, and its consequences made an end to all pretense of parliamentary democracy in Germany.

On April 1, 1933, there was a country-wide boycott of Jewish storekeepers, doctors, lawyers. On September 15, 1935, legislation was passed threatening all Germans with "non-Aryan" rightlessness unless they were able and willing to prove their "Aryan" ancestry. To be sure, it may not have been obvious prior to the Munich pact of September 30, 1938, that the Führer would plunge the world into the most devastating war of all time, just as it may not have been obvious until the Kristallnacht of November 10, 1938, that the Nazi persecution of the Jewish people would not stop at mass murder. However, the clear-sighted had long seen that not until the NSDAP placed anti-Semitism into the center of its "program" was it able to reconcile its contradictory goals and become a "movement." The clear-sighted knew, too, that the so-called "night of long knives" of June 30, 1934, marked the end of a possible overthrow of the Hitler tyranny by Germans alone, unaided by outside powers.* And when on September 30, 1939, two outside powers—Britain and France—at last declared war on the Third Reich it was, albeit in vastly different ways, too late for Germans and Jews and almost too late for the world. The world has forgotten. The world always forgets. However, a hidden dread still lurks beneath the surface.

What the Führer Adolf Hitler did in 1934 and 1935, respectively, to Germans and Jews, was no more than what the Denker Martin Heidegger had endorsed in advance when, on November 3, 1933, as rector of Freiburg University, he addressed his students as follows: "The Führer himself and he alone is Ger-

---

*With regard to the judgments expressed in the preceding paragraph, I owe a special debt to discussions with Professor George Mosse. Concerning the "first great internal crisis"—between "nationalism" and "socialism"—that occurred within Hitler's 6,000-member party in 1921, Mosse writes: "Hitler adroitly avoided coming to grips with the problem. . . . Instead, he brought up the issue of the Jews and launched into a diatribe against their religion, race and culture that was climaxed by the demand that force be used against the Jewish threat. There was no disagreement within the party; rather, the members united behind him . . . in the enthusiasm for the anti-Jewish revolution. . . . With this issue, Hitler emerged as party leader on July 29, 1921." (The Crisis of German Ideology [New York: Schocken Books, 1981], pp. 297 ff.). In the following it will emerge that what united the party from the start remained the core of the Reich to the end.

man reality and its law, today and henceforth. Learn to realize ever more deeply: from now on each thing demands decision, and every action accountability."* Earlier, on assuming the post of rector on May 27, 1933, Heidegger had endorsed the Nazi regime fully and unequivocally. And as late as 1935 he gave a series of lectures entitled "Introduction to Metaphysics" in which he still spoke of the "inner truth and greatness of the [National Socialist] movement" and the "cleansing of the sciences"[23]—an expression which at that time could refer, or at least could be taken as referring to, only "non-Aryans," anti-Nazis or both.

All this, to quote an American Heidegger scholar, is "embarrassing."[24] More instructive is the fact that, had the "Aryan" thinker Heidegger been a "non-Aryan,"—as was, to seek no further, his "revered friend and teacher" Edmund Husserl†—these events could not possibly have occurred. For a vast abyss had been created and legislated between Germans and German Jews; to employ the language of *Being and Time,* while the two groups continued to inhabit—for a while at least—the same space in the same "vulgar" time, this was not true of their ontic-historical situation or of the "decision" and "accountability" that was possible or necessary. Yet apparently not a single one of the countless inquiries into Heidegger's behavior during the ten months of his rectorship of Freiburg University—in fairness one must add that he soon dissociated

---

*See G. Schneeberger, *Nachlese zu Heidegger* (Bern, 1962), p. 136. The later Heidegger observed a near-total silence about his Nazi period—until the famous *Spiegel* interview of September 25, 1966, this latter intended for posthumous publication only. Asked by the *Spiegel* interviewer about the statement quoted by us, Heidegger replied that it had appeared not in his *Rektoratsrede* but only in the Freiburg student newspaper, and that as early as 1934 he would no longer have made it ("Only a God . . . , " p. 271). One asks: What bearing do the occasion and the time have on the only important issue—the horrendous *content* of Heidegger's statement and the need, in hindsight, for philosophical repentance?

†*SuZ* had been dedicated to Husserl with these words. The dedication was omitted in the fifth edition of the work, published in 1941, since otherwise its appearance would have been endangered. However—so Heidegger reports—he agreed to this only on condition that his acknowledgment of debt to Husserl in the text itself remained untouched (*On the Way to Language* [New York: Harper and Row, 1971], p. 199).

himself from Nazism, though the nature of this dissociation remains to be considered—has focused on this abyss. This is a scandal in scholarship.

The scandal would be minor if at issue were merely Heidegger's personal behavior. The indisputable and undisputed fact is, however, that when he endorsed in advance the Führer's actions as German "reality" and "law," he did so not, like countless others, impelled by personal fear, opportunism, or the hysteria of the time, but rather deliberately and *with the weight of his philosophy behind it*. If, as it surely is, this fact is of considerable philosophical significance, this may conceivably be true also of the fact that a "non-Aryan" Heideggerian could have endorsed Heidegger's own philosophical endorsement of the Reich only at the price of a masochism bordering on the suicidal.* In short, the abyss created and legislated in "ontic" condition between "Aryan" and "non-Aryan" philosophers was so vast and deep as to have, conceivably, "ontological" significance.

Yet no good purpose is served by still another investigation of Heidegger's actions during the early Nazi years. As regards personal behavior, it was no worse than that of countless others, some of whom later appointed themselves his judges. As regards his philosophical utterances, the final judgment will probably be that whereas the thought of *Being and Time*

---

*Georg Picht reports that in the summer of 1933 the classical historian Felix Jacoby, "a great scholar and man of immaculate character," opened his lectures on Horace at Kiel University as follows: "As a Jew I am in a difficult position. But as a historian I have learned not to view historical events from a private perspective. I have voted for Adolf Hitler since 1933 and consider myself lucky to be permitted to lecture on the poet of Augustus in the year of the national uprising. For Augustus is the only figure in world history comparable to Adolf Hitler." Picht further reports that, having fled from Hitler to Oxford, Jacoby's German nationalism remained unshaken even after World War II. He adds: "No one today is able to imagine what confusion then gripped the most significant spirits" ("Die Macht Des Denkens," in *Erinnerung*, pp. 199 ff.).

Not all significant spirits were confused. My own teacher Eugen Taeubler, himself a great classical scholar, resigned his Heidelberg professorship in protest against Nazism, with the result that his students, moved by his courage, demonstrated to obtain his reinstatement. The demonstration, needless to say, was unsuccessful.

and of the years immediately following did not "compel" surrender to Nazism it was "unable to prevent it."[25]

Before passing on, however, we must pause to specify this
judgment somewhat more fully. *Being and Time* has exalted
an ontological "decisiveness" that is prescriptive of no particular ontic decision and hence ominously hospitable to all
decisions. This stance, easy to criticize but more important to
understand, arises because Heidegger's thinking in *Being and
Time* hovers between an "ontological" historicity and an "ontic" history. By virtue of the required ontic "root and ground"
(*Boden*), his thinking, rather than cut off from history, is open
to history even as it is grounded in it. By virtue of its ontological universality, however, it eschews all specific involvement
either in historical study or historical action. (What Hegel and
Nietzsche say about Germany is still worth serious attention.
As we shall see, what Heidegger says is not.) Thus it may be
said that his thinking claims the best of both worlds, and that
the nemesis in 1933 was that he obtained the worst. Here is
the final reason why a further consideration of this period in
Heidegger's career is philosophically sterile.

Far from sterile, in contrast, is a consideration of the long
decades when, driven back from the "shock of the collision" of
his thought with the harsh political realities "back into his
residence" (i.e., the realm of thought), Heidegger set about settling "in his thinking what he had experienced."* We agree
with the author of the appraisal just cited that this is one way in
which to view Heidegger's entire later thought. (We shall argue
that, radically considered, it is the only way.) However, the
same critic who suggests to us our task also shows that, had she

---

*Hannah Arendt, "Heidegger at Eighty," in *HMPh*, p. 303. Arendt is wrong in
terming Heidegger's Nazi involvement an "episode" (p. 302). She is right,
however, in stressing that in Germany the philosophical habit of making pon-
derous political pronouncements without bothering with political facts—even
to the extent of reading the newspapers—was not confined to Heidegger.
Having stated that Heidegger had never read *Mein Kampf*, she continues:
"This misunderstanding of what it was all about is inconsiderable when compared with the much more decisive 'error' that consisted in not only ignoring
the most relevant 'literature' but in escaping from the reality of the Gestapo
cellars and the torture-hells of the early concentration camps into ostensibly
more significant regions" (p. 302).

herself undertaken it, she would have gone astray on at least two fundamental points. That "the wind which blows through Heidegger's thinking does not spring from the century he happens to live in" is an assertion strangely at odds with Heidegger's own self-understanding which is increasingly, consciously, historical. And that "Plato and Heidegger" may be compared in their respective turning to "tyrants and *Führers*"* is to ignore two differences between them. Plato attempted to convert the tyrant of Syracuse; Heidegger exalted the Führer as the "sole reality and law" of all things German, and hence of all philosophical things German. This is the first difference. Surely it is grave. However, though grave, it is dwarfed by a second: there is nothing in the tyranny of Syracuse, or indeed in any other tyranny in all recorded history, to compare to the horror of Auschwitz. This horror is unique.

6. The Age of Technology and the Age of Auschwitz

A(1)

The lecture series of 1935 that still speaks of the "greatness" of the "movement" and the "cleansing" of the sciences already contains a criticism—qualified, well hidden, possibly designed to elude informers but nevertheless unmistakable—that strikes at the core of Nazism. "Spirit" is "emasculated" when it is reduced (as in Marxism) to "the regulation and domination of the relations of material production," or (as in positivism), to "the intellectual ordering or explaining of what is already at hand," or, finally, to "the organizing management of the life-mass and race of a *Volk*." Heidegger names the perpetrators of the first two forms of emasculation. He does not name those of the third. However—which is, after all, the main thing—he *does* excoriate the deed and this, to be sure, well after the boycott of April 1, 1933, but at least (to give due credit) some months prior to the "Aryan" legislation of Sep-

*Arendt, "Heidegger at Eighty," in *HMPh*, p. 303. The day after Heidegger resigned from his Freiburg rectorship a colleague reportedly asked him: "Have you returned from Syracuse?" (*Erinnerung*, p. 246).

tember 15, 1935. Not "life-mass" or "race" are fundamental
but rather "Spirit" (*Geist*), and this latter term is defined as
"primordially attuned and knowing resolve toward the essence of Being."[26]

Heidegger does not move from this point on in a straight
anti-Nazi direction. The definition of Spirit just cited, as its
author himself mentions without signs of qualms, is taken
from the notorious *Rektoratsrede* of May 27, 1933. Some
months after that *Rede*, this definition had failed to prevent
the identification of the Führer as the German "reality" and
"law." Doubtless Heidegger never meant by those two terms
what was to come—the "reality" of the "night of long knives"
(which doomed the Germans) or the "laws" of Nuremberg
(which—to be sure, in vastly different and more terrible
ways—doomed the Jews). However, neither these terms nor
the definition of Spirit from which they derive expressly excluded what in fact did come. Heidegger's definition, then,
first formulated in 1933 and reasserted in 1935 permits, to put
it mildly, much latitude.

But perhaps all this is because Heidegger is still "on the
way." Perhaps to understand and do him justice we must
move forward, however briefly, to the very end of that way (or
as far as he ever came or wished to come), and only then move
back to the events of 1933 and thereafter—how he "settled in
his thinking what he had experienced."

A(2)

There is no more precise, profound or for our purpose suitable
way of describing Heidegger's final position with the necessary brevity than in contrast with the final or mature position
of Hegel. Unlike Rosenzweig, Heidegger considered Nietzsche
not as a fellow "new thinker" but rather as the last of the
metaphysicians. Yet like Rosenzweig he found his essential
antagonist in Hegel, and in his case (unlike that of Rosenzweig), the struggle with Hegel was lifelong. On the very first
pages of *Being and Time* it is asserted, against Hegel's *Logic*,
that the concept of Being, far from the "clearest" because the
"most general," is on the contrary the "darkest." This is Hei-

degger, as it were, at the start. "On the way," as we have already seen, there is the unmistakably Hegelian term *Geist* (Spirit) which is given, however, an unmistakably anti-Hegelian significance: rather than having *overcome* all otherness, *Geist* is "attuned" to an Other. And in the lecture *Time and Being* (a work with an air of finality if only by dint of its title, but by no means for that reason alone) Hegel alone is mentioned in the role of antagonist. The lecture itself refers to Hegel's *Logic* as "the most powerful thinking of modern times."[27] And in an account of a seminar on that lecture conducted by Heidegger himself the "unbridgeable difference" between him and Hegel is summed up as follows:

Since for Hegel man is the place of the Absolute's coming-to-itself, that coming-to-itself leads to the *Aufhebung* of man's finitude. For Heidegger, in contrast, precisely finitude comes to view—not only man's finitude but the finitude of the *Ereignis itself*.[28]

The two key terms of this passage have been untranslated because they are untranslatable. We must therefore explain them. Hegel's *Aufhebung*—this the cited passage fails to mention—reinstates finitude. As a necessary prerequisite to such an act, however—and this is rightly stressed in the cited passage—it *overcomes* finitude, and this occurs in a single act of *Geist* which at once raises thought to absoluteness and discloses pure Being as identical with pure vacuity. Heidegger has rejected from the start *both* these aspects of Hegel's *Aufhebung* and hence also *Geist* itself in its Hegelian significance. (*Dasein* is finite in all its aspects, that of thought included; and *Sein*, far from the most "vacuous" and hence "clearest" of concepts, is on the contrary the "darkest"—one that only *seems* vacuous to a tradition that has "forgotten" it.) This, as we say, is from the start. "On the way" from *Dasein* to *Sein*, to be sure, Heidegger falls back on the notion of *Geist* as a link between these two; however, the very notion of a mere link is un-Hegelian and indeed anti-Hegelian. Then why, at the end of the road, is this link no longer necessary? Because, we reply, *Being has, at long last, disclosed itself, fully and unequivocally, as itself finite. It is* Ereignis.

We are well-advised to ponder closely this last-named term, along with the thinking that leads to it. Earlier in this work we considered at length the Hegelian "Overcoming" and its post-Hegelian derivates, and found that at least vis-à-vis one event—the Holocaust—every would-be "overcoming" thought founders, and indeed runs the risk of being itself overcome. It is therefore a matter of no small moment, in itself as well as for us, that Martin Heidegger, though far removed from a philosophical concern with the Holocaust, found himself compelled to reject the notion of overcoming for reasons of his own. Moreover, this occurred at the climax of his career, in a crucial encounter with Hegel, and at a point of his thinking than which none could be philosophically more ultimate. (How can there be an overcoming of finitude if Being itself is finite?) We must therefore ask: precisely what, in contrast with the Hegelian Absolute-Coming-To-Itself, is the Heideggerian Being-as-*Ereignis*?

To begin with, it is a *Presence,* for in its ultimate sense *Truth* is a Presence. But this much is true of Hegel's Absolute as well. However, Hegel's absolute Truth is present *in* man and his thought which is why, as Spirit rises to absoluteness, Truth discloses itself as "the Whole." Heidegger's Truth-of-Being, in contrast, is present *to* man and his thought, such that *both* man and thought *remain* finite in the moment of Presence; indeed, their *ultimate* finitude "comes to view" precisely *through* that Presence. All this is because of one bold, fateful, monumental turn in Heidegger's thought: *the Presence of Being is itself finite; and since Being is inseparable from its Presence, Being is finite as well. It is* Ereignis—*the Ereignis par excellence.*

Ereignis, then, is an event that happens. However, this translation of the German colloquial word, while correct, is inadequate. (It correctly connotes the finitude and occurrence of a presence but fails to convey the nature of *this* Presence.) Being is present to *man* and *his thought,* and—shades of Hegel, but also opposition to Hegel!—neither the man nor the thought can *take this* Presence without *taking it over* as well. The *Ereignis*-of-Being is therefore *appropriation* as much as event, and *event* as much as appropriation. Heidegger expresses this duality in images such as of man as the "shepherd" of Being, and of thought as its "clearing."[29] *The duality of these two aspects is ultimate.*

The irreducibly-dual aspect of Being-as-*Ereignis* bids fair to fulfil a promise which Heidegger's thought has held out ever since *Being and Time.* We have stressed from the start that this work excites the thoughtful reader to this day with its suggestion that the Western metaphysical search for Being, for all its lengthy and arduous labors, has a hidden ground which has yet to disclose itself. That suggestion would be quite unexciting if man and his thought were, ultimately considered, a metaphysical subject standing over against a metaphysical object. (In that case, if there is no such object, *all* metaphysical thought entertained by the subject is simply false; and, if there *is* such an object, all except the thought "corresponding" to it is false, and the true or corresponding thought would be either an "-ism" already existing or else—an unlikely contingency—a new "-ism" which, for all their lengthy and arduous labors, past metaphysicians have not yet thought of.) However, like Hegel's Absolute, Heidegger's *Ereignis* undercuts the ultimacy of the subject-object dichotomy; and unlike that Absolute, it achieves that result without letting go—indeed, by ultimately confirming—the sternly adumbrated finitude of both *Dasein* and its thought. Thus is made possible—the main object of the labor of Heidegger's later years—a "destructive recovery" of the whole history of Western metaphysical thought in which this latter, because limited *to* the subject-object dichotomy, emerges as *concealing* the Presence of Being but also—it is no mere subjective conceit but rather an aspect of Being-as-*Ereignis* itself—as *revealing* it. In short, Heidegger's career, which begins with an exposition of the historicity of *Dasein,* has its climax in a disclosure of, and participation in, *Seinsgeschichte*—the history of Being itself.

A(3)

This must suffice as an account of the "end" of Heidegger's "way." It *may* suffice for, as will be recalled, we have moved forward to that end only so as to gain a fair perspective as to how Heidegger "settled" in his thinking what, in 1933 and the years thereafter, he "had experienced." Our forward-moving account has produced three results. One is to have corroborated Heidegger's singular, not to say unique, qualifications as a stern historicist witness against eternity—both the eternity-above-time of the "old" thinking and the eternity-within-time of Rosenzweig's "new" thinking. What historicity could be more inescapable than that of Being itself? And what "curse of historicity?"

This is the first result—strictly speaking, an unnecessary one. Not unnecessary are the second and third results. Heidegger asserts that Being-as-*Ereignis* is taken, and taken over, by *both* man and his thought. What relation obtains between the two? How is *Seinsgeschichte* related to what Rosenzweig referred to as the history of *Mord und Totschlag*? The question has clearly come to light, and we shall have to ask it when we reach our grim task of confronting a murder and manslaughter without equal in human history.

Another question—this is the third result—must be dealt with at once, for it defines our whole future course. Being-as-*Ereignis* situates all thought. It therefore situates Heidegger's thought as well. Then how can this latter *recognize* the situatedness of *all* thought, and the Being-as-*Ereignis* that, hitherto concealed, situates it? Is this possible, without, after all—once again shades of Hegel!—rising above history as a whole, thus doing away with Being-as-*Ereignis* itself?

Heidegger in effect replies as follows. We are *between* the "metaphysics" that has ended and the "thinking" that has yet to come, too late for the gods and too early for Being. Moreover, the *recognition* of this situation, far from an autonomous result of autonomous thought, is itself *part* of the event that is *happening* even though, to be sure, a taking-over goes with the taking. And the result of this double "between" is that the truth of Being-as-*Ereignis* is disclosed in *our Ereignis*—and ours is the age of technology. Such is the complex turn of thought (traces of which are detectable soon after the events of 1933) that points to the way in which Heidegger "settled in his thinking what he had experienced."

Heidegger's occupation with the age of technology does not begin auspiciously. We have stressed that as early as in 1935 Heidegger excoriates the "emasculation" of "Spirit" through "race." We cannot now fail to mention that in the same context there is talk of an "historic" German "mission," of a Germany as the "metaphysical *Volk*" par excellence, of that *Volk* as "in the pincers between Russia and America," and of these two countries as manifesting, "metaphysically considered," "the same desolate frenzy (*Raserei*) of a rootless and groundless (*bodenlos*) organization of mediocre humanity."[30] One asks—and this in kindness, for nastier questions come easily to mind: Is this Heidegger speaking, or a thinker of the caliber of Richard Wagner or Kaiser Wilhelm II?* This combination of Teutonic megalomania and "metaphysical" indifference to the difference between Roosevelt's freedom and Stalin's terror—is it a merely personal aberration? Or are these the first signs of a fateful split between *Seinsgeschichte* and the history of ordinary mortals? A split causing Heidegger to talk dangerous nonsense? But does Heidegger talk nonsense?†

Despite these unpromising beginnings Heidegger has made a productive start. It is true that not until long after World War II—the war had provided ample opportunity for reflection on this particular subject—did Heidegger give the important lecture *The Question concerning Technology*, a discourse first fully explicating technology-as-*Ereignis*. (The term does not appear in this essay.) However, the theme began to appear in

*On June 1, 1918, at a banquet at General Headquarters to celebrate the thirty years of his reign, Kaiser Wilhelm II asserted that this war was a struggle between two world philosophies. He went on: "Either the Prusso-German-Teutonic world philosophy—justice, freedom, honour, morals—persists in honour, or the Anglo-Saxon—which means succumbing to the worship of the Golden Calf. In this struggle one or the other philosophy must go under. We are fighting for the victory of the German philosophy" (cited by Fritz Fischer, *Germany's Aims in the First World War* [New York: W.W. Norton, 1967], p. 618). This statement deserves only a one-word comment, namely, the German *Quatsch*—*vicious Quatsch*. There is a great deal of *Quatsch* in German philosophy, the Heideggerian not excluded.

†Much German philosophy prior to Nazism was marred by a vague and pretentious language. Thus even good and decent philosophy was vulnerable when an attempt was made to transform a metaphysical *Durchbruch zum Sein* into the Nazi *Umbruch*.

his thought in the years immediately following 1933: this is the sense in the talk, otherwise nonsensical, about a Russian and American—but un-German—technological *Raserei*.

On the surface, "Heidegger on technology" is classifiable with all the latter-day anti-Baconians for whom the once promising Baconian dream has turned into a nightmare. Or, in case this seems too broad, he is classifiable with such as Oswald Spengler, a thinker with a "metaphysical" concern. But the resemblance between Heidegger's thought and *The Decline of the West*, a superficial work by comparison, is itself superficial, and instructive only by way of contrast. Spengler stands in one sense at the end of history, and in another over against it; Heidegger stands *within* history, *between* past and future, unable to transcend his situatedness, and refusing to make the attempt. Spengler makes pessimistic predictions; Heidegger can make no predictions and hence no pessimistic ones. Most important is the third contrast. For Spengler, the whole metaphysical tradition is a product of human creativity, a view which retroactively destroys that tradition. (It is "culture," i.e., a human product without objective truth.) For Heidegger—who seeks to help reopen an original access to Being itself—this Spenglerian view is but an expression, or even a mere symptom, of modern *Seinsverlassenheit*. This last contrast, above all, serves to show Heidegger's special—nay, unique—philosophical stance toward his age. From the start, we have observed in this thinker a resolute togetherness of a resurrected reverence for the age-old quest for Being with a stern insistence on human historicity. As his thought moved from *Dasein* toward *Sein*, we saw this togetherness culminate in the notion of Being-as-*Ereignis*. Now that we hark back so as to see him come face to face with his own age within *Seinsgeschichte*, we find him grappling with two questions, and they are intertwined. Heidegger's *Seinsfrage* is inseparable from his *Frage nach der Technik*.

The conjunction of these questions has two major consequences. First, the current, ever-expanding technological malaise is not for Heidegger, as for others, the effect of modern science but rather the result of a loss of Being which is prior to

science and technology alike: thus technology becomes an uncanny "frenzy" as it moves, as it were, into the vacated
sphere. Second, there can be no authentic escape from this
frenzied present, either into the past (in a vain, romantic-reac-
tionary attempt to restore it) or into the future (in a vain uto-
pian-revolutionary attempt to produce it). Heidegger finds
himself sternly situated in the technological present, yet is
able to write:

In the realm of thinking, a painstaking effort to think through still
more primally what was primally thought is not the absurd wish to
revive what is past, but rather the sober readiness to be astounded
before the coming of the dawn.

In this vein, too, he quotes Hölderlin:

> But where danger is, grows
> The saving power also.[31]

Only a stance enduring the grim present can generate hope.
Moreover, such a stance aids the growth of the saving power,
thus augmenting the grounds for hope. So far is Heidegger's
thought removed from fatalism when it first confronts technology.

His thought remains far from fatalism to the end. To be sure,
by then not much hope is left. Thus the famous interview
published posthumously in *Der Spiegel* bears the title "Now
Only a God Can Save Us." Thus, too, whereas once the noteworthy fact had been that machines, meant to work, break
down, now the "uncanny" fact is that everything "functions,"
that the machinery does *not* break down, that technology has
come to dominate our "planet" so thoroughly that attempts at
self-liberation, too, become enmeshed in it.

But even so Heidegger's thought does not become fatalistic.
Given its basic characteristics, it cannot: if nothing else, a
"god" can save us still. For, first, Being, whether present to us
or absent from us, is never manipulatable by us. Second, Being-
as-*Ereignis* is Presence even in the midst of the most radical
absence. Third, inasmuch as Being-as-*Ereignis* is appropriation

as much as event, thought is not, even in extremity, reduced to impotence. It is true that in our extremity thought, willing to transcend the technological frenzy, is by this very willing drawn, willy-nilly, into that frenzy. What still remains—and this is the freedom of thought in the age of technology which, once actual, ipso facto points beyond that age—is a will-not-to-will, a *Gelassenheit* which is "absolute composure" because it "lets things be." Such is Heidegger's final stance toward the age of technology.[32] What light does it shed on the way in which he settled in his thinking what he had experienced?

A(4)

The following, presumably written during World War II but for obvious reasons not published at the time, is probably the strongest attack on Nazism Heidegger ever made:

"World wars" and their "totality" are already consequences of the prior loss of Being. They press toward securing a constant form of using things up. Man himself is drawn into this process, and he no longer conceals the fact of being the most important raw material of all. Man is "the most important raw material" because he remains the subject of all using-up, and this in such a way that he lets his will be dissolved into the process unconditionally. Thus he becomes the "object" of the loss of Being. World wars precede the elimination of the difference between war and peace. The elimination is necessary because the "world" has become an unworld (*Unwelt*) in consequence of the abandonment of beings by a Truth of Being. For "world" in the sense of *Seinsgeschichte* . . . means the non-objective Presence of Being for man who is essentially beholden to it. . . . The moral outrage of those who do not yet know what is the case often aims at the arbitrariness and claim to dominance of the "leaders" (*Führer*)—the most fatal form of perpetually giving them dignity. . . . People think that the Führers have arrogated everything unto themselves entirely on their own, in a blind frenzy (*Raserei*) of egotism. But in fact they are merely the necessary consequence of the fact that what-is has gone astray, so that an emptiness expands which in turn requires a single ordering and securing of what-is.[33]

This statement should not be underestimated. To some extent, it captures the eerie-but-empty infinity of the Führer's Reich, its mythology, its celebrations, its marches, its language, to say nothing of its total war. But neither should we be blind to a fundamental flaw in it. The pro-Nazi Heidegger has endorsed the "law" and "reality" of *the one Führer*. The subsequent, anti-Nazi Heidegger speaks of Führers in the plural. This is no mere matter of arithmetic, but rather a telltale sign. This subsequent, anti-Nazi Heidegger, to be sure, has reappraised Nazism. However, he has in no way reappraised his own philosophy which, while not responsible for his surrender to Nazism, had been unable to prevent it. His *Weg* of thought moves through World War II as though all that had happened was an intensification of technology. Hence after the war as before, America and Russia are forms of technological *Raserei*: to them is but added yet another form—the Führer, with a *Raserei* of their own. Hence, too, in the *Spiegel*-interview already cited, he recognized his disastrous statement of 1933 about the Führer's "reality" and "law," to be sure, as a political error, but in no way as a symptom of a philosophical catastrophe. And as late as 1953 Martin Heidegger was still able to write:

What has World War II decided? (Let us be silent about its terrible consequences for our *Vaterland*, and in particular about the split through its middle.) This world war has decided nothing, if we take the term "decision" in so high and wide a sense as to concern solely the essential destiny (*Wesensgeschick*) of man on this earth.*

B

World War II decided at least one thing: it destroyed the world of the Holocaust. We use the word "world" advisedly. Auschwitz and Treblinka were a world, with a structure of their own, a logic of their own, a horizon of their own, even a language of their own; but they were unlike any world ever dreamt of in

---

*WhD, p. 65; *What is Called Thinking?* (New York: Harper and Row, 1968), p.66. Heidegger prefaced one lecture in this cycle as follows: "Ladies and Gentlemen: An exhibition 'Prisoners of War Speak' has been opened in Freiburg today. I ask you to pay a visit, so that you may hear that soundless voice and never again lose it from your inner ear"(WhD, p. 159; this passage is omitted in the English edition of the work). Heidegger heard the soundless voice of victims who were fellow Germans. (German prisoners of war in Russia were victims, whatever Nazi Germany had done to produce or even justify Russian vengeance.) But did he also hear the soundless voice of the victims of his fellow Germans? I have searched for evidence—in vain.

Heidegger's or any other philosophy. They were unlike Heidegger's technological *Unwelt* as well. This was the world of children not used as "raw material" for a purpose, but rather—this *was* the purpose—thrown alive into the flames. It was the world of the *Muselmänner*, no longer fit for any sort of "using up," and no longer able to be-toward-death, for "one hesitates to call them living, one hesitates to call their death death." And the terrible screams of the first and the no less terrible silence of the second are a reminder, as lasting as it is compelling, that at work in that *Welt*—or *Unwelt*—was a *Raserei* quite other than an "unfettered technology and groundless and rootless organization of average man." This description may fit adequately, even admirably, the necessary means. It comes nowhere near the ends which were degradation, torture and murder. These ends had no higher purpose but were themselves both highest and "unshakable."*

We have already made one attempt to come to philosophical terms with that world—but where the "overcoming" Hegelian (or post-Hegelian) thought is at work, there the Holocaust is not.† Now that we are with a philosophical thinking that accepts its historical situatedness, we must accept *this* situatedness, and expose thought to the event situating it. And it is well to bear in mind Theodor Adorno's warning, to the effect that a philosophical thinking that does not test itself in the light of extremity is comparable to the music by which the SS customarily drowned out the cries of their victims.[34]

In due course we must consider the victims, their suffering, their resistance, their identity. For the present, let us be silent

---

*That his important decisions were *unerschütterlich* was Hitler's most characteristic boast. It was also entirely truthful. Even Himmler, *der treue Heinrich*, in the end wanted to stop the murders, as part of an abortive attempt at a separate peace with the Western Allies. Hitler's last will and testament is proof enough that any such act on the Führer's part is inconceivable.

†See above, ch. III, section 11. In our first exploration (ch. II, in which thought rises above history), the Holocaust came as a shocking surprise. In our second exploration (ch. III, in which thought moves through history, in an attempt to overcome it), our thought tried but failed to confront the Holocaust. Only now that our thought *is and remains situated in history* is a confrontation possible—with results that remain to be seen.

of them and consider the technicians, administrators, rulers and philosophers.

Lest unauthentic refuge be sought in the most obvious place, it must be stressed from the start that the sadists, perverts, madmen—the kind that may be found anywhere and at any time—were least in significance. (They were probably least in number as well: only so many of them can be enlisted by even the most sedulous organizers.) More significant were the ordinary men and women who performed their new, extraordinary jobs in much the same manner in which they had once performed—and would soon again perform—their ordinary jobs. However, most significant of all—indeed, setting the tone— were the idealists: these were much like other idealists, except that their ideals were torture and murder. (They did not just "use" torture, but "worshiped" it.) On their part, these idealists were subdivided into those who practiced the ideals and those who provided the theory. And the theory and practice, in the last analysis, had their "reality" and "law" in the Führer himself.*

Of the last-named two groups, the practitioners and the philosophers, one should give examples. Rudolf Hoess was brought up in the Black Forest, which he loved. His great, life-long ambition was to return to the soil and till it. He was good to his wife and his children. He was dedicated to his *Volk* and thus abominated Julius Streicher's "pornographic anti-Semitism that was harmful to German women and children." Yet this man was commandant of Auschwitz. In all likelihood, he was the greatest torturer and mass murderer in history.

To Kommandant Hoess the Führer himself was law. That law left some small room for doubt as to the fate to be meted out to the "enemies of the state" that were within his jurisdic-

---

*This brief synopsis is indebted to the work of Holocaust historians such as Yehuda Bauer and Raul Hilberg. Their work uncovers a reality rarely perceived by general historians who, if they do not dismiss the Holocaust in a footnote, resort with amazing regularity to metaphors such as "racist madness," as if they, rather than explain anything, did not themselves stand in need of explanation. See also below, p. 231n.

tion. In the case of Jews there was no room for doubt. To be a Jew was in itself a capital crime: such was the essence of Hoess's "serious"—as contrasted with Streicher's "pornographic"—anti-Semitism.[35]

Hoess practiced this law. The Führer's philosophers furnished the necessary theory. Once the University of Jena had been home, successively, to Fichte, Schelling, and Hegel, thinkers of whom Heidegger quite rightly said that they expressed a "grandeur, breadth and originality" of a "spiritual world" to which a subsequent age was no longer equal.[36] Now it was home to Professor Johann von Leers, the author of learned arguments to the effect that states harboring Jews were harboring the plague, and that the Reich had the moral duty and, by the principle of hot pursuit, the legal right to conquer such countries, if only in order to wipe the plague out.*

Such was the theory. It was so well in tune with practice that practitioners such as Kommandant Hoess—by his own voluntary confession—could be both deeply moved by the innocent play of Gypsy children—considered "non-Aryan" by one school of Nazi thought, though considered "Aryan" by another—and yet cold-bloodedly plot their murder.[37] And the theory and the practice had both their ultimate source in the Führer himself. As early as in September 1919, Hitler had written:

Antisemitism arising out of purely emotional causes finds its ultimate expression in pogroms. Rational antisemitism must be directed toward a methodical legal struggle. . . . The final aim must be the deliberate removal [Entfernung] of the Jews as a whole.†

*Die Verbrechernatur der Juden (Berlin, 1944), p. 8. On the Nazi concept of Jews as bacilli, see Erich Goldhagen, "Weltanschauung und Endlösung," Vierteljahreshefte für Zeitgeschichte (1976), p. 379. In a letter to me Professor Goldhagen stresses that whereas of course the bacilli idea was common among Nazis, von Leers had the unusual distinction of not bothering to veil his call for mass murder in euphemistic language. Goldhagen also informs me that after the war von Leers, his Nazi ardor undiminished, launched the first neo-Nazi journal in Argentina where he had fled. Later he went to Egypt and under an assumed Arabic name wrote anti-Zionist pamphlets for the Information Ministry, until his death in 1967. His widow (who shared his views) returned to Germany, where she embarrassed neo-Nazis by defending Hitler's "extermination" of the Jews openly, instead of classifying it among his "mistakes."
†This letter is cited in nearly all Hitler biographies.

Only a few years later the sentiments of this letter became the core of the "program" of a party—its core, if not its sole unambiguous content. By 1935 the "legal struggle" had become a legislation distinguishing between "non-Aryan" guilt and "Aryan" innocence. And in the end the "final aim"—"the deliberate *Entfernung* of the Jews as a whole"—became the "Final Solution."*

The roles of Führer, philosopher and practitioner were remarkably united in the person of Reichsführer Heinrich Himmler. It is therefore necessary for us to consider him. On a noted occasion Himmler addressed his idealistic subordinates as follows:

I want to make reference before you here, in complete frankness, to a really grave matter. Among ourselves, this once, it shall be uttered quite frankly; but in public we will never speak of it. Just as we did not hesitate on June 30, 1934 to do our duty as ordered, to stand up against the wall comrades who had transgressed, and shoot them, so we have never talked about this and never will. It was the tact which, I am glad to say, is a matter of course to us that made us never discuss it among ourselves, never talk about it. Each of us shuddered, and yet each one knew that he would do it again if it were ordered and if it were necessary. I am referring to the evacuation of the Jews, to the annihilation of the Jewish people. This is one of those things that are easily said. "The Jewish people is going to be annihilated," says every party member. "Sure, it's in our program, elimination of the Jews, annihilation—we'll take care of it." And then they all come trudging, eighty million worthy Germans, and each has his one decent Jew. Sure, the others are swine, but this one is an A–1 Jew. Of all those who talk this way, no one has seen it happen, not one has been through it. Most of you know what it means to see a hundred corpses lie side by side, or five hundred, or a thousand. To have endured this and—excepting cases of human weakness—to have re-

*Exactly when and how the Final Solution was decided on is for historians to determine. For our part we assert only this much, that the extremes in the historians' debate are both absurd: that Hitler planned the Final Solution from the start, so that the whole process was ultimately the execution of but one man's plan; and that, since Hitler's Reich was a "totalitarian anarchy" composed of conflicting "fiefdoms," the "road" was so "crooked" as to reach Auschwitz only by accident. (See also *Jewish Return*, p. 68 ff.) Clearly, the genocidal impulse was in the "movement" from the start, but it also took decisions on the road for it to be accelerated and intensified.

mained decent, that is what has made us hard. In our history, this is an unwritten and never-to-be-written page of glory.[38]

Himmler, as is well known, was himself not hard enough; on a visit to Auschwitz he was sick to his stomach. Not so well known is that on another visit

he stopped beside the burning pit and waited for a pair of gloves. Then he put on the gloves, picked one of the dead bodies off the pile, and threw it into the fire. "Thank God," he cried with a loud voice. "At last I too have burned a Jew with my own hands."[39]

We must take Himmler's speech—one of several—as an authoritative document. (Hence we have cited it at some length.) The leading Nazi spirits were not perverts or opportunists or even ordinary jobholders but rather extraordinary idealists, i.e., criminals with a good conscience and a pure heart. This is one lesson of Himmler's speech, already known to us but now authoritatively confirmed. The other, however, is new and more important still, for it concerns not the Holocaust alone but rather the Führer's Reich as a whole. Most of the eighty million Germans, Himmler states, fell short of sufficient loyalty to the Führer's law; yet they all subscribed to it. This is, of course, a gross lie on Himmler's part, a crude Nazi joke and an insult to countless decent Germans, never converted to "Aryan" ideology. Alas, no lie but rather a brute fact is that the eighty million, the countless decent ones included, obeyed the Führer's law and owed life itself to this compliance. By the laws of every other world, a person is punished for *doing*, i.e., the breaking of the laws. By the "Aryan" laws of the Führer's world, "non-Aryans" were "punished" for *being*, i.e., their accidental ancestors. By the laws of every other world—in theory if never wholly in practice—a person is presumed innocent until proven guilty. By the laws of the Führer's world, *all* persons were suspect of "non-Aryan" criminality unless they proved, or were prepared to prove, their "Aryan" innocence. Hence the awesome fact is *that all giving such proof, prepared to give it, or even simply surviving on the presumption of "Aryan" descent—i.e., no less than all the eighty million Germans as well as many in Nazi-*

occupied Europe—are implicated, however remotely, indirectly, and innocently, in the crime crying to heaven in the screams of the children of Auschwitz and in the no less terrible silence of the Muselmänner. Only those defying the Führer's law (and in so doing risking or forfeiting lives) are wholly exempt. One searches all history in vain for a parallel to this German tragedy.

We use the term "tragedy" advisedly. One must emphasize that *subjectively* many or most Germans were innocent—all those who knew nothing or could do nothing. Yet it is just to these that the term "tragedy" applies. (To apply it to the criminals is a mistake.) Indeed, the more one has reason to insist on subjective innocence the more starkly comes into view the contradiction between it and objective implication—survival on the presumption of an "Aryan" innocence that implies "non-Aryan" guilt. Deliberately, insidiously, diabolically, the laws of the Third Reich drew, spiderlike, the *whole* German people into a web, the core of which was the Holocaust. And the gulf created and legislated since 1933 was between German (and, subsequently European) Jewry as a whole and—with exceptions noted—the *entire* German people and much of Nazi-occupied Europe. No wonder the mind shrinks from this scandalous fact. No wonder the Holocaust is widely viewed as an accident—for historians a footnote—in the history of Germany, Europe, the world.

To disprove this last-named view one need go no further than the dynamics of Nazism itself, i.e., to consider how, as the inner logic of the Führer's law and reality unfolded, the Third Reich took its terrible historical course. The Nazi Empire had not one but two aims that brooked no compromise. One was the annihilation of the Jewish people. The other—this in behalf of social Darwinist "principles" freely mixed with dreams, ambitions, and myths harking back to Kaiser Wilhelm II, to some German romantics, to Frederick the Great, and to Kaiser Barbarossa—was the conquest of *Lebensraum* and of lesser races by the master race, all this with an ultimate (if vague) view to world conquest. (The secret code name for the war on Russia was "Operation Barbarossa"; the public slogan since 1933 had been "today Germany—tomorrow the world.") All this, however, was when the Third Reich was at the height of its power. At the time of the apocalypse, only the first of these aims proved itself to be absolute. As for the second—this still in behalf of social Darwinist principles, though Barbarossa was by then forgotten—the German people were now being handed over for destruction cynically and even enthusiastically—and of all "races," to the once-despised Slavs. Thus the *sole absolute* article of faith that remained was expressed in the burning of Jewish children. That otherwise this was a "revolution of nihilism" was expressed in a *Führerbefehl* in the doomed Berlin bunker. Hitler ordered the flooding of the Berlin subways, the hiding place of men, women, and children. This would not stop the Russian armies. However, it would drown German children.

Such was the essence of Nazism as revealed in the end. Such, revealed in part, had been its essence all along. As early as 1936, Julius Streicher was quoted in print as follows:

Who fights the Jew fights the devil!
Who masters the devil conquers heaven!*

Streicher no more than echoed the Führer himself who earlier still had written: "In defending myself against the Jew, I fight for the work of God."[40] The distinction between "porno-graphic" and "serious" or "idealistic" Nazi anti-Semitism dis-solves. *In extremis* they became in fact, as in essence they were all along, one and the same.†

Such was the *Welt* (or *Unwelt*)—its inner core the Holocaust,

---

The Yellow Spot: The Extermination of the Jews in Germany (London: Gol-lancz, 1936), p. 47. The very title of this book refutes those who, years later, still claimed that they did not know and could not guess. In his moving (but unheeded) introduction the Bishop of Durham confessed—in 1936!—that in the records of persecution, many and sombre as they are,' he could not find "anything quite equivalent to the persecution of the Jews which now proceeds in Germany" (p.6).

†This completes our first account of the Holocaust world, with the focus on the criminals. It will be followed in section 8 by a deeper account, in which the focus is on the victims. For the language employed in both these accounts, see above, ch. I, section 8.

its outer expression the Nazi Reich as a whole—in which the German tragic contradiction between subjective innocence and objective implication-by-dint-of-"Aryan"-survival assumed its unheard of, unprecedented reality. Once the German philosopher Schelling had written deeply, compellingly about innocent guilt in Greek tragedy—a mere conceit of poets.[41] One asks: Where is the philosopher—he ought to be, *can only be* German—to face a German tragedy which is no mere poetic conceit and which no poet could ever have conceived?

Martin Heidegger was not the required philosopher. We shall have further, deeper reasons for parting company with Heidegger from this point on. His obtuseness to the German tragedy would be quite enough. A thinker failing to notice a unique tragedy in his own land, associated with a war, has poor credentials for adopting so "high and wide" a viewpoint as to judge what that same war has or has not "decided" for nothing less universal than "the essential destiny of man on earth."

That World War II *has* changed nothing *for some or even most* people was expressed unforgettably by a German poet of Jewish origin who survived and returned from Theresienstadt. She writes:

> *Nur ein paar Menschen—wer hat sie gekannt!*
> *Nur ein paar Menschen, ermordet, verbrannt.*
> *Nur ein paar Menschen sind nicht mehr da.*
> *Und alles ist wieder, als ob nichts geschah.*
>
> Just a few people—who ever knew them?
> Just a few people—murdered, burnt!
> Just a few people—no longer there.
> And all is again as if nothing had happened.[42]

In endorsing the view that World War II had decided nothing Heidegger arraigned himself on one side of the great gulf between "Aryans" and "non-Aryans" that had been created and legislated since 1933. And in so doing he contributed to its perpetuation. In this failure personal idiosyncrasies are of no account. Of great account, however, are those aspects of Heideggerian thought that made the failure possible. Above we asked but did not answer the question of the relation between Heidegger's *Seinsgeschichte* and the history of ordinary mortals. Now we reply: his *Seinsgeschichte* is cut loose from at least one *Mord und Totschlag,* and this despite or because of the fact that it is without precedent in all history. Only because in his generalized *Seinsverlassenheit* the screams of the children and the silence of the *Muselmänner* are not heard is there any possibility of adopting toward the age, as the ultimate philosophical stance, a "composure" that "lets things be."*

But after Auschwitz there are some things that thought *cannot* let be, and toward which a stance far removed from composure is necessary. Devotees of Heidegger's later thought must face the fact that the Holocaust world—or *Unwelt*—should have been for him—but was not—an *Ereignis.* As for students prepared to take seriously no Heideggerian work beyond *Being and Time,* these are forced to recognize that, even by Heidegger's own standards, vis-à-vis the Holocaust and the Third Reich as a whole, his thought lapses into unauthenticity.

7. *Unauthentic Thought after the Holocaust*

In 1957 there occurred a chance meeting in a Swiss resort between Martin Heidegger and Martin Buber, and the meeting turned into a lengthy and friendly discussion. One participant was the greatest German philosopher of the age. The other was—in the West at least—its greatest, most authoritative Jewish thinker. The two occupied the same intellectual universe of discourse, yet were at opposite sides of the great abyss that had been created and legislated since 1933. The meeting thus represented a rare, perhaps unique, opportunity for bridging, or at least narrowing, the great abyss at the highest, most authoritative level. Yet the Heidegger-Buber meeting was a failure.

---

*With all the due respect already expressed (see above, p. 181n), what happened to German prisoners of war in Russia is, alas, not new in the history of human *Mord und Totschlag.* (Indiscriminate revenge is human, if evil.) In contrast (as will emerge ever more inescapably), both the victims and the victimizers of the Holocaust are without precedent.

We mention this incident because it raises questions which, having left Heidegger's *Denkweg*, we now see loom on the horizon. Heidegger's thought has lapsed into unauthenticity vis-à-vis the Holocaust: given its nature, could it have done otherwise? And does such lapsing, perhaps, extend to other thinkers, not excluding many at the other side of the abyss? But perhaps no thought can exist in the same space as the Holocaust; perhaps *all* thought, to assure its own survival, must be elsewhere. This is the radical question behind all the others.

What occurred at the Heidegger-Buber meeting? A philosophical journalist who interviewed both men reports that Heidegger "hardly reacted to the name of Buber, as though he did not know him personally but only by name." As for Buber, he reports him as remarking that whereas the past had remained *unbewältigt* ("un-overcome") this very avoidance of the past had made possible a "straightforward speaking" about other matters, among them "guilt and forgiveness, the guilt of thought included." If our informant can be trusted, Buber if not Heidegger regarded the meeting as at least a partial success.*

And yet a failure it was. For one must ask: *If a dialogue between two thinkers of the first rank, sharing the same universe of discourse but placed at opposite sides of the great abyss created and legislated since 1933, still requires in 1957 evading das Unbewältigte and ignoring the great gulf, how can the dialogue take up, without radical distortion, anything else?* Both thinkers were close to Kierkegaard. Each might have remembered the Dane's insistence that a single event of inexplicable horror "has the power to make everything inexplicable, including the most explicable events." But while Buber if not Heidegger may have remembered, in his meeting with Heidegger he chose not to act on his knowledge.

Yet whereas his purpose was surely to narrow the abyss the Heidegger-Buber meeting, if anything, only widened it. On an

---

*Hans A. Fischer-Barnicol, "Spiegelungen—Vermittlungen," in *Erinnerung*, pp. 90 ff., 101. As will be seen, there is doubt as to the extent to which our informant can be trusted, and he himself reports that Buber made his remark about the "un-overcome past" "mockingly."

unnamed authority the indefatigable journalist reports that the "conciliatory, nay, friendly meeting" between Buber and Heidegger led to "heated quarrels" in Buber's "circle of Jerusalem friends," and that "a continuation of the conversation, or even a friendship, with Heidegger would have been, on Buber's part, impossible since it would have led to a rupture of all relations to Buber in Israel." Indefatigable still, the reporter passed this information on to Gabriel Marcel, whose reaction was that Buber should have risked this danger. Marcel went on to exclaim: "What Pharisees are these, who want to prohibit reconciliation and forgiveness!" Thus it seems, Buber's noble intentions notwithstanding, that the main result of the Buber-Heidegger meeting was to cause a venerable Christian thinker to resort to an anti-Jewish New Testament stereotype. As for the "heated quarrels" (*Auseinandersetzungen*) in Buber's "circle of Jerusalem friends," they never took place. To cite a letter of Gershom Scholem to this writer, they "belong definitely to the realm of fantasy."*

Undoubtedly Marcel lapsed into his anti-Jewish stereotype unconsciously. Undoubtedly, too, it was unconsciously that he took refuge in reconciliation-in-general and forgiveness-in-general when the ineluctable task was, before all else, to confront the Holocaust in its scandalous particularity. Yet unconscious or not, the taking-refuge did occur, and was a lapse into unauthenticity. Nor was Marcel alone either among Christian or philosophical thinkers in making things easy for himself in this manner. Buber's hope notwithstanding, Heidegger never faced German "guilt," to say nothing of the "guilt of thought." On his part, Karl Jaspers did write *The Question of German Guilt*;[43] but he stayed away from the Holocaust. Among Christians, as already mentioned, the neo-orthodox Karl Barth was unorthodox enough to describe the Holocaust as the greatest Jewish catastrophe in history; that it might also be a Christian catastrophe does not seem to have entered his mind. Nor did other great Christian theologians do better. Paul Tillich wrote

---

*Fischer-Barnicol, "Spiegelungen—Vermittlungen," p. 93. In his letter, dated January 24, 1979, Professor Scholem reports not only his own opinion and recollections but also those of Professor Ernst Simon.

about idolatry during and after World War II much as he had written after World War I. And Rudolf Bultmann wrote about Old Testament, New Testament, and hermeneutics as though nothing had happened. Nor—with some notable exceptions to be mentioned later on—has this failure among the great ones in this century been remedied by philosophers or theologians coming after them.* Thus, for the first time in this work, we are faced with the possibility that *the Holocaust may be a radical rupture in history*—and that *among things ruptured may be not just this or that way of philosophical or theological thinking, but thought itself.*

If this is a serious possibility, then intimations of it must exist among "non-Aryan" as well as "Aryan" thinkers. Critics often dismiss any special preoccupation with the Holocaust on the part of Jewish thinkers as a mere "compulsion" and result of a "trauma"—understandable, no doubt, but without claim to objective validity. Such dismissals are best disposed of by examples of significant Jewish thinkers who, despite their "Jewish trauma," dissolve both their own Jewishness and the Holocaust into generalities—and lapse into unauthenticity.

Isaac Deutscher foresees no end to communist violence. Also, as already mentioned, he views the Holocaust as a unique event of horror which no theory, the Marxist included, will ever explain or overcome. Then what of Marxism remains for this maverick Marxist? Having solved little else, Marx has at least "solved" the Jewish "problem," by dissolving Jews into men-in-general. But what hope remains for *mankind-in-general*? This painful, post-Holocaust question pushes Deutscher into a strange, not to say weird, combination of universalist-humanist utopianism and Jewish chauvinism. After Stalin and Hitler, the future may be precarious for post-capitalist, liberated, universal Man: he has at least *one* firm vanguard in *some* men *already* universal, i.e., "non-Jewish Jews" such as Marx, Trotsky, and Deutscher himself. Such is the nemesis, and *reductio ad absurdum*, of a thinking which—forced to recognize the Holocaust but refusing to confront it,

*See below, section 13 of this chapter.

compelled to be Jewish but wishing to be "non-Jewishly Jewish"—lapses into unauthenticity.[44]

If Deutscher lapses into utopianism, Ernst Bloch consciously adopts it. Indeed, in his thought utopianism is no less than a metaphysical principle: hope is not something clung to but rather an all-embracing ultimate by which are judged all societies, cultures, and philosophies. Moreover, his thought is not so much "non-Jewish" as *post*-Jewish, for in its grand sweep Judaism and Christianity are both contained and superseded. And yet the bold radicalism of his thought, in the end, only radicalizes the escapism. In 1954 the Stalinist outcome of Lenin's "proletarian dictatorship" was unmistakable; yet for Bloch it still contained a future end of all violence "immanently" and "inescapably." Unmistakable, too, was the starkly unique horror of the Holocaust; yet in Bloch's thought it is trivialized into a by-product of the "late bourgeoisie," to the extent to which it appears at all. Thus Bloch's post-Jewish Jew is only slightly less chimerical than Deutscher's non-Jewish Jew—and nearly as alone. As for the flight of his thought from the post-Holocaust present, it is into a future that is, as it were, absolute.[45]

If "non-Jewish-Jewish" escapism, at least when it is profound, is apt to be into the future, the escapism of "Jewish-Jewish" thinkers, if and when it occurs, is apt to be into the venerable Jewish past. Not that a resort to that past must be a case of escapism. (Nor is a resort to the Messianic future.) On the contrary, before allowing the hallowed Jewish tradition to be threatened—and exposure to the Holocaust inevitably *does* threaten it—the "Jewish-Jewish" thinker is required to cherish it, to nurture it, to bring to life its wisdom, its faith, its God. And this must have been why Jewish thinkers of unquestionable Jewish authenticity such as Martin Buber and Abraham J. Heschel said little about the Holocaust—and that little with great reticence. Yet, as much current Jewish opinion has it, little was said by Buber and Heschel because little needed to be said, because "theologically" if not historically, the Holocaust "poses no new problems": it is a "a chapter" in Jewish history, and nothing more. In this manner not a few current

Jewish writers invoke two great Jewish thinkers, both no longer alive, in order to justify their own escapism.[46]

How was it in fact with Buber? We have seen him lapse into unauthenticity in dialogue with another. We now owe him a consideration of his thought in its own right: did he—could he—confront the Holocaust? That the prospects in this regard are unpromising is recognized by any student of Buber's thought. Buber had a lifelong difficulty with the recognition of evil. Religiously, he was predisposed to hold "no one to be absolutely unredeemable." Philosophically, his basic framework, the celebrated "I-Thou/I-It," leaves room for decay and dehumanization, but not for an evil that is truly radical. In this whole matter, the thinking and teaching of a lifetime may be said to have found its climax in the statement that "evil cannot be done with the whole soul; good can only be done with the whole soul." In a moving passage, Buber applies this doctrine to an "important poet" who grieved to his death for having allowed himself to accept a high Nazi honor. However, against all this one must face the stern, bitter truth that a repentant Hoess or Eichmann, Himmler or Hitler cannot be conceived.* Indeed, even Heidegger, if ever he repented at all, failed to do so in public. Yet the sin that required repentance had been committed in the glare of worldwide publicity.

Buber's difficulties with radical evil may help explain some strange moral lapses on his part. In the preface to a book written in Jerusalem during the Arab siege in the first

Philosophical Interrogations, ed. S. and B. Rome (New York: Holt, Rinehart and Winston, 1964), pp. 110 ff.; *Good and Evil* (New York: Scribners, 1953), pp. 133 ff.; *The Philosophy of Martin Buber*, ed. M. Friedman and P. A. Schilpp (La Salle, Ill.: Open Court, 1967), p. 720. In a letter to Maurice Friedman, Buber adds "such as Goebbels" to " . . . no one to be absolutely unredeemable." Yet in Goebbels's case repentance—surely the indispensable condition of redemption—is least conceivable. Such big Nazis as Hoess, Eichmann, Himmler, and Hitler were, each in his fashion, "true believers," so that in their case, had someone *per impossibile* shaken their belief, repentance is not wholly inconceivable. (However, the notion of "true belief" requires, in the Nazi case, a deeper reflection than it has yet received.) Goebbels is the paradigm of the Nazi who is wholly cynical about Nazi doctrines—certainly about Jews—and yet passionately spreads them as truth. His speech in the Berlin *Sportpalast* alluded to by us elsewhere (see below, section 14) is the speech of a liar who has made evil his god.

Arab-Israeli war, Buber wrote the following: "The work involved [in the writing of this book] has helped me to endure in faith this war, *for me the most grievous of the three.*"[47] The wars referred to, in addition to the first Arab-Israeli war, are World Wars I and II. One understands this grief when Zionism is seen as bound up with the prophetic pursuit of justice and peace. One understands and cannot but sympathize. Even so, since World War II includes the Holocaust, this statement is a lapse in judgment.

Remarkably enough, Buber's thought was, despite all, shaken by the Holocaust, and this not at its political periphery but rather at what may be called its religious center. (The center of Buber's thought is dialogical speech, and since it is divine-human speech that confers meaning on *all* speech, his thought may be said to have a religious center.) In *I and Thou,* Buber had taught that God speaks constantly. Many years later he was moved to fall back on the traditional Jewish doctrine of the "hiding of the Face" and asserted that an "eclipse of God," possible at any time, is actual in our time. However, in falling back on the traditional doctrine Buber was concerned not with "belief in God" or "explaining" His ways, but rather with the possibility of divine-human *speech.* Thus in crisis the religious center of Buber's teachings—the dialogical reality and its fate—remained undamaged.

Against this background one must understand Buber's lecture "The Dialogue between Heaven and Earth," originally delivered in 1951. Buber writes:

In this our time, one asks again and again: how is a Jewish life still possible after Auschwitz? I would like to frame this question more correctly: how is a life with God still possible in a time in which there is an Auschwitz? The estrangement has become too cruel, the hiddenness too deep. One can still "believe" in a God who allowed those things to happen, but *how can one still speak to Him? Can one still hear His word?* Can one still, as an individual and a people, enter at all into a dialogical relationship with Him? Can one still call on Him? Dare we recommend to the survivors of Auschwitz, the Job of the gas chambers: "Call on Him, for He is kind, for His mercy endureth forever?"

Buber addresses these questions, not only to them, to the survivors, but rather to "all those who have not got over what happened and never will get over it." Rather than consider the Holocaust as a "chapter" in Jewish history—with the next, perhaps, already under way—he saw his generation "at the turning" between the *whole* Jewish past and a Jewish future yet to come. How then does Buber's post-Holocaust Jew face the future? Buber writes:

Do we stand overcome before the hidden face of God as the tragic hero of the Greeks before faceless Fate? No, rather even now we contend [like Job] with God, with the Lord of Being Himself whom once we, not our fathers only, chose for our Lord. We do not accept the world as it is but rather struggle for its redemption, and in this struggle appeal for help to our Lord, who on His part is once more, and still, One who hides. In this condition we await His voice, whether it comes out of the storm or the stillness that follows it. And although His coming manifestation may resemble no earlier one, we shall nevertheless recognize again our cruel and merciful God.[48]

This answer, arresting and thought-provoking in many ways, is, in one sense, no answer at all. Called into question is *speech*—not just this or that speech, spoken by this or that speaker, but rather *all significant* speech, divine and human, believing-human and unbelieving-human; both the speech of the Job of the gas chambers and the speech of all those who have not got over what happened and never will get over it. Moreover—Kierkegaard said it when he spoke of the fall of Jerusalem—all significant speech is called into question *ever after*, for that either man or God should ever "get over it" is inconceivable.* It is this circumstance that made us judge

---

*That all this did not escape Buber is indicated, it would seem, in a letter of his to Ernst Szilagyi, dated July 2, 1950, which ends as follows: "How is a Jewish life possible after Auschwitz? Today I no longer really know what this is—a Jewish life. Nor do I expect ever again to experience it. But this I know: what it is to stay with Him [*bei Ihm ausharren*].Those who in our time stay with Him lead over to that which one day may be called a Jewish life" (Ms. Var. 350/801a in the Martin Buber Archives, Jewish National and University Library, Jerusalem. I wish to thank the library for giving me access to these archives, and permission to cite this passage. The translation is mine.) Buber here speaks of *ausharren* and not of speech. In the case of the "philosopher of dialogue," this can hardly be considered insignificant.

earlier that the Buber-Heidegger conversation was a failure, and that made Theodor Adorno once remark—truly yet absurdly, absurdly yet truly—that after Auschwitz a poem is impossible.*

This absurd truth and true absurdity was, so to speak, put into practice by a great poet. Paul Celan was a survivor. If there can be Holocaust poems, his *Todesfuge* ("Fugue of Death") is surely one of the greatest. Yet, as a critic asserts, its very greatness makes this poem a "highly problematic achievement," inviting as it does "against the writer's intent" "an escape in literature from troublesome reflection." The critic continues:

In West Germany (where, according to the revised statute of limitations, concentration-camp murderers who did not act from base personal motives can no longer be prosecuted), Celan's "Fugue of Death" has become a popular textbook piece, and one of the academic commentators admonishes the classroom teacher to stick to the text, lest "student discussion deviate from the work of art to the persecution of the Jews."†

*In 1949 Adorno wrote: "To write a poem after Auschwitz is barbaric" ("Kulturkritik und Gesellschaft," *Prismen* [Berlin: Suhrkamp, 1961], p. 31). In 1961: "I do not wish to qualify (*mildern*) the statement that to write lyric after Auschwitz is barbaric" ("Engagement," *Noten zur Literatur, III* [Berlin: Suhrkamp, 1961], p. 125). Finally, in 1966 we are told: "Ceaseless suffering has as much right to express itself as does the victim of torture to screaming. Therefore it may have been false [on my part] to say that after Auschwitz one cannot write poetry. But it is not false to ask . . . whether after Auschwitz it is possible to live at all; whether . . . he can do so who escaped by accident, and who by every logic should have been murdered" (*Negative Dialektik*, p. 355; the translation is mine).
†Peter Demetz, *Postwar German Literature* (New York: Schocken, 1971), pp. 80 ff. I must confine myself to quoting the opening lines of *Todesfuge*:

"*Schwarze Milch der Frühe wir trinken sie abends*
wir trinken sie mittags und morgens wir trinken sie nachts
wir trinken und trinken
wir schaufeln ein Grab in den Lüften da liegt man nicht eng
Ein Mann wohnt im Hause der spielt mit den Schlangen der schreibt
der schreibt wenn es dunkelt nach Deutschland dein goldenes Haar
    Margarete
er schreibt es und tritt vor das Haus und es blitzen die Sterne er pfeift seine
    Rüden herbei
er pfeift seine Juden hervor lasst schaufeln ein Grab in der Erde
er befiehlt uns spielt auf nun zum Tanz. . . ."

Celan did not wish his language to come between the reader and the Holocaust. He would not permit it to come between the event and himself. Hence his later poems turned against the "beauty" of language and indeed against language itself. Yet *being* poems, they were also bound to language. Celan had come to a point where the poet needs a thinker.

On his part, and for reasons quite unrelated, Heidegger had reached the view that thinker and poet dwell in close proximity. Heidegger and Celan were acquainted and are said to have had friendly relations. Celan addressed a poem to Heidegger, and this contained the line "Hoping for the coming Word of a Thinker," with the urgent clause added, "coming immediately." But the word hoped for from Heidegger never came in Celan's lifetime. (The poet committed suicide soon thereafter.) The word never came.[49]

"Black milk of dawn we drink at dusk
we drink it at noon and at daybreak we drink it at night
we drink and we drink
we are digging a grave in the air there's room for us all
A man lives in the house he plays with the serpents he writes
He writes when it darkens to Germany your golden hair Margarete
he writes it and steps outside and the stars all aglisten he whistles for his
    hounds
he whistles for his Jews he has them dig a grave in the earth
he commands us to dance."
    (Paul Celan, *Speech-Grille and Selected Poems*, tr. Joachim Neugroschel
    [New York: Dutton, 1971], pp. 28 ff.)
    The *Kommandant* in this poem, of course, is Hoess, but also, as Demetz
remarks, "in his blend of aesthetic inclinations and cold brutality closely
resembles Reinhard Heydrich" (p. 80). Anyone attempting to read Hoess's
autobiography—or, for that matter, Heydrich's biography by his widow (Lina
Heydrich, *Leben Mit Einem Kriegsverbrecher* [Pfeffenhofen: W. Ludwig,
1978])—ought to have *Todesfuge* in mind; and anyone doing so will ask
whether, if the poem did not exist, one could read these biographies in any
kind of truthful perspective at all. Truth being "objective," one normally
wishes to look at an issue not only from one side but also from the other side.
With this excuse North American media have been known to try to stage
debates between Nazis and Jews, presumably with the former arguing why
Jews should be "removed" and the latter, why they shouldn't be. But is
looking at Hoess from the side of Hoess *any fragment* of truth? Or not rather
the absolute lie? On this question, see below section 9, C–E, in some respects
the climax and turning point of this work in its entirety.

Could it have come? Earlier we saw Heidegger's thought lapse, vis-à-vis the Holocaust, into unauthenticity, and suggested that this was by his own standards. Now we must wonder whether, given these standards, it can be otherwise and whether, for an historically-situated thinker, other or deeper standards are available. On Heidegger's later *Denkweg*, thought achieves the freedom it requires only by adopting, toward its age of technology, a stance of "composure" that "lets things be." But if Auschwitz permits *no* composure—thought *cannot* let it be—how can thought be at all? Must it not either perish or else, for the sake of survival, flee back into the age of technology and deny Auschwitz? Again, in the earlier *Being and Time* philosophical thought, though situated in *Dasein*, has the necessary transcending power because *Dasein* itself has a transcending power, i.e., its being-toward-death. But, as we have already seen, "with the administrative murder of millions" at Auschwitz "the individual was robbed of the last and poorest that until then still remained his own," i.e., dying his own death, so that it was "no longer the individual that died but rather the specimen." Must not, then, thought either be robbed of its transcending power or else deny that death at Auschwitz "affects the dying also of those who escaped the procedure?" In an earlier exploration we concluded that thought cannot overcome the Holocaust, that where the Holocaust is overcoming thought is not, and that where overcoming thought is the Holocaust cannot be—a conclusion forcing us to assent to a way of philosophical thought that, immersed in history, is fully exposed to it. Now that our thought *is* exposed, and exposed to *that* history, must we not conclude that where the Holocaust is, *no* thought can be, and that where there is thought it is in flight from the event? Is, for thought vis-à-vis Auschwitz—philosophical, theological, other—unauthenticity the price of survival? Or, as Theodor Adorno put it, in a remark less famous than that about poetry but more ominous still, must it be and remain the case that, when confronted with the "real hell" of Auschwitz, "the metaphysical capacity is paralyzed"?[50]

8. The Spectrum of Resistance during the Holocaust:* An Essay in Description and Definition

A

The Holocaust may paralyze thought, even *after* the event. Astoundingly, it did not *wholly* succeed in paralyzing the existence singled out by it—the victims—during the event itself, i.e., while the Holocaust world held undisputed sway. This fact is astounding in itself. It will also be of pivotal importance for the whole present inquiry. A recurring and central theme in our inquiry has in any case been a certain dialectic of life and thought—a theme central in all post-Hegelian thought. On our part, we have not been able to find a way of settling the relation once and for all between the two. (At times thought, like Hegel's owl of Minerva, has seemed merely to comprehend life; at other times, like the Marxian cock, it has announced and helped produce a new day; at other times still, it seemed somehow to partake of both functions.) Now, however, we come upon a *novum* in that relation. The paralysis of the metaphysical capacity is a *novum* in history. So is the Holocaust, the event that produces the paralysis. *But the pivotal fact for us will be this, that a novum too is to be found in the resistance offered by the most radically singled-out victims.*

"Resistance during the Holocaust" is, of course, a much discussed subject. But the *novum* that is in that resistance cannot begin to come to light except for a prior self-immersion in what was being resisted. This has aptly been called a "logic of destruction." *The Nazi logic was irresistible, yet was being resisted:* this is the enormous fact that must be grasped. And thought, if it grasps but a single instance of such resistance, and of but the most prosaic sort, has no choice but to be radically, permanently astonished. Its surprise, like the surprise of the faithful at a redeeming Word, can never grow old.

*This section had its first origins in several public discussions between Yehuda Bauer and Raul Hilberg in which I had the good fortune of being the third participant.

It would be foolish to suggest that the resistance of the victims had a role in the destruction of the Third Reich. (Even the gas chambers destroyed in the Treblinka revolt were quickly rebuilt.) This vast task could be accomplished only by the Allied armed forces; and even the resistance movements in occupied Europe—occupied, but not behind ghetto walls or barbed wire—could contribute only negligibly to victory. The exploits of these armed forces belong in the pages of political and military history but also—since the Third Reich aimed at nothing less than world conquest, at the Concentration-Camp-As-New-Order—in the pages of resistance. As such, these exploits are world-historical, and place all future generations in the debt of all the Allied forces.

The Allied forces destroyed the Third Reich, and with it ipso facto the Holocaust world. However, they destroyed the first essentially, and the second only accidentally. In contrast, the resistance of the victims was to the Holocaust world essentially, even if it could be to the Nazi Reich even at best only insignificantly. The two forms of resistance are, as it were, at opposite ends of a spectrum.

It will be our task to move from one end of this spectrum to the other. (The one extreme is well documented, and is securely part of the historical consciousness; the other is known to few, grasped by fewer and not yet part of the historical consciousness. Moreover, it is difficult to document, for the murderers destroyed most of the evidence.) And as we move from one end of the spectrum to the other, we shall at the same time have to move from the outside of the Third Reich to what has already been described as its inner essence. This latter move—from the Reich to the Holocaust world—has already been made once in the present exploration. But our renewed move, rather than a redundancy, is an advance in thought. Previously we considered the rulers, administrators, and operators of the Holocaust world. Now we shall consider the victims—their anguish, their suffering and, when it was possible and actual, their resistance.

On occasion the two extremes of the spectrum of resistance were to meet, and when this happened the meeting changed the very lives of those who experienced it. Language cannot describe the mixture of ecstasy, relief, despair, joy of the survivors when they beheld the redeeming figures of their liberators. (Except that many, "the divine spark dead within them," no longer noticed—no longer could notice.) Nor can it describe the mixture of horror, disgust, hate, pity, love felt by even the most battle-hardened Allied soldiers when they came to Auschwitz and Buchenwald. Generals Eisenhower and Patton visited the concentration camp of Ohrdruf. An eyewitness describes the visit:

Even before reaching the entrance, the smell of death and corruption was almost overpowering. An officer from XX Corps, still pale and shaken, received us. "They tried to eliminate the evidence before we arrived," he said, "but as you see, they were not very successful."

Lying individually and in piles throughout the area, the bodies of recently murdered inmates, in most cases shot at close range through the base of the skull. An ex-guard acted as guide. We were spared nothing. The building piled to the roof with emaciated naked bodies. The gallows—contrived to effect death as slowly and painfully as possible. The whipping racks, the butcher's block for the cleaving of jaws and smashing out of gold teeth. The half-filled and still smoking ovens in the crematories.

The officers present all are men who have seen much of life in the raw, yet never on any human faces have I witnessed such horror and disgust. At one point General Patton [the very symbol of the tough soldier; "old blood and guts," they called him (E.L.F.)] frankly disappeared behind the corner of a building and was violently sick to his stomach.

As we stood by the entrance waiting for our transportation to draw up, one of our enlisted men accidentally bumped into the Nazi ex-guard, and from sheer nerves began to giggle. General Eisenhower fixed him with a cold eye and when he spoke, each word was like the drop of an icicle.

"Still having trouble hating them?" he said. Before leaving, General Eisenhower addressed the others.

"I want every American unit not actually in the front lines to see this place," he said. "We are told that the American soldier does not know what he is fighting for. Now, at least, he will know what he is fighting *against*."[51]

This is one thing that those at the other extreme of the spectrum of resistance, however filled with disbelief at the start, had known for endless days, months and—in the case of those either very perspicacious or very lucky—for years.

Up to a point, the existence of a spectrum of resistance is recognized in a noted historian's definition of resistance as "maintenance of self-respect and . . . [the refusal to] yield to the blandishments of collaboration."[52] This definition recognizes the blandishments—that the New Order was an unheard-of universe of intimidation, seduction, and psychological warfare so that to resist was heroic and extraordinary, and to yield was easy and even "natural." Recognized too is that while the assault was new, quite old could be the resources required for resistance: old-fashioned "self-respect" either right-wing-patriotic, or left-wing-socialist, was quite enough. This definition of resistance, then, moves with admirable clarity from one end of the spectrum of resistance—the valor of the Allied soldiers—toward the other. However, it does not encompass the other extreme. It does not even bring it into view. Thus its scope is parochial, and its value limited.

For this insight we need only turn from the French (or Polish or Czech) to the German resistance—or what little of it there was. The German resistance was faced not with "blandishments" to be "resisted," but rather with orders to be evaded, subverted, or openly defied. Moreover, whereas the French or Polish or Czech resistance could rely on old-fashioned self-respect there was need, in the German case, for a prior discovery of the self to be respected. Precisely what, especially in a time of war, was "true patriotism"? (Martin Niemoeller, though an open foe of the Nazi regime almost from the start, offered his services as submarine commander when war broke out—from Sachsenhausen. Dietrich Bonhoeffer could not bring himself to pray for the defeat of Nazi Germany until he recognized that the throne of Caesar was occupied by the Antichrist).* What, vis-à-vis the claims of "national socialism," was *true* socialism?

---

*The allusion is to Dietrich Bonhoeffer, *True Patriotism*, ed. Edwin H. Robertson (London: Collins, 1973). The title of this collection of letters, lectures, and notes between 1939 and 1945 is the editor's. It is well chosen since by 1939 Bonhoeffer no longer had any doubt as to what, for him, true patriotism was. In the United States at the time, he decided in June of that year that he must return to Germany, and wrote to Reinhold Niebuhr as follows: "I have made a mistake in coming to America. I must live through this difficult period of our

(The Social Democratic leadership, while holding out bravely in 1933 by the standards of the time, was soon undermined by its own commitment to legality—and Hitler's "solution" of the unemployment problem.) Clearly, for an understanding even of the German resistance—a task beyond our present scope†—the above definition of resistance is inadequate.

The task is beyond our scope only because of the necessity to move, in as direct and goal-directed a manner as possible, to the opposite end of the spectrum of resistance—offered to the Holocaust world essentially, even if it contributed to the destruction of the Third Reich only negligibly. This was resistance *in extremis* to an assault with an extremity of its own. The assault itself was on three kinds of "criminal." There were those whose crime was a *doing*—political opponents, common criminals, Jehovah's Witnesses, some clergymen, selected homosexuals. And there were those whose crime was a *being*. These latter again were subdivided into those, mostly Slavs, whose crime was that there were too many of them, and those whose crime was that they were at all. Slavs were decimated so as to create *Lebensraum* for Germans. With the possible exception of the Gypsies, in the case of Jews alone existence itself was a crime unpardonable, and punishable by degradation, torture, and death. In the following, all types of victims of the Nazi assault must be constantly kept in mind. However, it is the Jewish "criminals"-by-birth that are our essential subject.

We cannot attempt a description, classification, or even bare summary of the countless ways in which individuals, groups, whole communities attempted to resist the Nazi system of assault as, step by step, it moved toward the near-total annihi-

---

national history with the Christian people of Germany. I will have no right to participate in the reconstruction of Christian life in Germany after the war if I do not share the trials of this time with my people. . . . *Christians in Germany will face the terrible alternative of either willing the defeat of their nation in order that Christian civilization may survive, or willing the victory of their nation and thereby destroying our civilization. I know which of these alternatives I must choose; but I cannot make that choice in security.* " (Cited in Eberhard Bethge, *Dietrich Bonhoeffer* (New York: Harper and Row, 1970), p. 559; italics added.) On Bonhoeffer, see further below, note 110 and p. 293n.
† See, however, below, section 12.

lation of European Jewry. This vast task lies within the province of the historian. Our philosophical task is merely a *definition* of resistance, in these extreme, nay, unique circumstances. To call this task "mere," however, is by no means to say that it is negligible. Resistance to the Holocaust world—this latter a *novum* in history—is a *novum* as well. We have already made this assertion. Our definition must consider this *novum* and describe its essence. One must add, however, that any *concept* or *definition* of resistance we might arrive at would be an empty conceit unless it were both illustrated and validated by acts of resistance that *actually occurred.*

B

Resistance *in extremis* cannot be considered without a prior consideration of the assault in its own extremity—the Nazi "logic of destruction." We have already repeatedly used this phrase, coined by Jean Améry. Now it is necessary to explore the reality. And this is done best by considering how the extraordinary emerged from the ordinary—how the normal could give birth to an evil without precedent.

It is not necessary to assume that the Nazi logic of destruction, like Athene from the head of Zeus, leapt fully-armed from some Nazi bureaucratic mind. (Indeed, this assumption is farfetched.) It is more reasonable to assume a progress in which design and chance gradually—from the Nazi point of view, by good fortune or a stroke of genius—reached a sort of synthesis. We have elsewhere described the Sachsenhausen of 1938 (midway in the process) as "groundwork for Auschwitz,"[53] and will here briefly return to one aspect of this theme. Labor at Sachsenhausen had three components. One was meaningful work—tiles and uniforms for the Reich. The second was meaningless work—carrying sand from spot A to spot B one day, back the next day from spot B to spot A, always on the double. Both these aspects had an obvious purpose—the one, needed products, the other, torture of the prisoners—and were, so to speak, innocuous: they were open and above board. Each had many precedents—the one in economic history, the other in the history of torture—and left guards and prisoners in no doubt as to their role. All this was untrue of the third aspect of labor in Sachsenhausen: yet it was this that was the sole original aspect and also the most important. This was *meaningless labor endowed with a fictitious meaning.* Thus the daily march to and from the tile factory (a) had to be orderly, (b) was so organized as to produce inevitable chaos, and (c) was also so arranged that in the midst of chaos the fiction of order was maintained. The procedure was simple. Yet the principle was new and, in its implications, enormous and all-shattering. The two obvious purposes—the production of tiles and uniforms, and the torture of the prisoners—were synthesized into a whole, indeed, a world. And in this synthesis a new, eerie reality was given for all occupants of this world—on the one hand, the Kommandant and his henchmen, on the other, the victims—to an old, time-honored, once-decent Prussian principle. The principle was: *Ordnung muss sein.* One considers the synthesis of the old and the new principles and already seems to visualize human beings marched to gas chambers by the sound of military music, greeted by the legend *Arbeit Macht Frei.*

Such was the labor aspect of the Nazi logic of destruction, while it was still taking shape. The complete shape of that logic was well described by Jean Améry as follows:

In relation to the prisoner the SS was applying a logic of destruction that operated just as consistently as the logic of the preservation of life operated in the outside world. You always had to be cleanly shaven, but it was strictly forbidden to possess a razor or scissors, and you went to the barber only once every two weeks. On threat of punishment no button could be missing on the striped inmate suit, but if you lost one at work, which was inevitable, there was practically no chance of replacing it. You had to be strong, but were systematically weakened. Upon entrance into the camp everything was taken from you, but then you were derided by the robbers because you owned nothing. . . . The intellectual revolted [against this logic] in the impotence of mere thought. In the beginning he subscribed to the rebellious wisdom of folly that that which ought not to be cannot be. However, this was only in the beginning. The rejection of the SS logic, the rebellious murmuring of incantations such as "but this is not possible" did not last long.[54]

That this was quite literally a logic of *destruction*—not one of mere petty chicanery—is corroborated by Filip Müller, "the only man who saw the Jewish people die and lived to tell what he saw."[55] Müller writes:

Among the many slogans adorning the walls of our block [in Auschwitz] there was one which . . . warned us that "one louse may be your death." This was no exaggeration either, for a louse might infect its host with typhus, a disease which in Auschwitz spelled certain death. Alternatively, any louse discovered during a shirt check might have grave consequences in question. The reason for this could be found in the strange logic of what was known as Auschwitz justice. It argued that any prisoner on whom a louse was found after a delousing order had been issued, had obviously failed or, worse still, refused to obey orders and must therefore be severely punished. To be lousy in Auschwitz was a serious crime and liable to cost a man his life. That water came out of the taps only on special occasions or that we prisoners had neither soap nor towel was something in which nobody was interested.[56]

The last sentence in this passage should not be taken too literally. Some people—not necessarily everyone—were very much interested in the absence of soap and towels, and in the scarcity of water, and in the fictitious concern for the health of prisoners soon to be murdered.

But does even "destruction" exhaust this "logic"? The Gulag has rightly been called a "destructive labor camp."* The SS logic of destruction aimed at their victims' *self*-destruction as well. This found no clearer or more systematic expression than what is called—this too rightly—"excremental assault."[57] Again we ask how the system originated; and again we hazard the guess that in the origins—say, some time in 1933 or 1934— chance and design were intermingled. On the one hand, the prisoners must keep clean, which is to say that they must relieve themselves at places set aside for the purpose. But on the other hand, they cannot just wander off from work or roll call at any time of their own choosing. Both rules are innocuous in the sense defined above, and could be supported by the old Prussian principle already cited—that *Ordnung muss sein*. All innocuousness vanished, however, when sometime, somewhere, some bright architect of torture discovered—from the Nazi

*By Aleksandr I. Solzhenitsyn.

point of view, by good fortune or a stroke of genius—that while the two rules are not *intrinsically* in conflict, they can be *made to be so* quite easily, for the simple reason that "death . . . [is] planted in a need which . . . [cannot], like other needs, be repressed or delayed or passively endured, [for] the needs of the bowels are absolute."[58] A survivor writes:

Imagine what it would be like to be forbidden to go to the toilet; imagine also that you were suffering from an increasingly severe dysentery, caused and aggravated by a diet of cabbage soup as well as by the constant cold. Naturally, you would try to go anyway. Sometimes you might succeed. But your absences would be noticed and you would be beaten, knocked down and trampled on. By now, you would know what the risks were, but urgency would oblige you to repeat the attempt, cost what it may. . . . I soon learned to deal with the dysentery by tying strings around the lower end of my drawers.[59]

Clearly, excremental assault was *designed* to produce in the victim a "self-disgust" to the point of wanting death or even committing suicide. And this—nothing less—was the essential goal. The Nazi logic of destruction was aimed, ultimately, at the victims's *self*-destruction.

One must ask why the Nazi logic took this further, unsurpassable step. The question must be pondered carefully. But no matter how hard one ponders it, any answer can only come to this: if Bolshevism can seek nothing higher from the "class"-enemy than a conversion, accompanied by confession to never-committed crimes, then Nazism can seek nothing higher from the "non-Aryan" "race"-enemy than self-destruction, preceded by self-transformation into the loathsome creature which, according to Nazi doctrine, he has been since birth. This answer may seem wrong, for the Nazi logic of destruction destroyed millions who were by no means loathsome since birth, among them not only political enemies but also members of "inferior races." (Women of Slavic origin *could* be chosen for the breeding policies of the master race.) Yet no other answer is intelligible. We are therefore forced to view "Aryans" subjected, say, to excremental assault, as being as it were, honorary

Jews, and we do so in full knowledge of the fact that "a conquered Europe passed before the *Kommandant* at the [Auschwitz] gate, on their way to and from work: Polish, French, Russian, Yugoslav, Dutch, Belgian, Greek."*

That the Nazi logic of destruction aimed at Jewish self-destruction may be learned from no less an authority than the Führer himself. Hitler once remarked that the only decent Jew he ever heard of was the Viennese writer Otto Weininger who, desperately wanting but unable to be an "Aryan," committed suicide at the age of twenty-three in a fit of self-loathing. Much the same idea, transposed into Nazi humor, was expressed by Josef Goebbels when the *Anschluss* produced a rash of Jewish suicides in Vienna.

There is talk of mass Jewish suicide in Vienna. It is not true. The number of suicides remains the same. The difference is that whereas Germans committed suicide before, it is now Jews. We cannot provide every Viennese Jew with a special policeman to protect him from committing suicide.[60]

From the Nazi point of view, the ideal "solution" of the "Jewish problem" was wholesale Jewish suicide, but only if preceded and motivated by Jewish self-loathing, or wholesale Jewish self-loathing, but only if it was extreme enough to lead to Jewish suicide. This ideal, to be sure, was not universally shared—not, for example, by those "SD intellectuals" who "wanted to be regarded as 'decent'" and merely wished to "solve the so-called Jewish problem in a cold, rational man-

---

*Lewinska, p. 71. In an essay dated July 1979, unpublished but widely circulated, John Murray Cuddihy asks why such as myself consider the Holocaust unique, proceeds to state the "obvious first answer" that it "*was* unique," but manages to ignore this answer in the whole rest of his essay, in favor of a largely irrelevant mixture of liberal-Christian apologetics and sociological ruminations. Had he stayed with his own "first answer," he would have had to notice that, with the sole possible exception of Gypsies, only Jews were condemned by Nazi doctrine to "removal"(*Entfernung*) *solely because they were.* And he might also then have understood that my previous description (*Jewish Return*, p. 93) of non-Jewish "innocent victims" as "quasi-Jews," reflects not a placing of them into some lesser "residual category" but rather the fact that they too—as if they were Jews—were murdered simply because they *were.*

ner."* However, its acceptance was wide enough to set the tone for the world of Auschwitz and to dominate its logic.

This is not to deny that even in the highest SS circles there was room for some strange, not to say weird, exceptions. Rumor had it at the time that none other than Reinhard Heydrich had a "non-Aryan" ancestor. Refutations were produced, yet the rumor persisted. (It is believed by some to this day.)[61] After Heydrich's assassination by Czech patriots, Himmler delivered himself of the following:

He had overcome the Jew in himself by purely intellectual means and had swung over to the other side. He was convinced that the Jewish elements in his blood were damnable; he hated the blood which played him so false. The *Führer* could really have picked no better man than Heydrich for the campaign against the Jews. For them he was without mercy or pity.

For the rest it will interest you to know that Heydrich was a very good violinist. He once played a serenade in my honor; it was really excellent—a pity he did not do more in this field.[62]

The opportunity to "overcome the Jew in himself" was given to the chief architect of the Final Solution. It was not given to his victims.

Hitler's ideal "solution" of the "Jewish problem" was hampered less by insufficient zeal on the part of his operators than by recalcitrance on the part of his Jewish victims. Jews sick with self-hatred rarely reached the point of suicide. Jews committing suicide did so far less frequently out of self-loathing than out of despair or self-respect.† Most serious of all, so long

---

*See Heinz Höhne, *The Order of the Death's Head* (London: Pan, 1969), pp. 301 ff. I have already criticized Höhne for failing to ask whether the "cold, rational manner" in which the "problem" was "solved" at Auschwitz does not make the "decent" "SD intellectuals" more deadly than the Streicher-type "fanatics" (see *Jewish Return*, pp. 69 ff.). In any case, as is recognized by historians more reflective than Höhne, without the cooperation of the "decent" ones the aim wanted by the "fanatics" would have been unattainable.

†An instance in which despair and self-respect were combined is reported from Mauthausen. Eugen Kogon writes: "The second day after their arrival the Jews were shunted into the quarry. They were not allowed to use the steps to the bottom of the pit: they had to slide down the loose stones at the side and . . . many died or were severely injured. The survivors then had to shoulder hods, and two prisoners were compelled to load each Jew with an

as they were still able to choose at all, they chose life much rather than death, and loathed (or despised) their persecutors rather than themselves. From the Nazi point of view, this was one obstacle to the ideal goal. Still more serious was another: Jewish babies, like all babies, are incapable of either self-loathing or suicide. In their case, the ideal Nazi "solution" of the "Jewish problem" was impossible. There were not many adult Weiningers. Baby Weiningers do not exist.

If Jews would not commit suicide in self-loathing, then driving them into death was, from the Nazi point of view, the next best thing. Perhaps it was even the best thing. For, as Jean Améry has written, "There was a Germany that drove Jews and political opponents into death, since it believed itself capable of self-realization only in this manner.[63] (Would not widespread Jewish suicide frustrate this form of self-realization?) These are two ways of looking at the matter. It is hard to say which is more adequate.

In any case, one characteristic action of the Holocaust world was the most painful possible murder of Jewish babies, conducted, whenever possible, in the hearing or sight of their mothers. The reader will remember—how could he forget—the testimony of a Polish guard at the Nuremberg trials.* We

---

excessively heavy rock. The Jews then had to run up the steps. In some instances the rocks immediately rolled downhill, crushing the feet of those behind. Many of the Jews were driven to despair the very first day and committed suicide by jumping into the pit. On the third day the S.S. opened the so-called 'Death Gate' and with a fearful barrage of blows drove the Jews across the guard line, the guards on the watchtowers shooting them down in heaps with their machine-guns. The next day the Jews no longer jumped into the pit individually. They joined hands and one man would pull nine or twelve of his comrades over the lip into a gruesome death." *The Theory and Practice of Hell* (New York: Berkeley, 1964, p. 180).

This passage recalls nothing so much as the opening words of a prayer probably composed during the Crusade of 1096 for the Jewish victims of Mayence and Worms: "May the Merciful Father who dwells on high in His infinite mercy remember those saintly, upright and blameless souls . . . who gave their lives for the sanctification of the divine Name. They were lovely and amiable in their life, and were not parted in their death. . . ."

*See above, p. 131. The Polish guard's testimony should now be quoted more fully, as follows:

"*Witness:* Women carrying children were always sent with them to the crematorium. The children were then torn from their parents outside the

have already cast doubt on the witness's opinion that the children were thrown into the flames alive for reasons of economy alone. That this hypothesis is false is proved by the testimony of a Ravensbrück survivor. She reports:

In 1942 the medical service of the Revier were required to perform abortions on all pregnant women. If a child happened to born alive, it would be smothered or drowned in a bucket *in front of the mother.* Given a newborn child's natural resistance to drowning, *a baby's agony might last for twenty or thirty minutes.*[64]

The italics are ours. They are not by the eye-witness author. Perhaps a survivor of Auschwitz or Ravensbrück no longer knows what, and what not, to italicize.

Such, in the case of Jewish babies and their mothers, was the Nazi "solution" of the "Jewish problem" that approximated most closely the ideal or even expressed it perfectly. With adults there was greater variety, as well as much room for ingenuity. To follow one line of thought, if one could not make Jews destroy themselves one could, perhaps, make them destroy each other. By making some Jews rule over others one could achieve this aim equally by using the base and the noble. Base Jewish rulers would destroy the Jews ruled by them, so as to save themselves. Noble Jews would sacrifice some Jews they ruled so as to save others. Neither type of Jewish ruler, of course, would himself be spared. The base would not long survive their victims. The noble, in addition, would not wish to survive them, for—so they thought—their own souls were already destroyed. Was there ever a nobler

---

crematorium and sent to the gas chambers separately. When the extermination of the Jews in the gas chambers was at its height, orders were issued that the children were to be thrown into the crematorium furnaces, or into the pit near the crematorium, without being gassed first.

"Smirnov (Russian prosecutor): How am I to understand this? Did they throw them into the fire alive, or did they kill them first?

"Witness: They threw them in alive.

"Smirnov: Why did they do this?

"Witness: It is very difficult to say. We don't know whether they wanted to economize on gas, or if it was because there was not enough room in the gas chambers."

and more tragic Jewish ruler than Adam Czerniakow, who "stood at the helm" of the Warsaw Ghetto and "died with his people"?*

This was an indirect method of making Jews—collectively if not individually—destroy themselves, and it called for much ingenuity. But there were also direct methods, some of which required no ingenuity at all, and of these—since all men must defecate—excremental assault was probably the most universally effective. (Other worlds have dreamt of making men equal in possessions, rights, dignity, holiness: the Auschwitz world sought to reduce its victims to the equality of the bowels.) The action most revelatory of the Gulag world is assault-by-psychiatry on dissidents, on the grounds that critics of the already-existing, perfect society can only be insane. The action most revelatory of the Holocaust world was excremental assault on Jews—and, as we have seen, all honorary Jews sucked into the system—on the grounds that, before dying, they must be *made* into the self-loathing vermin that, according to Nazi thought, they *are*. Hence Treblinka Kommandant Franz Stangl lied when he said that the purpose of all the humiliation and cruelty was to make killing easier on the nerves of the operators. ("It is easier to kill a dog than a man, easier still to kill a rat or frog, and no problem at all to kill insects.")† At best he spoke a half-truth. Is shooting a person—quickly, cleanly—harder on the nerves than conducting the slow, methodical process by which a person is reduced to a dog, a rat, an insect—or, if to none of these, to a

*Raul Hilberg sent to this family a copy of The Warsaw Diary of Adam Czerniakow, ed. Raul Hilberg, Stanislaw Staron, Josef Kermisz (New York: Stein and Day, 1979). This he inscribed as follows: "For Emil and Rose Fackenheim—this incomparable log from one who stood at the helm and died with his people."

†A remark of Hannah Arendt's quoted by Des Pres, The Survivor, p. 61. Gitta Sereny asked Stangl: "If they were going to kill them anyway, what was the point of all the humiliation, why the cruelty?" Stangl replied: "To condition those who actually had to carry out the policies; to make it possible for them to do what they did." Sereny comments: "And this, I believe, was true" (Gitta Sereny, Into That Darkness [London: Andre Deutsch, 1974], p. 101). Despite certain weaknesses that may be guessed from the last-cited comment, Sereny's interviews of Stangl are of the greatest importance. Like Hoess's autobiography, they must be read to be believed. And even then they remain past belief.

human being who is already dead while he is still alive? Beyond doubt this living death was not a means to death only, but also an end in itself. The most characteristic success of the Gulag world is one new man—the former dissident who voluntarily undergoes psychiatric treatment on the grounds that his erstwhile dissent was ipso facto insanity. The most characteristic success of the Holocaust world—other than the screams and gasps of the children and the agony of their mothers—is another new man: the *Muselmann* who is already dead while still alive. (The reader will remember—how could he forget?—the above-cited testimony by a survivor about the living dead.)* And since the screams and gasps of Jewish children are no different from those of other children, we must conclude that the *Muselmann*—"one hesitates to call him living, and hesitates to call his death death"—is the most notable, if indeed not the sole, truly original contribution of the Third Reich to civilization. He is the true *novum* of the New Order.†

C

Such, in the extremity that discloses its inner truth,‡ was the Nazi assault on the Jewish people. As we have insisted from the start, it was necessary to dwell on it, and do so at length and without mercy, if the whole question of Jewish resistance was to be seen in its true perspective. Now that we *have* dwelled on the Nazi assault, most of the many discussions of

*See above, p. 99; and below, p. 287.
†This concludes my second, and more difficult, attempt to write in the language of "restrained outrage" (see above, ch. I, section 8, and p. 188).
‡This formulation—an allusion to Heidegger's 1935 statement about the "inner truth and greatness" of the national socialist "movement" (see above, sections 5 and 6A1) is, I fear, not devoid of malice. The malice, however, is fully deserved. When Heidegger was preparing the 1935 lectures for publication in 1953, an assisting friend suggested what amounted to changes in the text. To his credit Heidegger refused to falsify the record but went on to say: "If the reader of today does not want to understand what, within the lecture in its totality, was said with these words, then I cannot help him" (reported by Hartmut Buchner, "Fragmentarisches," in *Erinnerung,* p. 49). Nearly twenty years later Heidegger was still unprepared to consider that his endorsement of Nazism had not been some small, philosophically inconsequential, political error but rather an indication of philosophical catastrophe.

Jewish resistance appear as a mixture of folly and obscenity. The unsuspecting Jews in small towns and villages gunned down by motorized murder squads in a blitzkrieg, first in Poland, subsequently in Russia; the men, women, children herded into cattle cars with floors covered with lime so as to maximize the deaths even prior to arrival; the arrivals in a Treblinka decorated with false storefronts, false café-fronts, false barbershop-fronts, all designed to conceal the gas chambers behind them: in these and countless other cases the philosophizing person, like other flesh-and-blood persons, can think no thoughts and ask no questions but can only be appalled by the criminals and filled with grief for the victims. Nor can this philosophizing person, without gratuitous, posthumous insult to all the *Muselmänner*, ask about even one why he let himself be reduced to a state of death while still alive. And, rather than be quick to raise the question of resistance, one may well ask how one can raise it at all.

Let us begin with Jewish mothers. Nazi thought took a serious view of Jewish pregnancies. Pregnant women at Auschwitz were sent to the crematorium on arrival or, if they managed to conceal their condition then and until birth, immediately on discovery and together with their babies. Orthodox rabbis, considering the situation, permitted abortions despite the stern Halakhic opposition to the practice. Then why did even a single pregnant Jewish woman refuse an abortion, give birth to her baby, and show the energy and ingenuity to conceal it for a day, a week, a month, or even by good fortune until all was over? After the destruction of Jerusalem in 70 C.E., the rabbis had wondered whether there should be any further Jewish children. (In the end they decided in favor of it.) Then why did these Jewish women not decide *against* it for ever after? *Decide against it:* What hope was there of saving them from the buckets or the flames? *Forever after:* a Holocaust, having happened once, would be possible for all future time. To be sure, it is natural for women to want to give birth, to love their children even before they are born. In the Holocaust world, however, was this not unnatural by all ordinary standards? Did natural love for the unborn not dictate their abortion? Or can we ascribe to the will what is not attributable to nature? But no will-power, within ordinary standards, is that strong. In his musings culminating in "composure," Heidegger came upon the limits of "will" and "nature," and the need to transcend that dichotomy. In a search of our own, and in a sphere undreamt of in Heidegger's or any other philosophy, we have now come upon limits to the concepts "will" and "nature" ourselves. In the mothers, we have touched an Ultimate.

We move on. One asks: Why did so many become *Muselmänner*? One ought to ask: How did even one *not* become a *Muselmann*? The logic of destruction was irresistible: then how was it, nevertheless, resisted? Some, made into each-for-himself-and-against-every-other, rediscovered—recreated— the truth that "the need to help [is] . . . as basic as the need for help." The demands of the bowels overcame them; yet some washed in water that made them no cleaner, or attempted to shave, to comb their hair. Why did they do it? How *could* they do it? Pelagia Lewinska writes:

At the outset the living places, the ditches, the mud, the piles of excrement behind the blocks, had appalled me with their horrible filth. . . . And then I saw the light! I saw that it was not a question of disorder or lack of organization but that, on the contrary, a very thoroughly considered conscious idea was in the back of the camp's existence. They had condemned us to die in our own filth, to drown in mud, in our own excrement. They wished to abase us, to destroy our human dignity, to efface every vestige of humanity, to return us to the level of wild animals, to fill us with horror and contempt toward ourselves and our fellows.

But from the instant that I grasped the motivating principle . . . it was as if I had been awakened from a dream. . . . I felt under orders to live. . . . And if I did die in Auschwitz, it would be as a human being, I would hold on to my dignity. I was not going to become the contemptible, disgusting brute my enemy wished me to be. . . . And a terrible struggle began which went on day and night.[65]

This is an historic statement. Above we saw unauthentic thought shrink from the Holocaust world. (Below we shall find that *any* thought can confront it only with great difficulty and within severe limits.) Now we have come, for the first time, upon an unimpeachable testimony to the effect that some—not learned or profound thinkers but ordinary men and women—*confronted and grasped this whole-of-horror even while they were in it and trapped by it, and that, without this confronting grasp, they could not have done what in fact they did.*

This is a monumental discovery. (For us in this book it will be pivotal.) We must therefore ask of Lewinska'a statement some crucial questions. She felt under orders to live. We ask: *Whose* orders? Why did she wish to obey? And—this above all—where did she get the strength? We answer the last question by discovering that it is unanswerable. Once again "will-power" and "natural desire" are both inadequate. Once again we have touched an Ultimate.

Pelagia Lewinska does not say who gave the orders. We must respect this silence. (Nietzsche once said that "one takes and does not ask who gives"; Buber, though far removed from Nietzsche, cites this statement with approval.)[66] But we must equally respect other witnesses, no less unimpeachable, for whom the Source of the orders is not in doubt. Once at Buchenwald a Ukrainian *kapo* offered to sell a pair of *tefillin* to a group of Hasidim. (There were two conflicting Nazi doctrines about the disposal of sacred Jewish objects. What may be called the idealistic doctrine dictated that they should be destroyed, on the grounds that, like Jews themselves, they defiled. What may be called the utilitarian doctrine dictated that they should be used. In the present case, the utilitarian doctrine prevailed, for the confiscated *tefillin* had been "placed into a pile with other leather objects for salvage," and the *kapo* had stolen a pair.) The Ukrainian's price—four rations of bread—created a moral problem for the Hasidim. To do without this much bread was to risk death; to sell the bread was therefore to risk committing the sin of suicide. What did they do? They sold the bread, bought the *tefillin* and then, to quote a survivor, "prayed with an ecstasy which it would be impossible ever to experience again in . . . [their] lives." Then what of their moral problem? Rabbi Zvi Hirsch Meisels writes:

We could not possibly explain or understand what was occurring and why. The only course was to become stronger in perfect faith through the mystic symbolic effect of the *tefillin*. This is why the *mitzvah* of *tefillin* was so beloved in Auschwitz, for it kept broken spirits from losing their complete faith even for a moment when they had no grasp or understanding of the reason for their plight.

The moral problem had solved itself, for the *tefillin*—"a much more valuable kind of merchandise" at Buchenwald than bread—were bread also: they strengthened the spirit, and hence the body as well. They were an "elixir of life."[67]

Unlike Pelagia Lewinska, the Buchenwald Hasidim identified the Source of the orders to live. But like her they leave us in doubt as to why, in these circumstances, they had any wish to obey. Unauthentic theological thought now, Jewish or Christian, may discover the divine purpose of Buchenwald, or at least claim that it had such a purpose. What made the prayers of these Hasidim great was not their ability to explain or understand what was happening, but precisely the insight that this was impossible; not a classification on their part of the Holocaust with other Jewish catastrophes, but the recognition of it as unclassifiable. Then why did they obey the *mitzvah* of *tefillin*? More important still, where did they get the strength? For a third time we find that the concepts of nature and will are inadequate and—one must add in this case, and especially in view of what Rabbi Meisels wrote—so is recourse to a mystic dimension. (Was there no Hasid, Kabbalist or other mystic among the living dead?) Once again we have touched an Ultimate.

We have now described three instances of Jewish "behavior in extremity." In due course we must consider whether we were justified in describing them as "ultimate."* For the present we must ask whether we were justified in classifying them as "resistance"—whether they were "resistance proper." This turns the mind to *armed* Jewish resistance, in the forests, the ghettoes, and even in the murder camps themselves. If viewed

*See below, section 9.

as simply part of the "European resistance," then of these three doubtless the first was most and the third least important: Jewish partisans, like others, were able to blow up trains and ammunition dumps; the Treblinka gas chambers, having been destroyed by the inmates, were quickly rebuilt. However, while with such a view one may perceive that the "role" of the "Jewish" in the "European resistance" was "honorable" and "in some respects even exemplary,"[68] one cannot perceive its essence. Rather than reach the end of the spectrum of resistance one remains somewhere in the middle. The astounding fact about the Treblinka revolt is not that the gas chambers were quickly rebuilt; it is that the inmates, who can have had no illusions on this score, nevertheless attempted to destroy them, and succeeded.

There are of course many similarities between Jewish and non-Jewish armed resistance. (A Jewish Molotov cocktail does not differ from a French, Czech, or Polish one, nor does it require a different kind of courage to throw it.) The differences, however, are more profound. We shall pass over the "Polish partisan bands" who, "imbued with an ineradicable antisemitism," "did not welcome Jews into their ranks."[69] We cannot pass over the vast gulf between would-be Jewish and non-Jewish resistance fighters, simply because of their situation. Jean-Paul Sartre describes the moral conflict of a young Frenchman who must choose between staying with his ailing mother—her other son is dead—and joining De Gaulle's Free French abroad.[70] Yitzhak Zuckerman describes the moral conflict of young Jews in Warsaw, Bialystock, and other ghettoes who had to choose between staying and fighting in the ghetto, and joining the partisans outside.[71] Sartre rightly refuses to pass a moral judgment on the young Frenchman, whatever his choice. The same applies to the young Jew in Warsaw or Bialystock. Still less can one make moral comparisons between resisting Frenchmen and resisting Jews. (Should Sartre's Frenchman pass himself off as a "non-Aryan" and expose himself to the Nazi logic of destruction—to prove, perhaps, that he could resist it? Should the trapped Warsaw Jew miraculously transport himself into Paris and make himself into an "Aryan" Frenchman, so as to be able to fight more effectively?) We cannot, then, judge between the Jewish and the non-Jewish dilemma; but we must identify the difference. Sartre's Frenchman could hope to help liberate his people; the Warsaw or Bialystock Jew could hope only to help save a small remnant. This was if the two left: what if they stayed? Sartre's Frenchman could hope to save and brighten his mother's life; his Jewish counterpart could hope only to share his mother's death—and that of his whole people. It is true, as Zuckerman reports, that the youth of the ghettoes did not see their choice in quite so grim a light; that instead they asked themselves whether they

had the right to abandon [their] ... parents, [their] ... children, [their] ... infirm, the centers of [their] ... creativity ... [leaving them] ... without any possibility of defending themselves, so that [they themselves could] ... get away to where the war [offered] ... better prospects, where life and victory [were] ... more assured.

Still, in their heart of hearts there were no illusions or self-deceptions.[72]

Then why was it that

it was the Zionist pioneering youth, they who had rejected the Diaspora, who had no faith in Jewish survival in a foreign land, who had left their homes to prepare themselves for a new life in Eretz Yisrael—that it was precisely these young people who upheld the case for struggle within the Ghettoes and clung to the Ghetto walls?

Zuckermann rightly finds this "remarkable" and replies as follows:

The Polish partisans are on Polish soil, while the Jewish partisans are outside the Ghetto. If we remove the best of our forces outside the walls, who will remain to fight within the Ghetto? Do we have the right to desert the Ghetto in its extremity, depriving it of its young people, of its fighting strength? The Jewish youth, bred and educated in the narrow streets, in the *yeshivot*, nurtured on the literature of our people, whose fate is bound up with the fate of the Jewish nation—is not the place of the Jewish youth in the Ghetto?[73]

Their people, already caught and helpless in the ghettoes, were about to be subjected to the Nazi logic of destruction in its extremity: just then these young fighters decided that they must share the Jewish fate. Why? Not—a perverse and even obscene suggestion—because of some subconscious masochistic wish to submit. On the contrary, because of an unprecedented and wholly conscious decision to resist. Why did the Warsaw Ghetto hold out longer than, a few years earlier, the whole Polish army? Why did it take place at all when, unlike other uprisings, it was not inspired by hope but began, and could begin, only when all hope had come to an end?* (They occasionally spoke of "Jewish honor"—but mass-suicide would have been less agonizing and painful and, in the circumstances, no less honorable; and they did have the precedent of Masada. But the Jews of Warsaw did not need to defend Jewish honor to a world that was spared the Jewish fate.)

By deciding to stay, the fighters in Warsaw, Bialystock, and all the other ghettoes had already chosen to share their people's fate. Now they chose, so far as was possible, to *defy* that fate. The Nazi logic of destruction was meant to drive the Jewish people into self-loathing and suicide. *The Warsaw Ghetto Uprising was a unique affirmation*—unique except only for similar, less known uprisings—*of Jewish self-respect.* (We have seen that the German resistance, such as it was, had to discover a true self to be respected. The Jewish resistance had to *recreate* Jewish selfhood and self-respect, and even while engaged in this struggle was ignored by the world and slandered by the Nazis as "banditry.")† What is more, since it was a defiance even of honorable suicide, *it was also, and at*

*One Molotov cocktail thrown by one Jew at one German would produce gruesome German reprisals. This moral objection to throwing it was removed once it was clear that, no matter what they did, all Jews in the Warsaw Ghetto were doomed.

†See *The Stroop Report*, tr. Sybil Milton (New York: Pantheon, 1979). In this report by the SS officer in charge of the Warsaw Ghetto *Grossaktion*, German soldiers are praised for their courage in fighting (with machine-guns and flamethrowers) against Jews (armed with a few pistols and Molotov cocktails). Even so their foes—who as Jews are "intrinsically cowardly"—are not respected now that they are formidable fighters. In the report, they are merely "bandits" to be "smoked out" (pp. 8 ff.).

the same time, during the long, terrible weeks that it lasted, a unique celebration of Jewish life, and thus of life itself. Once again the categories "willpower" and "natural desire" seem inadequate. Once again we have touched an Ultimate.

It emerges, therefore, that the armed Jewish resistance in the Holocaust world belongs less closely with other European resistance movements than with the prayers of the Hasidim, the solitary struggle of Pelagia Lewinska, and the mothers who gave birth to children. The Nazi logic of destruction was an assault on the Jewish people without precedent in history. Jewish resistance in all the above forms, all interrelated, was equally unprecedented. Here at last is the other extreme in the spectrum of resistance to the Holocaust world.

How shall we define that extreme? Up to a point, a definition was already hinted at by Rabbi Yitzhak Nissenbaum in the Warsaw Ghetto itself. He said:

This is a time for kiddush ha-hayyim, the sanctification of life, and not for kiddush ha-Shem, the holiness of martyrdom. Previously the Jew's enemy sought his soul and the Jew sanctified his body in martyrdom [i.e., he made a point of preserving what the enemy wished to take from him]; now the oppressor demands the Jew's body, and the Jew is obliged therefore to defend it, to preserve his life.[74]

Nissenbaum's exaltation of kiddush ha-hayyim became justly famous in the camps and ghettoes, and this despite the fact that his dictum was not wholly adequate. *This* oppressor attacked *both* body and soul with an ever-increasing savagery. Hence initially, (i.e., in all stages leading to, but not yet including, the Final Solution), kiddush ha-hayyim could be understood as excluding armed resistance (provoking as it did murderous reprisals) but including the smuggling of food and medicine for the body, and prayer, study, lectures, and concerts for the soul. (The victims, like the murderers, played Beethoven. But whereas for the murderers he meant relaxation after a hard day's work, for the victims he meant sanctification of life: the abyss between the two was absolute.) This was initially. In extremity—when the Nazi logic of destruction had become the Final Solution—kiddush ha-hayyim revealed it-

self as a *unique form of resistance no longer distinguishable
from life itself—whether the life meant survival for an hour, a
day, a week, or even by good fortune until after the evil Unwelt was destroyed.* For to all the resistance fighters inside
and outside Nazi-occupied Europe, resistance was a *doing.*
For Jews (and semi-, quarter-, or honorary Jews) caught by the
full force of the Nazi logic of destruction, resistance was a way
of *being.* The Warsaw Ghetto "secularist" fighters expressed
this way with revolvers and Molotov cocktails. The "religious," unarmed, unmilitary Hasidim with their *tefillin* expressed it with prayer, dancing, and song. The two ways were
no longer antagonistic or even wholly distinct. Here at last we
have reached the Ultimate that holds together and unites all
these forms of resisting, all these ways of being.

One may well ask whether these forms of resisting and being should not be viewed much rather as forms of madness.
(We have ourselves stressed that they are not "natural" and
that—if "the will" must have rational goals—that they are
also not in the sphere of the voluntary.) But then one considers that the *Unwelt* in which they occurred was a topsy-
turvy world, and concludes that, rather than madness, this
resistance, this existence was a case of sanity. It was a sanity
the like of which the world has never seen.

This sanity found an unsurpassable expression in an incident that occurred in an empty field outside Lublin, early in
the war. A certain German officer named Glowoznik, having
rounded up a group of Hasidim, ordered them to sing and
dance. (He had heard about Hasidic songs. Also, he shared
Goebbels's sense of humor.) The terrified victims began the
kind of song that the pious sing in the face of death—*lomir
zich iberbeten, Ovinu she-ba-Shomayim,* "Let us be reconciled, Our Father in Heaven!" But their voices quavered.
Glowoznik then shouted at them to sing louder, more heartily.
(Picture the shouting Nazis, the barking dogs, the insults, the
blows—and the frightened victims, most of them old, all of
them helpless.) In the midst of this pandemonium suddenly
"an anonymous voice broke through the turmoil with a ...
piercing cry: *Mir welen sei iberleben, Ovinu she-ba-Sho-*

mayim—'We shall outlive them, Our Father in Heaven.' " A moment of silence. Then the song took hold of the whole group in an instant, transporting it into a "stormy and feverish dance." Glowoznik, now enraged, screamed at the Hasidim to stop.[75] Doubtless—though the chronicler does not tell us—he succeeded in stopping them, in one way if not another. But he could not destroy a moment of truth. *In an Unwelt whose sole ultimate self-expression is a system of humiliation, torture, and murder, the maintenance by the victims of a shred of humanity is not merely the basis of resistance but already part of it. In such a world—this is the testimony of the mothers, the countless individuals who had a spokesman in Pelagia Lewinska, the fighters in the ghettoes and camps, and the Hasidim in Buchenwald and Lublin—life does not need to be sanctified: it is already holy.* Here is the definition of resistance, sought after for so long.

Many performed the *mitzvah* of *kiddush ha-hayyim* by enhancing, defending, or even just barely clinging to life. Some could sanctify life only by choosing death. Adam Czerniakow, the president of the Warsaw Ghetto *Judenrat*, had sacrificed some in order to save others. More and more, the awful suspicion dawned on him that none could be saved at all. At length he was asked to sign an expulsion order. The order included the children. Then he knew what he must do. A note left by him states that the SS wanted him to kill the children with his own hands. Then Adam Czerniakow took his life. When Chaim Kaplan heard of his suicide, he recorded these words in his Warsaw Ghetto diary: "There are those who earn immortality in a single hour. The President, Adam Czerniakow, earned his immortality in a single instant.[76]

9. Resistance as an Ontological Category: An Essay in Critical Analysis

The assertion that resistance to the Holocaust, as above defined (or redefined), discloses an ultimate dimension, is apt to be criticized—all the more so, of course, because after all we *have* redefined "resistance" in the process of moving from one end of its "spectrum" to the other. The critic is not likely to accept this "ultimate dimension" without analysis, and the analysis, whether philosophical, historical, or, most likely, psychological, is apt to be reductionist, with the result that the "ultimacy" disappears.

A

At first blush, a psychological critique of the reductionist sort does not seem unjustified. We all accept as fact that "behavior" is disoriented "in extremity," and that in order to understand it we must adopt a standpoint other than that of the disoriented person.* Surely this applies—applies especially—to the Holocaust. A normal extremity (such as the death of a father) disorients a person but does not rob him of a reorienting mother, brother, friend. The Holocaust, in contrast, was a *world* of extremity, a disorienting *universe*, as though designed (indeed, actually designed) to leave its victim with no reorienting—as it were, Archimedean—point outside it. Surely *this* victim is *totally* disoriented; and we must detach ourselves *wholly* from him and his world—as it were, adopt an Archimedean standpoint of our own—if we wish to understand behavior in this extremity! With the disoriented son or daughter we can seek at least a partial personal identification, for he or she has a reorienting mother, brother, friend. Can we identify with the disoriented victim of the Holocaust? If not, then, whereas the traumatized orphan remains at least partly a subject for the psychologist analyzing his behavior, the traumatized Holocaust victim is an object and nothing else.

---

*The expression "behavior in extremity" alludes to an essay of that title by Bruno Bettelheim ("Individual and Mass Behaviour in Extreme Situations," in *Surviving* [New York: Knopf, 1979], pp. 48 ff. In the following, the works considered are: Bruno Bettelheim, *The Informed Heart* (Glencoe: Free Press, 1960); Elie Cohen, *Human Behaviour in Concentration Camps* (New York: W. W. Norton, 1953); and S. M. Elkins, *Slavery* (Chicago: University of Chicago Press, 3rd ed., 1976). See also Terence des Pres's critique in *The Survivor*, ch. 6; Bettelheim's response in *Surviving* (pp. 274 ff.) and des Pres's rejoinder, "The Bettelheim Problem," *Social Research*, 46, no. 4 (1979), pp. 619 ff.

If this is the critic's stance, it is a foregone conclusion that all responses to the Holocaust assault which we have dignified above with the term "resistance" in fact reduce themselves to expressions of a trauma, of an escape mechanism; this may apply even to responses such as the Warsaw Ghetto uprising, which are not denied the title of resistance by anyone. In that case, the annual worldwide Jewish communal commemorations of the Uprising prove only this much, that the trauma of the Holocaust extends beyond its immediate victims. As for our above redefinition of "resistance" to the Holocaust, this is itself subject to psychological analysis, and becomes an ideological superstructure of a collective Jewish trauma.

What has just been summarized includes much popular, psychologically informed opinion. It also includes some professional-theoretical writing. However, in both cases, the popular and the professional, the question is whether it is not the critic, with his Archimedean-objective standpoint *outside* and *above* the Holocaust world, rather than the object of his criticism, that has lapsed into escapism. At the popular level, this may be suspected by the speed with which attention is diverted from the actions of the criminals to the reactions of the victims. Certainly all the loose talk about "sheep to slaughter" and "collaborationist" *Judenräte* stems, not only from not knowing about the Holocaust assault, but also not wanting to know: it is more comfortable to blame the victim.

More instructive than the popular is the professional case, for here the escapism has built for itself theoretical foundations. We read that the concentration camp, like the slave system in America, was a "kind of patriarchy" ("grotesque," to be sure), with the role of the fathers played by the storm troopers. We further read that just as the SS stereotyped their Jewish victims, so these latter stereotyped the SS, and in much the same terms; that, following "inner motive" rather than "outer pressure," they regarded them as "sadistic, uninhibited, unintelligent, of an inferior race, and addicted to sexual perversions." Further, the prisoners were "unable to plan for the future" because they had lapsed "into childlike devia-

tions from normal adult behavior."* All this, of course, is
arrant nonsense. (The prisoners treated the SS with respect
because of well-warranted caution; they stereotyped them to
the extent to which they *were* stereotypes, created in the image of Himmler's philosophy; and they failed to plan because
to do so—an unrealistic exercise under the circumstances—
would itself have been childish.) The nonsense reaches an
obscene height when Rudolph Hoess, the arch-murderer, is
categorized with the *Muselmänner*, his most characteristic
victims. True—the admission is made—Hoess was not a *Muselmann*, but—so the argument proceeds—only because he
was well fed and well clothed. The *Muselmann* and Hoess
alike had divested themselves of "self-respect" and "self-
love," and "given the environment total power over them."
And if in so doing Hoess had made at least one *decision*—total
loyalty to Hitler—this was equally true of the *Muselmann*, for
"so long as a prisoner fought in any way for survival, for some
self-assertion within and against the overpowering environment, he could not become a 'moslem.' "[77] In this manner
psychological theory is used to dispose of two terrible myster-
ies—*Kommandant* Hoess, the unprecedented criminal, and
the *Muselmann*, his unprecedented victim. However, the theory as here used—autonomy is good, childlike or heterono-
mous behavior is bad—does not explain the reality, but rather
ignores it or explains it away. Soon after liberation a young
psychiatrist arrived at Bergen Belsen.

After some days he came back and said that he did find one patient
who was in need of psychiatric treatment. The symptoms? Well, he
saw her combing her hair with a broken comb and looking into a
piece of broken mirror glass. When we asked him whether he tried to
give her a good comb and a good mirror and had she refused to take
them, he realized the tragedy of our situation and was genuinely
ashamed and left.[78]

*Elkins, *Slavery*, pp. 104, 112 ff.; Bettelheim, *Surviving*, pp. 221 ff., 168 ff.;
Cohen, pp. 177 ff. Elsewhere in his book Cohen states that the prisoners
treated the SS with respect only "because any show of disobligingness ...
might have the most disastrous results" (p. 153). Though relying heavily on
Cohen, Elkins does not cite passages such as these: they would not have
suited his absurd "concentration-camp-patriarchy" theory.

Perhaps the psychiatrist should not have left. But he was right in being ashamed.

In its professional-theoretical if not in its popular form, the escapism becomes systematic. This is the result of two interrelated moves of thought. The critic first focuses his attention away from the Holocaust assault on to the "behavior" of the victims, with the result that the uniqueness of the assault is flattened out into a generalized "extremity." (Thus the Holocaust becomes an easy subject of comparison with slavery and even the strains of the "mass age"; the differences become accidental.) Second, the critic rises in thought *above* both the unique assault and the unique victims and in so doing bestows on his own categories a universal validity that is not earned by crucial tests but rather presupposed from the start. (Bruno Bettelheim was *in* a concentration camp. In his psychological theorizing he is *above* it—as well as above his fellow victims.) Whereas the victim of the Holocaust assault is disoriented, the categories of his psychoanalyst are untouched. His escapism is a system.

To overcome this escapism, the psychological critic must undo the two moves of thought that are responsible. He must abandon his Archimedean standpoint outside and above it all and place himself *with* the resisting victims; and he must redirect his focus, away from their "behavior" torn out of context (resisting or not), onto *their* object, i.e., the Nazi assault in its unflattened-out uniqueness. To have done so is to be left with much scope for psychological criticism, as, for example, upon learning that "a strange wave of optimism swept the [Warsaw] Ghetto at the time of the Uprising." But this now has sober limits at points where *common sense and common decency both dictate that the victim's behavior should be understood exactly as he understood it himself*—as, for example, upon learning that "the leaders and rank and file fighters did not share [the] illusion of the Ghetto."[79] When asking why *such as these* did it, we cannot, dare not go beyond their own testimony.

Then *was* Pelagia Lewinska under orders to live? She heard these orders not because she misunderstood Auschwitz, but because she understood it. Were the prayers of the Buchen-

wald Hasidim *true* prayers? They prayed as they did not because they had found a pious explanation of the unique catastrophe, but because they had rejected them all. Was the dance
of the Lublin Hasidim a *genuine* dance? Inspired by a cry—
mir welen sei iberleben—it was, exactly like the Warsaw
Ghetto uprising in all its fully-recognized hopelessness, a
commitment, despite and because of the Holocaust, to future
Jewish life. It is not within the province of the psychological
thinker to endorse these testimonies—but also not to explain
them away. And, for a thought placing itself *with* the resisting
victims, and *against* an assault that in its fury transcends his
psychological comprehension (as much as it did theirs), this
testimony must be as ultimate as it must be, surely, for those
who were there.

B

That the Holocaust transcends comprehension is of course not
immediately accepted—or acceptable. Reason rightly rebels
against this assertion, until all avenues for understanding are
explored.* And the reason that comes on the scene, next to
the psychological, is that of the historian. This latter estab-
lishes facts and hence *these* facts. But he also goes beyond
facts toward their explanation. Yet the better a Holocaust historian succeeds in explaining the event, the closer he comes to
suspecting the inevitability of ultimate failure.

Why was it done? An historian is tempted to reply: "The
Nazis wished to save Germany, and perhaps the world, from
what they considered to be the 'Jewish virus.' " Then why,
when all came crushing down, was it more important to annihilate the few remaining Jews than to save all the Germans?
(Eichmann redirected trains from the collapsing Russian front
to Auschwitz. Hitler reacted to the plot of July 20, 1944, with
removing remaining "non-Aryans" from the civil service and
the Wehrmacht, thereby weakening these institutions in a
time of catastrophic need.) And how many Jews did Himmler

---

*In sections 6B and 8 we have described the Holocaust world, first with a
focus on the criminals, then with a focus on the resisting victims. In section 9
we are concerned with attempts to *explain* it.

have to murder in order to be shaken in his belief in Jewish omnipotence? Raul Hilberg has explored the "how" of the Holocaust as thoroughly as has any historian. Yet as to its "why," he recently said (in private conversation with this writer) that the more he ponders the question, the more his answer becomes an empty tautology. "They did it because they wanted to do it." The riddle remains.

A riddle remains with the "how" as well. *How was it done?* The historian has many partial answers to this question, but all, separately or jointly, point to an ultimate mystery. "Many little men obeyed escalating orders, and these caught them unawares, at times because the escalation was imperceptible, at other times because it occurred with breath-taking suddenness." But obey orders *such as these?* "Many big men were manipulated—bureaucrats into writing murderous paragraphs; generals into condoning or even committing heinous crimes; thinkers, poets and high-ranking clerics into silence." But are there *no* limits to *being* manipulated? (Is "human nature" capable of *all* things?) And were there none to the power of the manipulators—their cunning, their ingenuity, their industry, their single-minded zeal? A power so great and unfailing can in the last resort derive only from the purpose to which it is directed, so that, in this case, the historian's "how"-question is driven back, after all, willy-nilly to the "why"-question. Driven back to purposes, the historian can point to penultimate ones, such as the uses of anti-Semitism in the creation and maintenance of the Third Reich. That these were *only* penultimate, however, was unmistakably revealed when the "extermination" of the Jewish people became an end more ultimate than the Third Reich's very survival. When reaching this point, historians less reflective than Hilberg are wont to lapse into medical metaphors—the "racist mania," the "anti-Semitic madness," and the like.* These

---

*K. D. Bracher—an outstanding, thoughtful historian—writes: "The extermination [of the Jews] grew out of the biologistic insanity of Nazi ideology, and for that reason it is completely unlike the terror of revolutions and wars of the past" (*The German Dictatorship* [New York: Praeger, 1971], p. 430). This statement is completely correct——but "insanity" explains nothing.

metaphors, however, far from being explanations, are merely unwitting confessions of failure. Thus the mystery of both the "how" and the "why" of the Holocaust remains.

The mystery does not vanish but only deepens if the historian, in an attempt to fill "gaps" in his explanatory narrative, seeks help from psychology, thus turning into a "psychohistorian." Not that this turn is useless or inadmissible. Indeed, psychohistory, of doubtful validity in many other instances, has a rare, not to say unique, opportunity in the case at hand. By near-common consent, Nazism was the creation of a single person, and psychological speculations or guesses are surely more sound about one person than about dubious psychological entities such as a nation, a class, an historical period. Further, the thesis *"Hitler: The Psychopathic God"** supplies solutions of sorts to problems which otherwise would seem totally intractable. Why did Hitler attack Russia, thereby wilfully creating the long-dreaded, unnecessary two-front war? Why did the plan to "remove" the Jews turn into a vast system of murder, more important than victory, and persisted even in the shadow of defeat? To such questions psychohistory gives more plausible answers than either psychology without history or history without psychology.

It gives its answers, however, only at the price of raising still more intractable questions. How shall one "if not explain . . . , at least . . . make conceivable how a great and civilized nation could identify itself with" a dictatorial leader of "almost inconceivable spiritual, moral, and human inferiority?" How shall one "reconcile the gravity, the catastrophic magnitude of the event with the vulgar mediocrity of the individual who initiated them?"† These questions, in any case as inescapable as they are intractable, assume a dimension of utter absurdity if the initiating individual must be viewed as a psychopath. Were the German people led—did they *let themselves be* led—first into victory, then into catastrophic defeat because

---

*By Robert G. L. Waite (New York: Basic Books, 1977).

†Herbert Luethy, "Der Führer," *The Commentary Reader* (New York: Atheneum, 1966), pp. 63, 65. Luethy's essay, originally published in *Commentary* in 1954, remains to this day the equal in depth, substance, and perspective to much larger works, to say nothing of the recent revisionist literature that will be touched on below.

Hitler had a love-hate relation to his mother? Were six million actual "non-Aryans" and many additional honorary ones butchered and gassed because the Führer hated his father and thought of him as a half-Jew?[80] Must one—*may* one—extend the psychopathic hypotheses beyond Hitler to the German people, to much of Europe, to large parts of the world? An hypothesis so vast explains too little because it explains too much. Many psychopaths populate the world. So, if the larger hypothesis has any validity, do psychopathic groups. Yet none of them *does* what was done by *this* psychopath and, led and allowing themselves to be led by him, by his followers. The more plausible psychohistory becomes the more it points to an ultimate absurdity. The mystery remains.

The grounds of this mystery are existentially terrifying but logically of an astonishing simplicity. *To explain an action or event is to show how they were possible. In the case of the Holocaust, however, the mind can accept the possibility of both how and why it was done, in the final analysis, solely because it was done, so that the more the psychologist, historian, or "psychohistorian" succeeds in explaining the event or action, the more nakedly he comes to confront its ultimate inexplicability. In the paradoxical formulation of the philosopher Hans Jonas, "much more is real than is possible."*[81]

C(1)

It is precisely at this point that penultimate rational questions, such as those asked by the historian or the psychologist, turn into ultimate, i.e., philosophical ones. A fixed distinction between the humanly possible and impossible presupposes a fixed concept, so that what is or is not humanly possible is disclosed not by a permanent human nature but only by impermanent human history. This modern concept implies a malleability of man which, in the last analysis, is infinite. In earlier, more innocent periods of the modern West, philosophers could focus all attention on man's malleability for good—his "infinite perfectibility." In our own time—although many philosophers have yet to notice the fact—philosophical thought is forced to consider man's infinite malleability for evil as well.

This much could be, and was, considered earlier in the present work. However, now that we are at last forced to confront the Holocaust world nakedly—robbed of the philosophical means of rising above it, overcoming it, evading it—we are also forced to face the fact that *the precise point that marks the limit of penultimate rational intelligibility—psychological, sociological, historical—marks the end also of ultimate or philosophical intelligibility.* To be sure, one wonders about Schelling, the solitary figure in modern philosophy to brood and write about "radical" or "demonic" evil.* However, one wonders only momentarily, for the simple reason that when Schelling did his brooding and writing *the event known to us as the Holocaust had not yet happened.*† This event—a scandalous particularity—disclosed an evil quite other than the "radical" or "demonic" evil dreamt of in literature, philosophy, and theology. Indeed, our explorations have been haunted by the fact that the characteristic SS torturer or Gestapo paper-pushing murderer was neither a pervert or certifiable psychopath nor a God-defying Raskolnikov, but rather either a most ordinary job holder (whose job, however, was the daily commitment of unspeakable crimes) or else a most ordinary idealist (whose worship, however, was not of God or Man or even German Destiny but rather of torture and murder). Philosophers and theologians make things easy for themselves when they resort to a category—radical-evil-in-general or the demonic-in-general. Indeed, they lapse into escapism. For the true question is: How can philosophic thought—*any* thought—cope with *this* phenomenon?

It is true (as might be said in partial reply) that the jobholder and the idealist did what they did in the last resort because of

---

*Schelling's thought began to take this direction in 1804, when in his *Religion and Philosophy* he came upon a "fall" so radical as to be incapable of mediation in the system of absolute idealism which, in 1801, he himself had been the first to put forward. Kant too wrote about radical evil, but only in a single essay. See my article cited in ch. I, n. 6.

†Above I stressed the need for thought to "place itself *between* the concept 'epoch-making event' and *this* epoch-making event" (ch. I, section 6). My present refusal to dissolve the Holocaust into the demonic-in-general is in an attempt to do justice to this need, and consequences of this attempt will necessarily permeate the whole remainder of this book.

the Führer, the one ordered by him, the other inspired by him. It is true too—and here philosophic probing falls back on historical facts and reflection—that Hitler was an "evil genius" of a magnitude that continues to fascinate, defy, and in any case necessarily to occupy the historian. However, the historian's occupation with this, possibly penultimate, question—the relation in the Third Reich between *Volk* and Führer*—does not, whatever the answers, dissolve the ultimate or philosophical question but only serves to accentuate and deepen it.

The philosophical question may be stated in the form of a dilemma. If we locate all the inexhaustible, groundless evil of the Holocaust, in the last analysis, in but a single "demonic" individual, then we at once falsely endow this one individual with a diabolical omnipotence that is *beyond* all humanity and, equally falsely, ascribe to all those ordered or inspired by him an all-encompassing manipulability that is *beneath* all humanity: between these two extremes, man is lost. Yet if, rejecting this alternative, we hold fast to man, then the men we in fact find among the rulers and jobholders of the Holocaust-world—whether it be Hitler or Himmler, Eichmann, Hoess, or the unknown soldier who was an SS murderer—are, whatever else they may be, human beings like ourselves. But while this finding chills the marrow and numbs the mind, it must under no circumstances mislead us into the seemingly "liberal" but in fact trite, cowardly and escapist weakening of the distinction between those who *might have* done it—you, I, the greengrocer next door—and those who *in fact did it*. As the previous reflections have shown, the leap from possibility to actuality is, in this case, radical.† While the doers of the

---

*On that relation, see *Encounters*, ch. 4

†Two opposite forms of escapism must be avoided. We cannot make the Nazi murderers into a species separate from all humanity, with the results that their actions become a product of (historical, genetic, or medical) fate; that their postwar return to ordinary existence becomes a mystery; and that neither the first nor the second has any relation to ourselves. And we cannot, on the grounds that all men are sinners, dissolve or weaken the distinction between those who *might have* done it and those who *did* it. This latter is especially tempting to Christians. Thus, e.g., in William Styron's Holocaust novel *Sophie's Choice*, Josef Mengele, the notorious Auschwitz SS doctor (see below, ch. 5, section 3), becomes "Dr. Jemand von Niemand"—Dr. Anyone and No one.

deed were ordinary, the evil that they leapt into by doing the deed was absolute and unsurpassable. And here lies the enigma.

This enigma has given rise to the doctrine—widely cited, widely popular, widely accepted—of the banality of evil.[82] Reduced to its barest essentials, this doctrine may be stated as follows. Eichmann—the one "only taking orders"—is a nobody wanting to be a somebody. So is Himmler, the one both taking orders and giving them, a "Grand Inquisitor," to be sure, but also a "petty bourgeois."[83] It would not be difficult to extend this reasoning to Hitler himself. Historians may rightly warn us not to underestimate the Führer, an error made to their grief by his erstwhile opponents and subsequent victims. Even so, and after the consumption of myriads of words and the consideration and reconsideration of every angle of the question, no thoughtful reader can have any doubt as to the "almost inconceivable spiritual, moral and human inferiority" of Adolf Hitler. His ideas, though blown up into a pretentious Weltanschauung, are unoriginal and trite. So, for all the posturing designed to conceal the fact, is the man. Only the passion locked into this trite man and his trite ideas is a devouring fire; and even the passion, unbelievably, is for the most part fed by long-nursed, petty resentments, by a mean thirst for vengeance for old but never-forgotten slights: by a determination to "show them"—whom?—that the "poor devil" is a somebody. (He stopped "the Jews" from laughing at him by murdering them.) Jean-Paul Sartre has given a classic account of the anti-Semite as a nobody who makes himself into a somebody by elevating his petty hatred into a principle—his anti-Semitism is "unrelenting and pure"—and the fact of his "Aryan" birth into a virtue and an accomplishment. This account recalls nothing so vividly as the passage in *Mein Kampf* which describes how its author became an anti-Semite.[84]

The "extreme" evil, then, which is unarguably present in the Holocaust world lies not—so the argument for the banality of evil concludes—in the doers, right up to and including the ultimate one, all of them banal, but rather in the deeds; and the doers yielded to the deeds only because they were enmeshed in a dynamic, escalating, "totalitarian" system—ever-escalating, as it were, by itself. Thus the evil is "*only* extreme" and not "radical," spreading "like a fungus on the surface." It is "thought-defying" in the sense that thought, "trying to reach some depth," is "frustrated because there is nothing."[85]

This argument is not unreasonable. Indeed, it is only because it was advanced by its author in conjunction with less reasonable but more sensational assertions—Jews collaborating in their own destruction—that it has failed to receive the philosophical attention that it deserves. Even so, it is quite untenable. The single incident of Himmler and his gloves at Auschwitz would be quite sufficient to demolish it. So would a single incident that occurred during Eichmann's trial in Jerusalem. (The accused had preserved a stolid composure throughout his trial. One day the courtroom was darkened and pictures of Eichmann's victims were flashed on a screen. Secretly, a camera was trained on him in the dark. Believing himself unobserved, Eichmann saw what he saw—and smirked.) So would every one of Hitler's *Führerbefehle*, quite regardless of content. (The Final Solution was one of them.) For the mere *form* of these *Befehle*—the elevation of whim into an absolute principle—made both the giving and the taking of these orders into acts of idolatry that cause those of a thousand Raskolnikovs to pale into insignificance. We say "acts" because *any* such giving and taking was *the deed of a doer*, hence more than banal, hence more than a yielding or—if we cannot but speak of a yielding—a *doing* that was *in* the yielding.

These reflections apply to the "totalitarian" Third Reich as a whole. They also apply to the Holocaust world that we have already shown to be its inmost essence. And the conclusion to be drawn is that the doctrine of the banality of evil is only half a thought and half the truth, and that the complete thought and the complete truth is that *just as the "totalitarian" system produced the rulers and operators, so the rulers and operators produced the system.* In however varying degrees, those manipulated *let themselves be* manipulated; those obeying ever-escalating orders *chose* to obey without limits; those surrendering in a blind idealism *made a commitment* to blindness. Not only Eichmann but *everyone* was more than a cog in the wheel. (The Nazis viewed their "non-Aryan" victims as less than human. We cannot view *them* as less than human—will-less automata: we must view them as human beings like ourselves.)

This, as has been said, chills the marrow and numbs the mind. It also haunts it. The philosophical mind must resist the temptation to evade the haunting fact but must rather *let itself be* haunted. And, as it seeks out the fact that haunts it, it is driven from the "banal" doers to the evil system, and from the evil system back to the doers—these latter, after all, *not* banal *only*, for they created, sustained and escalated the system. *Thought, in short, moves in a circle.* This was meant by the above assertion that the limit of penultimate or scientific intelligibility marks also the end of ultimate or philosophical intelligibility.

The limit of philosophical *intelligibility*, however, is not quite yet the end of philosophical *thought*. The circular thought-movement that fails produces a result in its very failure, for it grasps, to the extent possible, a *whole*. The grasp of a whole by a circular thought is no novelty in philosophy. It is abundantly present in Hegelian thinking, nowhere as profoundly as in Hegel himself. For Hegel, however, to grasp a whole in a circular thought is to comprehend it, to transcend it, and, from a higher standpoint, perceive the meaning of the whole by placing it into a perspective. On our part, in contrast, we confront in the Holocaust world a *whole of horror*. We cannot comprehend it but only comprehend its incomprehensibility. We cannot transcend it but only be struck by the brutal truth that it cannot be transcended. Here the very attempt to see a meaning, or do a placing-in-perspective, would *already* constitute a dissipation, not only blasphemous but also untruthful and hence unphilosophical, of either the *whole* of horror—the fact that it was not random, piecemeal, accidental, but rather integrated into a *world*—or else *of the horror* of the whole—the fact that the whole possessed no rational, let alone redeeming purpose subserved by the horror, but that the horror was starkly ultimate.

The philosopher may feel—he believes that nothing human is alien to him—that this whole is not unintelligible after all. He wants to understand Eichmann and Himmler, for he wants to understand Auschwitz. And he wants to understand Auschwitz, for he wants to understand Eichmann and Himmler. Thus his understanding *gets inside* them and their world, bold enough not to be stopped even by Eichmann's smirk and Himmler's gloves. To get inside them is to get inside the ideas behind the smirk and the gloves; and whereas this is not necessarily to accept these ideas it is in any case to obtain a kind of empathy. And thus it comes to pass, little by little, that a philosopher's *comprehension* of the Holocaust whole-of-horror turns into a *surrender,* for which the horror has vanished from the whole and the *Unwelt* has become a *Welt* like any other. In this way, one obtains a glimpse of the Ph.D.s among the murderers, and shudders.

The truth disclosed in this shudder is that to grasp the Holocaust whole-of-horror is not to comprehend or transcend it, but rather *to say no to it,* or resist it. The Holocaust whole-of-horror *is* (for it *has been*); but it *ought not* to be (and *not* to have been). It ought *not* to be (and have been), but it *is* (for it has been). Thought would lapse into escapism if it held fast to the "ought not" alone; and it would lapse into paralyzed impotence if it confronted, nakedly, the devastating "is" alone. *Only by holding fast at once to the "is" and "ought not" can thought achieve an authentic survival. Thought, that is, must take the form of resistance.*

This resistance-of-thought, however, cannot remain self-enclosed in thought. The tension between the "is" and the "ought not"—the more unendurable to philosophical thought, the deeper, the more rational, the more philosophical it is—would lose all depth and seriousness if the resulting no were confined to thought alone. Having reached a limit, *resisting thought must point beyond the sphere of thought altogether, to a resistance which is not in "mere" thought but rather in overt, flesh-and-blood action and life.*

Such a pointing-by-thought-beyond-itself is no novelty in the history of philosophy, any more than a circular thought comprehending a whole. Indeed, it is in response to this latter that it first appeared in history. For Hegel "the Whole" came to be "the Truth." Schelling—his dispute late in his career with the already-deceased Hegel remains significant to this day—rejoined that such a total comprehension only serves to disclose absolute incomprehensibles, among them existence as such, the absolute Existent or God, and radical evil. Schelling's comprehending thought therefore reached a limit where thought becomes "ecstatic," i.e., discloses a reality that yet lies beyond it.[86] In our explorations in the present work, we have already come upon two post-Schellingian "ecstatic" thinkers, i.e., Kierkegaard (whose thought points to the leap into faith) and Marx (for whom thought points to revolutionary action).

But the ecstatic thought required of us is not found in any of these thinkers. Schelling and Kierkegaard point to an Absolute—but in an affirmative pointing to God. Marx does a negative and resisting pointing, issuing as he does a call to revolutionary action; but the evil pointed to is only relative which is why the revolution called for is an overcoming. Schelling's pointing-to-evil is both negative and to an absolute. (Thought cannot overcome it, nor can human action.) However, the evil pointed to is, first, general, and, second, already overcome by Grace. None of these thinkers ever came where we have come, nor could they have. For—here we repeat an assertion made earlier—the Holocaust whole-of-horror had not yet occurred. Only Heidegger might have reached this point, for his *Denkweg* was self-immersed in history, and he lived to witness the *Ereignis*. However, as we have seen, Heidegger dissolves Auschwitz in the Age of Technology, and assumes toward this latter a "composure" which "let things be."

We are therefore led into uncharted territory. That which thought cannot "let be" is a *world* of evil, a *novum* in human history just *because* it was a world. The thought that resists it must therefore be a *novum* as well. What is this thought? What the reality it points to? And are both possible at all?

C(2)

These questions are of so grave an import that it is wise for us to retrace our steps and corroborate our previous sketchy outline with an account that follows, step by step, the circular movement by which thought assumes its resisting stance.

Let us begin by considering the actual torturers and murderers and take both them and their victims as "conditioned." ("It is easier to kill a dog than a man, easier yet to kill a rat or frog, and no problem at all to kill insects.")* But then we *resist* our having-taken-them-thus as a *having-been* taken, as an amoral indulgence and an intellectual weakness, with the spectre not far away of a yielding to the lure of the evil kingdom: the victims, including the *Muselmänner* and to say nothing of the babies, are *not* and *never became* insects; and *not a single one* of the torturers and murderers was *simply* "conditioned" to view or treat them as such.

We consider next, Kommandant Hoess, the immediate conditioner. No person in his senses, of course, will take him as he portrays himself in that unbelievable autobiography of his which we have already cited, for he is a criminal and a liar who shows no signs of repentance. However, we *do* take him on *some* things as he takes himself. After all, we do and must see the system as dynamic, ever-escalating, all-absorbing, overwhelming. Also, we do and must see the Kommandant himself as a brutal soldier-type, to be sure, but not as a raving sadist or maniac but rather well within the bounds of human normalcy. Hence we will wish to take his word to the effect that his last truly free act was the voluntary joining of the "ranks of the active SS," and that thereafter there "was no returning." Hence, too, we will wish to take him—the one who directly gives the orders and is at hand to see the results—as being "not indifferent to human suffering." Having taken both, we are then led to see the strange—nay, unique—spectacle of Hoess watching the torture and the murders as though not he but someone else had ordered them, and of the Kommandant commiserating, not with his victims

*See above, p. 214n.

but rather with his own tender self that is compelled to watch such scenes.*We see the spectacle, and end up understanding it, if understand it we can, as a strange case of "schizophrenia."† We *take* all this, and then *resist* our having taken it thus as a snare and a horrifying temptation. It is *not true* that there was "no returning" for Hoess. Like other, less highly placed ones, Hoess was at *all* times free to volunteer for the Russian front: he *chose not to use* that freedom.‡ He was not sick with schizophrenia; his condition was self-induced, hence not schizophrenia at all. Doubtless there is a sense in which one can speak of all of Nazi Germany as suffering from a universal split consciousness, and say that this condition made possible the committing and condoning of heinous crimes with a well-conditioned conscience. But in speaking in

---

*Hoess writes: "On one occasion two small children were so absorbed in some game that they quite refused to let their mother tear them away from it. Even the Jews of the Special Detachment were reluctant to pick the children up. The imploring look in the eyes of the mother who certainly knew what was happening, is something I shall never forget. The people were already in the gas-chamber and becoming restive, and I had to act. Everyone was looking at me. I nodded to the junior non-commissioned officer on duty and he picked up the screaming, struggling children in his arms and carried them into the gas-chamber, accompanied by their mother who was weeping in the most heart-rending fashion. My pity was so great that I longed to vanish from the scene: yet I might not show the slightest trace of emotion. I had to see everything. I had to watch hour after hour . . ."(*Commandant of Auschwitz*, pp. 172 ff; see also pp. 66, 72, 86). Martin Broszat comments: "His psychological egocentricity enabled Hoess to transform a vicious murder of defenseless children into a tragedy for the murderer" (*Kommandant in Auschwitz*, ed. Martin Broszat [Stuttgart: Deutsche Verlags-Anstalt, 1958], p.18).

†Fest, *The Face of the Third Reich*, pp. 425, 427; Broszat, *Kommandant in Auschwitz*, p. 17. Broszat writes: "Hoess is an extreme case of the universal split consciousness that made it possible for countless human beings in Nazi Germany to serve the regime of Hitler and Himmler with a feeling of selfless devotion and undisturbed consciousness, even when it was no longer possible to ignore its criminal character" (p. 18).

‡Otto Friedrich writes: "Dr. Ella Lingens, a prisoner, recalled at the Frankfurt trial that there was one island of peace—at the [Auschwitz] Babice subcamp, because of an officer named Flacke. 'How he did it I don't know,' she testified. 'His camp was clean and the food also.' The Frankfurt judge, who had heard endless protestations that orders had to be obeyed, was amazed.

" 'Do you wish to say,' he asked, "that everyone could decide for himself to be either good or evil at Auschwitz?'

" 'That is exactly what I wish to say,' she answered" ("The Kingdom of Auschwitz," *Toronto Globe and Mail*, October 2, 1981, p. 10).

this manner we must not fail to notice that "conditioned con-science" is a moral and intellectual scandal. As for such as Kommandant Hoess, they were the *producers* of the split in question, as much as its products. Who produced it if not such as he?

In answer to this question we turn from Hoess, the immediate conditioner, to more remote conditioners such as Eichmann and Himmler—more remote, and hence better able to avoid watching the results of their orders. The one is a model bureaucrat who admits quite readily to the desk murder of millions that conforms to regulations, but at the same time denies hotly (and quite possibly truthfully) the charge of having killed just a single Jew personally—an action that he would presumably consider highly irregular. The other is an ideologue who supervises it all, makes speeches boasting about it all, but who cannot stand the sight when he witnesses it. Thus we take Eichmann and Himmler as removed from the flesh-and-blood torture and murder by the abstractions, respectively, of bureaucracy and ideology. But then we remember—we must *force ourselves* to remember, for the thought slips away—Eichmann's smirk in Jerusalem and Himmler's gloves at Auschwitz, and we catch ourselves as being, as it were, on the brink of philosophical blasphemy—the dissipation of an unspeakable evil into the product of a faceless, impersonal, possibly even "value-free" (though ideologically-inspired) technological apparatus that is the work of everyone and no one. (Are we to return to Heidegger's technological frenzy which belongs to everyone and no one?) We must resist it. But can we do more?

We can do at least one thing more, namely, consider the ultimate author of the Final Solution. In the case of Hitler we find that while the "doctrine" is always both clear and public there is nothing but a "striking silence" about the ultimate "consequences" of the doctrine: indeed, "not a single concrete reference of his to the practice of annihilation has come down to us." Thus we are inclined to take a noted historian's "guess" as to the "motives" of the Führer's "silence about the central concern of his life," listed by him as composed of a "characteristic mania for secrecy, a remnant of bourgeois morality [and] the desire to keep what was happening abstract and not weaken his own passion by letting him see what it led to."[87] We take this guess, and indeed take it as natural, in view of what was said earlier about Hitler's triteness. Yet we must then resist our having-taken it, for it pushes us in the direction of the ultimate absurdity. Formerly our thought, following conventional wisdom, was driven toward the view that only one was responsible, that all the others, ultimately considered, were cogs in the wheel. Now that at length we reach this one, are we to point back to all the others as responsible for the "consequences," while this one is guilty of nothing more than the "doctrine"—a nineteenth-century platitude until it was acted on?* Or, more precisely, that having given the "abstract" *Führerbefehl,* he withdrew from the scene and the responsibility? In its search of the *doers* of the evil deed, is our thought to point from the lower to the higher and highest in the order of command, only in order to lapse, once having reached the highest, into the vast absurdity of pointing back to the lower and lowest? (Are we to end up with the unknown soldier who was an SS torturer and murderer, and with him alone?) *Is the evil—the doers are inseparable from the deeds, and the deeds are inseparable from the doers—to be located wherever thought is not?*

The most extreme outcome of such a way of thinking—or rather, of *not* thinking that which is most of all in need of being thought—is the thesis that the Holocaust never happened at all. This, of course, is a Nazi or neo-Nazi thesis which is not respectable. (It should be mentioned, however, that at this time of writing there are learned professors who advance this thesis, and that others defend them in the name of academic freedom.) However, quite respectable, it seems—or in any case neither

---

*After having shown that Hitler's "ideas," far from original, had by 1914 "become the common-places of radical anti-Semitic and pan-German journalism and cafe-talk in every city in Central Europe," the historian Alan Bullock goes on: "Hitler's originality lay not in his ideas, but in the terrifyingly literal way in which he set to work to translate fantasy into reality, and his unequalled grasp of the means to do this" (cited in *Encounters,* p. 193). See also below, p. 296n.

Nazi nor neo-Nazi—is the thesis that while the Endlösung doubtless happened, nobody really wanted it, that it was "what the Germans call a Verlegenheitslösung—the way out of an awkward dilemma." True, Hitler ordered the wholesale persecution, deportation, ghettoization of the Jewish people. That he did not order their wholesale murder is argued by the respectable work under consideration not only from the absence of conclusive documentary evidence but also—an argument given much greater weight by the author—from the fact that, if one studies Hitler with some empathy and through the testimonies of those who knew him, followed him, admired, or even loved him, then the Führer emerges as a figure not lacking in humanity. (If one studied them in the same manner one would presumably reach a similar conclusion about Himmler and Heydrich, Eichmann and Hoess.) Then why did anybody do it? David Irving, the author of the massive, two-volume work under review, writes as follows:

Hitler had unquestionably decreed that Europe's Jews were to be "swept back" to the east.... But the SS authorities, Gauleiters and regional commissars and governors in "the east" proved wholly unequal to the problems caused by this uprooting in midwar. The Jews were brought by the trainload to ghettos already overcrowded and underprovisioned.[88]

It seems that if a bureaucrat has sleepless nights because he cannot house and feed masses of men, women, and children entrusted to his care, then the best Lösung of the problem (and an end to the sleepless nights) is wholesale murder. Such is the absurd outcome of not thinking what is above all in need of being thought.

It is present in a "revisionism" that has come to be widespread. Above we showed that the Holocaust was the climax of the sole firm commitment—the "removal" of the Jews—in what was otherwise a revolution of nihilism. The passage of time has produced a total perversion of the truth, to the effect that the Holocaust was some sort of Betriebsunfall ("factory accident") and that Hitler was nothing worse than a conventional (if "extreme") nationalist politician—at least until, plagued by gastric troubles, a maxillary sinus needing irrigation, and a quack physician who gave him poison instead of medicine, he lost his grip. Such is the perverse revisionism that has been produced by the passage of time. The passage of time alone, of course, would never have produced it, were it not for the inherent difficulty—and widespread unwillingness—to think the unthinkable.

That even minds wholly immune to perversity may lapse into locating the evil where thought is not, is illustrated by an incident that occurred during the Nuremberg Trials. (Many other illustrations could be given.) With Hitler dead, Goering was Nazi number one, and Captain G. M. Gilbert, a U.S. Army psychologist, interviewed him and all the other big Nazi criminals almost every day while the proceedings were under way. In these interviews, Goering proved that he had not been Nazi number two for nothing, by the jovial bluster with which he managed to give tit for tat on such charges as waging aggressive warfare and committing war crimes. Only with the Holocaust was this impossible, but this subject Goering adroitly avoided. One day this could not be done, for a witness had testified how the children were thrown into the crematorium alive. Goering responded by denying all knowledge. He said: "You know how it is even in a battalion—a battalion commander doesn't know anything that goes on in the line. The higher you stand, the less you see of what is going on below." Goering's response no longer surprises us. Hoess had blamed the tortures, if not the murders, on those below him—and was himself the immediate conditioner who watched the results. Goering blamed the whole crime on those beneath him—and was himself the man who had charged Heydrich with the Final Solution. In both cases the "schizophrenia," if any, was self-induced, and is, in this exploration, no longer remarkable. What is remarkable is the reaction of Gilbert who reports the incident. The American captain was a shrewd, tough-minded, high-minded interviewer. He was well-equipped to understand Goering's kind of "schizophrenia" or (to put it bluntly) to recognize a liar when he heard one. Yet though he criticizes Goering's "explanation" he nevertheless accepts it. He writes: "I could hardly have thought of a more damning argument against the military hierarchy, but Goering, in his militaristic perversion, thought he had given a reasonable explanation."[89] Such is the fate of a thought that lapses into not thinking or, which is the same thing, that locates the evil that must be thought where thought is not.

This fate—in its high-minded version, to say nothing of its perverted, low-minded version—can be avoided only by a thought that is determined *to place itself and the evil to be thought, as it were, into the same space.* Yet, since the evil systematically eludes it, thought can abide by this determination only indirectly, i.e., by means of a pursuit radical enough so as to move circularly and thus to grasp the evil *as a whole.* But just what is this grasp? We have already insisted that it is not a comprehension. It is, rather, at once a *surprised acceptance and a horrified resistance.* It is a horrified surprise and, since the thought that is in this surprise is forced to accept what is yet in all eternity unacceptable, *thought is required to become "ecstatic," such as to point beyond resistance within its own native sphere, to a resistance that is beyond the sphere of thought altogether, and in the sphere of life.* Kant's moral will would not be moral at all if, instead of willing-to-act, it withdrew into the enjoyment of its own purity. Resistance-in-thought to the Holocaust would degenerate into academic self-satisfaction unless it climaxed in calling for, praying for, working for, resistance in life.

D

What, then, of the banality of evil? Thought is, indeed, "frustrated" by the Holocaust not, however, because the evil to be thought is "banal" or "on the surface"—because thought looks for "depth" and there is "nothing" since "only good has depth and can be radical." In truth the frustration occurs because the circular thought that grasps the whole-of-horror—it grasps it only if it confronts it *as* whole at *every* point of its circular movement—in no way *comprehends* but merely *confronts* it, in a horrified surprise, or a surprised horror. Hence we reach a fundamental conclusion. *The evil of the Holocaust world (which is radical and far removed from banality) is philosophically intelligible after Auschwitz only in the exact sense in which it was already understood in Auschwitz—and Buchenwald, Lublin, and the Warsaw Ghetto—by the resisting victims themselves.* When Pelagia Lewinska "grasped the true meaning of Auschwitz" she "awakened from a dream" and "felt under orders to live." *No deeper or more ultimate grasp is possible for philosophical thought that comes, or ever will come, after the event.* This grasp—*theirs no less than ours*—is *epistemologically ultimate.*

This is our first conclusion. But it is not all. Doubtless our thought is richer than theirs. We possess historical facts beyond their ken. We have hindsight knowledge. We have the leisure that has enabled us in this exploration (to employ two Kierkegaardian expressions) to "circumnavigate" the Holocaust whole-of-horror in detached "reflection" before confronting it in the "immediacy-after-reflection" of horrified surprise. All this they did not have. Even so, our knowledge is not superior. Though without our hindsight knowledge and our leisure, they were able to "grasp the motivating principle" of the whole. Moreover, whereas *our* resisting thought is merely a pale, *intellectual* struggle, *theirs* was a "terrible" life-and-death- "struggle . . . which went on day and night"—a struggle so total that "to abandon [it] meant letting oneself be broken, [that] capitulating meant going under."[90] We have seen that our resisting thought must point beyond thought itself, to resistance in life. In *their* case, resisting thought not only went together with resistance in life. Their *recognition* of the Nazi logic of destruction *helped produce resistance to it*— a life-and-death struggle that went on day and night.

We are thus led to a second conclusion. We have previously identified the Holocaust world as *novum* in human history. We have also suggested that resistance to it is a *novum* as well. Now our ecstatic thought must point to *their* resistance—the resistance in thought and the resistance in life—as *ontologically ultimate. Resistance in that extremity was a way of being. For our thought now, it is an ontological category.*

E

With this monumental conclusion what may be called a necessary excursus, extending over the last two sections of the present exploration, has come to a climax and an end. Prior to these sections we reached an impasse with the question whether perhaps *no* thought can be where the Holocaust is; whether perhaps *all* thought is "paralyzed" vis-à-vis that event; and whether perhaps paralysis at this catastrophic point calls into question significant post-Holocaust thought everywhere. The two sections that followed were an excursus in that that question was suspended; and the excursus was necessary because only the astounding fact that *existence* was not wholly paralyzed *during* the Holocaust *itself* could give our thought any hope of breaking the impasse. Now that the astounding fact has been confronted, contemplated, explored, the suspended question returns; and there arises for future thought—the focus of our concern is Jewish thought, but also involved are philosophical and, to a lesser extent, Christian thought—an imperative that brooks no compromise. *Authentic thought was actual during the Holocaust among resisting victims; therefore such thought must be possible for us after the event: and, being possible, it is mandatory. Moreover, their resisting thought pointed to and helped make possible a resisting life; our post-Holocaust thought, however authentic in other respects, would still lapse into unauthenticity if it remained in an academically-self enclosed circle—if it failed to point to, and help make possible, a post-Holocaust life.*

But can this imperative be obeyed? Only through a new departure with the help of a new category. In this whole work we have been engaged in thinking—philosophical, Jewish, and within proper limits, Christian. When it was "old" thinking it required access to Eternity. When it was "new" thinking it still required historical continuity. (This is obvious in the case of Jewish and Christian thinking, with their need for access to the Scriptures. In the case of philosophical thinking it was demonstrated for us by Heidegger, for his earlier thinking needs "recovery" of "tradition," and his later must "think more primally still what was originally thought.") Our own thinking in this book, recover as it did the past, itself presupposed a continuity between present and past. Yet our question now is whether the continuity indispensable for thought is still available. This question first appeared when our own thought, surprised and horrified by the Holocaust, could only resist but not comprehend it.

The continuity is broken, and thought, if it is not itself to be and remain broken, requires a new departure and a new category. Only thus can the imperative that brooks no compromise be obeyed. Historical continuity is shattered because "at Auschwitz not only man died, but also the idea of man"; because our "estrangement from God" has become so "cruel" that, even if He were to speak to us, we have no way of understanding how to "recognize" Him.[91] We need a new departure and a new category because the Holocaust is not a "relapse into barbarism," a "phase in an historical dialectic," a radical-but-merely-"parochial" catastrophe. It is a total rupture.

10. Rupture, Teshuva, and Tikkun Olam

How has the Lord covered the daughter of Zion with a cloud in His anger, and cast down from heaven to earth the beauty of Israel. . . . The Lord has swallowed up without pity all the habitations of Jacob. . . . He has profaned the kingdom and its princes. . . . The Lord was like an enemy. He has swallowed up Israel. . . . He has increased in the daughter of Yehuda mourning and lamentation. (Lam. 2:1, 2, 5)

A

This passage from Lamentations takes us closer to total rupture than any passage in all philosophy. (Nietzsche or Sartre or Heidegger might find, mixed with mourning, exhilaration in the solitariness caused by an absent God, or a freedom caused by a God that has died. There is no exhilaration but only terror in a God present still—but become an enemy.) It takes us closer, too, than any passage in all Christianity. For a Christian, Good Friday is always before Easter, which is why even Kierkegaard, though horrified by the fall of Jerusalem, has the edifying thought of being *with* God in his knowledge of being always wrong over against Him. The Jewish author of Lamentations has no such certainty. He exists in an unredeemed world, in possession only of the promise of redemption. And since, unlike the Christian, he belongs not to a spiritual but rather a flesh-and-blood people, it is always possible—"so changeable are human affairs"*—that this promise is falsified by history, that a destruction so total might occur that no remnant is left. Then why is Lamentations in the Jewish Bible?

The commitment to include the book in the biblical canon is much the same that ordained its liturgical use. (Both are part of rabbinic or "normative" Judaism.) The way of its use on the ninth of Av demonstrates with great clarity just how close the rabbinic mind comes to the very brink of rupture—and that it is, nevertheless, able to withdraw. Lamentations ends with a stark question that remains unanswered: "Hast Thou utterly rejected us? Art Thou angry with us beyond measure?" (Lam. 5:22). However, after the liturgical reading of this verse, the second-to-last verse is repeated: "Turn us unto Thee, O Lord, and we shall be turned. Renew our days as of old" (Lam. 5:21). Here is the oldest, deepest life-and-death commitment of the Jewish people in its career in history. Even in extremity there still is a divine turning to the human, and a human being-turned by the Divine; and in the prayer itself there is a human turning to the Divine, even as it is being turned. This dialectic of turning and being-turned is the stance of the ninth of Av toward all past catastrophe. It is the stance toward future catastrophe as well. A remnant has always turned and returned. One always will. It is this remnant that stands between the threat of rupture and rupture itself.

B

But will a remnant *always* return? Will there always be a remnant? Or does normative Judaism behave like Kierkegaard's bourgeois Christianity, for which the catastrophic destruction of Jerusalem becomes ever dimmer with the passage

---

*This allusion to Spinoza—see above ch. II, p. 57—seems most fitting at this point.

of time? Astonishingly, as the centuries wore on, the catastrophe of 70 C.E. became ever more vivid in the Jewish mind.
In the Midrash we read:

When the Holy One, blessed be He, remembers His children who
dwell in misery among the nations, He sheds two tears into the sea,
and the sound is heard from one end of the earth to the other. It is an
earthquake.[92]

One imagines an earthquake, and thinks of floods, fires, collapsing houses. But what one thinks of above all is a rupture
of the earth.

Another Midrash has the following:

The night is divided into three watches, and in each watch sits the
Holy One, blessed be He, and roars like a lion: "Woe unto Me that I
have destroyed My house and burned My temple and sent My children into exile among the nations."[*]

The Midrash just cited belongs to the third century. Not until
the eleventh century did it come to be reflected in ritual. If
Rachel's children are in exile, are they not *His* children as
well as hers? Shall He not weep with her and on account of
her? And if He weeps at midnight, shall not *we* wake at this
appointed time and weep with Him and for Him? And if these
two laments—His and ours—reflect a rupture, shall not the
divine-human *community* of waking and weeping be a *Tikkun*—a mending of what is broken? Thus with the rite of
Tikkun Hatzot—the "midnight mending"—both a rupture and
a mending of it takes shape before our eyes. The rite begins,
and must begin, with *Tikkun Rachel*—the weeping for the
children in exile—and goes on to *Tikkun Lea*—a rejoicing in
the anticipated redemption. But it *can* go on only because
Tikkun Rachel is *already* a *Tikkun*. It is an at-oneness of God
and men because "men bewail not their own afflictions, but
the one affliction that really counts in the world, the exile of
the *Shekhina*."[93]

*Bab. Talmud, Berakhot 3a. Any rabbinic reference to children in exile would
at once call to mind Jer. 31:15 ff.—the passage in which Rachel weeps for her
exiled children and receives the promise of their return.

C

A "mending" takes place. But is there a real rupture? Normative Judaism shrinks from that assertion. Historical catastrophe is real. So is the divine involvement in it. However, the Midrash does not presume to penetrate the divine nature but is rather a human, metaphorical way of speaking. God only "as it were" weeps or roars like a lion. The Midrashic symbolism does not claim to have an ontological reference.

No such restraint is shown by kabbalistic Judaism in search of a truth beyond the Midrashic symbols. In its own symbolism, "a reality becomes transparent." "The vessels are broken." "The Shekhina is in exile." God Himself is in a state of Tzimtzum—a "retreat from the world"—without which the very being of the world would be impossible. These and similar symbols go in their reference beyond rupture in history, to a rupture of cosmic dimensions that involves no less than the "life and action" of Divinity itself.

It is not easy to say whether the kabbalistic impulse goes so far as to assert, at the price of "verging on the blasphemous," a rupture in the very "substance" of Divinity. Even so, the radical problematic in the logic of Tikkun comes clearly to light. The "exile of the Shekhina" and the "fracture of the vessels" refers to cosmic, as well as historical realities: it is that rupture that our Tikkun is to mend. But how is this possible when we ourselves share in the cosmic condition of brokenness? Yet just in response to this problematic the kabbalistic Tikkun shows its profoundest energy. It is precisely if the rupture, or the threat of it, is total, that all powers must be summoned for a mending. If the threat is to man, there is need to invoke divine as well as human power. If the threat is to God—the "exile" is "an element in God Himself"—then human power must aid the divine. And if this can be said without blasphemy, it is because the human aid is itself aided by the Divine. "The impulse below calls forth an impulse above."*

*Gershom Scholem, Major Trends in Jewish Mysticism (New York: Schocken, 1965), pp. 27, 260 ff., 232 ff., and passim. Like every other writer on the Kabbalah, I am greatly indebted to Scholem's work, all the more so because, in my case, a concern with the Kabbalah assumed real seriousness only with the present work.

Such was the way in which, in the greatest catastrophes experienced and indeed conceivable prior to the Holocaust, the age-old Jewish dialectic of *Teshuva* was both transformed and preserved.

D

After 586 B.C.E., and again after 70 C.E., the children of Rachel went into exile: at Ravensbrück and Auschwitz, they were drowned in buckets and thrown into the flames. For centuries the kabbalists practiced their *Tikkun*, their "impulse below"— "Torah, prayer and *mitzvot*"—calling forth an "impulse from above": in the Holocaust their bodies, their souls and their *Tikkun* were all indiscriminately murdered. No *Tikkun* is possible of *that* rupture, ever after.

But the impossible *Tikkun* is also necessary. Then and there, many doubtless thought of their "Torah, prayer and *mitzvot*" quite consciously in terms of a *Tikkun*. Others, when engaged in the act of *kiddush ha-hayyim*, doubtless did not. Yet we on our part must think of *all* such acts of *kiddush ha-hayyim* as a *Tikkun*. Does it or does it not matter whether or not Pelagia Lewinska lived or died or, had she died, whether she died with dignity? Is the world different or the same because the Buchenwald Hasidim decided to buy the *tefillin*, and found in them an elixir of life? Or because the Warsaw Ghetto fighters fought? A Tikkun, *here and now, is mandatory for a* Tikkun, *then and there, was actual.* It is true that because a *Tikkun* of *that* rupture is impossible we cannot live, after the Holocaust, as men and women have lived before. However, if the impossible *Tikkun* were not also necessary, and hence possible, we could not live at all.

This impossible necessity must have been in the mind of Rabbi Yissachar Shlomo Teichthal, a leading Hasid of the Munkacher Rebbe, when he composed his *Em Ha-Banim Smeha* [The mother of the children is happy]. Teichthal wrote his book in the Budapest of 1943, and saw it published in 1944, just three months before the Nazis occupied the city. The rabbi was soon sent to Auschwitz and murdered.

In his book Teichthal wrote the following:

Now if we shall rise and ascend to Zion we can yet bring about a
Tikkun of the souls of the people Israel who were murdered as martyrs since it is on their account that we are stimulated to return to our
ancestral inheritance.... Thus we bring about their rebirth [italics
added].[94]

The author of this statement, a religious Zionist, was surely
ignorant of the worst. However, what he knew was enough to
destroy any notion of the Holocaust as a providential means to
even the noblest Zionist ends: a state; a state blessed with
justice at home and peace abroad; a state home to all persecuted if not all Jews. The attempt to justify the Holocaust as an
evil means to any good however glorious would be blasphemous—and is impossible.

But Rabbi Teichthal's statement leaves us in no doubt that
its author was innocent of blasphemy. The Tikkun he envis-
aged was not a good requiring and thus retroactively justify-
ing the evil that it was to mend. Rather was it—both "the
impulse below" and the "impulse above"—of a wholly different order. The return would not be of some esoteric mys-
tics to an esoteric place in the land; it would be of the whole
people to the whole Land. Israel's exile would come to an
absolute end. So would the exile of the nations, of the cosmos, of the Godhead itself. The Muselmänner would live and
be whole. The drowned and burned children of Rachel
would be resurrected. And at that time—the End of all
Time—all the unspeakable anguish would be remembered
no more.* Such was the divine-human Tikkun that was en-
visaged by Rabbi Teichthal in his desperate ecstasy. After
that rupture no less a Tikkun would be adequate.

---

*Scholem writes: "A young German recently wrote to me expressing the hope
that Jews, when thinking of Germany, might keep in mind the words of Isaiah:
'Remember ye not the former things, neither consider the things of old.' I do
not know whether the messianic age will bestow forgetfulness upon the Jews.
It is a delicate point of theology. But for us, who must live without illusions
in an age without a Messiah, such a hope demands the impossible . . ." (On
Jews and Judaism in Crisis [New York: Schocken, 1976], pp. 91 ff.).

11. *Historicity, Hermeneutics, and* Tikkun Olam *after the Holocaust*

A

Rabbi Teichthal was not alone in his desperate ecstasy. How many there were will never be known. Among them was a certain Rabbi Israel Shapiro of Grodisk who, together with his Hasidim, was herded into box cars and transported from Warsaw to Treblinka. When they arrived he told his Hasidim that *these* were at last the *real* birthpangs of the Messiah, and that he and they were blessed, for their ashes would help purify Israel and thus hasten the end.[95]

We hear these words across the abyss and weep. Some of us may weep for the *Shekhina.* We all must weep not only for them but also for ourselves, for we cannot mystically either fly above history or leap forward to its eschatological End. The screams of the children and the silence of the *Muselmänner* are in our world. We dare not forget them; we cannot surpass or overcome them: and they are unredeemed. Rabbi Teichthal correctly foresaw a Jewish "return . . . to the place of ancestral inheritance." But the *Tikkun* that he quite rightly considered alone adequate to the rupture has not come to pass. Hence in our search for a post-Holocaust *Tikkun* we must accept from the start that at most only a fragmentary *Tikkun* is possible. This is because we are *situated in* the post-Holocaust world. We must accept our situatedness. We must live with it.

B

There has come into existence in our time a hermeneutical teaching that begins with the acceptance of historical situatedness. It confronts the problem of recovery of the past—the past itself and the Word of the past, human and divine—when the past itself is in one situation and we who seek access to it are in another. Moreover, a consensus of sorts has been reached in this teaching—inspired partly by Heidegger, but having many independent sources—among literary critics, philosophers, and theologians. And since our own concern is itself philosophical and theological—indirectly it is also literary—we therefore do well to seek help from this teaching. However— our own concern is a post-Holocaust *Tikkun*—we shall also have to ask where it falls short.

Since there *is* a consensus in the teaching in question we can spare ourselves independent labor and give instead a summary.

1. The present interpreter of the past, like the past itself, is situated *in* history; he cannot stand either "absolutely" *above* history or "objectively" *over against* it. His interpretation of the past arises from an always-already-existing "pre-understanding" of the past, "prejudiced" in that it is historically situated. And while his arising interpretation can broaden, widen, transform his "prejudice," it can transcend it only to the extent of recognizing its inescapability.

The overcoming of all prejudices, this global demand of the Enlightenment, will prove to be itself a prejudice, the removal of which opens the way to an appropriate understanding of our finitude; which dominates not only our humanity but also our historical consciousness.[96]

2. However, far from barring us from the past, this prejudice is, on the contrary, our sole means of access to it. The past is historical; so is the present: *and there is continuity between the two.* An already-existing, forward-moving continuity *from past to present* makes possible a backward-moving hermeneutical recovery *of the past in the present.*

3. Such a hermeneutical recovery is not confined to *thought*, to say nothing of it being confined to *academic* thought. (This latter view once gave rise to the abortive nineteenth-century positivistic search for an illusory "objectivity.") The recovery in the sphere of thought arises from an always-already-existing "pre-understanding" in the sphere of life. It remains tied to that pre-understanding and cannot cut itself loose from it. Is life, then, ever ahead of thought? Or, on the contrary, can thought, arising though it does from life, move ahead of it and legislate

for it? (In an older, still apt imagery, does thought remain the owl of Minerva that rises to flight only with the coming of dusk? Or can it become a cock that announces a new day?)* The answer is not immediately clear, if clear at all. But whatever the answer, *a truly human existence that is not already hermeneutical in its own right is impossible; not only thought but existence as well is hermeneutical.*

4. The interpreter may seek access through a text to a past beyond it. (This is true of the historian.) Or he may seek nothing beyond the text itself and its meaning. (This is true of the text-expositor.) In neither case may the past become purely passive material for a present hermeneutic that, on its part, is pure activity. (In that case there would be no truth in the past and no true past; the truth of the past and the true past would be *made* by the present activity.) It is true that the crucial historicist thesis (number 1) implies a gap between past and present, so that a hermeneutical *activity* is necessary if the gap is to be bridged. But the past itself has a many-faceted meaning in its own right, and this "speaks" to the hermeneutical activity only if this latter is also a faithful, receptive "listening." This is true of the past and its texts. It is eminently true of *great* past texts. Of these it has well been said that, while the conscious purpose of their finite human authors was limited, their meaning is inexhaustible. Here all else may *seem* to be, yet on account of the gap between past and present *cannot ever quite* be, overwhelmed by the hermeneutical task of being "ministerial to the text."†

5. An historicist hermeneutic may therefore be contrasted with alternative hermeneutics as follows. A Platonic-type hermeneutic (for which history is inessential) will recognize no hermeneutical gap, and hence will understand its own activity

---

*See above, ch. I, section 5, and, of course, most of ch. III. For the implications, see esp. sections 12, 13, and 14, below.

†The inexhaustibility of great human texts is set forth powerfully in Schelling's aesthetical thought of 1800. That of divine texts is, of course, a common thesis among both Jewish and Christian thinkers (see, e.g., *Pirke Abot* V 25). On the hermeneutical task of being ministerial to the text, see, e.g., the exchange between Leo Strauss and H. G. Gadamer in *The Independent Journal of Philosophy,* 2 (1978), pp. 5–12.

as being *purely* ministerial: the past text *can* be, and *ought* to be, understood exactly as its author intended. A Hegelian-type hermeneutic (for which history is essential, but for which past is "overcome" by present history) will not be ministerial at all, but will enter into the past only in order to absorb it: it understands the past better than the past understands itself. An historicist hermeneutic (for which past and present are situated *in different* historical situations but also part of *one continuous* history) understands itself as "dialogical"—and ever incomplete.

6. What speaks through past texts may be the word of man. But it may also be a reality-higher-than-human; and, in that case, it must *a fortiori* be possible that the texts in question are inexhaustible. For Heidegger, through great works of Western philosophy speaks nothing less than Being itself. One cannot be open to this possibility on behalf of Athens without also being open to a higher-than-human speech coming from Jerusalem—the "written" and "oral" Torah of Judaism and the "Old" and "New" Testament of Christianity. One must be *at least* as open. Possibly we must be *more* so, if only because, without any suspicion of Socratic irony, those works announce themselves as the revealed Word of God.

The "new hermeneutic" has many theological disciples. That they are by no means all *mere* disciples, was illustrated in the nineteenth century by Kierkegaard. Rejecting Hegel's "overcoming" of history but unable to reject history, he anticipated contemporary doctrine with his view that the Christian, here and now, can reach the Christ, then and there, only if—and because—"repetition" is possible. More telling still is, in this century, Martin Buber. So radically is Buber's thought immersed in history that even the divine "Thou," speaking *to* the human "I" *in* the moment, is a "God *of* the moment, a moment God." Yet so radical a gap as between past moments then and our moment now is hermeneutically bridged, for "in lived life out of the moment-gods there arises for us with a single identity the Lord of the Voice, the One." Hence, whereas the stone of the two Sinaitic tablets "at an unknown time . . . pass[ed] out of our ken," the "Word endures."[97]

C

This is our summary of the "new hermeneutic." All its principles save one will be valuable in our search of a post-Holocaust *Tikkun* in philosophical, Christian, and Jewish thought.
The principle that fails, however (number 2), affects all the
others—the assertion of an unbroken historical continuity
from past to present. That continuity is ruptured by the Holocaust. However, so far as the new hermeneutics is concerned—the vast majority of its literary, philosophical and
theological representatives—this fact has yet to come to consciousness. So do the consequences of it for hermeneutical
theory.

The fact is beginning to come to consciousness. Are all
works once considered inexhaustible *in fact* inexhaustible?
(Can *The Merchant of Venice* be read now as before? Can it be
read at all?)* Can inexhaustibility be claimed even on behalf
of texts considered more than humanly-inspired? Two decades ago a distinguished Christian theologian could still
argue that, being divinely inspired, the New Testament cannot
be anti-Semitic.[98] He has given up this argument; and other
Christian theologians—radical-yet-orthodox—recognize passages in the Christian Scriptures that cannot be hermeneutically reinterpreted and thus saved for the faith but can only be
repudiated.† And whether for Buber the "Word" still "endures" is questionable when this same thinker speaks of an
"estrangement" so "cruel" as to make any "life with God"

---

*Unquestionably Shakespeare's play is a great work of art. Equally unquestion-
ably, although the work is not "in praise of anti-Semitism," anti-Semitic stereotypes—the vengeful old Jew, the salvation of his daughter from his
clutches, and the clutches of Judaism, by a triumphalist Christianity—are
indispensable parts of it. Hence after the Holocaust, if not before, Sartre's
remark is relevant, to the effect that "nobody can suppose for a moment that it
is possible to write a good novel in praise of anti-Semitism" (J-P. Sartre, *What
is Literature?* [New York: Philosophical Library, 1949], p. 64).
†Thus, e.g., David Tracy at a recent conference. On another recent occasion
Roy Eckardt has gone even further. Since a merely human error within divinely inspired Truth could hardly have had power against that Truth, anti-
Jewish passages in the Christian Scriptures such as Matthew 27:25—"His
blood be on us *and our children*" (italics added)—are no merely human element; they are diabolical.

radically doubtful. In these and other instances a post-Holocaust hermeneutic stands or falls with the possibility of a
post-Holocaust *Tikkun.*

In the following we shall confine our attention to a post-
Holocaust *Tikkun* in philosophical, Christian and Jewish
thought. Before entering into these areas, we shall illustrate
the general problematic of a post-Holocaust hermeneutic with
a single example. There is no greater poem in the German
language than Goethe's *Über allen Gipfeln ist Ruh.** None
breathes a deeper, more universal tranquility. But how can we
gain access to, have a share in, that tranquility when alongside
Goethe's poem exists Celan's *Todesfuge?* This latter exists
alongside, in the realm of poetry, but it also points beyond
that realm to the realm of history—to the fact many a cultured
SS murderer may have read Goethe's poem of an evening, so
as to regain tranquility after a hard day's work. Our tranquility
is gone. We recall Adorno to the effect that poetry after Auschwitz is barbaric—not only the writing but also the reading of
it. Is Goethe's poem, then, destroyed?

One of course protests against such a conclusion. One wants
to say that this poem, and indeed every great poem, is timeless
in its truth—but this is to seek refuge in a Platonic hermeneutic. Cast back into an historicist hermeneutic, one wishes to
protest that this poem can be recovered in our time as much as
in any other time—but this is to act as though the Holocaust
had not happened. Goethe's poem can be recovered only if, its
tranquility having been ruptured, there can be a *Tikkun* of it—
both a recognition of the rupture and a mending of it. But how

---

*Wanderers Nachtlied

Über allen Gipfeln
Ist Ruh.
In allen Wipfeln
Spürest du
Kaum einen Hauch;
Die Vögelein schweigen im Walde.
Warte nur, balde
Ruhest du auch.

Wanderer's Nightsong

On the peaks of all mountains—
Tranquility.
In all treetops
You feel
Barely a breath.
The birds in the forest are silent.
Hush, soon for you too—
Tranquility.
                    (The translation is mine.)

such a *Tikkun* is possible and actual is, within the present context, not for us to attempt to say.

The above examples, of course, are all "parochial." It might be said that this is only natural, that the Holocaust itself is parochial. It is relevant to Germans and Jews. Perhaps it is relevant to Europe. Possibly it is relevant even to the whole West and all of Christendom. But, except for these, it is irrelevant to a world for which, therefore, the task of a post-Holocaust *Tikkun* does not arise.

But the Holocaust calls into question not this or that way of being human, but *all* ways. It ruptures civilizations, cultures, religions, not within this or that social or historical context, but within *all possible* contexts. Hence a *Tikkun* of the Holocaust (if a *Tikkun* there is) transcends its limited context in significance. It is Good News to the world. The thought we are in search of—philosophical, Christian, and Jewish itself—will therefore have one universality: that of a witness. Its *Tikkun* will be what in Jewish tradition *Tikkun* is always meant to be—*Tikkun Olam.*

12. On Philosophy after the Holocaust

A

In a veiled allusion to the Hitler regime and all its works, Leo Strauss writes:

It is safer to understand the low in the light of the high than the high in the light of the low. In doing the latter one necessarily distorts the high, whereas in doing the former one does not deprive the low of the freedom to reveal itself fully for what it is.[99]

This statement may be described as a superb expression of a grandiose philosophical failure. Hannah Arendt (who wrote extensively about totalitarianism, Adolf Eichmann, and the banality of evil) reached the view—untenable, as we have seen—that "only good has depth" whereas evil, even when it is "extreme," is "at the surface" and banal. Strauss (who pondered these and related subjects no less deeply but, with characteristic prudence and restraint, confined himself, at least in print, to a few terse statements) spent the best efforts of his philosophical career on the effort of recovering the eternal verities of the greatest of the "old" thinkers. Like other lovers of such as Plato and Aristotle—the names of Jacques Maritain and Etienne Gilson come to mind—Strauss immersed himself with profound regard in the great, Platonic-Aristotelian tradition known as the *philosophia perennis*. But unlike these thinkers, he had no less a deep grasp than any Heideggerian of the vast hermeneutical gulf between ourselves and just that tradition, the Greek originators of which he rightly cherished most highly. (To gain access to the eternal verities from Parmenides to Plato—or, according to viewpoint, to Aristotle, St. Thomas, or Hegel—was no mere matter of "refuting" modern "errors" or "heresies." It was also, and indeed above all, a matter of closing an historical gap existing not only between minds and ways of thought, but between forms of existence as well.) If Strauss's above-cited statement, for all that, expresses a failure, it is because the "low" that Strauss considered it prudent not to inspect too closely—the Third Reich, and its inmost essence, the Holocaust world—does not, alas, reveal itself fully for what it is to an understanding of the high but rather, to the extent to which it reveals itself at all, only (as we have seen) to a thinking confronting it, shattered by it, and saved from total destruction only if it opposes its horror with a sense of horror of its own. This devastating truth—a rupture of the tradition known as *philosophia perennis*, whether this latter is understood in Platonic, Aristotelian, Thomistic, or Hegelian terms—does not, to be sure, invalidate Strauss's insistence that to understand the "high" in terms of the "low" is necessarily to distort it, that the "high" must at all costs be understood in its own terms alone.* However, after the unique rupture that has occurred, the high is accessible only through an *act of recovery*, and this must bridge what is no mere gap but rather an abyss: the necessary recovery must be a

---

*A protest on Strauss's part against the kind of reductionism which we ourselves have repudiated in a different context above, section 9A of this chapter.

Tikkun. Indeed, Strauss's own philosophical efforts, so it would seem, must be understood in such terms. Or—as, following Rosenzweig, he himself might have put it—his return to the "old" thinking, manifesting as it does an ultimately unarguable commitment, is itself an act of "new" thinking. There is evidence to the effect that Strauss himself was aware of this fact.*

This turn of thought suggests the need for a return—brief and last but, for all that, climactic—from the deepest contemporary commitment to the *philosophia perennis* to its extreme opposite, i.e., the most radical contemporary philosophical self-immersion in history. Heidegger's thought has already been given much space in this work. (Too much, some may object.) Yet the last and crucial question still remains to be asked of it. Heidegger failed philosophically to confront the Holocaust; given the nature of both his earlier and his later thought, was this failure inevitable?

Let us consider Heidegger's view of Nietzsche. For Rosenzweig, Nietzsche is among the first representatives of the "new" thinking. For Heidegger, Nietzsche's thought is the unsurpassable and therefore last expression of the metaphysical tradition that begins with Plato. Metaphysics, originating in a primordial withdrawal of and from Being, ends with a *Seinsverlassenheit* so complete that an absolutized Will-to-Power moves—*must* move—into the vacated sphere. Hence God is dead and—so Dostoevsky might have added—everything is permitted. So much, for the present purpose, for Heidegger's view of Nietzsche. So much, for the present purpose, for Nietzsche himself.[100]

The Third Reich made much use of Nietzschean phrases. However, it revealed itself not as a Will-to-Power but rather as a Will-to-Destruction which, being universal, was a Will-to-*Self*-destruction as well. (The burning Jewish children at

---

*On February 4, 1962, Strauss delivered a lecture at the University of Chicago, entitled "Why We Remain Jews: Can Jewish Faith and History Still Speak to Us?" After a profound and sympathetic treatment of his subject he pointed to the *Aleynu* prayer as the "greatest expression" of Judaism, but refused to read it. To do so would be "absolutely improper" since it would imply a *commitment* that he, Strauss, admired but could not honestly say he shared. See above, ch. II, p. 89n.

Auschwitz was its climax, the drowning German children in Berlin its apocalypse.) As for the Reich's inner essence—the Holocaust world—it would be misdescribed as a "world in which God is dead and everything is permitted." It was much rather a world in which torture and murder were *commanded*, and the commanding voice—its ultimate source, a direct *Führerbefehl*—was the voice, as it were, of God.

Heidegger did not confront this scandal. Given the nature of his thought—it is necessary for us to insist—to do so was beyond its power. An *Ereignis*, manifesting a presence of Being even in its absence, is unique and good insofar as Being *is* present, and this includes also the Nietzschean Will-to-Power. The *sheer absence* of Being—what may be called the source of evil insofar as it appears in Heidegger's thought—comes in indefinite varieties the content and diversity of which is, in the last analysis, trivial and irrelevant. (Hence even the later, "anti-Nazi" Heidegger expressed philosophical scorn for those filled with "moral indignation" at the arbitrary Führers, on the grounds that such indignation was lacking in ontological profundity.)* Heidegger's entire stance vis-à-vis Nazism is therefore destroyed by an exceedingly simple dilemma. Either the Führer and his *Volk* manifest a Presence of Being, in which case, for Germans if no one else, the one Führer is "sole reality and law." Or else they manifest a sheer absence of Being, in which case they, together with the bond between them,[101] reduce themselves to but one of many forms—their number and diversity are trivial—of a universal technological malaise. *In either case the evil uniqueness of the Nazi Reich disappears. As for its inner core—the Holocaust world—it could never come into view.*

Its coming into view—a philosophical necessity, for the *Ereignis* has happened—threatens the Heideggerian recovery of "tradition" no less radically than it threatens its opposite, the attempt to recover the *philosophia perennis*. The thinking of the later Heidegger presupposes a philosophical tradition which, whatever its fate in other respects, is in any case un-

*See above, section 6A(4).

ruptured: only thus can this thinking attempt to "think through more primally what was primally thought," thus becoming "soberly ready" to be "astounded before the coming of the dawn." Less obviously but still unmistakably, the early Heidegger's *Sein and Zeit*, too, presupposes a continuous tradition, although not necessarily a philosophical one: how else can a present *Dasein*, projected as it is into the future, "recover past possibilities of *Dasein*?" We have, of course, already touched on the crucial issue of historical continuity, when speaking in general of the problematic of an historically situated hermeneutical recovery. But, now that our theme is post-Holocaust philosophic thought, the conclusions reached earlier are not only corroborated but also given a new focus. We have already confronted the Holocaust as a rupture. What is now coming into view is how it ruptures philosophy.

Already come into view has the fact that the extremes of the "old" and the "new" philosophical thinking are equally threatened with rupture. And since compromises between the two are hardly worth considering, the threat that looms is to philosophy *as a whole*. Hence there arises a question: the symbol of *Tikkun* is alien to philosophy; what happens—what can happen—if, to paraphrase Hermann Cohen, philosophy "borrows" this symbol "from the sources of Judaism"?*

B

A philosophical *Tikkun* is possible *after* the Holocaust because a philosophical *Tikkun* *already* took place, however fragmentarily, during the Holocaust itself. What the greatest German philosopher of the age failed to achieve in decades after the *Ereignis*, was accomplished, at least in principle, by an obscure German professor of philosophy in the midst of the *Ereignis* itself. (Here and in the following we do not mean that *this* one was *the only* one; we *do* mean that even a *single* case, provided it was *genuine*, is a *novum* that alters everything.)

It is obviously necessary to explain and defend this asser-

---

*Cohen writes: "Prophetic Messianism . . . is the most tremendous idea that ethics must borrow and absorb from a reality alien to philosophical methodology" (*Ethik des reinen Willens*, 2nd ed. [Berlin: Cassirer, 1907], p. 407).

tion. Above we made mention, in the context inevitably all-too-briefly, of the German resistance. There was no purer resistance to the Nazi regime than the handful of Munich students who called themselves the "White Rose." They knew that their action—distributing anti-Nazi pamphlets at the late date of 1943—was almost sure to be futile. They knew, too, that they were almost certain to be caught and put to death. They knew it: yet they did it. And they were caught and brutally, legally, murdered.[102]

Appropriately enough, the court decreeing their murder was a *Volksgericht*, the most assiduous of all institutions administering the Führer's law. Just as appropriately, the presiding judge was Doktor Roland Freisler, most assiduous among the Führer's officers of law. No less fitting, however, were the person and the ideas of the spokesman and mentor of the accused. Kurt Huber was a professor of philosophy. His posthumous papers contain a "Final Statement of the Accused," which in substance, if not in actual words, was delivered before the court. In this, Huber said that he had acted out of responsibility for all Germany; that his action was not illegal but rather an attempt to restore legality; that this was so because there were unwritten as well as written laws; and that although he was set by the court at the level of the lowest criminals, he would be vindicated by History. Huber's "Final Statement" ends as follows:

> Und handeln sollst Du so, als hinge
> Von Dir und Deinem Tun allein
> Das Schicksal ab der deutschen Dinge,
> Und die Verantwortung wär dein.

> And act thou shalt as though
> The destiny of all things German
> Depended on you and your lonely acting,
> And the responsibility were yours.[103]

The words are J. G. Fichte's. So is the philosophical teaching. Kant had ascribed a moral mission to all mankind. Fichte, his disciple, singled out the Germans for a special mission. The master, Kant, had seen the essence of a moral action not in its intended or actual consequences, but rather in the will that motivated it. Fichte, the one-time apprentice, considered an action morally impure if the agent thought of consequences at all. These two Fichtean doctrines, both un-Kantian, are dubious in the extreme. Each had a baneful effect in German history that needs no rehearsing here, for it is well known and obvious. Yet both had a moment of truth when Kurt Huber invoked them before the Munich *Volksgericht* on April 19, 1943, just before he and his fellow-conspirators were put to death. It was a truth and a moment never reached by the greatest philosopher of the age, during a lengthy, distinguished and on the whole quite peaceful and undisturbed career.

We do not, of course, mean to set above the thought of Heidegger that of Huber or, rather, the old-fashioned, Kantian-Fichtean idealism that he espoused. Earlier in this work, when we summarized the course of modern philosophy on the road to *Being and Time*, the name of Fichte was barely mentioned.* Now that his name most emphatically is mentioned, it is with the express reservation that his philosophy, or what of it is relevant in this context, had, perhaps, but a single moment of truth. (It had, in any case, only one *great* and *historic* such moment.) The import of Huber lies in his deed more than in this thought; in his thought insofar as it first motivated and then articulated the deed; and in both together by virtue of the unique place, time, and circumstances in which the deed was done and the thought expressed.

As regards the deed by itself, Huber, of course, was not unique. There were, first, the student members of the White Rose. Then there were others in other places who were not students, knew neither of philosophy nor of unwritten laws but who, nevertheless, defied the evil written laws out of an ordinary decency. What marks Huber off from the others is that he invoked philosophy in behalf of his action. However, the invoked philosophy—so we have said—was old-fashioned. Indeed, it is not too much to say that it was outlandish

---

*See above, section 3 of this chapter.

at any time, and that in Huber's time—and in ours—it was and is long out-of-date.

This last assertion needs no proof in the case of Fichte, who taught that all history was in necessary progress toward reason and moral freedom.*(Thus the moral agent could afford to ignore consequences; History-writ-Large would take care of them.) Proof is needed, however, in the case of Kant, for the concerned Kantian teaching, the categorical imperative, has been an inspiration from Kant's own time to our own, and not only to philosophers but also to ordinary folk.

What was soon to be at stake with this Kantian teaching is intimated by two contemporary philosophies, the Heideggerian and the Sartrean. Neither of them is old-fashioned nor out-of-date. Both, to this day, are rightly regarded as being among the great achievements of this century. A categorical imperative of sorts may be extracted from both Heidegger and Sartre. (Briefly: "be authentic!") It is, however, formalized to a totally un-Kantian extreme, with the result that Heidegger's thought, though not compelling his 1933 surrender to Nazism, was unable to prevent it; and that Sartre, though resisting Nazism, could find no adequate grounds for doing so in his philosophy. To Sartre—if not, as we have seen, to Heidegger— this was a source of philosophical anguish. And philosophers today, were they not forgetful of that time of philosophical testing, might find cause in this failure for uneasiness about philosophy itself in our age.†

---

*Fichte identified God as the "moral order of the world"—an ideal progressively shaping the real world.
†Hans Jonas writes: "When in 1945 I reentered vanquished Germany as a member of the Jewish Brigade in the British army, I had to decide whom of my former teachers in philosophy I could in good conscience visit, and whom not. It turned out that the 'no' fell on my main teacher . . . who by the criteria which then had to govern my choice had failed the human test of the time; whereas the 'yes' included the much lesser figure of a rather narrow traditionalist Kantian persuasion, who meant little to me philosophically but of whose record in those dark years I heard admirable things. When I did visit him and congratulated him on the courage of his principled stand, he said a memorable thing: 'Jonas,' he said, 'I tell you this: without Kant's teaching I couldn't have done it' " ("Contemporary Problems in Ethics from a Jewish Perspective," in *Judaism and Ethics*, ed. Daniel Silver [New York: Ktav, 1970], p. 31). Jonas's main teacher was Heidegger.

Still, philosophical powerlessness, as here displayed, is as old as Nietzsche's wrestling with nihilism, and is neither new nor unique to that time of testing. And a long distance exists between these intimations, coming from a time before the worst was known, and the philosophical horror that grips us when the worst is known and philosophically confronted. As friends of the categorical imperative, we are inspired by what Huber said in 1943 before the Munich *Volksgericht*, in support of what he had done. (He cited Fichte but referred to Kant as well.) Then what shall we think of what Adolf Eichmann said before the 1961 Jerusalem court, in support of what *he* had done? He too invoked the categorical imperative—and was not altogether mistaken. There is only one thing we *can* think: we must rethink Kant's *own* teaching, and consider its contemporary fate.

Let us summarize Kant's categorical imperative as succinctly as possible. (1) It is morally necessary to do duty for duty's sake. (2) It is morally necessary so to act that the "maxim" of one's acting could become, through one's will, universal law. (3) It is morally necessary to treat humanity, whether in one's own person or in that of another, never as a means only, always as an end as well. No lengthier summary than these three principles is necessary; none terser is possible. How did Eichmann stand related to them?

There is no doubt that he obeyed the first Kantian principle: he was a dutiful, idealistic mass-murderer, not merely a sadistic or opportunistic one. In this exploration, we have come in many contexts upon the Nazi idealist, from the Führer down to the unknown SS criminal with a pure heart. Now, however, the context is philosophy itself, and the horror of this idealist is philosophical.

The horror is increased by the fact that Eichmann obeyed the second Kantian principle as well. For there is no doubt that the "maxim" of his acting was to make through his own will the Führer's will into universal law. His idea of law was, of course, quite different from the Kantian. However, we cannot take philosophical refuge in this difference; the horror pursues us into the place of refuge itself.

What is the difference between the two ideas? Kant's universal law *is* law and universal only if it respects no persons and treats all as equals. (Thus no man has the right to lie, since *not all* men can have it.) Eichmann's universal law discriminates between "Aryans" and "non-Aryans," between "master-" and "slave-races," and, above all, is itself subject to arbitrary suspension at the Führer's whim. (Thus the "master-race" has the right to lie, and even the duty. And the Führer is beyond truth and falsehood, just as he is beyond good and evil.)* This is the difference between the two ideas of universal law. It is easy for us to know which to love and which to abominate. However, the philosophical question is: *Just where is it written that all are equal? that the law must respect no persons?†*

This question was asked by a young Jewish philosopher in 1935 as he sat in a Viennese coffee house, studying in a newspaper the Nuremberg laws which had just been promulgated. Jean Améry was no old-fashioned Kantian but close in philosophical outlook to Sartre. Also, he was a realistic observer of the then-dominant realities, not only in Germany but also beyond. Hence he put the philosophical question in the following terms: The Hitler regime is accepted as legitimate by the German people; it is accepted as legitimate by the world as well; then what substance is there to appeals against the laws enacted by this regime to a higher, unwritten, law which views all as equal, all as persons? There is no substance, he grimly replied to his own question. Such appeals are insubstantial gestures. And such as he himself were objects of a

---

*Arendt reports that, when one of the judges, indignant at Eichmann's invocation of Kant in connection with his crimes, decided to question him, the latter "to the surprise of everyone . . . came up with an approximately correct definition of the categorical imperative." In this context she also quotes Hans Frank's Nazi updating of Kant's doctrine: "Act in such a way that the *Führer*, if he knew your action, would approve of it" (*Eichmann in Jerusalem*, p. 136).

†In his *Freedom and Reason* (New York: Oxford University Press, 1970, ch. 9) J. M. Hare stages an imaginary debate between two philosophers, a liberal and a Nazi, concerning the "extermination" of Jews. First eliminated in the debate are the opportunists and sadists among the Nazis who act merely from inclination. Next eliminated are those principled but not principled enough. When at length the liberal is confronted with a Nazi principled enough voluntarily to go to Auschwitz when he is discovered to be himself "non-Aryan," the liberal, to be sure, can abominate the Nazi principles, but he can do no more.

"death sentence," "corpses on vacation." Still alive only by accident, as a Jew he had the "sole duty to disappear from the face of the earth."[104]

Three years later, following the *Anschluss*, Eichmann came to Vienna, in pursuit of the maxim of making the Führer's will into universal law.

Adolf Eichmann thus obeyed the first two principles of Kant's categorical imperative if, to be sure, in a fashion Kant never dreamt of. The same cannot be said of the third principle, for this—also in a fashion never dreamt of by Kant and indeed inconceivable prior to the event itself—was defied by Eichmann and his like, not only at Auschwitz, but throughout the length and breadth of the Third Reich. That human personality is an end in itself is the heart and soul of Kant's categorical imperative. As for the Third Reich, *its* heart and soul was the aim to destroy just this principle—by no means only in the case of Jews, "inferior races," and enemies of the Reich, but also, and perhaps above all, in the case of the "master race" itself. From the start the great dream was to stamp out personality as the *Volk* marched in unison at the Führer's behest; and the dream was not destroyed when, at the time of the apocalypse, it turned into a nightmare. For philosophy, the grim fact is this: Kant's own principle is not immune to this unheard of, unprecedented, unique assault.

Concerning Kant's own principle, the respected scholar H. J. Paton writes:

As Kant well knows, men are not saints. Nevertheless—and this is a fundamental conviction of Kant—a good will is present in every man, however much it may be overlaid by selfishness, and however little it may be manifested in action. Because of this he is still entitled to respect and is not to be treated as a mere instrument or a mere thing. As a being capable of moral action, a man, however degraded, has still an infinite potential value; and his freedom to work out his own salvation in his own way must not be restricted except insofar as it impinges on the like freedom of others. We shall never understand Kant aright unless we see him as the apostle of human freedom and the champion of the common man.[105]

Doubtless Paton is correct. Doubtless Kant's "treat all as persons, as endowed with dignity!" rests on the belief that

real, empirical humans *are* persons, endowed with dignity.
Many take Kant as doing no more than express his own personal convictions, whether or not these are due to his Christian upbringing. Taken as a serious philosophical doctrine, his
philosophical *Idea* of Humanity *must* have, and according to
Kant *does* have, a matrix or *Boden* in *actual* humanity. Kant,
in short, *believes* in humanity: *but is that belief warranted?*
Perhaps it was so in Kant's time. Arguably it was once warranted at *any* time if only because, while undemonstrable, this
belief was at least also irrefutable. (Who can refute a "good
will" in the "common man" which is admittedly "overlaid
with selfishness" and hence "not manifest in action"?) But is
this belief warranted in the age of Auschwitz? Then and there,
one kind of common man—the *Muselmann*—was made into a
uniquely uncommon victim, while the other, the manufac-
turer of the victim, was made—*let himself* be made—into a
uniquely uncommon criminal. And "uniquely uncommon" in
both cases was this, that personality was destroyed. It is true
that Kant's belief in humanity could at no time be verified.
However, not until the advent of the Holocaust world was this
belief *refuted*, for here the *reality* that is object of the belief
was *itself systematically annihilated*. That this was possible is
the awful legacy of Auschwitz to all humanity. The awful
legacy for philosophy is that the annihilation of human personality robs the Idea of Humanity of its indispensable basis.
And thus it could come to pass that Kant's categorical imperative, with its heart and soul destroyed, was invoked by its
most dedicated enemies. Kant had formulated his imperative
in behalf of human dignity. The Eichmanns of the Third Reich
invoked it in behalf of a destruction of that dignity so total
that, were the dream to come true, no remnant would be left.
No more terrible illustration can be found of Elie Wiesel's
dictum that at Auschwitz not only man died; that the Idea of
Man died as well.[106]

C

Then what did the philosophy professor Kurt Huber think he
was doing when he invoked an old-fashioned philosophy before the Munich *Volksgericht?* More precisely—since the term

"old-fashioned" suggests that he did not quite *know* what he was doing—*what was he doing?* (This, as will be seen, is in any case the central question.) We cannot say that he proved in his own person that goodness is part of a human "substance" and hence indestructible. (If so, why were there so few? Why not a great army of professors, poets, priests, philosophers?) The "good in man" *can* be destroyed. It *was being* destroyed, and by no means only among those exposed to the Nazi logic of destruction. Then did the "good" in *this* "man" escape *actual* destruction only through an accidental circumstance? But Huber did not belong to the aristocratic, still privileged and shielded officer class. He was no part of a conspiratorial group whose members strengthened each other's resolve. He was not, personally, a man of superhuman courage. In fact, he and the other members of the "White Rose" were rather ordinary. The students had grown up and been indoctrinated in the Third Reich, and some had been soldiers on the Russian front. Huber himself still made a distinction, long robbed of moral validity, between serving the Third Reich and serving in its armed forces.* Then what made Huber do it?

In a different context, we would have to ask this question about all those "righteous Gentiles," few in number and mostly ordinary folk, who had no more reason for defying the Nazi regime than the millions that went along, and yet did defy it.† Here we must ask it about Huber, for he invoked a philosophical Idea in support of his action. Shall we say that the Idea *caused* his action, made it *necessary?* This would have been Fichte's view, in his own Age of Progress. In *our own* century—part of the age of progress no more—Hermann Cohen could still cling to this view prior to World War I. (To the orthodox Jewish objection that unlike the existing God of tradition, the God of Cohen's philosophy, the *Idea* of God, had

---

*Since Hitler's attack on the Soviet Union regular German army units were systematically implicated in SS crimes.

†In traditional Jewish thought "righteous Gentiles" are those who, obeying the laws given to Noah, "have a share in the world-to-come" and are "priests of God." In the Holocaust world this term acquired a new, deeper meaning, as yet unfathomed by Jewish—or any other—thought, since in that world even ordinary decency, when shown to Jews, was little short of miraculous.

no power, Cohen still replied that *only* the Idea has power.) However, this could not be Huber's view during World War II and after ten years of Nazi rule. In Huber's time, the Idea—of God, of Man, of God and Man—was weak. It was ignored when it was not actually scorned, and among the scorners were professors of philosophy. As for the unwritten law deriving from the Idea, this was ignored by all except the victims of the written law, and their appeals to it were futile gestures. Huber himself had sought not to restore this or that law but legality itself.

Did the Idea, then, have no power over his action? But then his words before the Munich *Volksgericht* were, at worst, the words of a liar and a charlatan; even at best, his declared reason for acting was a mere rationalization. From such a view of Huber's trial—the most significant trial for philosophy since that of Socrates—there is but one step to the view that the reasons for philosophical beliefs or actions are *always* other than those given; that—except when it is engaged in scholastic debates of no relevance to human life—*all* philosophical reason is mere rationalization. However, we have seen long ago that "the high" must be understood in its own terms, not "in the light of the low"—and earlier still that there are situations of great moment in which common sense and common decency both dictate that a person's behavior be understood exactly as he understood it himself.*

What we must say, then, is the following. If Huber, in contemplating the great but fearful deed, was irresolute—and what reflective man would not have been?—then it was the Idea that strengthened his resolve. And if the Idea was weak—abandoned, betrayed, assailed, and mocked on all sides—then it was just this weakness that so intensified his resolve as to make him act (if act he must) without regard to consequences, and—except only for a few comrades—alone. Thus he *gave* strength to the Idea even as, in turn, he *was given* strength by it. This dialectic bears a remarkable resemblance to the dialectic of *Teshuva* and also, once self-exposure to the threat of

---

*See above, section 9A.

rupture made it come into view, the kabbalistic dialectic of Tikkun.*

Huber's action *was* a *Tikkun*. He was old-fashioned enough to invoke the unwritten law as if, dwelling in a Platonic heaven, it were always accessible when in fact his own present was so divorced from it that only a *Tikkun* could *make* it accessible. However, his action *was itself* the required *Tikkun*. In obeying the unwritten law he *restored* that law—it must be written *somewhere*—by *writing it into his own heart*. In acting in behalf of Kant's Idea of Humanity, he *mended* that Idea—it was broken—for he recreated the matrix or *Boden* of it in *actual* humanity, even if only in his own person. Such was Huber's *Tikkun* of philosophy, in the age of its most catastrophic rupture.

This *Tikkun*, then and there, created the possibility and necessity of a post-Holocaust philosophy, here and now. This cannot consist of a return to Huber's—or any other—old-fashioned philosophy. Rather must it bring the *Tikkun*, performed by Huber in behalf of an old-fashioned philosophy, to a post-Holocaust philosophical consciousness. The Idea of Man can be—has been—destroyed, for humanity can be—has been—destroyed. But because humanity itself *has been* mended—*in* some men and women *by* some men and women—the Idea of Man *can* be mended. In the foregoing, we have come upon two *nova* of our age, a rupture and a *Tikkun*. Now we have come upon these same two *nova*, in the form that makes a post-Holocaust philosophy both necessary and possible.

The necessity of somehow rescuing philosophical thought has weighed heavily on us in this exploration, ever since first we cited the dread dictum that Auschwitz does not paralyze this or that philosophical thought but the whole metaphysical capacity. Now that, at long last, the possibility has emerged, it has come to us not without irony. Fichte's idea of a world-saving mission of the Germans never had more than fragments of truth, and what little truth it once had was corrupted long before the advent of the Third Reich. It is ironical that its sole

*See above, section 10C.

unquestionable moment of truth should have occurred when a small band of German men and women took upon itself the responsibility for all things German, brushed aside all thought of consequences, and acted in order to save the world, and hence Germany herself, not through but from Germany. However, it was fitting, in the *Volk der Dichter und Denker*, that this *Tikkun* included philosophy, and that the person articulating it was a philosopher.

D

Is this philosophical *Tikkun*, potentially in the making ever since Huber's action and his appearance in the Munich court, a way of the "old" or the "new" thinking? Philosophically to "recover" what "once was" is possible only if the "what was" is no mere fleeting appearance but rather "what *always* was."* Yet it cannot *quite* be what *always* was, for it could be—and was—ruptured. And because it was ruptured the recovery of it is an *act* that is not inessential and will not leave the "what was" unchanged.

Perhaps the answer can come only from the actual process of recovery, i.e., from a new reading of the old great texts of Western philosophy. Such a reading may well find new, unexpected evidence confirming the belief in their inexhaustibility. It may also find new meaning in the person and the teaching of Socrates. Socrates, like Huber, was on trial for his life. But whereas, in Socrates' case, it was for initiating the philosophical quest, in that of Huber it was for defending its noblest achievement—the Idea of Man, and hence the dignity of actual men—against the most thorough, most dedicated enemies. Future philosophers must therefore remember the trial of Kurt Huber, just as through the ages they have remembered that of Socrates. Those remembering it will find much new meaning in Socrates' remark that he had no leisure to study the stars; that all his attention was focused on man, with a view to discovering whether he was a monster more terrible than tryphon or, perhaps, after all, a being of a gentler sort.[107]

*An allusion to Aristotle's "essence" in temporal things that is an intimation of Eternity.

13. Concerning Post-Holocaust Christianity

Was the generation then living more wicked than the foregoing generations? . . . Was the whole nation corrupt, was there none righteous in Jerusalem, not a single one who could check God's wrath? . . . No, its destruction was determined; in vain the besieged city looked in anguish for a way out, the army of the enemy crushed it in its mighty embrace, and heaven remained shut and sent forth no angel except the angel of death. . . . Shall then the righteous suffer with the unrighteous?

What answer should me make? Should we say, "There now have elapsed now nearly two thousand years since those days; such a horror the world never saw before and never will again see; we thank God that we live in peace and security, that the scream of anguish from those days reaches us only very faintly. . . ."

Can anything be imagined more cowardly and disconsolate than such talk? *Is then the inexplicable explained by saying that it has occurred only once in the world? Or is not this inexplicable, that it did occur? And has not this, the fact that it did occur, the power to make everything inexplicable, even the most explicable of events?* [My italics.][108]

We have already cited previously from the above Kierke-gaardian passage. Now, however, we cite it at greater length, for whereas our previous concern with it was proleptic, now that we confront Christianity with the Holocaust, our concern with it is thematic—as thematic as it can ever be. And we need not go beyond this passage in order to suspect from the start that, like philosophy, Christianity is ruptured by the Holocaust and stands in need of a *Tikkun*. Even in his own time Kierkegaard—surely the greatest, boldest, most uncompromising modern Christian thinker—gave an uncharacteristically lame answer to his own bold question: Man is always wrong over against God, and this thought "edifies." A lame response to the destruction of Jerusalem in 70 C.E., vis-à-vis the Holocaust, is it not blasphemous toward man and without glorification of God? Were the children wrong over against God? Their mothers? The *Muselmänner*? Are *we* wrong if we weep, protest, accuse on their behalf? Can any conceivable relation to God *edify* us as we hear those screams and gasps, and that no less terrible silence?

Surely the Christian Good News that God saves in the Christ is itself broken by this news.

We must stress at the outset that the following is not a post-Holocaust resumption of the ancient Jewish-Christian debate concerning redemption. This debate, in any case proved to be fruitless by the experience of two millennia, could well degenerate into obscenity if it became involved in the comparison of sufferings, and if the Holocaust itself became a theological debating point. Rather than resume that debate, or any other Jewish-Christian debate, we shall attempt to enter into the Christian self-understanding, with a view to helping it confront the Holocaust. This is to serve the wider purpose of renewing—*of mending*—Jewish-Christian dialogue.

We speak advisedly of a renewal and a mending. We began this work with Franz Rosenzweig, who found himself standing both within and above Judaism, and able, for the first time in the history of Jewish thought, to give recognition to the Christian covenant from a Jewish point of view. Later we discovered the need for a post-Constantinian, post-Hegelian dialogical openness in which, from a Jewish point of view, dialogue with Christianity—though the future is open—is of central significance for a modern confrontation with revelation, this latter essential to both. Now that we have placed ourselves firmly within the stern limits of our post-Holocaust situation, these exalted aspirations are all unreal in comparison with the arduous task of narrowing the abyss between "Aryans" and "non-Aryans"—i.e., most Christians and all Jews—created and legislated in 1933, and made into an overwhelming reality with the rule of the Antichrist in Christian Europe. And that this was "only once" and "long ago" would be "cowardly and disconsolate talk" even if one glance at the newspapers—for instance, the report of a session of the United Nations—did not prove that the talk is false. One fervently prays that the Holocaust is over, and that it could have happened "only once." But anti-Semitism in the USSR, Nazis at large in Argentina, a declining Jewish birthrate and the isolation of Israel are all part of the sobering evidence that its aftereffects are still here.

B

No Christian Tikkun is possible unless the rupture is recognized. With few exceptions, Christian theologians avoid this
recognition. Some argue that this "horror" "occurred only
once" and "long ago"—not, to be sure, two thousand years,
but at any rate well over thirty. Others argue that it was not
just once, that today there are other "Holocausts" so that, lest
attention be diverted from these new ones, the "old" one is
best assimilated to the others if not forgotten.* We do not of
course deny that the horrors of the present age—hunger in
Africa, torture in the Gulag and, at this moment of writing,
what some Cambodians do to others—require a deep moral
concern by Jews and Christians alike. In some cases, a theological concern is required as well. But these concerns become
flawed the moment they are abused to avoid the unique scandal that Auschwitz constitutes for Christianity. And since current Christian theology, not lacking in boldness, is not afraid
of scandals, we must suspect a deep, unacknowledged Christian trauma.

We shall attempt to reach this trauma with three questions in
an ascending order of theological gravity. Even the first seems
traumatic enough, for Christians though asked the question,
have mostly ignored it.† *Where would Jesus of Nazareth have
been in Nazi-occupied Europe?* If he was who he is said to have
been, he would have gone to Auschwitz or Treblinka voluntar-

Auschwitz: Beginning of a New Era?, ed. Eva Fleischner (New York: Ktav,
1977), is a Jewish-Christian dialogue that attempts to focus on the Holocaust
without diversions or evasions. Yet its editor included a piece—except for a
few poems, the last, i.e., climactic contribution!—which in effect undermines
the whole effort. In this piece Auschwitz is flattened out into a case of atrocity-
in-general. (Others are Dresden, Vietnam, and Hiroshima.) Further, it is reduced to a parochially Western European atrocity, and for this reason to be left
behind in the advance to a less parochial stage of history. The piece climaxes in
the call for a "correction" of the whole concept of Jewish-Christian dialogue.
Such dialogue, on the one hand, is to be broadened by the inclusion of Muslims
and, on the other, to be narrowed in that only "Oriental and non-Zionist Jews"
are to be admitted. The author of the article, Gabriel Habib, seems unaware of
the fact that most "Oriental Jews," having fled to Israel from Arab and Muslim
persecution, are vigorous Zionists—for excellent reasons.
†I have already raised the first of these questions in *Jewish Return*, ch. 4. The
second and third I have not raised previously.

ily even if, as Nazi-Christian doctrine asserts,* he had been an "Aryan." If not going voluntarily, he would have been dragged into a cattle car involuntarily, for he was not an "Aryan" but a Jew. A Jesus that goes voluntarily reveals the scarcity of his disciples in the great time of testing—that saints, those Christian included, were few. A Jesus dragged off involuntarily reveals the still more terrible truth that, without Jew-hatred in Christianity itself, Auschwitz, in the heart of Christian Europe, would have been impossible.

Here more is at stake than the need to acknowledge sin. Christians have always known how to acknowledge sin, including the sin of crucifying the Christ all over again. However, the crucifixion of Christ-in-general is one thing; quite another is the crucifixion-in-particular of six million human beings, among them the helpless children, their weeping mothers, and the silent *Muselmänner*.[109] To be sure, only the actual jobholders and tone-setting idealists knew the exact project and carried it out. But Christian theologians need no instruction in the guilt of complicity; and the complicity, in this case, included giving "only" lip service to the "Aryan" Gospel, passing by on the other side, not wanting to know what was suspected by everyone, and keeping silent when "the Jews are our brothers" or "we are all Jews" would have been the redemptive Word. Dietrich Bonhoeffer has charged that "the church has not raised her voice on behalf of the victims and has not found ways to hasten to their aid; . . . she is guilty of the deaths of the weakest and most defenseless brothers of Jesus Christ."[110] Nearly half a century later, what need one add to this charge, made by a great Christian thinker and martyr during the Holocaust, except a simple but devastating question: Why has the Christian theological response, in this nearly half a century, been so feeble, and so superficial? Why has it been even ambiguous?

The answer can be sought only in a deep, unadmitted, reli-

---

*Once, in a Jerusalem lecture, I employed the term "Nazi Christian." Afterward a visiting Christian stormed forward to protest that "Nazi-Christian" is a contradiction in terms. I could only agree—and add that, at least for twelve years, the conceptually impossible had been empirically factual.

gious and theological trauma. Toward non-Christian worlds—
especially toward the so-called Third World—Christians are
currently seeking to replace their former missionary stance
with one of "outreach." This change, rightly seen as required,
is considered to be bold, radical, risky, for it threatens, or
seems to threaten, the universality of the Christian claim to
Truth. Yet this boldness, radicalism and risk all pale in comparison with those involved in the other required Christian
change—repentance of supersessionism vis-à-vis Judaism and
the Jewish people. The first change requires a new openness
toward worlds hitherto unknown or unrecognized; the second,
no less than a revolution in attitude toward a world—that of
Judaism—known all along but explicitly denied recognition.
Moreover, since negating-of-Judaism has generally been part
and parcel of the Christian affirmation itself—it originates in
the Christian Scriptures—Christian dialogue with Jews and
Judaism, if seriously engaged in, is no mere species of the
genus Christian-dialogue-in-general with non-Christians-in-
general. It involves on the part of the Christian thinker no less
radical an enterprise than (to fall back on a Heideggerian conception) the "destructive recovery" of the *whole* Christian
"tradition"—an enterprise whose outcome and consequences
are unforeseeable.

So radical is the risk. The demand to run it, of course, has
existed ever since the age *post Hegel mortuum* has made Christian Constantinianism into an anachronism. In the age of
Auschwitz, however, the demand not only has a new existential urgency. It is also the case that a theology that heeds the
demand finds itself permeated with a new, unprecedented religious trauma. Without doubt an abyss yawns between Christian
supersessionism and Auschwitz: the Holocaust world sought
the death of Jewish bodies and souls, whereas to Christian faith
human life, and hence Jewish life, is sacred, so that even at
their worst—e.g., in the Inquisition—Christians burned Jewish
bodies so as to save Jewish souls. Even so, the terrible fact is
that there is a thread that spans the abyss. In seeking to Chris-
tianize Indians or Chinese, Christians never sought to make an
end to Indians or Chinese. Just this was—and is—involved in

the attempt to make the "old" Israel over into part of the "new."* And since the *very existence* of Jews—believing Jews, unbelieving Jews, agnostic Jews, but in any case human beings who have not ceased to be Jews—is a stumbling block to super-sessionist Christian theology, the Christian theologian J. Coert Rylaarsdam gave expression, hyperbolic to be sure, to a reli-gious if not a literal truth when he wrote that Christians gener-ally have recognized only two good Jews, a dead Jew and a Christian.[111] The thread that spans the abyss, then, is the idea that, strictly speaking, Jews—and no one but Jews—should not exist at all.

The Christian thinker prepared to face this trauma in the sphere of religious life comes, when persisting in his task, on yet another trauma—this in the sphere of theological thought. He must ask: What can be the weight and inner truth of his own theological thinking, conducted in the safety of Western seminaries now, when it pits itself against the cowardice, in-ner falsehood and downright depravity of Christian life and thought then and there—when there was a cost to disciple-ship? Hitler, Himmler, and Eichmann, baptized Christians all, were never threatened with excommunication; neither were the ordinary murderers. Vatican protests, on the rare occa-sions when they occurred, by the confession of their own au-thors did not spring "from a false sense of compassion." (Compassion, when extended to Jews, was considered false.)†
And while the heroic Protestant Confessional Church did fight on behalf of "non-Aryan" Christians it abandoned the Jews.[112]
At stake in this melancholy litany is not only the "mere

---

*"Jews-For-Jesus" is clearly a post-Holocaust phenomenon in that an old impetus of Jewish flight-into-Christianity is combined with a new reluctance to abandon the post-Holocaust Jewish remnant. However, the "movement" combines the uncombinable: unless its members propose in perpetuity to marry only other Jews-for-Jesus, their distant offspring may conceivably be for Jesus, but they will not be Jews.

†See *Eichmann in Jerusalem*, p. 200. The Papal Nuncio used this phrase when he explained, or rather excused, the Vatican's intervention with Admiral Horthy in behalf of Hungarian Jews. Arendt comments that the phrase "is likely to be a lasting monument to what the continued dealings with, and the desire to compromise with, the men who preached the gospel of 'ruthless toughness' had done to the mentality of the highest dignitaries of the Church."

Christendom" of Christian sinners, among them the confused, the opportunists, and co-opted establishments. For the Christian thinker, it is also, and more significantly and painfully, the Christianity of Christian saints—and their theology more than their personal lives. (Indeed, the Christian failure vis-à-vis Nazi Jew-hatred would have been impossible without a history of Jew-hatred on the part of Christian saints, among them St. Chrysostom, St. Augustine, St. Thomas, and Martin Luther.)[113] Then how can the Christian thinker trust the Holy Spirit to speak to his own thought now, when on Jews and Judaism it failed to speak, or spoke at best ambiguously, through the whole Christian tradition—and when, at the time of supreme testing, the Christian catastrophe was all but complete? The theological trust—one can say nothing else—is ruptured. And the question is: Can there be a *Tikkun?*

Karl Barth, the last great Christian supersessionist thinker—and one if anyone in his dark time surely in many ways guided by the Holy Spirit—still thought theologically *about* Jews.* A Christian thinker repenting of supersessionism can surely think theologically about Jews only *with* Jews—and seek the Holy Spirit only *between* himself and his Jewish partners in dialogue. How can he hope for its presence? An abyss was created and legislated since 1933 between "Aryans" (i.e., most Christians) and "non-Aryans" (i.e., all Jews). No dialogue between Jews and Christians is possible today unless it aims at narrowing if not closing that abyss. No narrowing is possible unless the abyss is first of all recognized. And all recognition must disclose that Jews and Christians come to this dialogue with different priorities.

For Christians, the first priority may be theological self-understanding. For Jews it is, and after Auschwitz must be, simple safety for their children. In pursuit of this goal, Jews seek—are *morally required* to seek—independence of other people's charity. They therefore seek safety—are morally required to seek it—through the existence of a Jewish state. Except among the theologically or humanly perverse, Zionism—

---

*Barth made a few attempts to speak with Jews toward the end of his life—when, so far as his *Church Dogmatics* is concerned, it was too late.

the commitment to the safety and genuine sovereignty of the State of Israel—is not negotiable. Nor can it be weakened or obscured in dialogue with Christians.

But Zionism, as just defined, must after Auschwitz be a Christian commitment as well. No less than Jews themselves, Christians must wish Jewish existence to be liberated from dependence on charity. On behalf of their partners in dialogue, they must wish independence from charity-in-general. On behalf of their own Christianity, they must wish it from Christian charity-in-particular. The post-Holocaust Christian must repent of the Christian sin of supersessionism. One asks: How can he *trust* in his own repentance—that it is both genuine and complete? There is only one answer: If he supports firmly and unequivocally the Jewish search for independence not only from the power of its enemies but also from that of Christian friends. Without Zionism—Christian as well as Jewish—the Holy Spirit cannot dwell between Jews and Christians in dialogue.

The Holocaust is a trauma today for Christian-Jewish relations: Is it a trauma also for Christianity quite apart from those relations? With this question we turn from the first to the second question raised by the Holocaust for the Christian faith. In the Christ God is said to have taken upon Himself in advance *all possible* suffering, and vicariously to have atoned in advance for *all possible* sin. But we have already seen that in the Holocaust "more was real than is possible." The Holocaust was a *world* of evil—an *Unwelt* or antiworld—that was previously unthought and unthinkable. It ruptures philosophical thought. It also ruptures—though this was only marginally our subject—art and literature. Are not then Christian thought and faith ruptured as well? Where is the sting of *that* death removed? Where is *that* sin vicariously atoned?

Up to a point, a response to these questions may be said to be given in a "leftward" move of contemporary Christian thought that, at the risk of the Easter paling in comparison to the Good Friday, hears the Christian Good News as a promise and a beginning rather than as an accomplished fact. (Thus a connection of sorts may exist between such phenomena as "liberation theology" and "political theology," and the trauma, otherwise unacknowledged, of the Holocaust.) If a connection there is, then the most apt illustration of this leftward move in Christian theology was given by Philip Maury with an episode about World War II. Maury was in the French resistance. There had been years of hiding, of resisting, of betrayals—and of the ever-present fear that it would all be in vain. Then, at the risk of both their lives, a friend telephoned him with the Good News that the Allies had landed; and he, Maury, proceeded to spread the news at the risk of his and other lives. Darkness was still holding sway. But there now was a light so *all*-sustaining that to see it, and help others see it, was worth the risk of life. It is a compelling parable.

Compelling too, however, is that the parable points to its own limitations. The sustaining light was *itself* limited. So far as the children, the mothers, the *Muselmänner* were concerned, the Allies had landed too late. What is worse, they had failed to bomb the Auschwitz railways while there was time. *Has the Good Friday, then, overwhelmed the Easter? Is the Good News of the Overcoming itself overcome?*

This is our second question. We move to the third, most traumatic of all; this arises if we transport Christian faith and thought into the Holocaust world itself. One would wish to ask about the children, unable to choose, and hence unfree to choose martyrdom; but Jesus of Nazareth was not a child. One would wish to ask, too, about the mothers wanting to die in their children's stead but denied this choice; but Jesus of Nazareth was not a parent.* He was a free person and is said by Christians to have been *the* free person. Surely all Christian doctrine centers on this freedom. Yet just this freedom gives rise to a traumatic question. At Auschwitz, other free persons were reduced to *Muselmänner*, to the living dead. This is a *novum* in human history and an unprecedented scandal. We ask: *Could Jesus of Nazareth have been made into a* Muselmann?

Liberal Christian theology (for which Jesus is human, nothing but human) cannot dismiss this possibility without a gra-

---

*In the light of the Holocaust, a renewed future Christian emphasis on the person of Mary seems a distinct possibility.

tuitous, posthumous insult to every person who in fact did become a *Muselmann*. We have already cited a great text on this subject. We must re-cite it now, more fully even than before:

On their entry into the camp, through basic incapacity, or through some banal incident, they are overcome before they can adapt themselves; they are beaten by time, they do not begin to learn German, to disentangle the infernal knot of laws and prohibitions until their body is already in decay, and nothing can save them from the selections or from death by exhaustion. Their life is short, but their number is endless; they, the *Muselmänner*, the drowned, form the backbone of the camp, an anonymous mass, continually renewed and always identical, of non-men who march and labour in silence, the divine spark dead within them, already too empty really to suffer. One hesitates to call them living: one hesitates to call their death death, in the face of which they have no fear, as they are too tired to understand.[114]

Was Jesus free of "basic incapacities," i.e., not human after all? Or a lucky one that was spared "misfortune" and "banal incidents"?

Liberal Christian theology cannot evade the *Muselmann*. Its orthodox (or neo-orthodox) counterpart is forced into new, desperate forms of age-old Christian theological dilemmas. If the incarnate Son of God was as fully human as all humanity, then the trinitarian Christian, like the liberal Christian and lest he heap a posthumous insult on all actual *Muselmänner*, must acknowledge the possibility of an incarnate *Muselmann*. And if the incarnate Son of God *remains* divine in spirit and power even in his incarnate state in Auschwitz, then, to be sure, the "divine spark" within him remains untouched, for it is untouchable. However, this very untouchability cruelly mocks all who were *not* untouchable—equally those who were destroyed and those who remained undestroyed only by dint of a desperate, day-and-night, life-and-death struggle. We have already asked whether at Auschwitz the Christian Good News of the Overcoming is not itself overcome. Only one question, for Christianity, is grimmer still: Whether, with both alternatives open to trinitarian thought, the once-Good News does not become a savage joke. In the first case—an incarnate Son of God fully human and made into a *Muselmann*—do not the Nazis laugh their kind of laughter at the victims, the Father, the Son, the Good News itself? ("Where is your God now?") In the second case—a Son of God incarnate and untouchable, hence detached by a gulf from the victims—do not Father and Son, as it were, join in the Nazi laughter? For whereas the process endured by the victims is grimly real, the trinitarian process is only a divine play. With this alternative, the conclusion, long suspected but suspended in the preceding, can no longer be postponed or avoided. However the Christian theologian seeks to understand the Good News that is his heritage, it is ruptured by the Holocaust. One ponders this awesome fact and is shaken.

The one who is shaken need not himself be a Christian. He may also be a Jew. As such he is far removed from Christian Trinitarianism. He may even suspect it of being mixed with paganism if not idolatry. Even so, he need by no means be indifferent. And if he ever had but a single true Christian friend—a true Christian and a true friend—indifference is impossible. This Christian was his friend. When the law made friendship with a Jew into an "Aryan" crime, this Christian— unlike too many others to remember—remained his friend, and risked his life. In this he felt guided and instructed by the Holy Spirit. A Jew must ask: Can this feeling have been a mere sham and a delusion?*

---

*I write these words in memory of Adolph Lörcher. Lörcher, a German patriot and a Christian, was my high school teacher at the *Stadtgymnasium* in the German city of Halle, until my graduation in 1935. In addition to Greek he taught religion, and while Jews were exempt I attended his classes voluntarily, for with Lörcher teaching Christianity was inseparable from attacking Nazism—at a time when other teachers no longer wanted (or dared) to speak. After my graduation we stayed in touch at his insistence, and in 1938 he wrote to a friend abroad in my behalf, thereby risking his life. After my release from Sachsenhausen in February 1939 I no longer visited my remaining "Aryan" friends before leaving Germany: I had no wish to endanger them. Lörcher phoned to say that he would never forgive me if I did not visit him. When visit him I did, he had in readiness two copies of Martin Buber's *Kingship of God*, one to give to me and the other to keep for himself. I have my copy to this day. It bears Lörcher's inscription: *dyoin thateron*—"one of two."

C

With this question in mind, we now approach a unique, unprecedented Christian prayer. The place, appropriately enough, was Berlin, the capital of the Third Reich. The date was November 10, 1938, the day of *Kristallnacht*. This too was appropriate, for this day revealed to the whole world that the Nazi persecution of the Jewish people would stop at nothing. (Jewish stores were plundered in broad daylight. Synagogues burned all over Germany. Jewish males vanished one did not know, but could guess, where.) On that day, anyone walking the streets of Berlin saw.* Few did anything. *Domprobst* [Prior] Bernhard Lichtenberg of the Hedwigskirche walked, saw, and did just one thing. He went back to his church and prayed publicly "on behalf of the Jews and the poor concentration camp prisoners." And he continued to recite his public prayer every day until, on October 23, 1941, he was at length arrested.[115]

Not until May 22, 1942 was Lichtenberg brought to trial. (Here, too, there was a trial.) He was found guilty under a variety of paragraphs of law. As for clemency, he was denied it on the grounds that he "had shown no signs of repentance or of a change of attitude" during the six months of his imprisonment. Thereupon the *Domprobst* asked for permission to speak and said the following:

Herr Staatsanwalt, the many paragraphs which you read to me—these do not interest me in the slightest. However, the last point you made—[and here, according to an eyewitness, his voice suddenly became clearer and stronger]—to the effect that I have not changed and would speak and act exactly as before, that, *Herr Staatsanwalt*, is completely accurate.

*I was among those walking the streets of Berlin on that day. On the fashionable Kurfürstendamm I saw the windows of elegant stores broken, and well-dressed people step in to help themselves. In another street a piano, thrown out of a Jewish window, was lying on the sidewalk. People stood around watching. A solid citizen walked over, touched a key, and produced a sound. (It seemed like mutilating a corpse.) The citizen laughed. "The Jew still can play!" he exclaimed.

The presiding judge then asked Lichtenberg how he came to pray on behalf of the Jews. Lichtenberg replied:

This question I can answer quite precisely. It happened in November 1938, when the store windows were smashed and the synagogues burned. . . . When I saw this destruction, with the police looking on doing nothing, I was scandalized by all this vandalism and asked myself what, if such things were possible in an ordered state, could still bring help.

Then, emphasizing every word, he concluded:

Then I told myself that only one thing could still help, namely, prayer. That night I prayed for the first time as follows: "Now let us pray for the persecuted 'non-Aryan' Christians and Jews."*

When, soon thereafter, Lichtenberg died, an anonymous non-Catholic who had been in prison with him walked over to a Catholic after the funeral and said: "Today they buried a saint."

We do not know how the venerable old priest expected his prayer to help. We *do* know how it *did* help. The twelve years of the Third Reich were a unique devil's *kairos* in the history of the Christian church. They were also, potentially, a unique *kairos* of God, in that even a silent, secret Christian prayer on behalf of Jews, whenever it was sincerely spoken, had a redemptive effect on the Christian soul. So long as it was on behalf *of Jews*—not merely mankind-in-general or "all-oppressed-in-general" or even "Semites-in-general,"† such a prayer went far toward closing the abyss that had been created and legislated between "Aryan" Christians and such as the Buchenwald Hasidim. (They too believed that

---

*In the context Lichtenberg had to use the Nazi term "non-Aryan." But this in no way suggests that he agreed with any part of Nazi doctrine.

†Pius XII on occasion spoke up on behalf of "the oppressed." His predecessor, Pius XI, is justly praised for going further, with his famous statement that spiritually Christians are Semites. Even so he still only opposed one code word with another. He did not unmask and oppose the Jew-hatred disguised in "anti-Semitism" by publicly declaring Christian love of Jews.

prayer helps and *were* helped.) Indeed, it went far toward narrowing the far older gulf created and legislated by the *laos* of the "new" covenant against the people of the "old."

But the full and unique nature of the divine *kairos*, in the midst of the diabolical *kairos*, was disclosed by the fact that Lichtenberg's prayer was *public rather than merely private*, and that even so it did not resort to evasions or circumlocutions. Nor was his choice of words thoughtless or a passing whim. In prison he decided that he would join the Berlin Jews after his release. They had been deported to the Lodz Ghetto, were in need of pastoral care, and he would be a *Judenseelsorger*. (He was taken to Dachau instead and died on the way.) When visited in prison by his bishop, Lichtenberg told him of his plan, wondering what the Holy Father would think of it. Had he lived to the end of the war and learned all, he would have been dismayed, though surely unwavering. For what at great risk and finally the cost of his life was done by Lichtenberg every day for nearly three years—pray for Jews *in public and by name*—was not done even once by the Vicar of the Christ in the safety of the Vatican. Excuses and explanations have been given. They will continue to be given. Some may have a certain pragmatic validity. None will ever obscure the pragmatic and transpragmatic truth that had masses of Christians, Protestant and Catholic, within and without Nazi-occupied Europe, prayed sincerely, publicly, and *by name* for the maligned, hounded, martyred Jews of Nazi Europe, their prayers would have moved more than mountains: *they would have caused the collapse of the kingdom of the Antichrist, the inner core of which was the Holocaust world.* Nazism originated as a system of words. To the end it continued to require and rest on a system of words. And the key-word in the whole vocabulary was "Jew," used as a hissing and a by-word, and unutterable except with a sense of ineffable horror. Never in the bimillennial history of the Church was there a greater *kairos* for changing the world with the Word. Never were the gates of Christian prayer more open, the Holy Spirit at once more clearly present and more vulnerable. *And never was a* kairos *more betrayed, the Holy Spirit more wounded, than when the Word was not spoken, and instead there was a dead, murderous silence.**

Lichtenberg's prayer, then, is an abiding indictment of the silence of the churches. As such it "helps" in that it discloses a rupture in Christianity and ipso facto inspires a search for a *Tikkun*. This, however, is the negative aspect of its "help" alone. Lichtenberg's prayer is *itself* a *Tikkun*: this is the positive aspect of the help given by it.

One may doubt whether this *Tikkun* can be recognized, let alone explicated by a theology that understands itself as a thought deducing truths from the revealed, authoritatively interpreted Scriptures. (Such a thought, resting as it does on authority, is open to no threats and no surprises.) This, however, is a form of the "fanatical," "old" thinking which we have long seen reason to abandon in favor of the "unfanatical" "new" thinking. Theology, within the "new" thinking, may be defined as "astonished response, articulated in thought," and within Christianity the central astonishment is the wonder of its Good News. But after the Holocaust, there can be no radical wonder that is not threatened by radical horror; and it is therefore not surprising that most Christian theology today, to protect the wonder, ignores that horror, minimizes it, flattens it out into a universalized horror that is at everything and nothing. But there is no salvation in such theologizing: to flatten out the horror is to flatten out the wonder as well. Only through self-exposure to the horror can Christian faith and thought preserve their integrity—and hope to be astonished anew by its old Good News. In our time, this old-new News is not that all is well, that nothing has happened, that now as before it is Good Friday after Easter.† It is rather that in a world in which *nothing* was well, *all* was happening, a terrible new Good Friday was every day overwhelming the old Easter, *Lichtenberg's prayer was actual, and, therefore, possi-*

---

*Beata Klarsfeld has said: "If only the Pope had come to Berlin in 1933 and told the Nazis '*Ich bin ein Jud*,' millions might have been spared. Instead, it was a Catholic President [John F. Kennedy] who told the Communists he was a Berliner" (reported by William Stevenson, *The Borman Brotherhood* [New York: Harcourt Brace Jovanovitch, 1973], p. 238).

†An allusion to the teaching of Karl Barth, see above p. 133.

ble. The Good News is in the prayer itself, and in the Holy Spirit that dwells in it. This *Tikkun* is the *Boden* on which Christian theology can undertake the "destructive recovery" of the Christian Scriptures, of the Christian tradition, of the Christian faith. It is the rock on which Christian faith can rebuild the broken church.

D

This is the limit of our reflections. They are, as was said at the outset, the reflections not of a Christian or crypto- or quasi-Christian, but those of a Jew.* As was also said at the outset (but must be repeated), there could be no thought of using (or, which in this case is the same thing, abusing) the Holocaust for any kind of Jewish-Christian debate, one about redemption included. Irving Greenberg has written that Judaism and Christianity are equally religions of redemption, and that the Holocaust is the radical "countertestimony" to both.[116] The most fitting beginning of an attempt to narrow, and eventually close, the gap between Jew and Christian, made into an abyss since 1933 but existing through the centuries, is for the alienated brothers to share in a sorrow that is unique to our time, and belongs to all humanity in our time. Of this Primo Levi has written:

---

*They would have been quite impossible, however, without the comradeship and friendship of Christians that have accompanied me all my life. I have already mentioned Adolph Lörcher. I must also mention Ernst Tillich, an inspiring comrade during my three months in Sachsenhausen. (We Jews were there because of our "race." He was there from choice—a Christian foe of Nazism.) Finally I must mention Alice Eckardt, Roy Eckardt, and Franklin Littell who, in long years of friendship and shared labor, have taught me that for a Jew to be "soft on Christians" would be no act of help or love but rather a betrayal.

In addition to personal Christian friends, I must also mention some Christian thinkers. In a letter to me dated April 20, 1979, Eberhard Bethge writes that Dietrich Bonhoeffer "belongs to those making possible a [Christian] theology [after the Holocaust]," and this despite the fact that "to expect such a theology from him is impossible." I agree with this assessment. Next, the unique figure of Reinhold Niebuhr is surely foremost among the pioneers—and sorely missed today. Further, some presently perceive the task and are at work on it. Johann Baptist Metz has written that Auschwitz was "the apotheosis of evil"; that anyone wanting to "comprehend" it has "comprehended

If I could enclose all the evil of our time in one image, I would choose this image which is familiar to me: an emaciated man, with head dropped and shoulders curved, on whose face and in whose eyes not a trace of thought is to be seen.[117]

14. *Jewish Existence after the Holocaust*

A

What is a Jew? Who is a Jew? These questions have troubled Jews, ever since the Emancipation rendered problematic all the old answers—those of Gentiles and those given by Jews themselves. Today, however, these same old questions, when asked by Jews, bespeak a hidden dread. It is true that the old post-Emancipation answers are still with us: a "religious denomination," a "nationality," a "nation like other nations," or, currently most fashionably in North America, an "ethnic group." Also, the much older Halakhic answer—"a child born of a Jewish mother or a convert to Judaism"—has gained a new lease on life; and, whether it is admitted or not, this is very largely thanks to the existence of the State of Israel. Finally, the fact of Israel itself, a modern state in the modern world, has shaken and confused all the old answers, i.e., the old post-Emancipation ones and the still older Halakhic ones, lending the question of Jewish identity a new kind of urgency. (The state exists. It is a state. It has problems that brook no postponement.) All this is true. Not true, however, is that all the above definitions, whether taken separately or together, today either exhaust the depth of the question or even so

---

nothing"; that a Christian theodicy in this sphere is "blasphemy"; that Christians, still unready to listen to Jews, must at last do so, instead of "offering dialogue to victims"; and that all this is a theological as well as a human necessity, since "by Auschwitz everything is to be measured" ("Ökumene nach Auschwitz," in *Gott nach Auschwitz* [Freiburg: Herder, 1979], pp. 121–44). Finally, I must mention two Christian thinkers who, each in his own way, have prepared the way for a post–Holocaust Christianity: Franklin Littell, by initially single-handedly placing the Holocaust on the Christian agenda, and Roy Eckhardt, by penetrating into theological realms as yet unapproached, so far as I can see, by any other Christian thinker.

much as touch a dimension that is now in it. As for confer-
ences on Jewish identity conducted in such terms alone, in
these the hidden dread is shut out.

*A Jew today is one who, except for an historical accident—
Hitler's loss of the war—would have either been murdered or
never been born.* One makes this statement at a conference on
Jewish identity. There is an awkward silence. And then the
conference proceeds as if nothing had happened.

Yet the truth of the statement is undeniable. To be sure, the
heroism and sacrifices of millions of men and women made
the Nazi defeat no mere accident. But victory was not inevitable. Thus without as brief a diversion as the Yugoslav campaign Russia might have been conquered. Thus, too, Hitler
might have won the war had he not attacked Russia at all
when he did—a gratuitous, suicidal lapse into a two-front war
that is surrounded by mystery to this day.

No mystery, however, surrounds the condition of a world
following a Nazi victory—the "New Order," as it already was
called, or the "Free New Order," as in due course it might have
been called. (As it was, the Auschwitz gate already bore the
legend *Arbeit macht Frei*.) Such are the names and the propa-
ganda. The reality would have resembled a vast, worldwide
concentration camp, ruled by a *Herrenvolk* assisted by dupes,
opportunists, and scoundrels, and served by nations conditioned to slavery. We say "worldwide," although a few semi-independent satellite states, modelled, perhaps, after Vichy
France, might have been tolerated at the fringes. Of these the
United States would surely have been the most prominent.

Such is the outer shape of a worldwide Nazi "New Order." Its
inner essence would have been a murder camp for Jews, for
without Jews to degrade, torture, and "exterminate," the rulers
could have spiritually conditioned neither themselves to mastery nor the world to slavery. (Had Julius Streicher not said:
"Who fights the Jew, fights the devil; who masters the devil,
conquers heaven"?) However, with all, or almost all, Jews long
murdered, the New Order would have had to invent ever-new
Jews for the necessary treatment. (Had not Hitler himself once
remarked that, if there were no Jews, it would be necessary to

invent them?) Or alternatively, in case such an inventing were impossible—who except *real* Jews are the devil?—one would have had to maintain the fiction that Jews long dead were still alive, a mortal threat to the world.* (Had not Goebbels declared in the Berlin *Sportpalast* that Jews alone of all peoples had not suffered in the war but only profited from it—this in 1944, when most Jews of Europe were dead?) We speak advisedly of *all*, or almost all, Jews being dead. A worldwide Nazi New Order that permits semi-independent satellite states at its fringes is conceivable; Jews permitted refuge in them are not. (Had not Professor Johann von Leers argued that, by the principle of hot pursuit, the Third Reich had the legal right and the moral duty to invade surrounding countries, for the purpose of "exterminating" the "Jewish vermin"?) And if nevertheless only *almost* all Jews were dead, if a *few* still survived, this would be due to the help of some Gentiles whose ingenuity, endurance, and righteousness will always pass understanding.

Such would be our world today if, by ill fortune, Hitler had won the war. But by good fortune he lost the war; then why, for the sake of a future Jewish identity, conjure up the spectre of his victory? The answer is simple. One survivor, a poet, rightly laments that, except for a few missing persons, the world has not changed. Another, this one a philosopher, charges just as rightly that the world refuses to change, that it views the reminding presence of such as himself as a malfunctioning of the machinery. Long before either Jewish plaint— long before the *Ereignis* itself—the Christian Sören Kierke-

*Hitler's remark is reported by Hermann Rauschning and is integrated into the latter's "revolution of nihilism" thesis. In an attempt to refute that thesis Eberhard Jäckel's *Hitlers Weltanschauung* (Tübingen: Wunderlich, 1969) starts out by asserting that Hitler was no nihilist but rather had a coherent, if evil, *Weltanschauung* composed of "principles." The book ends up, however, with the unwitting demonstration that with Hitler all except Jew-hatred was compromisable, and that what is grandiloquently called Hitler's "coherent *Weltanschauung*"—indeed, no less than a "thought system" with "theoretical foundations"—amounts only to this, that the nineteenth-century anti-Semitic slogan "the Jews are our misfortune" is made into a cosmic principle. In *Mein Kampf* Hitler himself writes: "If, with the help of the Marxist creed, the Jew is victorious over the other peoples of the world, his crown will be the funeral wreath of humanity and this planet will, as it did thousands [second edition: millions] of years ago, move through the ether devoid of men . . ." (p. 60).

gaard had spelled out the abstract principle—that a single ca-tastrophic event of monumental import is enough to call all things into question ever after.[118] We have cited such wit-nesses against others. As we now turn to our native realm of Jewish self-understanding, we can do no other than cite them against ourselves.

Even to do so only tentatively—preliminarily, as it were by way of experiment—is to discover, quite independently from all the previous complicated reflections and simply by looking at the facts, that to minimize, ignore, "overcome," "go beyond" the dark past for the sake of a happy and healthy future Jewish self-understanding is impossible. Empirically, to be sure, all this *is* possible: the phenomenon exists on every side. But mo-rally, religiously, philosophically, humanly it is an impossibil-ity. Shall we trust in God because we—though not they—were spared? Shall we trust in man because here and now—though not then and there—he bears traces of humanity? Shall we trust in ourselves—that we, unlike them, would resist being made into *Muselmänner*, the living dead, with the divine spark within us destroyed?

We can do none of these things; they are all insults, one hopes unwitting, to the dead. And behind these unintended insults lies the attempt to repress the hidden dread, to deny the rupture that is a fact. Above we asserted that philosophy and Christian theology can each find its respective salvation not by avoiding the great rupture, but only by confronting it. We must now turn this assertion against ourselves.

B

The move from non-Jewish to Jewish post-Holocaust thought is not a step but a veritable leap. This is so by dint of a single fact the implications of which brook no evasion. "Aryan" victims of the Third Reich, though robbed, enslaved, subjected to humil-iation, torture, and murder, were not *singled out* unless they *chose to single themselves* out; Jews, in contrast, were *being singled out without choice of their own.* We have already con-sidered this difference as it was manifest during the Holocaust itself. We must now consider its implications for today.

There are two such implications. First, whereas much of the post-Holocaust world is ruptured, the post-Holocaust *Jewish* world is *doubly* ruptured, divorced by an abyss not only from its own past tradition but also—except for such as Huber and Lichtenberg who, even then, bridged the gulf from the non-Jewish side—from the Gentile world. Second, whereas post-Holocaust philosophical and Christian thought finds a *Tikkun* in such as Huber and Lichtenberg, post-Holocaust Jewish thought finds itself situated after a world which spared no effort to make a *Jewish* Huber or Lichtenberg systematically impossible. For "Aryans," "crime," then as always, was a *doing*, so that in their case the Nazi tyranny, like other tyrannies, *created* the possibilities of heroism and martyrdom. For "non-Aryans," however, the crime was *being itself*, so that in their case—a *novum* in history, all previous tyrannies included—every effort was made to *destroy* the very possibility of both heroism and martyrdom, to make all such choosing, actions, and suffering into an irrelevancy and a joke, if indeed not altogether impossible.[119] The Jewish thinker considers the choiceless children; their helpless mothers; and finally—the achievement most revelatory of the essence of the whole Nazi world—the *Muselmänner*, these latter once free persons, and then dead while still alive: and he is filled not only with human grief but also with a metaphysical, religious, theological terror. Ever since Abraham, the Jewish people were singled out, for life unto themselves, and for a blessing unto the nations. And again and again throughout a long history, this people, however weary, responded to this singling-out act with the most profound freedom. (No response is as profoundly free as that to a singling-out act of God.)* Ever since 1933, this people was singled out for death, and no effort or ingenuity was spared to make it into a curse to all those befriending it, while at the same time robbing it of the most elementary, most animal freedom. (No freedom is either more elementary or more animal than to relieve the bowels at the time of need.) The Reich had a research institute on the "Jewish question." Its work included serious, scholarly,

*See above, ch. III, section 12.

professorial studies. These can have had no higher aim than to discover the deepest roots of Jewish existence and, after four thousand years of uninterrupted life, destroy them. The Jewish thinker is forced to ask: Was the effort successful?*

C

It is unthinkable that the twofold rupture should win out. It is unthinkable that the age-old fidelity of the religious Jews, having persisted through countless persecutions and against impossible odds—Yehuda Halevi expressed it best†—should be destroyed forever. It is unthinkable that the far less ancient, no less noble fidelity of the secular Jew—he holds fast, not to God, but to the "divine spark in man"—should be smashed beyond repair. It is unthinkable that the gulf between Jews and Gentiles, created and legislated since 1933, should be unbridgeable from the Jewish side so that the few but heroic, saintly attempts to bridge it from the Gentile side—we shall never forget such as Lichtenberg and Huber—should come to naught. It is this unthinkability that caused in my own mind, on first confronting it, the perception of a "614th commandment," or a "commanding Voice of Auschwitz," forbidding the post-Holocaust Jew to give Hitler posthumous victories. (This is the only statement of mine that ever widely caught on, articulating, as one reviewer aptly put it, "the sentiments . . . of Jewish shoe salesmen, accountants, policemen, cab-drivers, secretaries.")[120]

But we must now face the fact—and here my thinking is forced to move decisively beyond the earlier perception just mentioned—that the unthinkable has been real in our time, hence has ceased to be unthinkable; and that therefore the "614th commandment" or "commanding Voice of Auschwitz" may well be a moral and religious necessity, but also, and at the

*With this question we are forced to go beyond Buber's stance toward the Holocaust, see above, section 7. This is not to say, however, that it ceases to be relevant, or that there may not be ways of recovering it.

†In the *Kuzari* he asserts that the great Jewish virtue is not saintliness or humility but rather fidelity, and implies that this belongs not to some but to the whole people. Jews could "escape degradation by a word spoken lightly" (IV, pp. 22, 23). Only because they stay in fidelity at their singled-out Jewish posts do they exist as Jews at all.

same time, an ontological impossibility. In his time, as sober a
thinker as Immanuel Kant could argue that since moral freedom, while undemonstrable, is at any rate also irrefutable, we
all *can* do that which we *ought* to do. On our part and in our
time, we need but visualize ourselves as victims of the Nazi
logic of destruction in order to see this brave doctrine dissolve
into the desperate cry, "I cannot be obligated to do what I no
longer can do!" Indeed, such may well have been the last silent
cry of many, just before, made into the living dead, they were
no longer capable of crying even in silence.* Nor are we re-
scued in this extremity by the Jewish symbol of *Tikkun* in any
of its pre-Holocaust uses, even when, as in the most radical of
them, a rupture is admitted and confronted. We have seen that
during the Holocaust the Nazi logic of destruction murdered
kabbalistic no less than nonkabbalistic Jews—and their *Tikkun*
with them. A would-be kabbalistic *Tikkun* of our own post-
Holocaust rupture would inevitably be a flight from *that* rupture, and hence from our post-Holocaust situation as a whole,
into an eternity that could only be spurious.

We are thus driven back to insights gained earlier in the
present work:[121] the moral necessity of the "614th commandment" or "commanding Voice of Auschwitz" must be "rootless and groundless" (*bodenlos*) unless it is an "ontological"
possibility; and it *can* be such a possibility only if it rests on
an "ontic" reality. With this conclusion all our Jewish thinking and seeking either comes to a dead halt or else finds a
novum that gives it a new point of departure.

D

The Tikkun *which for the post-Holocaust Jew is a moral necessity is a possibility because during the Holocaust itself a
Jewish* Tikkun *was already actual.* This simple but enormous,
nay, world-historical truth is the rock on which rests any authentic Jewish future, and any authentic future Jewish identity. (As is gradually emerging, it is also the pivotal point of

---

*The careful reader will notice that, compared to my *Encounters* (in which all
of ch. II is taken up with the Kantian "ought"), the role of Kantianism has
diminished in the present work. This is so because of considerations which
reach their climax in the present section.

the developing argument of this whole work.) We have already seen that the singled-out Jewish resistance *in extremis* to the singling-out assault in its own extremity is ontologically ultimate.[122] As we now turn from the Jewish past to a prospective Jewish future we perceive that this ontological Ultimate—a *novum* of inexhaustible wonder, just as the Holocaust itself is a *novum* of inexhaustible horror—is the sole basis, now and henceforth, of a Jewish existence, whether religious or secular, that is not permanently sick with the fear that, were it then and there rather than here and now, *everything*—God and man, commandments and promises, hopes and fears, joys and sorrows, life itself, and even a human way of dying—would be *indiscriminately* prey to the Nazi logic of destruction. The witnesses cited earlier all crowd back into the mind. We recall those we named. We also think of many we did not name and, above all, of the countless ones whose memory can only be nameless. As we ponder—ever reponder—their testimony, we freely concede that we, or others before us, may have romanticized it. We also concede that, yielding to all sorts of delusions, they may have done much romanticizing themselves. (Both errors are human.) But such concessions reveal only the more clearly that the astounding fact is not that many succumbed to the Nazi logic of destruction but rather that there were *some* who did *not* succumb. Indeed, even one would suffice to warrant a unique astonishment—and deny the evil logic its total victory.

We have reached this conclusion before. Our task now is to consider its implications for an authentic Jewish future. Above we repudiated the belief—an outworn idealism then, a case of humanistic twaddle now—that there is a core of human goodness that is indestructible. Now we must repudiate the belief—an outworn theology then, a case of Jewish twaddle now—that there is a Jewish substance—an *inyan enoli*, as it were*—that cannot be destroyed. Rather than in any

---

*An allusion to Yehuda Halevi's *Kuzari*, II, pp. 34 ff. Halevi attempts to establish the continuity of the Divine-Jewish covenant through the dubious doctrine of a "divine content" planted hereditarily into the Jewish people. That he does not embrace racism is proved by the fact that the whole work is addressed to a would-be convert. Nor is any respectable modern Jewish thinker a racist. However, not a few have affirmed an absolutely indestructible Jewish tradition—religious, moral, or, more vaguely, cultural.

such terms, the Jewish resistance to the singling-out Holocaust assault must be thought of as a life-and-death, day-and-night struggle, forever threatened with collapse and in fear of it, and saved from actual collapse—if at all—only by acts the source of whose strength will never cease to be astonishing. Their resistance, in short, was the *Tikkun* of a rupture. *This* Tikkun *is the* ultimate ground *of our own*.

E

To this theme—*their* Tikkun as the basis of *our* present and future Jewish Tikkun—we shall turn in detail forthwith. For the present, it is necessary, for a last time, to hark back to the theme of post-Holocaust philosophy and Christianity. We have seen that when Huber and Lichtenberg made their momentous choices—had their momentous trials—they each created a Tikkun, the one for future philosophy, the other for future Christianity. But what if, treated like Jews, they had been robbed of all choice, denied any trial, and had been subjected to the Nazi logic of destruction? (Other "Aryans" were treated in just this way.) Would they—*could* they—have resisted the irresistible? We did not ask this question when we considered their testimony. (It would then have been out of place.) We must ask it now. And, remembering the *Muselmänner*, we cannot answer it. (The question is—will always be—unanswerable.) Moreover, if we *can* say that they *might* have resisted, it is solely and exclusively because the irresistible Nazi logic of destruction was *in fact* resisted by some who were subjected to it, i.e., by Jews and those many non-Jews who were treated as if they were Jews themselves.* Hence we must say of a philosophical and Christian future exactly what we said of a Jewish future: Were it not for the Jewish Tikkun then and there—and that of quasi- and honorary Jews of whom Pelagia Lewinska has served as our symbol in this ex-

---

*See the above argument (section 8B) to the effect that insofar as the Nazi logic of destruction aimed at the self-destruction of its victims, it can be understood in terms of the Nazi scheme of things only if these victims are Jews.

ploration—all authentic future philosophers and Christians would be sick with a permanent fear—in this case, the fear that, were they then and there rather than here and now, they, their prayers, their philosophical thoughts, would all be indiscriminately prey to the Nazi logic of destruction. This is what was meant (or some of what was meant) by the above assertion that the Jewish *Tikkun* in the Holocaust world is not only enormous in significance but world-historical.

Directly, then, the *Tikkun* of such as Pelagia Lewinska, the Lublin and Buchenwald Hasidim, the Warsaw Ghetto fighters, is the basis of a future Jewish *Tikkun*. Indirectly, it is also a pillar—not, to be sure, the sole pillar, but indispensable—of a future philosophy and Christianity. We thus arrive at a strange, unexpected, even paradoxical conclusion. Then and there, no effort was spared to make the Jewish people into a curse for all those befriending it. Yet philosophers and Christians today and tomorrow—no other group of Gentiles can be considered within the limits of the present exploration—are reached by a blessing across the abyss, coming to them from the darkest Jewish night. It is a blessing the like of which the world has never seen.

F

Christians after the Holocaust, we have seen, must be Zionist on behalf not only of Jews but also of Christianity itself. Jews after the Holocaust, it now emerges, must be Zionist on behalf not only of themselves but also of the whole post-Holocaust world. That a Jewish state is an authentic modern project without need for justification through the Holocaust has already been shown.* Yet to be shown in pages to come is its place within a post-Holocaust Jewish self-understanding. At stake in the present context is the role of a Jewish state in a post-Holocaust mending of Jewish-Gentile relations. Such a mending is needed after the Holocaust. During the Holocaust, Jewish powerlessness placed Jews absolutely at the mercy of Nazi enemies and democratic friends alike, encouraging murder among the

*See above, ch. III, section 12. That Zionism and the State of Israel became thematic in this book before the Holocaust is, of course, not accidental.

first and among the second, half-heartedness in opposition, or even total indifference. After the Holocaust, the Jewish people owe the whole world the duty of not encouraging its vices—in the case of the wicked, murderous instincts, in the case of the good people, indifference mixed with hypocrisy—by continuing to tolerate powerlessness. Without a Jewish state there could be no post-Holocaust *Tikkun* of Jewish-Gentile relations, from the Jewish any more than from the Gentile side. The "Jewish emergence from powerlessness,"[123] occurring when it did, has been and continues to be a moral achievement of world-historical import.*

This, of course, is not universally recognized. The United Nations Organization condemns Zionism as a form of racism. Clerical councils exalt a "moderate" PLO that shows no signs of moderateness. A world indifferent to Jerusalem in Arab hands is greatly concerned when she is in Jewish hands. To go beyond Zionism and Israel in this melancholy litany, Nazi criminals are widely at large, unmolested. Anti-Jewish hate literature flourishes. Synagogues are bombed in Paris. There are even Jews who wish the State of Israel would "go away." And since Vietnamese boat-people now, much like Jewish boat-people then, roam the seas, one wonders whether today Hitler is not winning posthumous victories throughout the world. Despite the new reality that is Israel, one must there-

---

*Persistent attempts to obscure or deny this fact arise from a combination of repressed guilt on the part of the good people, and a new form of Jew-hatred on the part of the wicked. Arnold Toynbee's equation of Israeli behavior toward Palestinian Arabs with Nazi behavior toward Jews is, one hopes, a case of the first. A case of the second is the PLO National Covenant's denial of the same right to self-determination to Jews that is claimed on behalf of Palestinian Arabs themselves. And the two combine whenever the wicked succeed in persuading the good that the State of Israel is a radical injustice—a punishment of the innocent (i.e., the Palestinian Arabs) for sins committed by others (i.e., the German Nazis). The British White Paper of 1939 that stopped Jewish immigration into Palestine at the time of greatest need was inspired by Arab protests. When the 1946 Anglo-American committee recommended, not a Jewish state but only the admission to Palestine of 100,000 Jewish survivors, the Arabs, by then fully aware what *these* were survivors *of*, flatly rejected the recommendation and declared a general strike. These two examples are sufficient proof to the effect that if any state or political leadership at the time was innocent of the shedding of Jewish blood, the Palestinian Arab leadership was not among them.

fore ask a radical question. *Jewish trust in the Gentile world was ruptured by the Holocaust: how, in the world of today, can it be mended?*

Of course one wants to avoid this question. Any Jew today wants to say that there *is* no such rupture any longer, and hence no need for a mending, and this in gratitude to Allied soldiers then (without whom no Jews would survive); in friendship with many Gentiles now; and also, perhaps above all, in simple fairness to a new generation of Germans that knows not Auschwitz and bears no guilt. (Not all anti-Zionists are anti-Semites; not all anti-Semites are murderers; and, above all, the post-Holocaust world is not the Holocaust world itself.) A Jew *wants* to say all this; but he cannot say it. For he remembers Kierkegaard—having cited him against others, we must also cite him against ourselves—and he is forced to spurn a course at once so easy and so obvious. The Holocaust ruptured Jewish-Gentile relations once. If unmended, the rupture would haunt Jewish-Gentile relations forever, even if learned professors could give proof absolute to the effect that a repetition is impossible. Thus a question arises for Jews and Gentiles alike that brooks no evasion. For Gentiles it is: If *per improbabibile aut impossibile* there were a repetition, could they trust themselves? (This question extends to Jews as well—just in the unlikely case that, next time, they were among the "Ayrans.") For Jews it is: Profoundly and radically rather than merely superficially, can they ever again trust the world? For four millennia of uninterrupted existence, the Jewish people, even when totally abandoned, has managed to keep a bond with the world, if only because it understood its existence as meant for a blessing. The post-Holocaust Jew must ask: Is this bond broken forever? Is Jewish existence henceforth condemned to utter solitariness?

Meant for a blessing, the Jewish people was treated time and again as though it were a curse. Yet except for moments of despair, its prophets and sages have never in turn wished a curse upon the nations. The tone was set by Lamentations, following the first fall of Jerusalem: "Let it not come unto you, all ye that pass by!" (1:12). Following the second fall of the City, a Midrashic author commented: "The community of Israel says to the nations of the world: 'May that not come upon you which has come upon me! May not happen to you what has happened to me!' " This Midrash is last and climactic in *Midrashim of Lament and Comfort*, an anthology published for German Jews in Germany by a German rabbi in 1935, the year of the Nuremberg laws.[124] So early was an attempt made, on the Jewish side, to narrow (if not close) the Jewish-Gentile abyss.

This was, of course, before the gulf had *become* an abyss. After that catastrophe Jews cannot speak the biblical words to unrepentant Nazis, accomplices, bystanders, for they cannot speak to them at all. They can and must speak to those upon whom it, or something resembling it, has come—starving African children, Gulag slave laborers, boat-people roaming the seas. But can the Jewish people speak to a world which, first, let it happen and, now, lets all this happen? Can there be a *Tikkun* of the ruptured Jewish trust?

From the Gentile side of the Jewish-Gentile relations, what will happen will happen. From the Jewish side, it is clear enough what ought to happen. Gentile friends, many or few, are spending themselves in the attempt to repair the great rupture of trust. Jews cannot abandon these efforts made on the Gentile side, but must respond to them on the Jewish side. This much, we say, is clear enough. It is even trivially clear, since not sharing in the mending of Jewish-Gentile relations would be handing posthumous victories to Hitler. Yet here as before we must ask whether what is morally necessary is also ontologically possible. For what haunts Jews and Gentiles alike in their search for mutual trust—what *cannot but* haunt them—is whether, if they were then and there rather than here and now, they could trust themselves—and, therefore, each other. It is the crucial question. And so long as it remains unasked, or if asked remains wholly without answer, every expression of "Never again," Jewish or Gentile, belongs into the realm of mere pious hopes, gestures, or prayers that, rather than mend the broken trust, are themselves untrusted.

A Tikkun *of Jewish-Gentile trust, genuine even if fragmentary, is possible from the Jewish side, here and now, because a* *corresponding* Tikkun *was already begun from the Gentile side then and there.* Above we came upon a blessing that reaches post-Holocaust philosophy and Christianity from the darkest Jewish night. We come upon a blessing now, no less unique, that reaches post-Holocaust Jewish life and thought from this same night. (This is no symmetry constructed by armchair philosophy. Coming as it does from the testimony of survivors, it is rather a stumbling block to all armchair understanding.) In other worlds, a hero or martyr serves, and is himself sustained by, a great and noble cause as, going beyond all ordinary decency, he risks or gives his life. In the Holocaust world, a Gentile's decency, if shown toward Jews, made him into something worse than a criminal—an outlaw, vermin—just as were Jews themselves; and, as he risked or gave his life, there was nothing in the world to sustain him, except ordinary decency itself. Above we saw, in Huber and Lichtenberg, a *Tikkun*, respectively, of the Idea of Man and the Christian Word. Now we have come upon something greater still: in the Holocaust world there occurred a *Tikkun* of ordinary decency. Those that performed this *Tikkun* may insist that they did nothing unusual. However, a post-Holocaust Jew—and the post-Holocaust world—can never cease to be amazed.*

This is by no means to say that ordinary decency has inherited the earth. Then and there, the number of the "righteous among the nations" was small. If *per improbabibile aut impossibile* there were a repetition, their number, for all the far-reaching efforts to learn lessons from the Holocaust, might be no larger. Conceivably—our age is grim—it might even be smaller, so that the "contracting logic" which Rosenzweig once found applicable to Jews might come to dominate the decency of humanity. Even so the post-Holocaust Jew must stake much—almost all—on the trust that it is these, many or few, who represent humanity; and that, like Rosenzweig's

---

*Eliezer Berkowitz has rightly remarked that according to some Jewish writers "righteous Gentiles" were so numerous during the Holocaust that he must wonder how it could happen that most of his relatives were murdered. It is true that these righteous ones were few, that their number is depressing; the quality of these few, however, is an abiding wonder.

"eternal people," they will never vanish wholly from the earth.

G

What is a Jew? Who is a Jew? After *this* catastrophe, what is a Jew's relation to the Jewish past? We resume our original question as we turn from one rupture in post-Holocaust Jewish existence—of the bond with the Gentile world—to the other—of the bond with his own past history, past tradition, past God.

After all previous catastrophes ever since biblical times, a Jew could understand himself as part of a holy remnant. Not that the generation itself was holy, a presumptuous view, and one devoid of any real meaning. The generation was rather *heir* to holy ones—not to the many who had fallen away but rather to the few that, whether in life or the death of martyrdom, had stayed in fidelity at their singled-out Jewish post. Was there ever a self-definition by a flesh-and-blood people that staked so much—staked *all*—on fidelity? It is the deepest definition of Jewish identity in all Jewish history.

It cannot, however, be the self-definition of this Jewish generation for, except for an accident, we, the Jews of today, would either have been murdered or never born. *We are not a holy remnant. We are an accidental remnant.* However we may wish to evade the grim fact, this is the core definition of Jewish identity today.

The result is that we, on our part, cannot consider ourselves heir to the few alone. (For the religious among us, the martyrs and their prayers; for the secularists, the heroes and their battles.) We are obliged to consider ourselves heir to the *whole* murdered people. We think of those made into *Muselmänner* by dint of neither virtue nor vice but some "banal incident." We think of the children; their mothers; of the countless saints, sinners, and ordinary folk who, unsuspecting to the end, were gassed in the twinkling of an eye. And what reaches us is nothing so much as *the cry of an innocence that shakes heaven and earth; that can never be stilled; that overwhelms our hopes, our prayers, our thought.* Maimonides is said to have ruled that any Jew murdered for no reason other than being a Jew is to be considered holy. Folk tradition, already existing, cites Maimonides to this effect and views *all* the Jewish victims of the Holocaust as *kedoshim*—as holy ones. Only in this and no other sense are we, the accidental remnant, also a holy remnant. *In this sense, however, our holiness is ineluctable and brooks no honest escape or refusal.*

This circumstance places us into a hermeneutical situation that, after all that has been said about a post-Holocaust *Tikkun*, is new and unique still. Indeed, the dilemma in which we are placed is so extreme, so unprecedented, so full of anguish as to seem to tear us in two; and as to cause us to wonder whether, at the decisive point where all comes to a head, a post-Holocaust *Tikkun* of any kind is not seen, after all, to be impossible.

The dilemma is as follows. If (as we must) we hold fast to the children, the mothers, the *Muselmänner*, to the whole murdered people and its innocence, then we must surely despair of any possible *Tikkun*; but then we neglect or ignore the few and select—those with the opportunity to resist, the will and strength to resist, deriving the will and strength we know not whence—whose *Tikkun* (as we have seen) precedes and makes mandatory our own. And if (as also we must) we hold fast to just these select and their *Tikkun*, then our *Tikkun*, made possible by *theirs*, neglects and ignores all those who performed no heroic or saintly deeds such as to merit holiness and who yet, murdered as they were in utter innocence, must be considered holy. Not accidentally, "Holocaust theology" has been moving toward two extremes—a "God-is-dead" kind of despair, and a faith for which, having been "with God in hell," either nothing has happened or all is mended.* How-

---

*The most influential expression of the first extreme is Richard Rubenstein's *After Auschwitz* (Indianapolis and New York: Bobbs-Merrill, 1966). A poignant expression of the second is Eliezer Berkowitz, *With God in Hell* (New York: Sanhedrin, 1979). As is clear from his *Faith after the Holocaust* (New York: Ktav, 1973), Berkowitz does not assert either that nothing has happened or all is mended. He does, however, affirm a *faith* for which this is true, i.e, one which, though deeply shaken by the Holocaust, is not altered in consequence.

ever, post-Holocaust thought—it includes theological concerns but is not confined to them—must dwell, however painful and precariously, between the extremes, and seek a *Tikkun*
as it endures the tension.

The *Tikkun* emerging from this tension is composed of three
elements: (a) a recovery of Jewish tradition—a "going back
into possibilities of [Jewish] *Dasein* that once was *da*";* (b) a
recovery in the quite different sense of recuperation from an
illness; and (c) a fragmentariness attaching to these two recov-
eries that makes them both ever-incomplete and ever-laden
with risk. Without a recovered Jewish tradition—for the religious Jew, the Word of God; for the secular Jew, the word of
man and his "divine spark"—there is no Jewish future. Without a recuperation from the illness, the tradition (and hence
the Jewish future) must either flee from the Holocaust or be
destroyed by it. And without the stern acceptance of both the
fragmentariness and the risk, in both aspects of the recovery,
our Jewish *Tikkun* lapses into unauthenticity by letting *theirs*,
having "done its job," lapse into the irrelevant past.

To hold fast to the last of these three elements is hardest but
also most essential. Once Schelling and Hegel spoke scath-
ingly about theological contemporaries who were momentarily awakened from their dogmatic slumber by the Kantian philosophy but soon used that philosophy as a soporific: every
old dogma, bar none, could become a "postulate of practical
reason." Jewish thought today is in a similar danger. We remember the Holocaust; we are inspired by the martyrdom and
the resistance: and then the inspiration quickly degenerates
into this, that every dogma, religious or secular, is restored as
if nothing had happened. However, the unredeemed anguish
of Auschwitz must be ever-present *with* us, even as it is past
for us. *Yom Ha-Shoah cannot now, or ever after, be assimilated to the ninth of Av.*

The attempt, to be sure, is widely made; but it is impossible.
The age-old day of mourning is for catastrophes that are punishment for Jewish sins, vicarious atonement for the sins of

---

*An allusion to Heidegger, see above, section 3.

others, or in any case meaningful, if inscrutable, divine decrees. The new day of mourning cannot be so understood, for it is for the children, the mothers, the *Muselmänner*—the whole murdered people in its utter innocence. Nor has the *Yom Ha-Shoah* ceremonial any such content, for it commemorates not Jewish sin but innocent Jewish suffering; not sins of others vicariously atoned but such as are incapable of atonement; not an inscrutable decree to be borne with patience but one resisted then, and to be resisted ever after. As for attempts to find a ninth-of-Av-meaning in the Holocaust—punishment for the sins of Zionism; or of anti-Zionism; or a moral stimulus to the world—their very perversity confirms a conclusion reached earlier in the present work: *Galut* Judaism, albeit most assuredly not *Galut* itself, has come to an end.[125]

Even so the attempt to assimilate *Yom Ha-Shoah* to the ninth of Av must be viewed with a certain sympathy. The cycle of the Jewish liturgical year—Rosenzweig described it sublimely—is an experience anticipating redemption. The ninth of Av, though a note of discord, fits into this cycle: but does *Yom Ha-Shoah?* The ninth of Av does not touch the Yom Kippur—the Jewish "experience" of the "end" not through "dying" but living.[126] *Yom Ha-Shoah* cannot but touch it; indeed it threatens to overwhelm the Yom Kippur. Martin Buber has asked his post-Holocaust Jewish question—not whether one can still "believe" in God but whether one can still "speak" to Him.[127] Can the Jew still speak to God on Yom Kippur? If not how can he speak to Him at all? The Jewish fear of *Yom Ha-Shoah*—the wish to assimilate it to the ninth of Av—is a fear, in behalf not only of *Galut* Judaism but also of Judaism itself.

"Judaism and the Holocaust" must be the last, climactic question not only of the present exploration but also of this whole work.[128] Meanwhile we ask what ways of Jewish Tikkun there could be even if the climactic question had to be indefinitely suspended. These ways are many; their scope is universal. (The task is *Tikkun Olam*, to mend the world.) Yet they would all become insubstantial without one *Tikkun* that is a collective, particular Jewish response to history. This *Tik-*

kun may be said to have begun when the first Jewish "DP" gave a radical response to what he had experienced. Non-Jewish DPs, displaced though they were, had a home to which to return. This Jewish DP did not—and even so was barred by bayonets and laws from the land that had been home once, and that Jewish labor was making into home once again. Understandably, many of his comrades accepted these facts with a shrug of centuries, and waited for someone's charity that would give them the blessings of refuge, peace, and oblivion. (They waited in camps, often the very places of their suffering—and for years.) This Jewish DP took his destiny in his own hands, disregarded the legal niceties of a world that still classified him as Pole or German, still without Jewish rights, and made his way to the one place where there would be neither peace nor oblivion but which would be, without ifs and buts, home.

The *Tikkun* that is Israel is fragmentary. This fact need not be stressed, for it is reported almost daily in the newspapers. The power of the State is small, as is the State itself. It can offer a home to captive Jews but cannot force captors to set them free. Limited abroad, it is limited at home as well. It cannot prevent strife. It cannot even guarantee its Jewish citizens a culture or a strong Jewish identity. *Galut* Judaism may have ended; but there is no end to *Galut* itself, inside as well as outside the State of Israel.

If the *Tikkun* is fragmentary, the whole enterprise is laden with risk. (This too the papers report assiduously.) Within, *Yerida*—emigration of Israelis—threatens to rival or overtake *Aliyah*, the Ingathering. Without, for all the talk of a comprehensive peace, implacable enemies remain; and while enemies elsewhere seek to destroy a regime, or at most conquer a state, *these* enemies seek destruction of a state—and renewed exile for its Jewish inhabitants.

What then is the *Tikkun*? It is Israel itself. It is a state founded, maintained, defended by a people who—so it was once thought—had lost the arts of statecraft and self-defense forever. It is the replanting and reforestation of a land that—so it once seemed—was unredeemable swamps and desert. It is a people gathered from all four corners of the earth on a territory with—so the experts once said—not room enough left to swing a cat. It is a living language that—so even friends once feared—was dead beyond revival. It is a City rebuilt that—so once the consensus of mankind had it—was destined to remain holy ruins. And it is in and through all this, on behalf of the accidental remnant, after unprecedented death, a unique celebration of life.

It is true—so fragmentary and precarious is the great *Tikkun*—that many want no share of it, deny it, distort it, slander it. But slanders and denials have no power over those who are astonished—ever again astonished—by the fact that in this of all ages the Jewish people have returned—*have been* returned?—to Jerusalem. Their strength, when failing, is renewed by the faith that despite all, because of all, the "impulse from below" will call forth an "impulse from above."

15. *Epilogue*

Simha Holzberg is an orthodox Jew and a Hasid. He fought in the Warsaw Ghetto Uprising. He survived, made his way to Israel, and prospered. Holzberg, in short, was fortunate. But he was also haunted and without peace, rushing from school to school, kibbutz to kibbutz, synagogue to synagogue, always urging Jews to do more, to mourn more deeply, to remember more profoundly. It was not enough. It could not have been enough. Then came the Six-Day War, and with it its widows and orphans, and Simha Holzberg made the deepest commitment of his life. He became the adoptive father of orphans, vowing to care for them until they were married.

Holzberg has remained a man of anguish. The great wound is not healed nor can it be healed. The unprecedented rupture is not "overcome" or reduced to a "problem" about to be "solved" or already solved. But this Israeli Jew has ceased to be haunted. He has even found a measure of peace. When last heard of by this writer, he was already the adoptive grandfather of more than a hundred grandchildren.

V

Conclusion: *Teshuva* Today: Concerning Judaism after the Holocaust

1. The Problematics of Teshuva in Our Time

THE explorations of this work may all be said to have concerned a single theme—*Teshuva* for the Jewish people in our time. We first came upon that theme with Franz Rosenzweig, the Jew who became a *Ba'al Teshuva* virtually at the portals of the Christian Church—and the greatest Jewish thinker since Spinoza.[1] The theme appeared next with Spinoza himself, the first great modern Jewish man-in-general who would be required today by his own principles to return, not to be sure to the old Jewish God, but to his old-new people in their old-new land.[2] The theme appeared again with Hegelianism, the modern way of thought that preserves and supersedes rather than rejects or abandons the past, and that therefore may seem least in need of any turning or returning; and that yet in our time must repent of its Constantinianism, nowhere more clearly so than vis-à-vis Jews and Judaism.[3] From these forms of *Teshuva*, all at best peripheral to Jewish history (but not to modernity), we were finally led to its Jewish core, and this, appropriately enough, not until our own thought was self-immersed in history.[4] Yet just this self-immersion helped disclose also most fully the problematics of *Teshuva* in our time. Even in other times *Teshuva* was problematic whenever catastrophe produced (or seemed to produce) a rupture in history, so that *Teshuva* had to assume the form of *Tikkun* if the rupture was to be mended. The problematics have become radical, inescapable in our time, with a rupture so complete that any *Tikkun* can at best only be fragmentary. Hence our climactic question remains yet to be asked: *Can Teshuva after the Holocaust be the same as before? Is it possible at all?*

Teshuva is at the core of all Jewish existence. Enemies (and sometimes also dubious friends) have invented and perpetuated the myth of the Jew as Ahasverus, that ancient restless wanderer who only seeks—but cannot find—a peaceful death. If the real Jewish people, while often without peace, were rarely without vibrant life, it is because of the ever-renewing, ever-rejuvenating power of *Teshuva*. A castigating Jeremiah conjures up the affection of Israel's youth, when she followed after God in the wilderness, a land not sown (Jer. 2:2)—a useless exercise unless youthfulness can be recovered. Lamentations—according to tradition, the work of the same prophet— confronts radical catastrophe with *Teshuva:* it is the sole alternative to despair. And just this vision of the "old-new," as found in its ancient-religious context, inspired Theodor Herzl, in his modern-secular context, when he conceived of a return of the old-new people to its old-new land. (Even so, his vision was not visionary enough. The old language he considered dead is renewed.)*

Yet *Teshuva*, occurring in history, was also always threatened *by* history, never more so than when pagan experience seemed to be the simple truth—when the past seemed lost beyond recovery. Is not Jeremiah's vision of the desert one of a past that never was? Is not the culminating cry of Lamentations—"Turn us, O Lord, unto Thee, and we shall be turned; renew our days as of old" (5:21)—either a fruitless hankering after a dead past, or else a present reconstruction of the past in the present's own image? As for Herzl's project, is it not either an anachronistic, romantic attempt to revive the old, or else a modern nationalism that, like others, puts a mythical past to present uses? Doubts such as these have existed at all times. They have increased in modern, more historically-conscious times. And they can be stilled only if *Teshuva*, though ever-situated in history, is at the same time endowed with a transcendent dimension. Hence, the quest for *Teshuva* in our time must be so expanded as to include transcendence for our time.

The preceding explorations have furthered this latter quest—

---

*In *The Jewish State* (London: Zionist Organization, 1936), Herzl writes: "We cannot, after all, converse with one another in Hebrew. Which of us knows enough Hebrew to ask for a railway ticket in that language? It cannot be done" (p. 134).

and come to a halt. In Rosenzweig and Spinoza we came upon
two antithetical commitments to transcendence—both no less
than to eternity—but found both ruptured in our time: the one
because the eternal people, witness to the eternal Truth, have
barely survived; the other because a radical evil then impossible—"contrary to human nature"—has become actual. Thus
our first exploration reached an impasse.

A coming to a halt occurred also in our second exploration.
In a post-Hegelian encounter with Hegel we came upon a variety of commitments to transcendence (whether or not to eternity),* and were left in a state of dialogical openness, in point
of fact to some of these commitments, potentially to them all.
However, this openness too was ruptured—by a world of radical evil that (being radical) has a transcendent dimension of
its own, and that yet (being evil) demands not dialogical openness but, on the contrary, an opposition uncomprising and
complete.

In these two explorations, a commitment to transcendence
was not in principle called into question. As we proceeded
from these two to the third exploration, we saw no reason for
dwelling on an external-reductionist kind of criticism that in
the last analysis presupposes what it claims to prove.† But we
did see every reason for exploring an internal criticism, i.e., a
stance that takes with total, non-reductionist seriousness the
traditional commitment to transcendence; that takes with total,
non-escapist seriousness man's historically situated finitude;
and that brings these two commitments of its own to bear on
each other. In pursuit of such a criticism we made two crucial
discoveries. First, the thinking most rigorously self-exposed to
history, the Heideggerian, is in principle unable to confront
that history—the Holocaust. Second, in our own attempt to
confront it we came not only upon a rupture of history but also

---

*The case of left-wing Hegelianism is sufficient proof that the two are not
necessarily identical. This is corroborated by the case of Heidegger which
does not appear until the third exploration.
†In the present book, empiricist reductionism, having been dealt with in
chapter I of *Encounters*, has no longer been an issue. In contrast, a dialectical
reductionism, even after chapter 3 of *Encounters*, still required and received
treatment in chapter III of the present work. See also *Presence*, ch. 2.

a *Tikkun* of it. That *Tikkun*, like every previous case of *Tikkun*, is a form of *Teshuva* in response to extremity. However—this is crucial—it differs from every previous case in that it is in principle fragmentary. The Holocaust is a *caesura*, not only for the historian, the poet, the philosopher. It is a *caesura* also for the Jewish faith. Hence we must redefine our quest for *Teshuva* yet again, to read as follows: What is the fate of eternity in our time?

2. *Rosenzweig after Heidegger*

With this paradoxical question we resume a theme long suspended but not forgotten. Franz Rosenzweig's "new thinking" is situated in history, yet reaches eternity—a "Jewish vigil of the Day of Redemption." Hence we tested it through another "new thinking"—the Heideggerian. (This latter, *remaining as it does* situated in historical finitude, recognizes a Jewish vigil of the Day of Redemption as little as it does the Christian's "Rebirth" or the philosopher's "Platonic Sun.")[5] As it has turned out, however, in this process the testing philosophy was being tested as well, and the overall result is ironical. Rosenzweig died prior to the advent of the Nazi regime; Heidegger survived it long enough to have all the leisure necessary to ponder it. Rosenzweig's thought, though situated in history, rises above it, and hence also above the evil that is part of it; Heidegger's thought in both its earlier and later periods remains in history, unable to rise above it. *Yet it is Heidegger's thought that cannot confront the Holocaust; and it is Rosenzweig's thought that—had the thinker lived long enough—would have found a confrontation with the* Ereignis *inescapable.*

The confrontation would have been necessary because of Rosenzweig's "absolute empiricism." The *Star of Redemption* requires empirical confirmation at many points, the crucial ones being the apex of Judaism (its highest experience) and the matrix of Judaism (the existence of Jews). As Rosenzweig sees it, the passage of time has done nothing to shake either apex or matrix. However, had he lived through the passage of our time, he would have seen both "confirmations" shaken.

Our quest seeks eternity in our time. Rosenzweig's own quest finds, in the Yom Kippur, an eternity-in-any-time, for in the highest Jewish experience a "love strong as death" breaks the "scythe of the grim reaper," carries the worshipper "beyond the grave while still alive," and thus reveals an "absolute transcendence" for all humanity.[6] We shall not, at this late stage, subject this teaching to a reductionist criticism. (To do so would be incongruous, out of keeping with the most basic commitments of this whole work and, indeed, would retroactively destroy its significance.) What we must and shall do is ask whether Rosenzweig's eternity-in-time is accessible in our time. That Eternity, being in time, requires a witness, and this latter cannot testify without an eternity of his own. The witness—the Jewish people—exists in time, but rises above it in his highest experience, the apex of Judaism. If it can so rise—if the apex of Judaism is possible—it is because the matrix of Judaism—the existence of the Jewish people—is taken for granted. A contracting logic may decimate the Jewish people through pogroms, apostasies, and other ravages of Jewish history. But that even a remnant should be destroyed—it is a holy remnant—is, or very nearly is—impossible.

But the nearly impossible has in our time become almost actual. The holy remnant has become an accidental remnant, and the question is whether this threat to the matrix of Judaism can leave its apex unaffected. For a last time therefore our quest must be redefined. We first inquired about *Teshuva* in our time. This led to a quest for transcendence, and this latter in turn to a quest for the fate of eternity in our time. For Jewish thought after the Holocaust, these questions all find their focus and concentration in a single one on which the future of Judaism depends. *After the Holocaust, can the Yom Kippur be what it was before? Is it still possible at all?*

3. Yom Kippur after the Holocaust

Once at Auschwitz a group of girls on forced labor decided, so far as possible, to observe Yom Kippur. Prayer, of course, was out of the question; but fasting, they thought, was not. So they applied to their SS supervisor for permission to fast, and for a lighter work load for that day for which, they hastened to assure her, they would compensate on other days. Furious, the woman denied both requests, imposed overtime work in honor of the holiday, and threatened that anyone lagging in work on account of the fast would be sent to the crematorium without delay. Undeterred, the girls worked and fasted through the long day, exhilarated by the thought of Jews the world over sharing in it. When the day was done, they tasted their piece of black bread, and their "satisfaction was full." Yet this "story" of their "victory" ended with a "bitter disappointment." They had miscalculated. They had fasted on the wrong day.[7]

Was a love strong as death *not* present on that day? Were these girls *not* beyond the grave while still alive? Did an absolute transcendence *not* become real in the midst of that time and on behalf of all humanity? Heaven forbid that we should say any such thing! If the prayer that was in that fast was not heard, then no prayer on any Yom Kippur ever was heard, or could be heard. If this human love had no response in a divine love, then every Good News about divine love anywhere is a sham and a mockery. In this book we have made no attempt to demonstrate the commitment to transcendence, whether within Judaism or without it. (Only the "old" philosophical "thinking" seeks proofs, while its theological counterpart seeks infallible authorities.) At the same time, we have found not a single reason—philosophical, religious, moral, to say nothing of reasons psychological or sociological—for rejecting that commitment. *We see no reason now.*

But Yom Kippur *after* Auschwitz cannot be what *at* Auschwitz it still was. *Their* Yom Kippur necessitates a change in *our own.* This is a change to be approached cautiously and with care, for much—to the religious Jew all—is at stake in it. We must therefore search, so far as possible, for a precedent.

When the Syrians attacked on the Sabbath, the Maccabees were faced with a dilemma. They could defend themselves: but then they, the defenders of the Torah, would themselves violate it. Or they could let themselves be slain, but in so doing would not defend the Torah: a Judaism without Jews is impossible. The dilemma was insoluble.

But it was also unacceptable. And since the Torah—its Giver is divine—has infinite resources, the dilemma must, after all, be capable of a solution. To "violate" the Torah in order to protect it was not a violation but rather an interpretation. And since the Torah, the Word of God, could not be interpreted by the mere word of man, the interpretation itself could not be merely-human. Thus, in due course, there emerged, alongside the "written Torah," the "oral Torah" of rabbinic Judaism. In this manner the Sabbath was changed, and saved in being changed. In this manner a new page was opened in Maccabean times, in the history not only of Jews but also of judaism.[8]

This is our precedent. But it helps us only up to a point. The Sabbath-attacks of the Syrians had a pragmatic purpose—to catch the Jews defenseless. No such purpose was in the Nazi mind when—a favorite practice—deportations and selections were conducted on the holy days of Judaism. (The Jews were defenseless on those days. But they were also defenseless on all other days.) The true Nazi purpose was expressed best by Dr. Josef Mengele. It was the Auschwitz doctor's task to separate those to be murdered at once from those to be made to work now and murdered at a future date. Dr. Mengele was fond of performing his task on Yom Kippur. He was familiar with enough Jewish theology to know that on Yom Kippur God judges who will live and who will die. To cite his own boast, it would be he, Dr. Josef Mengele and not God, that would judge what Jews were to live and what to die.

Dr. Mengele was no mere new Antiochus or Titus or even Hadrian. The Syrians sought no more than the destruction of the Jewish state. The same is true of the Romans under Titus. Even Hadrian attacked Judaism only because it seemed—and was—a political threat. This was until Hadrian. But after Hadrian Judaism ceased to be a political threat. A *Galut* Judaism arose that relied only on God; that expected from the world only Jewish survival; and that, persisting in the first and obtaining the second, culminated in the Yom Kippur experience. It was this Judaism that, along with the Jewish people, such as Dr. Mengele sought to exterminate.

Whether or not Dr. Mengele's Yom Kippur selections destroyed *their* Yom Kippur is a question that resurrects the deepest, most painful tensions that have beset our post-Holocaust Jewish thought. (We cannot forget the girls at Auschwitz who observed Yom Kippur. And we equally cannot forget those victims, innocent all, for whom Nazi terror destroyed it.)* The result is that *their* Yom Kippur must *alter ours.* For we cannot resort to the "cowardly and disconsolate talk" that it happened only once, that it is improbable or impossible for it to recur, and that in any case the Yom Kippur's transcendence-of-time dissolves into irrelevance *that* time. An *absolute* transcendence of time is not attainable in our time. *For to return the throne of judgment usurped by Dr. Mengele back to God has become a Jewish necessity, and the necessity does not exist beside the Yom Kippur experience but is part of it.†* And since this returning would be an impotent gesture without a Jewish state, we are forced to conclude that *if in our time there were no State of Israel, it would be religious necessity, with or without the help of God, to create it. Without such a state, the end of* Galut *Judaism would also be the end of Judaism.* Our generation has opened—has been required to open—a new page in the history, not only of Jews but also of Judaism.

This opening of a new page in the history of Judaism found a deeply symbolic expression on the first day of the Yom Kippur War. The surprise attack forced Israeli soldiers to rush helter-skelter from streets, homes, synagogues, to trucks, cars, any vehicle at all that would take them speedily to their units. It was then and there that some old men somewhere in Jerusalem interrupted their prayers, rushed into the streets and tore out pages from their prayer books in order to give them to the departing soldiers. These pious men did not hesitate to mutilate their holy books. On their part, religious and secularist soldiers alike did not hesitate to accept the gift. On that Yom

---

*In this and the following it is necessary to hold fast to the stance-between-the-extremes set forth above in ch. IV, section 14F.

†Presumably the custom of Israel Bond appeals during the Yom Kippur service originated pragmatically, in the need to reach large numbers in a receptive mood. Its implicit religious meaning, over and above the pragmatic, became fully explicit on one Yom Kippur—the first day of the Yom Kippur war.

Kippur, some fought so that others could pray; and some prayed so that others could fight. Both statements are true. But only both together, on *that* Yom Kippur, expressed the full truth. The full truth, however, includes secular Jews. Hence we must ask: What can Yom Kippur be for secularist Jews?

4. The Message of Beit Ha-Tefutsot

In Tel Aviv there is a museum that does not have its like anywhere. Beit Ha-Tefutsot, "the House of the Diaspora," houses no rare, expensive relics but is content with mere replicas. It is intended not for the delight of the connoisseur or the advancement of the scholar but rather for the instruction of a whole people—one that needs the instruction if it is to survive. The museum tells the story of this people in its own land but—so its very name indicates—says far more about its story in other lands. And the lands are so many and so far apart that the Ingathering, when at last it occurred, was from all four corners of the earth. At one time in its history, Zionist thought simply rejected all the stories in all these lands. The mere existence of a "House of the Diaspora" in an Israeli museum proves that Zionist thought in our time seeks to take up the old into the new. To do so, however, is to take up old diversities, and among these none is either more ultimate or more significant than that between religious and secular. Because of its ultimacy, the diversity between these extremes forever threatens to become an out-and-out conflict. Because of its significance, nothing is more essential than a mediation of just that conflict. On such a mediation a Jewish future—the page of history already opened—depends.

Beit Ha-Tefutsot contains a section devoted to the liturgical life of the Jewish people, and, in keeping with the whole spirit of the museum, this section cannot avoid making a commitment. One walks down a hall and sees depicted, on one side, the chief festivals of the Jewish *Heilsgeschichte*—Pesach, Shavuot, and Succot. On the other side are the "Days of Martyrdom and Resistance," among them Purim, Hanukkah, and the ninth of Av—but also *Yom Ha-Shoah* and *Yom Ha-Atzmaut*.

The commitment that is in this portrayal alters Jewish tradition in two respects. First, it raises to a level of equality "secular" Jewish festivals that tradition had made into "minor" ones, and moreover, made over into religious ones: thus it addresses itself to the *whole* Jewish people. Second, in including *Yom Ha-Shoah* and *Yom Ha-Atzmaut* it carries Jewish liturgical life forward into present reality. As a result of these two changes, the visitor has in mind two questions as he walks down the hall, toward the place assigned to the Yom Kippur. Can the whole Jewish people share in the Yom Kippur? And can the Yom Kippur itself fail to be overwhelmed by *Yom Ha-Shoah?* As he reaches the place he finds this Talmudic quotation:

> *The gates of prayer are sometimes closed.*
> *But the gates Teshuva are always open.*[9]

Thus, in our search for the meaning of *Teshuva* for the Jewish people in our time, we have come full circle.

5. *The Sharing of* Teshuva *after the Holocaust*

We have not returned, however, without lessons learned on the way, so that our original question may now be further specified as follows. How are the gates of *Teshuva* open on Yom Kippur today? What is a *Teshuva* shared by the whole people, despite the differences that divide them? And can, perhaps, the walking through these open gates help reopen those other gates—the gates of prayer that are closed?

These questions, of course, are all concerned with God, the ultimate (if largely hidden) Subject of all our preceding explorations. The subject was not hidden without good cause. Ever since, in the modern world, the shibboleth of revelation has divided Jews into religious and secularist, theology, the beginning with God, has served to widen rather than narrow the fateful gap. Ever since the Holocaust, it divides religious Jews as well. (Martin Buber—no theologian—has raised the question of whether today a Jew can still speak to God. Theologians are apt to answer the question, or at any rate to supply new, divisive "concepts of God" that are to make it answerable.)* A deep and much-quoted saying in the Zohar asserts as valid for all times, that God, Torah, and Israel are at one.[10] Perhaps, in ancient times, when the Jewish people were alone against idolatry, the true and all-uniting beginning was with God. In our time, this beginning deepens the divisions *within* Israel, and hence also those *between* Israel, Torah, and God.

A Halakhic beginning with "Torah" is no more promising. It is true that a commitment to a shared Jewish future involves a recovery of the Jewish past, and hence of Torah. However, a beginning with Torah—in place of a recovery of it—rules out from the start possibilities of sharing, for to the religious Jew, Torah is the Word of God, and to his secular brother, the word of man. Perhaps in medieval times, when the Jewish people in exile were tempted to apostasy by Islam and Christianity, they were a people only by virtue of the Torah.[11] In our time, this beginning, too, widens divisions within Israel, and hence also between Israel, Torah, and God.

We are therefore at length led to the third term in the mystical triad of the Zohar—a beginning with Israel. How can the *whole* Jewish people share in *Teshuva* on Yom Kippur in our time? The religious Jew, now as always, spends the day in the synagogue, praying and reading the Torah. The secular Jew, whether inside or outside the synagogue,† can at any rate read the Torah—the Book of the *whole* Jewish people. It is true that the two ways of reading are not one shared activity. Indeed, if each is performed within a self-enclosed world—the one, a system of religious certainties, the other, a system of anti-religious ones—the two ways of reading may exacerbate the poten-

---

*A currently fashionable Jewish theological resort is to the Whiteheadian God who can only inspire and not save. It is doubtful whether to this God there can be any kind of Jewish speech. (What remains of the Psalms when addressed to a God that cannot save? Or that can save only if "salvation" is so spiritualized as to be cut off from questions of life and death?) More doubtful still is, if Jewish speech to this God there is and can be, whether this God can survive the Holocaust, for that catastrophe casts into doubt the divine power to inspire as well as that of saving.

†In Israel, it is a custom for secular Jews to attend synagogue on Yom Kippur.

tial for conflict. However, what may in our time break through all systems of certainties is an *overwhelming—and shared—astonishment.*

It is an age-old truth that just as Israel has kept the Torah so the Torah has kept Israel. This old truth has become manifest in our time in a new form. The Torah itself asks whether this ever happened, that God took one nation from the midst of another (Deut. 4:34). In our time we must ask whether this ever happened that, after two millennia, a people was returned to its language, its state, its land. *Without a Book—this Book—this return could not possibly have taken place.* This is the shared astonishment behind all religio-secular diversities. This is the shared experience that makes possible a bond between all Israel and Torah. These are the gates of *Teshuva* open to the whole Jewish people today.

If gates of *Teshuva* are open for *every* Jew, are gates of prayer open for *any* Jew? In the *Mahzor*, the High Holy Day Prayer Book, we read:

> Now, Lord our God, put Thy awe upon all whom Thou has made, Thy dread upon all whom Thou hast created. Let Thy works revere Thee, let all Thy creatures worship Thee. May they all blend into one brotherhood to do Thy will with a perfect heart. For we know, our God, that Thine is the dominion, power and might. Thou art revered above all Thou hast created.*

Never was this prayer as necessary as after a world in which the power was Dr. Mengele's—and never as inaccessible. It is necessary because the prayed-for Messiah is necessary. It is inaccessible because a Messiah that can come yet at Auschwitz did not come, is himself inaccessible.†

The worshiper that reads on comes upon *Ele Ezkera*—a martyrology. With Bar Kochba defeated, Hadrian forbade the practice of Judaism on pain of death. Ten rabbis defied the edict,

---

*This prayer is part of High Holy Day services on Rosh Ha-Shana as well as Yom Kippur.

†In Elie Wiesel's *Gates of the Forest* the protagonist concludes that it is too late for the coming of the Messiah, and that it is necessary to manage without him (New York: Holt, Rinehart and Winston, 1966), p. 225.

were caught, and tortured to death by Roman soldiers. Then the angels in heaven cried, "Is this the Torah, and this its reward?" And a voice from heaven replied: "If I hear another word, I will turn the world into water!" The voice went on: "This is My decree: accept it, all you who love the Torah!"*

The Jew at prayer today reads these words. And considering that Rabbi Akiba, Rabbi Ishmael and others had all chosen to be martyrs, had died as martyrs, he can accept the decree that came from heaven; for God needs martyrs. He can accept it for *that* time: but he cannot accept it for *our* time. For the children, the mothers, and the *Muselmänner* had *not* chosen to be martyrs, had *not* died as martyrs: and that God needs *that* death is unacceptable. Hence even the most devout Jew at prayer today must ask, on the holiest day of Judaism: why is the world today not water? He must ask the question. But he cannot answer it.

For this reason the Jew at prayer today is gripped by the most radical of all human questions. Why does anything exist at all? Why is there not rather Nothing? In philosophy, this question is asked in abstract, sweeping generality.† For the Jew at prayer on Yom Kippur today, it arises in singling-out particularity. Why does anything—Man, World, God—*still* exist *now*—and not water? Why does *he himself* still exist—an accidental remnant? And where, if not even *he* were left, would be the witness to the divine Judgment? Where the divine Judgment? As his prayer is informed by these questions, it is transformed. It becomes a gift whereby is returned to God "His crown and His scepter."[12] And in this returning—a Messianic moment, a Messianic fragment—Israel, Torah, and God are one.

---

*This prayer is found in the Yom Kippur Mussaf liturgy only: to recite these things more than once during the Jewish liturgical year would be impossible. One may well ask: How is it possible to recite them even once?

†Greek philosophers did not ask this question at all. Among moderns, it was raised (under the influence, remotely but unmistakably, of the Jewish-Christian doctrine of creation) by Leibniz, Schelling, and Heidegger, with increasing radicalism. Leibniz's answer is a conventional recourse to God. Schelling too resorts to God, but can reach Him only through a leap. For Heidegger the question is no longer answerable, and its significance now lies in being asked.

An eternity so momentary, so fragmentary, so precarious cannot but give rise to the most profound metaphysical, theological, religious disquiet. One—anyone—wants to "overcome" it, "transcend" it, "go beyond" it. Thus some will seek to separate the witness-to-Judgment from the Judgment itself and, as did former generations, project this latter into the world-to-come. But if a Messianic future is inaccessible so is an otherworldly eternity: we must *stay with* our singled-out, this-worldly anguish, and cannot escape from it. On their part, others may wish to raise "Israel" to the same preworldly, postworldly universality the Jewish tradition already ascribes to "God" and "Torah."* But, heir to the *kedoshim*, to the "holy ones," the flesh-and-blood Israel cannot rise, or wish to rise, above a heritage that is itself holy. To "overcome," "transcend" or "go beyond" our fragmented, momentary, precarious eternity is impossible.

There is yet another attempt to avoid the disquiet, and this, of all attempts, is both the most understandable and least possible. The Jewish people has persevered at a singled-out post through the centuries. All too understandably, this people today may be tired of the post; leaving the task of witnessing to others, it may create the prospect of a world without Jews. This, of course, is not a new prospect. Throughout history many have predicted such a world. Not a few have wanted it. A generation ago, an unprecedented attempt was made to make an end to Jews, and some in this generation regret that it failed of complete success. However, whether or not the world today realizes it, it cannot do without Jews—the accidental remnant that, heir to the holy ones, is itself bidden to be holy. Neither, in our time, can God Himself. An ancient Midrash addresses itself to the world as follows:

> They have said: "Come, let us cut them off from being a nation, that the name of Israel may be remembered no more." (Ps. 83:5)
> Their enemies said: "As long as the nation of Israel abides,
> God will be named the God of Israel. But if Israel is uprooted, whose God will He be named?"[13]

*Traditional Jewish teaching contains a doctrine of a preworldly Torah. The world was created through the Torah which is itself uncreated.

Another Midrash addressed Israel itself:

"You are My witnesses, says the Lord"—that is, if you are
My witnesses, I am God, and if you are not My witnesses, I am,
as it were, not God."*

*Midrash Psalms, on Ps. 123:1. I first cited this Midrash nearly thirty years
ago (see *Quest*, p. 39). The careful reader will notice that its significance has
changed for me in these many years—with an immense burden now falling on
the "as it were."

Abbreviations

Adorno	Theodor W. Adorno, *Negative Dialektik* (Frankfurt: Suhrkamp, 1966)
Améry	Jean Améry, *At the Mind's Limits*, tr. S and S. P. Rosenfeld (Bloomington: Indiana University Press, 1980)
Cr.p.R.	Immanuel Kant, *Critique of Pure Reason*
Erinnerung	*Erinnerung an Martin Heidegger*, ed. G. Neske (Pfullingen: Neske, 1977)
HMPh	*Heidegger and Modern Philosophy*, ed. M. Murray (New Haven: Yale University Press, 1978)
I and Thou	Martin Buber, *I and Thou*, tr. W. Kaufmann (New York: Scribner's Sons, 1970)
Levi	Primo Levi, *Survival in Auschwitz*, tr. Stuart Woolf (New York: Orion Press, 1959)
Lewinska	Pelagia Lewinska, *Twenty Months at Auschwitz*, tr. A. Teichner (New York: Lyle Stuart, 1968)
Löwith	Karl Löwith, "M. Heidegger and F. Rosenzweig: A Postscript of *Being and Time*," in *Nature, History and Existentialism* (Evanston: Northwestern University Press, 1966)
Preface	Leo Strauss, "Preface to *Spinoza's Critique of Religion*," in *The Jewish Expression*, ed. J. Goldin (Toronto: Bantam Books, 1970)

Works by Emil L. Fackenheim

Encounters	*Encounters between Judaism and Modern Philosophy* (New York: Basic Books, 1973)
Jewish Return	*The Jewish Return into History* (New York: Schocken Books, 1978)
MH	*Metaphysics and Historicity* (Milwaukee: Marquette University Press, 1961)

Presence	*God's Presence in History* (New York: New York University Press, 1970)
Quest	*Quest for Past and Future* (Bloomington: Indiana University Press, 1968)
RD	*The Religious Dimension in Hegel's Thought* (Bloomington: Indiana University Press, 1967)

Works by G. W. F. Hegel

Einl. Gesch. Phil.	*Vorlesungen über die Geschichte der Philosophie, Einleitung: System und Geschichte der Philosophie,* ed. J. Hoffmeister (Leipzig: Meiner, 1944)
Enc.	*Encyclopaedia of the Philosophical Sciences*
E.Th.Wr.	*Early Theological Writings,* tr. T. M. Knox (Chicago: University of Chicago Press, 1948)
Hist.Phil.	*Lectures on the History of Philosophy,* tr. E. S. Haldane (London: Kegan Paul, Trench, Trübner, 1892)
Phen.	*Phenomenology of Spirit,* tr. A. V. Miller (Oxford: Oxford University Press, 1977)
Phil.Rel.	*Lectures on the Philosophy of Religion,* tr. E. B. Speirs and J. B. Sanderson (London: Kegan Paul, Trench, Trübner, 1895)

Works by Martin Heidegger

BT	*Being and Time,* tr. J. M. Macquarrie and E. Robinson (New York: Harper and Row, 1962)
B.Wr.	*Basic Writings,* ed. D. F. Krell (New York: Harper and Row, 1977)
EB	*Existence and Being,* ed. W. Brock (London: Vision Press, 1949)
EM	*Einführung in die Metaphysik* (Tübingen: Niemeyer, 1953)
IM	*Introduction to Metaphysics,* tr. R. Manheim (New Haven: Yale University Press, 1959)
"Only a God"	"Only a God Can Save Us Now," English trans. of *Der Spiegel* interview, appears in *Philosophy Today,* vol. 20, 1976
SD	*Zur Sache des Denkens* (Tübingen: Niemeyer, 1969)
SuZ	*Sein und Zeit* (Tübingen: Niemeyer, 1927)
TB	*On Time and Being,* tr. J. Stambaugh (New York: Harper and Row, 1972)
Vorträge	*Vorträge und Aufsätze* (Tübingen: Gunther Neske, 1954)
WhD	*Was heisst Denken?* (Tübingen: Niemeyer, 1954)
WiM	"What is Metaphysics," in *B.Wr.*
Wm	*Wegmarken* (Frankfurt: Klostermann, 1967)
ZS	"Zeit und Sein," in *SD*

Works by Franz Rosenzweig

Briefe	Briefe (Berlin: Schocken Verlag, 1935)
Healthy and Sick	Understanding the Sick and the Healthy, ed. N. N. Glatzer (New York: Noonday Press, 1953)
Kl.Schr.	Kleinere Schriften (Berlin: Schocken Verlag, 1937)
Life and Thought	Franz Rosenzweig—His Life and Thought, ed. N. N. Glatzer (New York: Schocken Books, 1953)
Star	The Star of Redemption, tr. Wm. W. Hallo (New York: Holt, Rinehart and Winston, 1971)
Stern	Der Stern der Erlösung (Frankfurt: Kauffmann, 1921)

Works by Baruch Spinoza

Ethics	Ethics, tr. R. H. Elwes (New York: Dover, 1955)
Short Treatise	Short Treatise on God, Man and His Well-Being, ed. A. Wolf (London, 1910)
Tr.	Theological-Political Treatise, tr. R. H. Elwes (New York: Dover, 1951)

Notes

Preface

1. Many years ago, in a public disputation with the late Yaacov Herzog, held at the Hillel House of McGill University in Montreal.
2. An adjective used by Bernard Lewis at a recent symposium on the Holocaust held at the University of Chicago.
3. A term used by the distinguished German historian K. D. Bracher; see below, ch. IV, section 9.
4. See my exposition of Martin Buber's treatment of this subject in my *God's Presence in History* (New York: Harper Torchbooks, 1970), ch. 1.
5. See *Judaism*, Summer 1967. My contribution is reprinted in my *The Jewish Return into History* (New York: Schocken, 1978), pp. 19–24.
6. Bloomington: Indiana University Press, 1967; paperback reprint, University of Chicago Press, 1982.
7. Milwaukee: Marquette University Press, 1961.
8. For these, see the remainder of *The Jewish Return into History* and especially *God's Presence in History*, the third chapter of which bears the title "The Commanding Voice of Auschwitz." This formula does greater justice than "the 614th commandment" to my intention to see "secular" as well as "religious" Jews addressed by a "voice," a divine source of which is identified only by "the religious."

   The reader interested in the development of my Jewish thought is referred to *The Jewish Thought of Emil Fackenheim*, ed. Michael Morgan (Detroit: Wayne State University Press, 1987).
9. See Irving Greenberg's sensitive treatment of Yom ha-Shoah in *The Jewish Way* (New York: Summit Books, 1988), ch. 10.
10. The book deals with philosophical thought only insofar as it bears on Jewish thought. I have recently turned to philosophy in its own right; see my "Holocaust and Philosophy," *Journal of Philosophy*, LXXXII, no. 10 (October 1985), pp. 505–14; and "Holocaust and Weltanschauung: Philosophical Reflections on Why They Did It," *Holocaust and Genocide*, 3, no. 2 (1988), pp. 197–208.
11. For a while a few doctrinaire Marxists affirmed a Hegel-style "negation of the negation" of Auschwitz, and identified, of all places, communist

East Germany as the country where it was being realized. This being too absurd for even the most doctrinaire, Marxist ideologues in the Soviet Union and elsewhere have instead fallen back on the device, appealing also to a good many liberals, of flattening out Nazism into "fascism," and the Jews murdered in the Holocaust into "victims."

12. For a desirable understanding of post-Hegelian thought, the reader is urged not to forget the Hegel section of this book as he passes beyond it. He may also wish to consult my book on Hegel, already cited, as well as ch. 3 of my *Encounters Between Judaism and Modern Philosophy* (New York: Schocken, 1980).

13. Susan E. Shapiro writes: "However admirable, exemplary and reorienting is the testimony of resistance, its categorical and ontological privileging necessarily excludes and negates the claims of other testimonies to the event. Although Fackenheim in no way wants to slight or make secondary the mute testimony of the *Muselmänner*, his privileging of physical and spiritual resistance issues is such a denigration." ("For Thy Breach Is Great Like the Sea: Who Can Heal Thee," *Religious Studies Review*, 13, no. 3 [July 1987], p. 211.) Shapiro's is an excellent review of *To Mend the World*, indeed, the best I have read. She recognizes the problem of the book and focuses on the crucial point in its argument for a solution. Her error in the cited criticism is due to her failure to recognize that post-Hegelian thought, like Hegel's own, *moves*. Hence the *Muselmänner* are not left behind as this thought reaches the resistance that mends its own ontological foundations: it can reach, come to possess, and continue to possess these foundations only as it, ever again, *moves through* the mute testimony of the *Muselmänner* by which it is paralyzed. Not accidentally does the present essay end with the statement that while a mending of the wound of Spirit is possible, a healing is not.

14. The Jewish reader will reach the end of this book with a quest for a Judaism the spirit of which, though wounded, is mended. For my own quest of this, see *What Is Judaism?* (New York: Summit Books, 1987; paperback, Collier-Macmillan, 1988).

Chapter I

1. *Kl.Schr.*, pp. 373 ff.
2. *Quest*, ch. 6.
3. See, e.g., Paul Tillich's so-called method of correlation.
4. *Preface*, pp. 352 ff.
5. See the earlier essays in *Quest*.
6. See, e.g., *Quest*, ch. 2; the opening pages of *MH*; "Kant and Radical Evil," *University of Toronto Quarterly*, 23, no. 4 (1954), pp. 339–54.
7. See *Jewish Return*, ch. 2.
8. "Cloud of Smoke, Pillar of Fire: Judaism, Christianity, and Modernity after the Holocaust," in *Auschwitz: Beginning of a New Era?*, E. Fleischner, ed. (New York: Ktav, 1977), pp. 9–11.
9. See *Quest*, pp. 231, 329 ff.
10. See *Quest*, *passim*.
11. See *Presence*, ch. 1.
12. New York: Meridian, 1958. Originally published in 1951.
13. This is demonstrated by Mary Jo Leddy, "The Event of the Holocaust in

the Philosophical Reflections of Hannah Arendt," Ph.D. dissertation, University of Toronto, 1980.
14. See *MH*.
15. *Kl.Schr.*, p. 376.
16. *Kl.Schr.* p. 379.
17. See *Presence*, p. 92.
18. See Levi, p. 82.
19. See Lewinska, pp. 41 ff., 50.
20. See *I and Thou*, p. 158.
21. New York: Penguin, 1977 (first published in book form in 1963).
22. *The Survivor* (New York: Oxford, 1976), p. vi. The terms "objective" stance and "clinical" detachment appear in Des Pres's reflections.
23. See *Phen.*, Preface.
24. See *E.Th.Wr.*, pp. 313, 255.
25. See G. Scholem, *On the Kabbalah and Its Symbolism* (New York: Schocken, 1965), p. 146; also below ch. IV, section 10.
26. See G. Scholem, *Major Trends in Jewish Mysticism* (New York: Schocken, 1961), p. 246. See also below, ch. IV, section 10.

Chapter II

1. *Healthy and Sick*, p. 30.
2. *Short Treatise*, pp. 145, 146.
3. *Healthy and Sick*, pp. 44, 45.
4. *Short Treatise*, p. 77.
5. *Healthy and Sick*, p. 44.
6. Munich and Berlin: Oldenbourg, 1920.
7. Because of their ready availability and despite their many flaws, unless otherwise noted, the Elwes translations will be referred to throughout.
8. *Tr.*, ch. IV, pp. 63–65; ch. XI, p. 164.
9. Carl Gebhard in his German translation of *Tr.* (Leipzig: Meiner, 1922), pp. xiv ff.
10. *Tr.*, Preface, pp. 5, 6.
11. *Preface*, p. 370.
12. *Tr.*, Preface, pp. 9, 10. See also ch. XIV, pp. 184 ff.; ch. XV, pp. 194 ff.
13. *Tr.*, Preface, p. 9.
14. *Tr.*, ch. VII, p. 99, Preface, p. 7.
15. See *Preface*, pp. 369, 368, 371.
16. *Tr.*, ch. XIV, p. 186; ch. XV, p. 199.
17. See, e.g., *Tr.*, ch. XVII, p. 232.
18. *Preface*, p. 370.
19. *Tr.*, ch. XIV, p. 187.
20. *Tr.*, ch. VII, p. 118.
21. Letter no. 43; *Tr.*, ch. VII, p. 119.
22. *Tr.*, Preface, p. 9.
23. *Preface*, p. 380.
24. *Ethics*, Part II, prop. 11 note.
25. *Ethics*, Part II, prop. 11; Part II, prop. 14.
26. Part II, prop. 47.
27. See esp. Part I, prop. 11 note, prop. 12.
28. Part II, prop. 29 Corollary.

29. Part V, props. 3, 4 note, 6, 10 note, 15, 20 note, 27, 38, 42.
30. Part V, prop. 38; Part VI, prop. 63. For the rabbis, see the Midrashim on this subject assembled in *Rabbinic Anthology*, ed. Loewe, Montefiore (London: Macmillan, 1938), pp. 378 ff. I have treated this subject in connection with Kant in *Encounters*, pp. 50 ff.
31. Part V, prop. 36.
32. Part III, prop. 59 note; Part VI, props. 20, 56, 53, 52.
33. Part II, definitions of the emotions, def. 4; Part IV, app. 22; Part V, prop. 41; Part III, prop. 59 note.
34. *Briefe*, p. 45; *Life and Thought*, p. 19.
35. A much cited dictum of Goethe's. See *Kl.Schr.*, p. 363.
36. *Kl.Schr.*, pp. 376 ff.
37. Letter no. 76.
38. *Kl.Schr.*, p. 380.
39. *Stern*, pp. 16, 20; *Star*, pp. 11, 13.
40. *Stern*, p. 18; *Star*, p. 12.
41. *Briefe*, p. 510; *Life and Thought*, p. 136.
42. *Tr.*, ch. III, end.
43. *Kl.Schr.*, p. 374.
44. *Kl.Schr.*, p. 398.
45. *Kl.Schr.*, p. 379.
46. *Stern*, p. 113; *Star*, p. 88.
47. *Kl.Schr.*, p. 379.
48. *Kl.Schr.*, p. 285.
49. *Kl.Schr.*, p. 390.
50. *Stern*, p. 113; *Star*, p. 88.
51. *Stern*, p. 131; *Star*, p. 101.
52. *Stern*, pp. 134, 135; *Star*, pp. 104 ff.
53. *Kl.Schr.*, p. 384.
54. See above, p. 66.
55. *Stern*, p. 124; *Star*, p. 97.
56. *Stern*, pp. 205, 204, 212, 207, 222 ff.; *Star*, pp. 161, 164, 162, 174 ff.
57. *Stern*, p. 209; *Star*, p. 164.
58. *Kl.Schr.*, p. 398.
59. *Briefe*, pp. 73 ff.; *Life and Thought*, pp. 341 ff.
60. *Stern*, pp. 375 ff., 360; *Star*, pp. 298 ff., 285.
61. See the letter cited in n. 59.
62. *Stern*, pp. 498, 430; *Star*, pp. 397, 342.
63. *Stern*, pp. 520 ff.; *Star*, pp. 415 ff.
64. *Stern*, pp. 397, 398; *Star*, pp. 316, 317.
65. *Stern*, pp. 410 ff., 257, 209 ff., 493; *Star*, pp. 326, 202, 164, 393.
66. *Stern*, p. 410; *Star*, p. 327.
67. See above, p. 68.
68. *Stern*, pp. 506 ff.; *Star*, pp. 404 ff.
69. *Stern*, pp. 383 ff.; *Star*, pp. 305, 329.
70. *Stern*, p. 463; *Star*, p. 369.
71. See *Briefe*, pp. 71 ff.; *Judaism Despite Christianity*, p. 36; *Stern*, p. 341; *Star*, pp. 428 ff.
72. *Ethics*, Part VI, prop. 18 note, props. 22, 35 note.
73. Strauss, *Persecution and the Art of Writing*, p. 180.
74. *Tr.*, ch. XVII, p. 214.

75. Améry, p. 7.
76. Levi, p. 82.

Chapter III

1. *Kl.Schr.*, p. 352.
2. *Healthy and Sick*, p. 30.
3. *Life and Thought*, p. 81.
4. *Hist.Phil.*, III, p. 258.
5. *Phil.Rel.*, II, i, p. 97.
6. *Phil.Rel.*, II, i, p. 99.
7. *Hist. Phil.*, III, p. 257.
8. *Phen.*, Preface.
9. *Phen.*, Preface.
10. *Phen.*, Preface.
11. *Philosophie der Weltgeschichte*, Lasson, ed. (Leipzig: Meiner, 1919), II, i, p. 456.
12. *Einl. Gesch. Phil.*, pp. 190 ff.
13. *Phil.Rel.*, III, pp. 149 ff.
14. Améry, p. 9.
15. Cited by Irving Greenberg, "Cloud of Smoke, Pillar of Fire: Judaism, Christianity and Modernity after the Holocaust," in *Auschwitz: Beginning of a New Era?*, E. Fleischner, ed. (New York: Ktav, 1977), pp. 9 ff.
16. *Negative Dialektik*, pp. 354 ff.
17. "The Jewish Problem and the Christian Answer," in *Against the Stream* (London: SCM Press, 1954), pp. 193 ff.
18. W. R. Beyer, *Vier Kritiken* (Köln: Paul Rugenstein, 1970), pp. 191, 194, also 177, 189.
19. *Either/Or* (New York: Anchor, 1959), II, 344, ff.
20. *Midrash Exodus Rabba*, Va'Era, III, 3.
21. See above, ch. II, p. 57.

Chapter IV

1. *Ethics*, Part V, prop. 38. The difference between reason and intuition is explained in Part II, prop. 40, note ii.
2. *Star*, p. 3; *Stern*, p. 7.
3. See, e.g., SuZ, pp. 18 ff., 227, 229, 423, 427n. (All references to SuZ are to the German edition, the pagination of which is printed in the margin of the English translation.)
4. See *Kl.Schr.*, pp. 354 ff.
5. See, e.g., S. Alexander, "The Historicity of All things," in *Philosophy and History*, ed. H. J. Paton and R. Klibanski (New York: Harper Torchbook, 1963), pp. 11 ff.
6. See my "The Historicity and Transcendence of Philosophical Truth," *Proceedings of the Seventh Inter-American Congress of Philosophy* (Quebec: Laval University Press, 1967), I, pp. 77–92.
7. See SuZ, pp. 226 ff.
8. See *A Treatise of Human Nature*, ed. L. A. Selby-Biggs (Oxford: Clarendon Press, 1888), p. 253. Hume immediately adds, however, that "the comparison of the theatre must not mislead us."

9. See Descartes's first and second *Meditations*, tr. L. J. Lafleur (New York and Indianapolis: Bobbs Merrill, 1951), pp. 17–33. On the Cartesian anticlimax, see Karl Jaspers, *Descartes und die Philosophie* (Berlin and Leipzig: De Gruyter, 1937), p. 10.

10. See *Werke* (Stuttgart and Augsburg: Cotta, 1856–61), X, 4 ff.

11. See, e.g., *Cr.p.R.*, A 369 ff.

12. I remember reading this in Fichte but do not recall where.

13. *WiM*, p. 35; *EB*, pp. 274 ff.

14. *SuZ*, p. 382.

15. *SuZ*, p. 384. I have dealt with this Heideggerian lapse in *Encounters* (p. 216). See also Otto Poeggeler, *Philosophy und Politik bei Heidegger*, 2nd ed. (Freiburg-München: Alber, 1974), pp. 17 ff.

16. *SuZ*, p. 385.

17. See *SuZ*, p. 312, also pp. 12 ff.

18. *SuZ*, p. 312. See also my essay cited in note 6.

19. See further on this point my essay cited in note 6.

20. Löwith, pp. 59 ff.

21. *Encounters*, pp. 213 ff.

22. Löwith, pp. 59 ff.

23. *EM*, pp. 152, 36; *IM*, pp. 199, 48.

24. Karsten Harris, "Heideger as Political Thinker," in *HMPh*, pp. 314, 316.

25. See John D. Caputo, as cited in *Encounters*, p. 216. For other writers on the same subject, see *Encounters*, p. 261.

26. *EM*, pp. 37–38; *IM*, p. 49.

27. *ZS*, p. 6; *TB*, p. 6.

28. *ZS*, p. 53; *TB*, p. 49.

29. See, e.g., *Humanismusbrief, Wm*, pp. 172 ff., 162, 180, 191; *B.Wr.*, pp. 221, 210, 239.

30. *EM*, p. 28; *IM*, p. 37.

31. *Vorträge*, pp. 22, 28, also 31; *B.Wr.*, 303, 310, 313.

32. See *Gelassenheit* (Pfullingen: Neske, 1969); "Memorial Address," in *Discourse on Thinking* (New York: Harper and Row, 1966).

33. *Vorträge*, pp. 84 ff.; The End of Philosophy (New York: Harper and Row, 1973), pp. 103 ff.

34. Adorno, p. 358.

35. Rudolf Hoess, *Commandant of Auschwitz* (London: Pan Books, 1961), p. 145 and *passim*.

36. *EM*, pp. 34–35; *IM*, p. 45.

37. Hoess, *Commandant of Auschwitz*, p. 41. See also below, p. 242n.

38. This speech of Himmler's, given on October 4, 1943, is quite rightly cited in many books dealing with the subject. See, e.g., Lucy Dawidowicz, *A Holocaust Reader* (New York: Behrman, 1976), pp. 120 ff.

39. Dov Shilansky, *Musulman* (Tel Aviv: Menora, 1962), p. 123. For Nazi *Einsatzgruppen* to wear gloves when dealing with Jews was not unusual; see Goldhagen, "Weltanschauung und Endlösung," p. 586.

40. *Mein Kampf*, tr. Ralph Manheim (Boston: Houghton Mifflin, 1943), p. 65.

41. See *Werke*, IV, pp. 650 ff. Also my article, "Schelling's Philosophy of the Literary Arts," *Philosophical Quarterly*, 1954, pp. 310 ff.

42. The last stanza of Ilse Blumenthal-Weiss, "Rückkehr aus dem KZ," anthologized in *Welch Wort in die Kälte Gerufen*, ed. Heinz Seydel (Berlin: Verlag der Nation, 1968), pp. 437 ff. The translation is mine.

43. New York: Capricorn, 1961.
44. See *The Non-Jewish Jew*, *passim*; see also above, p. 132n.
45. On Bloch see *Presence*, pp. 57 ff., and *Encounters*, pp. 151 ff., 165.
46. Currently the most vocal exponent of the opinions summarized in this paragraph is Jacob Neusner; see, e.g., his "A 'Holocaust' Primer," *National Review*, August 3, 1979, pp. 975 ff.
47. *Two Types of Faith* (London: Routledge and Kegan Paul, 1961), p. 15. Italics added.
48. *At the Turning* (New York: Farrar, Straus and Young, 1952), pp. 61 ff.
49. See Clemens Podewils, "Die Nachbarlichen Stämme," in *Erinnerung*, pp. 210 ff.
50. Adorno, pp. 335, 354.
51. Charles R. Cogman, *Drive* (Boston: Little, Brown, 1957), pp. 282 ff.
52. Henri Michel, *The Shadow War: Resistance in Europe, 1939–1945* (London: Deutsch, 1967), p. 247.
53. *Jewish Return*, ch. 5.
54. Améry, pp. 10–11.
55. Yehuda Bauer, in Filip Müller, *Auschwitz Inferno* (London: Routledge and Kegan Paul, 1979); p. xi.
56. Ibid., pp. 6 ff.
57. The apt title of ch. 3 in Terence des Pres, *The Survivor* (New York: Oxford University Press, 1976). That chapter, and indeed des Pres's entire book, should be read in conjunction with the present section.
58. Ibid., p. 55.
59. Micheline Maurel, *An Ordinary Camp*, tr. Margaret S. Summers (New York: Simon and Schuster, 1958), pp. 38 ff., quoted by des Pres, *The Survivor*, pp. 55 ff.
60. Quoted by Arthur D. Morse, *While Six Million Died* (New York: Random House, 1967), p. 204 ff.
61. For the decisive refutation, see Jacob Robinson. *And the Crooked Shall Be Made Straight* (Philadelphia: Jewish Publication Society, 1965), pp. 145 ff. The story is still accepted by Joachim C. Fest, *The Face of the Third Reich* (New York: Penguin, 1979), p. 163.
62. Cited from Kersten's *Memoirs* by Fest, *The Face of the Third Reich*, p. 165. Kersten was Himmler's masseur and confidant.
63. Améry, p. 11. I have altered the Rosenfeld translation slightly.
64. Germaine Tillion, *Ravensbrück* (New York: Anchor, 1975), p. 77.
65. Lewinska, pp. 141 ff., 150. See above, ch. I, section 7.
66. *I and Thou*, p. 158; see above, ch. I, section 7.
67. See Irving J. Rosenbaum, *Holocaust and Halakhah* (New York: Ktav, 1976), pp. 78 ff.
68. Henri Michel, "Jewish Resistance and the European Resistance Movement," in *Jewish Resistance during the Holocaust* (Jerusalem: Yad Vashem, 1971), p. 375.
69. Leon Poliakov, *Harvest of Hate* (London: Elek, 1956), p. 240.
70. *Existentialism* (New York: Philosophical Library, 1947), pp. 28 ff.
71. "Twenty-Five Years after the Warsaw Ghetto Revolt," in *Jewish Resistance*, pp. 26 ff.
72. Ibid., p. 27. On the subject of "no illusions" see further note 79.
73. Ibid.
74. See Shaul Esh, "The Dignity of the Destroyed," in *The Catastrophe of*

European Jewry, ed. Y. Gutman and L. Rothkirchen (Jerusalem: Yad Vashem, 1976), p. 355.

75. The incident is reported by Pessach Schindler, "Responses of Hasidic Leaders and Hasidim during the Holocaust," Ph.D. dissertation, New York University, 1972, pp. 146 ff.

76. Chaim Kaplan, *Scroll of Agony* (New York: Macmillan, 1965), p. 325.

77. Bruno Bettelheim, *The Informed Heart*, pp. 238, 153, and *passim*.

78. Hadassa Bimko-Rosensaft, "The Children of Belsen," in *Belsen* (Irgun Sheerit Hapleita, 1957), p. 107.

79. Yisrael Gutman, "The Genesis of the Resistance in the Warsaw Ghetto," *Yad Vashem Studies*, 9 (Jerusalem, 1973), p. 67.

80. See Robert G. L. Waite, *Hitler: The Psychopathic God* (New York: Basic Books, 1977), pp. 126 ff., 203 ff., 339 ff., 370 ff., and *passim*.

81. In verbal communication to Ernst Simon, reported in Ernst Simon, "Revisionist History of the Jewish Catastrophe," *Judaism* 12, no. 4 (Summer 1963), p. 395.

82. See Hannah Arendt, *Eichmann in Jerusalem: A Report on the Banality of Evil* (New York: Penguin, 1977), and *The Jew as Pariah* (New York: Grove Press, 1978), pp. 250 ff. Arendt wished to develop a full-fledged doctrine of the banality of evil, but did not do so in the published parts of her *The Life of the Mind*, 2 vols. (New York: Harcourt Brace Jovanovich, 1978).

83. Fest, *The Face of the Third Reich*, p. 171.

84. Sartre, "The Childhood of a Leader," in *Intimacy* (London: Panther Books, 1977), pp. 130 ff. Hitler, *Mein Kampf*, tr. R. Manheim (Boston: Houghton Mifflin, 1943), pp. 55 ff.

85. Arendt, *The Jew as Pariah*, pp. 250 ff.

86. *Werke*, II, iii, p. 163, and elsewhere.

87. Joachim C. Fest, *Hitler* (New York: Vintage, 1975), p. 681.

88. David Irving, *Hitler's War* (New York: Viking, 1977), I, pp. xiv ff.

89. G. M. Gilbert, *Nuremberg Diary* (New York: Signet, 1947), p. 163.

90. Lewinska, p. 50.

91. Elie Wiesel, *Legends of Our Time* (New York: Avon, 1968), p. 230; Buber, as cited above, section 7.

92. Bab. Talmud, Berakhot 59a.

93. Gershom Scholem, *On the Kabbalah and Its Symbolism* (New York: Schocken, 1965), pp. 146 ff.

94. Cited by Schindler, "Responses of Hasidic Leaders and Hasidim during the Holocaust," pp. 100 ff.

95. See *The Unconquerable Spirit*, ed. S. Zuker and G. Hirschler (New York: Mesorah, 1980), pp. 27 ff.

96. H. G. Gadamer, *Truth and Method* (New York: Seabury Press, 1975), p. 244. In addition to Heidegger and Gadamer, the writers thought of in this summary include Rudolf Bultmann and Paul Ricoeur, but also Buber and Rosenzweig.

97. Martin Buber, *Between Man and Man* (Boston: Beacon Press, 1955), p. 15; *Moses* (London: East and West Library, 1946), p. 140.

98. Gregory Baum, *Is the New Testament Antisemitic?* (New York: Paulist, 1965).

99. *Preface*, p. 345.

100. See M. Heidegger, *Nietzsche*, 2 vols. (Pfullingen: Neske, 1961). My few

comments on Nietzsche's relevance after the Holocaust, here and previously, (*Quest*, pp. 296 ff., and *God's Presence*, pp. 67 ff.) are of course not meant to do the subject justice.

101. Further on that bond, see *Encounters*, ch. 4.
102. See Inge Scholl, *Students against Tyranny* (Middletown, Conn.: Wesleyan University Press, 1970).
103. Ibid., pp. 63 ff. (The translation of Fichte's poem is mine.)
104. Améry, pp. 85–86.
105. *The Categorical Imperative* (Chicago: University of Chicago Press, 1948), p. 171.
106. *Legends of Our Time*, p. 230.
107. See Plato, *Phaedrus* 230A.
108. S. Kierkegaard, *Either/Or* (New York: Anchor, 1959), II, pp. 344 ff. See above, ch. III, section 11.
109. See Franklin H. Littell, *The Crucifixion of the Jews* (New York: Harper and Row, 1975).
110. *Ethics* (New York: Macmillan, 1965), p. 114. On Bonhoeffer, see further below.
111. Cited in *Jewish Return*, pp. 36, 156.
112. See *The German Church Struggle and the Holocaust*, ed. Franklin H. Littell and Hubert G. Locke (Detroit: Wayne State University Press, 1974).
113. See Rosemary Ruether, *Faith and Fratricide* (New York: Seabury Press, 1974), esp. ch. 3.
114. Levi, p. 82. See above, pp. 99, 131.
115. See *Das Dritte Reich und die Juden*, ed. Leon Poliakov and Josef Wulf, 2nd ed. (Berlin: Verlags GMBH, 1955), pp. 432–37.
116. See Irving Greenberg, as cited above, ch. I, section 4.
117. Levi, p. 81.
118. See above, pp. 134 ff., 189, 278.
119. See further, *Jewish Return*, ch. 15.
120. *Jewish Return*, chs. 2, 3, 8; *God's Presence*, ch. 3; David Singer in *Commentary* (Oct. 1978), p. 83.
121. See above, section 4 of this chapter.
122. See above, all of sections 8 and 9 of this chapter.
123. An allusion to the title of Yehuda Bauer, *The Jewish Emergence from Powerlessness* (Toronto: University of Toronto Press, 1979).
124. *Midraschim der Klage und des Zuspruchs*, ed. Max Dienemann (Berlin: Schocken, 1935); *Midrash Rabba*, Lamentation I 40.
125. See above, ch. II, section 4.
126. See Stern, p. 493; *Star*, p. 393; above, ch. II, section 3.
127. See above, section 7 of this chapter.
128. See below, all of ch. V.

Chapter V

1. See above, ch. II, section 3.
2. See above, ch. II, section 4.
3. See above, ch. III, section 120.
4. See above, ch. IV, section 10.
5. See above, ch. IV, note 20.
6. See above, ch. II, section 3.

7. See Moshe Prager, *Sparks of Glory* (New York: Shengold, 1974) pp. 70 ff.
8. On this subject, see further *Encounters*, pp. 106 ff.
9. *Midrash Deut. Rabba*, 2.12.
10. A popular summary probably based on Zohar V 73b and/or 93a.
11. A dictum attributed to Saadia Gaon (882–942).
12. Wiesel, *Gates of the Forest*, p. 225.
13. *Midrash Psalms*, on Ps. 83:5.

Index